BOLLINGEN SERIES

THE
LIMITS OF ART

2 · From Villon to Gibbon

POETRY AND PROSE CHOSEN BY
ANCIENT AND MODERN CRITICS

COLLECTED AND EDITED BY
HUNTINGTON CAIRNS

BOLLINGEN SERIES

PRINCETON UNIVERSITY PRESS

Printed in the United States of America
by Princeton University Press, Princeton, New Jersey

TO THE MEMORY
OF
MARY MELLON

1904–1946

Εἰ καὶ ἄπιστα κλύουσι, λέγω τάδε· φημὶ γὰρ ἤδη
τέχνης εὑρῆσθαι τέρματα τῆσδε σαφῆ
χειρὸς ὑφ' ὑμετέρης· ἀνυπέρβλητος δὲ πέπηγεν
οὖρος. ἀμώμητον δ' οὐδὲν ἔγεντο βροτοῖς.

This I say, even though they that hear believe not: I declare
that the clear limits of this art have been found under my
hand, and the goal is set that may not be overpassed, though
there is no human work with which fault may not be found.

PARRHASIUS

PREFACE

THIS WORK presents selections of poetry and prose that have been held by competent critics to touch, in one way or another, the limits of art. That is to say, the selections have been pronounced perfect or the greatest of their kind. With each selection there is printed the judgment of the critic. I have thus, in the compilation of the work, employed a method the opposite of that used in the conventional anthology. My starting point was neither the poet nor the poem, but the critic; the volume therefore differs from the customary anthology of selections from standard authors. The work of a recognized writer is not included here unless in the considered judgment of a responsible critic it is, in some sense, superlative.

It should also be remarked that this volume brings criticism itself to the bar of judgment. Here is what criticism has held, at various times and places since its beginnings in ancient Greece, to be supreme in poetry or prose. I venture to think that on the whole its estimates have been sound. I have asked only that the critic's appreciation of his selection be in terms of its value as poetry or prose, and that there be a basis for believing he is competent to make the estimate. Where a critic has a long-established reputation I have attempted no careful weighing of his position, although, in the course of editing, I may have rejected many of his judgments. Coleridge, of course, I have admitted without hesitation, although there are those who now deny that he is a critic at all; however, I have included none of his appreciations which rest upon the circumstances that the poems promote a virtuous life or a sound view of religion. I should add that American and German critics are so hesitant to cite examples of excellence that their literatures are perhaps not as widely represented here as they deserve. This characteristic may possibly be the product of local conditions, as it is in Germany, where the taught tradition of the university seminars forbids the use of superlatives; but it is also individual, as we can see in the frugality with which such well qualified critics as W. P. Ker and Oliver Elton engage in the practice.

It will be seen from the book's epigraph that I have borrowed the phrase the "limits of art" from the Greek Anthology; it suggests both the idea of perfection and the idea of greatness, a distinction recognized long ago by Longinus, when he remarked on the difference between the flawless and the sublime. Criticism unfortunately has not arrived at any generally accepted understanding of either idea. Nevertheless, it has been the practice of nearly every important critic, from ancient to modern times, to apply these ideas to concrete examples. Perhaps the most satisfactory approaches are still Aristotle's conception that a poem is perfect when it cannot be added to or subtracted from, and Longinus' view that a poem is great when it transports or overwhelms the reader. There is, of course, the further limit, the requirement discussed by Aristotle, that art must discover the universal, that which is enduring and essential. It is the essence of the critical function to judge literature; when the critic is in the presence of poetry or prose that is wholly excellent, it would seem that he violates no sound canon when he pronounces it so. Art is wayward and baffling, it tends always to escape the rigid formula; it is however possible to contrast, to search for, the specific qualities that give literature its character. When the critic who does this has also knowledge and a sense of form we find, as we can see from Saintsbury's *History of Criticism*, that we have described the practice and equipment of all great critics in the history of the craft. If the critic goes further and states why the arrangement of a handful of words in a certain order possesses excellence, he is also discharging a legitimate function of criticism. "To like and dislike rightly," Bosanquet once wrote, "is the goal of all culture worth the name." Why are the first four words of the *Republic* pleasing to the ear, if placed in one order, as Plato discovered, and displeasing if placed in another? In the present work, when the critic has attempted to answer this difficult question, I have allowed him the additional space for his exposition; but that task, unluckily, is one that the critic too often sidesteps.

In all cases save two—Walpole's letter to the Rev. William Cole and Cowper's to the Rev. John Newton—every extract has been specified by the critic; for that reason many of them are of a fragmentary nature. If the critic gave his approbation to a single verse and not to the whole poem, I have not attempted to enlarge the area of his selection. Similarly, if he has designated Homer or Shakespeare or Dante as the first poet of the world and has not exhibited a passage to enforce his estimate, I have not printed his views nor attempted to make his opinion more particular by extracting an example of quotable length. Dryden thought that the English language reached its highest perfection in Beaumont and Fletcher; Shelley believed that the truth and splendor of Plato's imagery and the melody of his language were the most intense that it was possible to conceive; but they were not specific and their judgments are thus omitted from this volume. The reader should not assume, therefore, that because a passage is not specified in the context of the criticism quoted in its support that it is not specified by the critic at all. In the few cases where the criticism has not been definite I have turned to other sources, as, for example, to the authorized life of Tennyson for his favorite Virgilian lines to associate with the general tribute

Wielder of the stateliest measure
ever moulded by the lips of man.

Considerations of space have sometimes compelled me to make a choice where the critic has given more than one example of perfection or greatness. In one instance I have ventured to shorten a passage: the *De Corona* extract from Demosthenes, which is supported by Lord Brougham's famous judgment. Some poems, of course, because of their length, I have not been able to present. Gautier, for example, insisted that Alfred de Vigny's *Eloa* was the most beautiful and the most perfect poem in the French language; while present-day taste undoubtedly would not accept this estimate, it is with regret that I have been forced to omit the poem.

I have not hesitated to print extracts that are no more than a sentence or even a phrase. However, it may well be that some emotional association is involved in the critic's choice of the single word or two. Henry James' selection, for example, of "summer afternoon", as the most beautiful phrase in the English language probably carries a personal connotation. It is significant that in *The Portrait of a Lady*, when Isabel Archer and Gilbert Osmond are engaged, the most that Osmond can promise is that life for them will be "one long summer afternoon". In any event, the element of the personal is here too plainly present and I have therefore excluded such examples.

Although the volume to a degree exhibits some of the vagaries in the history of taste, that aspect is largely fortuitous. My intention has been to include only such passages as informed criticism would be inclined to rank at the highest level, whatever the period of the critic—such passages, that is, as have come to my notice, for an anthology of this nature can of course lay no claim to completeness. I must add that my inclusion of a passage does not necessarily imply an endorsement of the degree of the critic's enthusiasm, although it does imply a recognition of the merits of his selection and of his own authority to speak in the particular case; I doubt, for example, that any critic of standing today would concur in Johnson's estimate of the Congreve passage; nevertheless, that it is a great passage I think scarcely anyone would deny.

For the most part I have avoided the appraisal of the biographer, on the ground that his enthusiasm for his subject is likely to prompt him to excessive judgment. Nevertheless, on several occasions I have admitted criticism written by the author in praise of his own work; but in all instances the opinions are not incompatible with the estimates of other good critics. Many of the passages could have been supported by additional critical statements, but a mere repetition of authority seemed to serve no purpose. I have attempted everywhere to exclude the rhetorical superlative as exemplified by the otherwise excellent criticism of Hazlitt.

The passages have been uniformly printed in the language that evoked the critic's praise; to do otherwise would amount to a misrepresentation. However, translations have been provided in all cases save that of La Harpe. As a substitute for a translation of La Harpe's *La Prophétie de Cazotte* I have appended Saintsbury's witty condensation, with its supplementary information. The translations which have been made especially for this work are intended as no more than literal versions of the original. Occasionally, as in the Balzac passage, the criticism stresses not the original language but the general character of the piece; in those instances the extracts are printed only in translation. Where translations themselves have been the object of the critic's praise, as in the case of Chapman's rendering of Homer, the selected passage is included under the translator's name, and is followed by the original text for the convenience of the reader.

HUNTINGTON CAIRNS

National Gallery of Art
Washington, D. C.

NOTE TO THE PAPERBACK EDITION

The Limits of Art has been trisected into more or less equal parts, which will appear successively. The texts and critiques are unchanged; the indexes have been adapted for each of the three parts, but the acknowledgments and glossary are given in full.

ACKNOWLEDGMENTS

THE EDITOR wishes to express his appreciation for special assistance on editorial problems from many sources. He is particularly indebted to the following: the late Dr. Joseph Quincy Adams, Mabel A. Barry, René Batigne, Ruth E. Carlson, Mary Elizabeth Charlton, Frances Cheney, Marie Compton, A. D. Emmart, Dr. Elio Gianturco, Edith Hamilton, Dr. George N. Henning, Burnley Hodgson, Macgill James, Dean Martin McGuire, Dr. James G. McManaway, David Mearns, Elizabeth Mongan, Christopher Saintsbury, John H. Scarff, Fern Rusk Shapley, Katherine Shepard, Everett E. Smith, E. Millicent Sowerby, Charles C. Stotler, L. O. Teach and John Walker. The editor wishes to thank Miss Kay Becker, of the Catholic University of America, Washington, D. C., and Professor John B. McDiarmid, of the Johns Hopkins University, Baltimore, Md., for undertaking the task of reading the proofs of the Greek passages, and Professor Leonard Dean, of Tulane University, New Orleans, La., for reading the proofs of the Chaucer selections. The epigraph from Parrhasius was translated by the late Professor J. W. Mackail.

The following libraries have been of assistance in making source material available: Boston Public Library, Boston, Mass.; Bryn Mawr College Library, Bryn Mawr, Pa.; Catholic University Library, Washington, D. C.; University of Chicago Library, Chicago, Ill.; Columbia University Library, New York, N. Y.; District of Columbia Library, Washington, D. C.; George Washington University Library, Washington, D. C.; Grosvenor Library, Buffalo, N. Y.; Harvard College Library, Cambridge, Mass.; Lehigh University Library, Bethlehem, Pa.; Library of Congress, Washington, D. C.; National Gallery of Art Library, Washington, D. C.; Peabody Institute Library, Baltimore, Md.; University of Pennsylvania Library, Philadelphia, Pa.; Princeton University Library, Princeton, N. J.; University of Rochester Library, Rochester, N. Y.; Smithsonian Institution Library, Washington, D. C.; U. S. Department of Justice Library, Washington, D. C.; University of Virginia Library, Charlottesville, Va.; Yale University Library, New Haven, Conn.

For permission to use the copyrighted material included in this work acknowledgment is made to the following publishers and others: from Henry Adams Bellows' translation of the *Poetic Edda*, by permission of the American-Scandinavian Foundation, New York; Aldous Huxley's translation of Mallarmé's "L'Après-midi d'un faune", by permission of

Basil Blackwell & Mott, Ltd., Oxford; from L. P. Wilkinson's *Horace and his Lyric Poetry*, published by the Cambridge University Press, by permission; from R. C. Jebb's translation of Sophocles' *Oedipus at Colonus*, by permission of The Cambridge University Press; from George Thomson's translation of Aeschylus' *Oresteia*, by permission of The Cambridge University Press; from J. T. Sheppard's translation of Sophocles' *Oedipus Tyrannus*, by permission of The Cambridge University Press; from E. M. W. Tillyard, *Poetry Direct and Oblique* (1945), by permission of Chatto & Windus, London; from John Addington Symonds' translation of "The Confession of Golias", in *Wine, Women and Song* (The Mediaeval Library, published in England by Chatto & Windus, in the United States by The Oxford University Press) by permission of Chatto & Windus, London; from Robert Bridges, *Ibant Obscuri*, by permission of The Clarendon Press, Oxford; from A. O. Prickard's translation of Longinus' *On the Sublime*, by permission of The Clarendon Press, Oxford; translation of Pericles' Funeral Oration from Sir Alfred Zimmern's *The Greek Commonwealth*, by permission of The Clarendon Press, Oxford; extracts reprinted from Mary M. Colum, *From These Roots*, by permission of Columbia University Press, New York; a translation by Malcolm Cowley from La Fontaine's "Adonis", by permission of Malcolm Cowley; from *Catullus*, translated by Horace Gregory; copyright 1931, by Covici-Friede, Inc.; by special permission of Crown Publishers; from Gladys M. Turquet's translation of Joachim Du Bellay's *La Deffense et illustration de la langue française*, by permission of J. M. Dent & Sons Ltd., London; from Anatole France, *On Life and Letters*, by permission of Dodd, Mead & Company, Inc.; Arthur Symons' translation of Mallarmé's "Hérodiade", from *The Poems of Arthur Symons*, used by permission of Dodd, Mead and Company, Inc.; Arthur Symons' translation of "Clair de Lune" by Paul Verlaine, reprinted by permission of Dodd, Mead & Company, Inc.; Arthur Symons' translation of Paul Verlaine's "Chanson d'Automne", reprinted by permission of Dodd, Mead & Company, Inc.; from Rudyard Kipling's poems: "Danny Deever" from *Departmental Ditties and Barrack-room Ballads*, by Rudyard Kipling, copyright 1899, reprinted by permission of Mrs. G. Bambridge and Doubleday, Doran and Company, Inc.; "Recessional" from *The Five Nations*, by Rudyard Kipling, copyright 1903, reprinted by permission of Mrs. G. Bambridge and Doubleday, Doran and Company, Inc.; "An Only Son", "The Coward", "The Beginner", "Common Form", "A Dead Statesman", "Salonikan Grave", from *The Years Between*, by Rudyard Kipling, copyright 1904, reprinted by permission of Mrs. G. Bambridge and Doubleday, Doran and Company, Inc.; from J. G. Legge, *Chanticleer* (1935), by permission of E. P. Dutton & Co., Inc., New York, publisher in the United States; from Samuel Butler's translation of Homer's *Iliad*, by permission of E. P. Dutton & Co., Inc.,

New York, publisher in the United States; from E. J. Trechmann's translation of C.-A. Sainte-Beuve's *Causeries du lundi,* by permission of E. P. Dutton & Co., Inc., New York, publisher in the United States; from Hilaire Belloc, *Avril* (1904), by permission of E. P. Dutton & Co., Inc., New York, publisher in the United States; from Sir Frank Marzial's translation of Geoffroi de Villehardouin's *La Conquête de Constantinople* (Everyman's Library) by permission of E. P. Dutton & Co., Inc., New York, publisher in the United States; from E. B. Pusey's translation of the *Confessions of St. Augustine* (Everyman's Library) by permission of E. P. Dutton & Co., Inc., New York, publisher in the United States; extracts taken from the *Nibelungenlied,* translated by Margaret Armour (Everyman's Library), published by E. P. Dutton & Co., Inc., New York; extracts taken from *Anglo-Saxon Poetry,* by R. K. Gordon, published by E. P. Dutton & Co., Inc., New York; from *The Collected Essays and Papers of George Saintsbury,* by permission of E. P. Dutton & Co., Inc., New York, publisher in the United States; Horace's "Celebration for Neptune", translated by Roselle Mercier Montgomery; reprinted from *Forum* by permission of the Events Publishing Company, Inc.; from George Frederic Lees' translation of Rimbaud's "A Season in Hell" by permission of The Fortune Press, London; from A. R. Waller's translation of Molière's *Tartuffe,* reprinted by permission from *Molière—Complete Works in French and English* (8 Vols. Cr. 8vo, cloth) published by John Grant, Edinburgh; from Henry Thomas' translation of Lope de Vega's *The Star of Seville,* by permission of The Gregynog Press, Newtown, Montgomeryshire, England; from Joan Redfern's translation of *History of Italian Literature* by Francesco De Sanctis, by permission of Harcourt, Brace and Company, Inc., New York; from T. S. Eliot's "The Love Song of J. Alfred Prufrock", from *Collected Poems,* by permission of Harcourt, Brace and Company, Inc.; Louis Untermeyer's translation of Heine's "Ein Fichtenbaum Steht Einsam" from *Heinrich Heine: Paradox and Poet,* Volume 2, by Louis Untermeyer, copyright 1937, by Harcourt, Brace and Company, Inc.; from Aldous Huxley, *Texts & Pretexts* (1933), by permission of Harper & Brothers, New York; poems and prose extracts from Algernon Charles Swinburne, *Collected Poetical Works,* by permission of Harper & Brothers, New York; Sir William Watson's "Hymn to the Sea", from *The Poems of Sir William Watson, 1878–19,* by permission of George G. Harrap & Company Limited, London; texts and translations reprinted by permission of the publishers from the Loeb Classical Library: from Aeschylus, *The Persians,* translated by Herbert Weir-Smyth; from Aristotle, *Metaphysics,* translated by Hugh Tredennick; from Aristotle, *Art of Rhetoric,* translated by J. H. Freese; from Cicero, *Pro Archia Poeta,* translated by N. H. Watts; from Demosthenes, *De Corona,* translated by C. A. and J. H. Vince; from Euripides, *Daughters of Troy,* translated by Arthur S. Way;

from Herodotus, translated by A. D. Godley; from Hesiod, translated by H. G. Evelyn-White; from Homer, the *Iliad*, translated by A. T. Murray; from Homer, the *Odyssey*, translated by A. T. Murray; from Horace, *Odes*, translated by C. E. Bennett; from Isocrates, *Areopagiticus*, translated by George Norlin; from Longinus, translated by W. Hamilton Fyfe; from Lucian, translated by A. M. Harmon; from Lucretius, translated by W. H. D. Rouse; from Pindar, translated by Sir John Sandys; from Plato, the *Apology* and *Crito*, translated by H. N. Fowler; from Seneca, *Medea*, translated by Frank Justus Miller; from Sextus Propertius, translated by H. E. Butler; from Sophocles, *Ajax*, *Electra* and *Oedipus at Colonus*, translated by F. Storr; from Tacitus, *Agricola*, translated by Maurice Hutton; from Tacitus, *Annals*, translated by John Jackson; from Theocritus, *Idylls*, translated by J. M. Edmonds; from Virgil, *Aeneid* and *Georgics*, translated by H. R. Fairclough; Cambridge, Mass.; Harvard University Press; extracts reprinted by permission of the publishers from Gilbert Murray—*The Classical Tradition in Poetry*, Cambridge, Mass.; Harvard University Press, 1927; J. B. Leishman's translation of "Der Blinde Sänger" from *The Select Poems of Friedrich Hölderlin*, by permission of The Hogarth Press, London; from Norman Macleod's *German Lyric Poetry* (1930) by permission of The Hogarth Press, London; Norman Cameron's translation of Rimbaud's "Bateau Ivre", by permission of The Hogarth Press, London; from Helen Waddell, *The Wandering Scholars* (1927) and *Mediaeval Latin Lyrics* (1929), by permission of Constable and Company, Ltd., London, and published in the United States by Henry Holt and Company; from Henry Adams, *Mont-Saint-Michel and Chartres*, by permission of Houghton Mifflin Company, Boston; from Amy Lowell, *Six French Poets* (1915), by permission of Houghton Mifflin Company, Boston; from Charles Eliot Norton's translation of Dante's *Divine Comedy*, by permission of Houghton Mifflin Company, Boston; from *The Trophies* (translation of *Les Trophées* of José-Maria de Heredia) by John Hervey, The John Day Company, New York, 1929; from C. K. Scott Moncrieff's *The Letters of Abelard and Heloise*, by permission of Alfred A. Knopf, Inc., New York; from Maurice Baring, *Have You Anything to Declare?* by permission of Alfred A. Knopf, Inc., New York; Emily Dickinson, "The Chariot", from *The Poems of Emily Dickinson*, edited by Martha Dickinson Bianchi and Alfred Leete Hampson, reprinted by permission of Little, Brown & Company, Boston; translations from *The Poems of Victor Hugo* (1909), by permission of Little, Brown & Company, Boston; from Jacques Chevalier, *Pascal*, translated by Lilian A. Clare, by permission of Longmans, Green & Co., Inc., New York; from J. W. Mackail, *Lectures on Greek Poetry* (1910) by permission of Longmans, Green & Co., Inc., New York; from J. W. Mackail, *Studies in Humanism* (1938) by permission of Longmans, Green & Co., Inc., New York; translations by

CONTENTS

xxii

xxvi

THE LIMITS OF ART

ANONYMOUS

FOURTEENTH CENTURY

LANGUAGE OF THE LAW

An heir in tail rebutted from his formedon by a lineal warranty with descended assets.

It is forgotten that during the later middle age English lawyers enjoyed the inestimable advantage of being able to make a technical language. And a highly technical language they made. . . . Precise ideas are here expressed in precise terms, every one of which is French: the geometer or the chemist could hardly wish for terms that are more exact or less liable to have their edges worn away by the vulgar.

F. W. MAITLAND
Year Books of Edward II (1903)

FRANÇOIS VILLON

1431 – AFT. 1463

BALLADE DES DAMES DU TEMPS JADIS

Dictes-moy où, n'en quel pays,
Est Flora, la belle Romaine;
Archipiada, ne Thaïs,
Qui fut sa cousine germaine;
Echo, parlant quand bruyt on maine
Dessus rivière ou sus estan,
Qui beauté eut trop plus qu'humaine?
Mais où sont les neiges d'antan!

469

Où est la très sage Heloïs,
Pour qui fut chastré et puis moyne
Pierre Esbaillart à Sainct-Denys?
Pour son amour eut cest essoyne
Semblablement, où est la royne
Qui commanda que Buridan
Fust jetté en ung sac en Seine?
Mais où sont les neiges d'antan!

La royne Blanche comme ung lys,
Qui chantoit à voix de sereine,
Berthe au grand pied, Bietris, Allys;
Harembourges, qui tient le Mayne,
Et Jehanne, la bonne Lorraine,
Qu'Anglois bruslèrent à Rouen;
Où sont-ils, Vierge souveraine? . .
Mais où sont les neiges d'antan!

Envoi

Prince, n'enquerez de sepmaine
Où elles sont, ne de cest an,
Que ce refrain ne vous remaine:
Mais où sont les neiges d'antan!

THE BALLAD OF DEAD LADIES

Tell me now in what hidden way is
Lady Flora the lovely Roman?
Where's Hipparchia, and where is Thais,
Neither of them the fairer woman?
Where is Echo, beheld of no man,
Only heard on river and mere,—
She whose beauty was more than human? . . .
But where are the snows of yester-year?

Where's Héloise, the learned nun,
For whose sake Abeillard, I ween,
Lost manhood and put priesthood on?
(From Love he won such dule and teen!)
And where, I pray you, is the Queen
Who willed that Buridan should steer
Sewed in a sack's mouth down the Seine? . . .
But where are the snows of yester-year?

470

White Queen Blanche, like a queen of lilies,
  With a voice like any mermaiden,—
Bertha Broadfoot, Beatrice, Alice,
  And Ermengarde the lady of Maine,—
  And that good Joan whom Englishmen
At Rouen doomed and burned her there,—
  Mother of God, where are they then? . . .
But where are the snows of yester-year?

Nay, never ask this week, fair lord,
  Where they are gone, nor yet this year,
Save with this for an overword,—
  But where are the snows of yester-year?

Le Grand Testament (1461)
Translated by Dante Gabriel Rossetti

*One of the master-songs of the world, with its gentle rhymes in -IS and
-AINE, the exquisite ache of its music, caressing and soothing to dreams,
and its lovely refrain. Its melancholy inquiry and evocation and its concern with Death are common to large masses of medieval poetry: but
it is incomparable.*

D. B. WYNDHAM LEWIS
François Villon (1928)

FRANÇOIS VILLON

1 4 3 1 — A F T. 1 4 6 3

BALLADE

*Que Villon feit a la requeste de sa mère,
pour prier Nostre Dame*

Dame du ciel, regente terrienne,
Emperière des infernaulx palux,
Recevez-moy, vostre humble chrestienne,
Que comprinse soye entre voz esleuz,
Ce non obstant qu'oncques rien ne valuz.
Les biens de vous, ma dame et ma maistresse,
Sont trop plus grans que ne suis pecheresse,
Sans lesquelz biens ame ne peult merir
N'avoir les cieulx, je n'en suis jengleresse.
En ceste foy je vueil vivre et mourir.

A vostre Filz dictes que je suis sienne;
Que de luy soyent mes pechez aboluz:
Pardonnés moi comme à l'Egyptienne,
Ou comme il feit au clerc Theophilus,
Lequel par vous fut quitte et absoluz,
Combien qu'il eust au diable faict promesse.
Preservez-moy, que point je ne face ce;
Vierge portant sans rompure encourir
Le sacrement qu'on celebre à la messe.
En ceste foy je vueil vivre et mourir.

Femme je suis povrette et ancienne,
Ne riens ne sçay; oncques lettre ne leuz,
Au monstier voy dont suis parroissienne
Paradis painct, où sont harpes et luz,
Et ung enfer où damnez sont boulluz:
L'ung me faict paour, l'autre joye et liesse.
La joye avoir fais-moy, haulte Deesse,
A qui pecheurs doivent tous recourir,
Comblez de foy, sans faincte ne paresse.
En ceste foy je vueil vivre et mourir.

Envoi

Vous portastes, Vierge, digne princesse,
JESUS regnant, qui n'a ne fin ne cesse.
Le Tout-Puissant, prenant nostre foiblesse,
Laissa les cieulx et nous vint secourir;
Offrist à mort sa très clère jeunese;
Nostre Seigneur tel est, tel le confesse,
En ceste foy je vueil vivre et mourir.

BALLAD

That Villon made at the Request of His Mother,
Wherewithal to do Her Homage to Our Lady

Lady of Heaven, Regent of the earth,
 Empress of all the infernal marshes fell,
Receive me, Thy poor Christian, 'spite my dearth,
 In the fair midst of Thine elect to dwell:
 Albeit my lack of grace I know full well;
For that Thy grace, my Lady and my Queen,
Aboundeth more than all my misdemean,
 Withouten which no soul of all that sigh

May merit Heaven. 'Tis sooth I say, for e'en
  In this belief I will to live and die.

Say to Thy Son I am His,—that by His birth
  And death my sins be all redeemable,—
As Mary of Egypt's dole He changed to mirth
  And eke Theophilus', to whom befell
  Quittance of Thee, albeit (So men tell)
To the foul fiend he had contracted been.
Assoilzie me, that I may have no teen,
  Maid, that without breach of virginity
Didst bear our Lord that in the Host is seen.
  In this belief I will to live and die.

A poor old wife I am, and little worth:
  Nothing I know, nor letter aye could spell:
Where in the church to worship I fare forth,
  I see Heaven limned, with harps and lutes, and Hell,
  Where damned folk seethe in fire unquenchable.
One doth me fear, the other joy serene:
Grant I may have the joy, O Virgin clean,
  To whom all sinners lift their hands on high,
Made whole in faith through Thee their go-between.
  In this belief I will to live and die.

Envoi

Thou didst conceive, Princess most bright of sheen,
Jesus the Lord, that hath nor end nor mean,
Almighty, that, departing Heaven's demesne
  To succour us, put on our frailty,
Offering to death His sweet of youth and green:
Such as He is, our Lord He is, I ween!
  In this belief I will to live and die.

Le Grand Testament (1461)
Translated by John Payne

One of the masterpieces of the world.

HILAIRE BELLOC
Avril (1904)

The verses of the third stanza are among the finest in the language.

FERDINAND BRUNETIÈRE
Nouvelles Questions de critique (1898)

FRANÇOIS VILLON

1 4 3 1 — A F T. 1 4 6 3

CHRISTMAS TIME

En ce temps que j'ay dit devant,
Sur le Noël, morte saison,
Lorsque les loups vivent de vent,
Et qu'on se tient en sa maison,
Pour le frimas, près du tison.

In this year, as before I said,
   Hard by the dead of Christmas-time,
When upon wind the wolves are fed,
   And for the rigour of the rime
One hugs the hearth from none to prime.

Le Petit Testament (1456)
Translated by John Payne

L'ÉPITAPHE EN FORME DE BALLADE

*Que feit Villon pour luy et ses compagnons,
s'attendant estre pendu avec eulx.*

Frères humains, qui après nous vivez,
N'ayez les cueurs contre nous endurciz,
Car, si pitié de nous pouvres avez,
Dieu en aura plustost de vous merciz.
Vous nous voyez cy attachez cinq, six:
Quant de la chair, que trop avons nourrie,
Elle est piéça devorée et pourrie,
Et nous, les os, devenons cendre et pouldre.
De nostre mal personne ne s'en rie,
Mais priez Dieu que tous nous vueille absouldre!

Se vous clamons, frères, pas n'en devez
Avoir desdaing, quoyque fusmes occis
Par justice. Toutesfois, vous sçavez
Que tous les hommes n'ont pas bon sens assis;
Intercedez doncques, de cueur rassis,
Envers le Filz de la Vierge Marie,
Que sa grace ne soit pour nous tarie,

Nous preservant de l'infernale fouldre.
Nous sommes mors, ame ne nous harie;
Mais priez Dieu que tous nous vueille absouldre!

La pluye nous a debuez et lavez,
Et le soleil dessechez et noirciz;
Pies, corbeaulx, nous ont les yeux cavez,
Et arrachez la barbe et les sourcilz.
Jamais, nul temps, nous se sommes rassis;
Puis çà, puis là, comme le vent varie,
A son plaisir sans cesser nous charie,
Plus becquetez d'oyseaulx que dez à couldre.
Ne soyez donc de nostre confrairie,
Mais priez Dieu que tous nous vueille absouldre!

Envoi

Prince JESUS, qui sur tous seigneurie,
Garde qu'Enfer n'ayt de nous la maistrie:
A luy n'ayons que faire ne que souldre.
Hommes, icy n'usez de mocquerie
Mais priez Dieu que tous nous vueille absouldre!

THE EPITAPH IN FORM OF A BALLAD

*Which Villon made for himself and his comrades
expecting to be hanged along with them.*

Men, brother men, that after us yet live,
    Let not your hearts too hard against us be;
For if some pity of us poor men ye give,
    The sooner God shall take of you pity.
Here are we five or six strung up, you see,
And here the flesh that all too well we fed
Bit by bit eaten and rotten, rent and shred,
    And we the bones grow dust and ash withal;
Let no man laugh at us discomforted,
    But pray to God that he forgive us all.

If we call on you, brothers, to forgive,
    Ye should not hold our prayer in scorn, though we
Were slain by law; ye know that all alive
    Have not wit alway to walk righteously;
Make therefore intercession heartily

With him that of a virgin's womb was bred,
That his grace be not as a dry well-head
    For us, nor let hell's thunder on us fall;
We are dead, let no man harry or vex us dead,
    But pray to God that he forgive us all.

The rain has washed and laundered us all five,
    And the sun dried and blackened; yea, perdie,
Ravens and pies with beaks that rend and rive
    Have dug our eyes out, and plucked off for fee
    Our beards and eyebrows; never are we free,
Not once, to rest; but here and there still sped,
Drive at its wild will by the wind's change led,
    More pecked of birds than fruits on garden-wall;
Men, for God's love, let no gibe here be said,
    But pray to God that he forgive us all.

Prince Jesus, that of all art lord and head,
Keep us, that hell be not our bitter bed;
    We have nought to do in such a master's hall.
Be not ye therefore of our fellowhead,
    But pray to God that he forgive us all.

Translated by Algernon Charles Swinburne

It is possible to say of Villon that he created French poetry, and that at the same time he lead it to one of its purest and most glorious summits.

THIERRY MAULNIER
Introduction à la poésie française (1939)

PHILIPPE DE COMINES

1 4 4 7 ? — 1 5 1 1 ?

THE DEATH OF ILLUSTRIOUS MEN

Or voyez-vous la mort de tant de grands hommes, en si peu de temps, qui tant ont travaillé pour s'accroistre, et pour avoir gloire, et tant en ont souffert de passion et de peines, et abrégé leur vie; et par adventure leurs ames en pourront souffrir. En ceci ne parle point dudit Turc; car je tiens ce poinct pour vuidé, et qu'il est logé avec ses prédécesseurs. De nostre roy j'ay espérance (comme j'ay dit) que nostre Seigneur ait eu miséricorde de luy et aussi aura-il des autres, s'il luy plaist. Mais à parler naturellement (comme homme qui n'a aucune littérature, mais quelque peu d'expérience et sens naturel) n'eust-il point mieux valu à eux, et à tous autres princes, et hommes de moyen estat, qui ont vescu soubs ces grands, et vivront soubs ceux qui régnent, eslir le moyen chemin en ces choses. C'est à sçavoir moins se soucier, et moins se travailler, et entreprendre moins de choses, et plus craindre à offenser Dieu, et à persécuter le peuple, et leurs voisins, et par tant de voies cruelles que j'ay assez déclarées par cydevant, et prendre des aises et plaisirs honnestes? Leurs vies en seroient plus longues. Les maladies en viendroient plus tard, et leur mort en seroit plus regrettée, et de plus de gens, et moins désirée; et auroient moins à douter la mort. Pourroit-l'on voir de plus beaux exemples pour connoistre que c'est peu de choses que de l'homme, et que cette vie est misérable et briefve, et que ce n'est riens des grands; et qu'incontinent qu'ils sont morts, tout homme en a le corps en horreur et vitupère? et qu'il faut que l'ame sur l'heure se sépare d'eux et qu'elle aille recevoir son jugement? Et à la vérité, en l'instant que l'ame est séparée du corps, jà la sentence en est donnée de Dieu, selon les œuvres et mérites du corps, laquelle sentence s'appelle le jugement particulier.

Thus have you seen the death of many illustrious persons in a short time, who had borne so much sorrow, and endured so many fatigues, only to extend their dominions, and advance their fame and glory, as perhaps tended not only to the shortening of their lives, but to the endangering the welfare of their immortal souls. I am not speaking here of the Turk, for I question not but that he is gone to his predecessors, but of our king and the rest, on whom I hope God will have mercy. But to speak freely (as one that is no great scholar or genius, but has had some experience in the world), would it not have been better for them, and for all other great princes and subjects whatever, to choose a middle course in all their desires; that is, not to be so solicitous and careful about temporal things, and have such vast and unreasonable designs in view; but to be more cautious of offending God, oppressing their subjects, and invading their neighbours, by so many cruel and unchristian ways, as I have mentioned before, and rather employ their time in tranquillity and innocent diversions? Their lives would be longer, their infirmities the later in coming, their deaths less desirable to other people, and less terrible to themselves. Can we desire any clearer examples to prove how poor and inconsiderable a creature man is, how short and miserable his life, and how little difference there is betwixt princes and private persons, since as soon as they are dead, whether rich or poor, their bodies become abominable, all people fly and shun them, and their souls are no sooner separated but they prepare to receive their doom, which is given by God at that very instant of time, according to every man's works, and bodily deserts.

Mémoires (1488–1501) vi, 12
Translated by Andrew R. Scoble

No historian voices more vividly than he the profound realization of the misery of the great, the kings, the powerful and the fortunate of the world.

C.-A. SAINTE-BEUVE
Causeries du lundi (1850)

SIR THOMAS MALORY

FL. 1470

HOW SIR LAUNCELOT DEPARTED TO SEEK THE QUEEN GUENEVER

Than came syr Bors de ganys and sayd my lord syr Launcelot what thynke ye for to doo now to ryde in this royame wyt you wel ye shal fynde fewe frendes be as be may sayd Syr Launcelot kepe you stylle here for I wyl forth on my Iourney and noo man nor chylde shall goo with me. So it was no bote to stryue but he departed and rode westerly & there he sought a vij or viij dayes & atte last he cam to a nonnerye & than was quene Gueneuer ware of sir Launcelot as he walked in the cloystre & whan she sawe hym there she swouned thryse that al the ladyes & Ientyl wymmen had werke ynough to holde the quene vp. So whan she myght speke she callyd ladyes & Ientyl wymmen to hir & sayd ye meruayl fayr ladyes why I make this fare. Truly she said it is for the syght of yonder knyght that yender standeth. Wherfore I praye you al calle hym to me whan syr Launcelot was brought to hyr. Than she sayd to al the ladyes thorowe this man & me hath al this warre be wrought & the deth of the moost noblest knyghtes of the world for thorugh our loue that we haue loued to gyder is my moost noble lord slayn. Therfor syr Launcelot wyt thou wel I am sette in suche a plyte to gete my soule hele & yet I truste thorugh goddes grace that after my deth to haue a syght of the blessyd face of cryst and at domes day to sytte on his ryght syde for as synful as euer I was are sayntes in heuen therfore syr Launcelot I requyre the & beseche the hertelye for al the loue that euer was be-twyxte vs that thou neuer see me more in the vysage & I comande the on goddes behalfe that thou forsake my companye & to thy kyngdom thou torne ageyn & kepe wel thy royame from warre & wrake for as wel as I haue loued the myn hert wyl not serue me to see the for thorugh the & me is the flour of kynges & knyghtes destroyed therfor sir Launcelot goo to thy royame & there take the a wyf & lyue with hir with Ioye & blysse & I praye the hertelye praye for me to our lord that I may amende my

478

myslyuyng. Now swete madam sayd syr Launcelot wold ye that I shold torne ageyn vnto my cuntreye & there to wedde a lady. Nay Madam wyt you wel that shal I neuer do for I shal neuer be soo fals to you of that I haue promysed but the same deystenye that ye haue taken you to I wyl take me vnto for to plese Ihesu & euer for you I cast me specially to praye. Ys thou wylt do so sayd the quene holde thy promyse but I may neuer byleue but that thou wylt torne to the world ageyn wel madam sayd he ye say as pleseth you yet wyst you me neuer fals of my promesse & god defende but I shold forsake the world as ye haue do for in the quest of the sank greal I had fosaken the vanytees of the world had not your lord ben. And ys I had done so at that tyme wyth my herte wylle and thought I had passed al the knyghtes that were in the sanke greal excepte syr Galahad my sone and therfore lady sythen ye haue taken you to perfeccion I must nedys take me to perfection of ryght for I take recorde of god in you I haue had myn erthly Ioye and ys I had founden you now so dysposed I had caste me to haue had you in to myn owne royame.

Le Morte Darthur (1485), xxi

Malory's language and style exactly suit his subject. In no work is there a perfecter harmony—a more sympathetic marriage—of this kind. This chronicler of knighthood is himself a knight. His heart is devoted to the chivalry he portrays, and his tongue is the faithful spokesman of his heart.

JOHN W. HALES
in Craik's English Prose (1893)

LODOVICO ARIOSTO

1 4 7 4 — 1 5 3 3

THE ROSE

Simile alla rosa
che nun chiuso horto in la natiua spina
mentre sola e sicura si riposa
ne gregge ne pastor se le auicina
l aura soaue, e l alba rugiadosa,
l acqua, la terra al suo fauor s inchina
gioueni uaghi e dōne inamorate
amano hauerne, e seni, e tempie ornate

Ma non si tosto dal materno stelo
rimossa uiene, e dal suo ceppo uerde,
ch el fauor e de li huomini e del Cielo
e de l Elementi e di Natura perde.

Like the blooming rose
Which on its native stem unsully'd grows;
Where fencing walls the garden-space surround,
Nor swains, nor browzing cattle tread the ground:
The earth and streams their mutual tribute lend,
Soft breathe the gales, the pearly dews descend:
Fair youths and amorous maidens with delight
Enjoy the grateful scent, and bless the sight.
But if some hand the tender stalk invades,
Lost is its beauty and its colour fades:
No more the care of heaven, or garden's boast,
And all its praise with youths and maidens lost.

Orlando Furioso (1516), i
Translated by John Hoole

*Never once does the poet let his own personality come into the story;
he is more a spectator than an actor—a spectator who is enjoying himself
looking on at his world, almost as though it were not his own creation,
the child of his own imagination. The result is the perfect objectivity and
lucidity that are known as "Homeric clearness." In this simplicity and
clearness of Ariosto Italian art touches perfection; simplicity and clearness are the two qualities that make him the prince of Italian artists—of
artists, not of poets. Ariosto cares nothing at all for the things themselves,
which are detached from reality and a game of the imagination, but he
cares immensely for their form, and at this he toils with the greatest
seriousness. No smallest detail escapes his attention, or is left without
its finishing touches. And the interest being not in the thing but in its
form, we no longer have the sober and comprehensive manner of Dante:
instead of the Dantesque sketches we have finished pictures. The
DECAMERON gave us the period; the ORLANDO gives us the octave, with
a perfect framework, and composed like a picture, with its protagonist,
its accessories, and its background. Politian gave us a series, with the
links left to the imagination. Ariosto gives us a real period, so well distributed and proportioned that it seems like a person. And the effect is
due not only to the material framework, so solid and well composed,
but also to that musical wave, to that flowing and facile surface which
makes us reach forward to the soul while we are following the events
and the motives and effects. In that century of great painters, when the
Italian artists aimed at depicting the image with the last possible touch*

of perfection, Ariosto is the perfect painter. . . . This sublime sim-
plicity combined with complete clearness of vision, is what Galilei rightly
described as the "divineness" of Ariosto.

FRANCESCO DE SANCTIS
Storia della letteratura italiana (1870)
Translated by Joan Redfern

LODOVICO ARIOSTO

1 4 7 4 — 1 5 3 3

HER MATCHLESS PERSON

Di persona era tanto ben formata
    quanto me pinger san pittori industri
    cō bionda chioma lunga, et annodata
    oro nō é che piú risplenda, et lustri
    spargeasi per la guancia delicata
    misto color di rose et di ligustri
    di terso Auorio, era la fronte lieta
    che finia il spatio suo, con giusta meta

Sotto duo negri, et sottilissimi archi
    son duo negri occhi, āzi duo chiari soli
    pietosi a riguardar a muouer parchi
    ītorno cui par ch Amor scherzi et uoli
    et ch indi tutta la pharetra scarchi
    et che uisibilmente i cori inuoli
    quindi il naso per mezo il uiso scende
    che non ritroua Inuidia oue l emende.

Her matchless person every charm combin'd,
Form'd in th' idea of a painter's mind.
Bound in a knot behind, her ringlets roll'd
Down her soft neck, and seem'd like waving gold.
Her cheeks with lilies mix the blushing rose;
Her forehead high like polish'd iv'ry shows.
Beneath two arching brows with splendor shone
Her sparkling eyes, each eye a radiant sun!
Here artful glances, winning looks appear,
And wanton Cupid lies in ambush here:

'Tis hence he bends his bow, he points his dart,
'Tis hence he steals th' unwary gazer's heart.
Her nose so truly shap'd, the faultless frame
Not envy can deface, nor art can blame.

Orlando Furioso (1516), vii
Translated by John Hoole

If painters wish to find easily a perfect example of the beautiful woman, let them read those stanzas of Ariosto in which he describes marvellously the beauties of the enchantress Alcina, and they will see likewise to what extent excellent poets are themselves painters.

LODOVICO DOLCE
L'Aretino. Dialogo della pittura (1557)

MARTIN LUTHER

1 4 8 3 — 1 5 4 6

DOMESTICITY

Ach solt ich das kind wiegen, die windell wasschen, bette machen, stanck riechen, die nacht wachen, seyns schreiens wartten, seyn grindt und blattern heylen, darnach des weybs pflegen, sie erneeren, erbeytten, hie sorgen, da sorgen, hie thun, da thun, das leyden und diss leyden?

Oh, should I nurse the child, wash the diapers, make the beds, smell the stench, remain awake through the night, wait for it to cry, heal its scurf and pimples, afterwards take care of the wife, feed her, work, care for this, care for that, do this, do that, suffer this and suffer that?

Predigt vom ehelichen Leben (1522)

We are not surprised to find in Luther (notoriously a musical man) a rich crop of every kind of vocalic and consonantal assonance. To turn from pre-Lutheran German prose to Luther is, in this respect as well, to pass from medieval night to Renaissance day, as even cursory comparison of Luther with his forerunners will show. . . . We may cite a familiar passage from VOM EHELICHEN LEBEN *that is perhaps the supreme example of this type of almost musical prose. . . . The perfection of this piece of early German prose is such that one does not immediately realize how it* MIGHT *have sounded. Something is undoubtedly due to the occasional omission of the definite article; compare for sound 'das kind wiegen, den stanck riechen, die windell wasschen, das bett machen, die nacht wachen' with Luther's arrangement. Or read the last dozen words with DISS and DAS transposed. It is not, of course, suggested that Luther deliberately selected or shaped his phrases; the assumption is merely that here a naturally associative mind has dictated words and clauses linked to one another by their sound.*

WALTER ETTINGHAUSEN

in German Studies Presented to H. G. Fiedler (1938)

FRANÇOIS RABELAIS

1 4 9 0 ? — 1 5 5 3

THE MOST HORRIBLE SPECTACLE

Il chocqua doncques si roydement sus eulx, sans dyre guare, qu'il les renversoyt comme porcs, frapant à tors et à travers à vieille escrime.

Es uns escarbouilloyt la cervelle, ès aultres rompoyt bras et jambes, ès aultres deslochoyt les spondyles du coul, ès aultres demoulloyt les reins, avalloyt le nez, poschoyt les yeulx, fendoyt les mandibules, enfonçoyt les dens en la gueule, descroulloyt les omoplates, sphaceloyt les greves, desgondoit les ischies, debezilloit les fauciles.

Si quelq'un se vouloyt cascher entre les sepes plus espès, à icelluy freussoit toute l'areste du douz et l'esrenoit comme un chien.

Si aulcun saulver se vouloyt en fuyant, à icelluy faisoyt voler la teste en pieces par la commissure lambdoïde.

Sy quelq'un gravoyt en une arbre, pensant y estre en seureté, icelluy de son baston empaloyt par le fondement.

Si quelq'un de sa vieille congnoissance luy crioyt:

"Ha, Frere Jean, mon amy, Frere Jean, je me rend!

— Il t'est (disoyt il) bien force; mais ensemble tu rendras l'ame à tous les diables."

Et soubdain luy donnoit dronos. Et, si personne tant feust esprins de temerité qu'il luy voulust resister en face, là monstroyt il la force de ses muscles, car il leurs transperçoyt la poictrine par le mediastine et par le cueur. A d'aultres donnant suz la faulte des coustes, leur subvertissoyt l'estomach, et mouroient soubdainement. Es aultres tant fierement frappoyt par le nombril qu'il leurs faisoyt sortir les tripes. Es aultres parmy les couillons persoyt le boiau cullier. Croiez que c'estoyt le plus horrible spectacle qu'on veit oncques.

He hurried therefore upon them so rudely, without crying gare or beware, that he overthrew them like hogs, tumbled them over like swine, striking athwart and alongst, and by one means or other laid so about him, after the old fashion of fencing, that to some he beat out their braines, to others he crushed their armes, battered their legs, and bethwacked their sides till their ribs cracked with it; to others again he unjoynted the spondyles or knuckles of the neck, disfigured their chaps, gashed their faces, made their cheeks hang flapping on their chin, and so swinged and belammed them, that they fell down before him like hay before a Mower: to some others he spoiled the frame of their kidneys, marred their backs, broke their thigh-bones, pash't in their noses, poached out their eyes, cleft their mandibules, tore their jaws, dung in their teeth into their throat, shook asunder their omo-plates or shoulder-blades, sphacelated their shins, mortified their shanks, inflamed their ankles, heaved off of the hinges their ishies, their sciatica or hip-gout, dislocated the joints of their knees, squattered into pieces the boughts or pestles of their thighs, and so thumped, mawled and be-laboured them every where, that never was corne so thick and threefold thresht upon by Plowmens flailes, as were the pitifully disjoynted mem-bers of their mangled bodies, under the mercilesse baton of the crosse. If any offered to hide himself amongst the thickest of the Vines, he laid him squat as a flounder, bruised the ridge of his back, and dash't his reines like a dog. If any thought by flight to escape, he made his head to flie in pieces by the Lambdoidal commissure, which is a seame in the hinder part of the scull. If any one did scramble up into a tree, thinking there to be safe, he rent up his perinee, and impaled him in at the funda-ment. If any of his old acquaintance happened to cry out, Ha Fryar Jhon my friend, Fryar Jhon, quarter, quarter, I yield my self to you, to you I render my self: So thou shalt (said he,) and must whether thou wouldst or no, and withal render and yield up thy soul to all the devils in hell, then suddenly gave them dronos, that is, so many knocks, thumps, raps, dints, thwacks and bangs, as sufficed to warne Pluto of their coming, and dispatch them a going: if any was so rash and full of temerity as to resist him to his face, then was it he did shew the strength of his muscles, for without more ado he did transpierce him by running him in at the breast, through the mediastine and the heart. Others, again, he so quashed and bebumped, that with a sound bounce under the hollow of their short ribs, he overturned their stomachs so that they died immedi-ately: to some with a smart souse on the Epigaster, he would make their midrif swag, then redoubling the blow, gave them such a home-push on the navel, that he made their puddings to gush out. To others through their ballocks he pierced their bum-gut, and left not bowel, tripe nor intral in their body, that had not felt the impetuosity, fiercenesse and fury of his violence. Beleeve that it was the most horrible spectacle that ever one saw.

Les fouaces destroussées, comparurent davant Picrochole les duc de Menuail, comte Spadassin et capitaine Merdaille, et luy dirent:

"Cyre, aujourd'huy nous vous rendons le plus heureux, plus chevaleureux prince qui oncques feust depuis la mort de Alexandre Macedo.

— Couvrez, couvrez vous, dist Picrochole.

— Grand mercy (dirent ilz), Cyre, nous sommes à nostre debvoir. Le moyen est tel:

"Vous laisserez icy quelque capitaine en garnison avec petite bande de gens pour garder la place, laquelle nous semble assez forte, tant par nature que par les rampars faictz à vostre invention. Vostre armée partirez en deux, comme trop mieulx l'entendez. L'une partie ira ruer sur ce Grandgousier et ses gens. Par icelle sera de prime abordée facilement desconfit. Là recouvrerez argent à tas, car le vilain en a du content; vilain, disons nous, parce que un noble prince n'a jamais un sou. Thesaurizer est faict de vilain.— L'aultre partie, cependent, tirera vers Onys, Sanctonge, Angomoys et Gascoigne, ensemble Perigot, Medoc et Elanes. Sans resistence prendront villes, chasteaux et forteresses. A Bayonne, à Sainct Jean de Luc et Fontarabie saysirez toutes les naufs, et, coustoyant vers Galice et Portugal, pillerez tous les lieux maritimes jusques à Ulisbonne, où aurez renfort de tout equipage requis à un conquerent. Par le corbieu, Hespaigne se rendra, car ce ne sont que madourrez! Vous passerez par l'estroict de Sibyle, et là erigerez deux colomnes, plus magnificques que celles de Hercules, à perpetuelle memoire de vostre nom, et sera nommé cestuy destroict la mer Picrocholine. . . .

— Mais (dist il) que faict ce pendent la part de nostre armée qui desconfit ce villain humeux Grandgousier?

— Ilz ne chomment pas (dirent ilz); nous les rencontrerons tantost. Ilz vous ont pris Bretaigne, Normandie, Flandres, Haynault, Brabant, Artoys, Hollande, Selande. Ilz ont passé le Rhein par sus le ventre des Suices et Lansquenetz, et part d'entre eulx ont dompté Luxembourg, Lorraine, La Champaigne, Savoye jusques à Lyon, auquel lieu ont trouvé voz garnisons retournans des conquestes navales de la mer Mediterrannée, et se sont reassemblez en Boheme, après avoir mis à sac Soueve, Vuitemberg, Bavieres, Austriche, Moravie et Stirie; puis ont donné fierement ensemble sus Lubek, Norwerge, Swedenrich, Dace, Gotthie, Engroneland, les Estrelins, jusques à la mer Glaciale. Ce faict, conquesterent les isles Orchades et subjuguerent Escosse, Angleterre et Irlande. . . .

Là present estoit un vieux gentilhomme, esprouvé en divers hazars et vray routier de guerre, nommé Echephron, lequel, ouyant ces propous, dist:

"J'ay grand peur que toute ceste entreprinse sera semblable à la farce du pot au laict, duquel un cordouannier se faisoit riche par resverie; puis, le pot cassé, n'eut de quoy disner. Que pretendez vous par ces belles conquestes? Quelle sera la fin de tant de travaulx et traverses?

— Ce sera (dist Picrochole) que, nous retournez, repouserons à noz aises."

Dont dist Echephron:

"Et, si par cas jamais n'en retournez, car le voyage est long et pereilleux, n'est ce mieulx que dès maintenant nous repousons, sans nous mettre en ces hazars?

— O (dist Spadassin) par Dieu, voicy un bon resveux! Mais allons nous cacher au coing de la cheminée, et là passons avec les dames nostre vie et nostre temps à enfiller des perles, ou à filler comme Sardanapalus. Qui ne se adventure, n'a cheval ny mule, ce dist Salomon.

— Qui trop (dist Echephron) se adventure perd cheval et mule, respondit Malcon.

— Baste! (dist Picrochole) passons oultre. Je ne crains que ces diables de legions de Grandgousier. Ce pendent que nous sommes en Mesopotamie, s'ilz nous donnoient sus la queue, quel remede?"

The carts being unloaded, **and** the money and cakes secured, there came before Picrochole the Duke of Smalltrash, the Earle Swash-buckler, and Captain Durtaille, who said unto him, Sir, this day we make you the happiest, the most warlike and chivalrous Prince that ever was since the death of Alexander of Macedonia. Be covered, be covered, (said Pichrochole.) Grammercie (said they) we do but our duty: The manner is thus, you shall leave some Captain here to have the charge of this Garrison, with a Party competent for keeping of the place, which besides its natural strength, is made stronger by the rampiers and fortresses of your devising. Your Army you are to divide into two parts, as you know very well how to do. One part thereof shall fall upon Grangousier and his forces, by it shall he be easily at the very first shock routed, and then shall you get money by heaps, for the Clown hath store of ready coine: Clown we call him, because a noble and generous Prince hath never a penny, and that to hoard up treasure is but a clownish trick. The other part of the Army in the mean time shall draw towards Onys, Xaintonge, Angoulesme and Gascony: then march to Perigourt, Medos, and Elanes, taking whereever you come without resistance, townes, castles, and forts: Afterwards to Bayonne, St. Jhon de Luz, to Fuentarabia, where you shall seize upon all the ships, and coasting along Galicia and Portugal, shall pillage all the maritime places, even unto Lisbone, where you shall be supplied with all necessaries befitting a Conquerour. By copsodie Spain will yield, for they are but a race of Loobies: then are

486

you to passe by the streights of Gibraltar, where you shall erect two pillars more stately than those of Hercules, to the perpetual memory of your name, and the narrow entrance there shall be called the Picrocholinal sea. . . .

But (said he) what doth that part of our Army in the mean time, which overthrows that unworthy Swill-pot Grangousier? They are not idle (said they) we shall meet with them by and by, they shall have won you Britany, Normandy, Flanders, Haynault, Brabant, Artois, Holland, Zealand; they have past the Rhine over the bellies of the Switsers and Lanskenets, and a Party of these hath subdued Luxemburg, Lorrain, Champaigne, and Savoy, even to Lions, in which place they have met with your forces, returning from the naval Conquests of the Mediterranean sea: and have rallied again in Bohemia, after they had plundered and sacked Suevia, Wittemberg, Bavaria, Austria, Moravia, and Styria. Then they set fiercely together upon Lubeck, Norway, Swedeland, Rie, Denmark, Gitland, Greenland, the Sterlins, even unto the frozen sea: this done, they conquered the iles of Orkney, and subdued Scotland, England, and Ireland. . . . There was there present at that time an old Gentleman well experienced in the warres, a sterne souldier, and who had been in many great hazards, named Echephron, who hearing this discourse, said, I do greatly doubt that all this enterprise will be like the tale or interlude of the pitcher full of milk, wherewith a Shoemaker made himself rich in conceit: but, when the pitcher was broken, he had not whereupon to dine: what do you pretend by these large Conquests? what shall be the end of so many labours and crosses? Thus it shall be (said Picrochole) that when we are returned, we shall sit down, rest and be merry. But (said Echephron,) if by chance you should never come back, for the voyage is long and dangerous, were it not better for us to take our rest now, then unnecessarily to expose our selves to so many dangers? O (said Swashbuckler,) by G——, here is a good dotard, come, let us go hide our selves in the corner of a chimney, and there spend the whole time of our life amongst ladies, in threading of pearles, or spinning like Sardanapalus: He that nothing ventures, hath neither horse nor mule, (sayes Solomon). He who adventureth too much (said Echephron) loseth both horse and mule, answered Malchon. Enough (said Picrochole,) go forward: I feare nothing, but that these devillish legions of Grangousier, whilest we are in Mesopotamia, will come on our backs, and charge up our reer.

La Vie treshorrificque du grand Gargantua (1552)
Translated by Sir Thomas Urquhart

I have re-read, after CLARISSA, *some chapters of Rabelais, such as the battle of Frère Jean des Entommeures, and the counselling of Picrochole (I know them, however, almost by heart). But I have read them again with very great pleasure, because they are the most vivid pictures in the world.*

It is not that I put Rabelais beside Horace, but if Horace is the first among the writers of good epistles, Rabelais, when he is good, is the first among good buffoons. It is not necessary that there be two men of this profession in a nation, but it is necessary that there be one. I repent having formerly spoken too much ill of him.

F. M. AROUET DE VOLTAIRE
Letter to Marquise du Deffand (April 12, 1760)

FRANÇOIS RABELAIS

1 4 9 0 ? — 1 5 5 3

FELICITY OF MARRIAGE

Et voyent les dolens peres & meres hors leurs maisons enleuer & tirer par **v**n incongneu, estrangier, barbare, mastin tout pourry, chancreux, cadauereux, paouure, malheureux, leurs tant belles, delicates, riches, & saines filles, les quelles tant cherement auoient nourriez en tout exercice vertueux, auoient disciplinées en toute honesteté: esperans en temps oportun les colloquer par mariage auecques les enfans de leurs voisins & antiques amis nourriz & instituez de mesme soing, pour paruenir à ceste felicité de mariage, que d'eulx ilz veissent naistre lignaige raportant & hæreditant non moins aux meurs de leurs peres & meres, que à leurs biens meubles & hæritaiges. Quel spectacle pensez vous que ce leurs soit? Ne croyez, que plus enorme feust la desolation du peuple Romain & ses confœderez entendens le deces de Germanicus Drusus. Ne croyez que plus pitoyable feust le desconfort des Lacedæmoniens, quand de leurs pays veirent par l'adultere Troian furtiuement enleuée Helene Grecque. . . . Et restent en leurs maisons priuez de leurs filles tant aimées, le pere mauldissant le iour & heure de ses nopces: la mere regrettant que n'estoit auortée en tel tant triste & malheureux enfantement: & en pleurs & lamentations finent leurs vie, laquelle estoit de raison finir en ioye & bon tractement de icelles.

May not these Fathers and Mothers (think you) be sorrowful and heavy-hearted, when they see an unknown Fellow, a Vagabond Stranger, a barbarous Lowt, a rude Curr, rotten, fleshless, putrified, scraggy, bily, botchy, poor, a forlorn Caitif and miserable Snake, by an open Rapt, snatch away before their own Eyes, their so fair, delicate, neat, wellbehavoured, richly provided for, and healthful Daughters, on whose Breeding and Education they had spared no Cost nor Charges, by bringing them up in an honest Discipline, to all the honourable and vertuous Employments becoming one of their Sex, descended of a noble Parentage, hoping by those commendable and industrious means in an opportune and convenient time to bestow them on the worthy sons of their well-deserving Neighbours and ancient Friends, who had nourished, entertained, taught, instructed and schooled their Children with the same Care and Sollicitude, to make them Matches fit to attain to the Felicity of a so happy Marriage; that from them might issue an Off-spring and Progeny no less Heirs to the laudable Endowments and exquisite Qualifications of their Parents whom they every way resemble, than to their Personal and Real Estates, Moveables and Inheritances? How doleful, trist and plangorous would such a Sight and Pageantry prove unto them? You shall not need to think that the Collachrymation of the Romans, and their Confederates, at the Decease of Germanicus Drusus, was comparable to this Lamentation of theirs? Neither would I have you to believe, that the Discomfort and Anxiety of the Lacedæmonians, when the Greek Helen, by the Perfidiousness of the Adulterous Trojan Paris was privily stollen away out of their Country, was greater or more pitiful than this ruthful and deplorable Collugency of theirs? . . . They wretchedly stay at their own miserable Homes, destitute of their well-beloved Daughters; the Fathers cursing the days and the hours wherein they were married; and the Mothers howling, and crying that it was not their fortune to have brought forth Abortive Issues, when they hapned to be delivered of such unfortunate Girls; and in this pitiful plight spend at best the remainder of their Time with Tears and Weeping for those their Children of and from whom they expected (and with good reason should have obtained and reaped) in these latter days of theirs, Joy and Comfort.

Le Tiers Livre des faicts et dicts
Heroïques du bon Pantagruel (1552)
Translated by Sir Thomas Urquhart

Rabelais, before Montaigne, is the father of that clear, robust and supple French prose, that is to be spoken rather than written, that is meant to fall from the lips, and that has never been more beautiful.

ÉMILE FAGUET
Seizième Siècle: Études littéraires (1894)

CLÉMENT MAROT

1 4 9 5 ? — 1 5 4 4

DE L'ABBÉ, & DE SON VALET

Monsieur l'Abbé et monsieur son valet
Sont faictz egaulx tous deux comme de cire:
L'un est grand fol, l'autre petit folet;
L'un veult railler, l'autre gaudir et rire;
L'un boit du bon, l'autre ne boit du pire;
Mais un debat au soir entre eulx s'esmeut,
Car maistre abbé toute la nuict ne veult
Estre sans vin, que sans secours ne meure,
Et son valet jamais dormir ne peult
Tandis qu'au pot une goute en demeure.

OF THE ABBOT AND HIS VALET

His grace the Abbot and his servynge ladde
Are of one claye as honey is of wax;
One is a loon, the other one is madde;
One loves a joke, the other his sides cracks;
One drinks goode wine, the other never lacks.
Thus a debate one nighte between them rose:
Wineless his worship would no more repose
Than he would die of all his friends bereft,
Wheras his valet's eyelids could not close
Whyle in the bowle a single drop was left.

Epigramme lxxxv (1536)
Translated by Wilfrid Thorley

The model of the two-edged epigram.

ÉMILE FAGUET
Seizième siècle: Études littéraires (1894)

CLÉMENT MAROT

1 4 9 5 ? — 1 5 4 4

L'AMOUR AU BON VIEULX TEMPS

Au bon vieulx temps un train d'amour regnoit
Qui sans grand art et dons se demenoit,
Si qu'un bouquet donné d'amour profonde,
C'estoit donné toute la terre ronde,
Car seulement au cueur on se prenoit.
Et si par cas à jouyr on venoit,
Sçavez-vous bien comme on s'entretenoit?
Vingt ans, trente ans: cela duroit un monde
    Au bon vieulx temps.

Or est perdu ce qu'amour ordonnoit:
Rien que pleurs fainctz, rien que changes on n'oyt;
Qui vouldra donc qu'à aymer je me fonde,
Il fault premier que l'amour on refonde,
Et qu'on la meine ainsi qu'on la menoit
    Au bon vieulx temps.

OLD-TIME LOVE

In good old days such sort of love held sway
As artlessly and simply made its way,
And a few flowers, the gift of love sincere,
Than all the round earth's riches were more dear:

For to the heart alone did they address their lay.
And if they chanced to love each other, pray
Take heed how well they then knew how to stay
For ages faithful—twenty, thirty year—
    In good old days.

But now is lost Love's rule they used t' obey;
Only false tears and changes fill the day.
Who would have me a lover now appear
Must love make over in the olden way,
And let it rule as once it held its sway
    In good old days.

Translation Anonymous

491

He is the foremost master of a genre which is peculiarly French.

C. D. D'HÉRICAULT
Les Poëtes français (1861)

ANONYMOUS

FIFTEENTH CENTURY?

CHEVY CHASE

The First Fit.

The Persé owt of Northombarlande.
 An a vowe to God mayd he,
That he wolde hunte in the mountayns
 Off Chyviat within dayes thre,
In the mauger of doughtè Dogles,
 And all that ever with him be.

The fattiste hartes in all Cheviat
 He sayd he wold kill, and cary them away:
Be my feth, sayd the dougheti Doglas agayn,
 I wyll let that hontyng yf that I may.

Then the Persé owt of Banborowe cam,
 With him a myghtye meany;
With fifteen hondrith archares bold;
 The wear chosen out of shyars thre.

This begane on a monday at morn
 In Cheviat the hillys so he;
The chyld may rue that ys un-born,
 It was the mor pitté.

The dryvars thorowe the woodes went
 For to reas the dear;
Bomen bickarte uppone the bent
 With ther browd aras cleare.

Then the wyld thorowe the woodes went
 On every syde shear;
Grea-hondes thorowe the greves glent
 For to kyll thear dear.

492

The begane in Chyviat the hyls abone
    Yerly on a monnyn-day;
Be that it drewe to the oware off none
    A hondrith fat hartes ded ther lay.

The blewe a mort uppone the bent,
    The semblyd on sydis shear;
To the quyrry then the Persè went
    To se the bryttlynge off the deare.

He sayd, It was the Duglas promys
    This day to meet me hear;
But I wyste he wold faylle verament:
    A gret oth the Persè swear.

At the laste a squyar of Northombelonde
    Lokyde at his hand full ny,
He was war ath the doughetie Doglas comynge:
    With him a myghtè meany,

Both with spear, 'byll,' and brande:
    Yt was a myghti sight to se.
Hardyar men both off hart nar hande
    Wear not in Christiantè.

The wear twenty hondrith spear-men good
    Withouten any fayle;
The wear borne a-long be the watter a Twyde,
    Yth bowndes of Tividale.

Leave off the brytlyng of the dear, he sayde,
    And to your bowys look ye tayk good heed;
For never sithe ye wear on your mothars borne
    Had ye never so mickle need.

The dougheti Dogglas on a stede
    He rode all his men beforne;
His armor glytteryde as dyd a glede;
    A bolder barne was never born.

Tell me 'what' men ye ar, he says,
    Or whos men that ye be:
Who gave youe leave to hunte in this
    Chyviat chays in the spyt of me?

The first mane that ever him an answear mayd,
    Yt was the good lord Persè:

We wyll not tell the 'what' men we ar, he says,
    Nor whos men that we be;
But we wyll hount hear in this chays
    In the spyte of thyne, and of the.

The fattiste hartes in all Chyviat
    We have kyld, and cast to carry them a-way.
Be my troth, sayd the doughtè Dogglas agayn,
    Ther-for the ton of us shall de this day.

Then sayd the doughtè Doglas
    Unto the lord Persè:
To kyll all thes giltless men,
    A-las! it wear great pittè.

But, Persè, thowe art a lord of lande,
    I am a yerle callyd within my contre;
Let all our men uppone a parti stande;
    And do the battell off the and of me.

Nowe Cristes cors on his crowne, sayd the lord Persè.
    Who-soever ther-to says nay.
Be my troth, doughtè Doglas, he says,
    Thow shalt never se that day;

Nethar in Ynglonde, Skottlonde, nar France,
    Nor for no man of a woman born,
But and fortune be my chance,
    I dar met him on man for on.

Then bespayke a squyar off Northombarlonde,
    Ric. Wytharynton was his nam;
It shall never be told in Sothe-Ynglonde, he says,
    To kyng Herry the fourth for sham.

I wat youe byn great lordes twaw,
    I am a poor squyar of lande;
I wyll never se my captayne fyght on a fylde,
    And stande my-selffe, and looke on,
But whyll I may my weppone welde,
    I wyll not 'fayl' both harte and hande.

That day, that day, that dredfull day:
    The first Fit here I fynde.
And youe wyll here any mor athe hountyng a the Chyviat,
    Yet ys ther mor behynde.

The Second Fit.

The Yngglishe men hade ther bowys yebent,
    Ther hartes were good yenoughe;
The first of arros that the shote off,
    Seven skore spear-men the sloughe.

Yet bydys the yerle Doglas uppon the bent,
    A captayne good yenoughe,
And that was sene verament,
    For he wrought hom both woo and wouche.

The Dogglas pertyd his ost in thre,
    Lyk a cheffe cheften off pryde,
With suar speares off myghttè tre
    The cum in on every syde.

Thrughe our Yngglishe archery
    Gave many a wounde full wyde;
Many a doughete the garde to dy,
    Which ganyde them no pryde.

The Yngglishe men let thear bowys be,
    And pulde owt brandes that wer bright;
It was a hevy syght to se
    Bryght swordes on basnites lyght.

Thorowe ryche male, and myne-ye-ple
    Many sterne the stroke downe streght:
Many a freyke, that was full free,
    Ther undar foot dyd lyght.

At last the Duglas and the Persè met,
    Lyk to captayns of myght and mayne;
The swapte togethar tyll the both swat
    With swordes, that wear of fyn myllàn.

Thes worthè freckys for to fyght
    Ther-to the wear full fayne,
Tyll the bloode owte off thear basnetes sprente,
    As ever dyd heal or rayne.

Holde the, Persè, sayd the Doglas,
    And i' feth I shall the brynge
Wher thowe shalte have a yerls wagis
    Of Jamy our Scottish kynge.

Thoue shalte have thy ransom fre,
　I hight the hear this thinge,
For the manfullyste man yet art thowe,
　　That ever I conqueryd in filde fightyng.

Nay 'then' sayd the lord Persè,
　I tolde it the beforne,
That I wolde never yeldyde be
　To no man of a woman born.

With that ther cam an arrowe hastely
　Forthe off a mightie wane,
Hit hathe strekene the yerle Duglas
　In at the brest bane.

Thoroue lyvar and longs bathe
　The sharp arrowe ys gane,
That never after in all his lyffe days,
　He spayke mo wordes but ane,
That was, Fyghte ye, my merry men, whyllys ye may,
　For my lyff days ben gan.

The Persè leanyde on his brande,
　And sawe the Duglas de;
He tooke the dede man be the hande,
　And sayd, Wo ys me for the!

To have savyde thy lyffe I wold have pertyd with
　My landes for years thre,
For a better man of hart, nare of hande
　Was not in all the north countrè.

Off all that se a Skottishe knyght,
　Was callyd Sir Hewe the Mongon-byrry,
He sawe the Duglas to the deth was dyght;
　He spendyd a spear a trusti tre:

He rod uppon a corsiare
　Throughe a hendrith archery;
He never styntyde, nar never blane,
　Tyll he came to the good lord Persè.

He set uppone the lord Persè
　A dynte, that was full soare;
With a suar spear of a myghtè tre
　Clean thorow the body he the Persè bore,

Athe tothar syde, that a man myght se,
    A large cloth yard and mare:
Towe bettar captayns wear nat in Christiantè,
    Then that day slain wear ther.

An archar off Northomberlonde
    Say slean was the lord Persè,
He bar a bende-bow in his hande,
    Was made off trusti tre:

An arow, that a cloth yarde was lang,
    To th' hard stele halyde he;
A dynt, that was both sad and soar,
    He sat on Sir Hewe the Mongon-byrry.

The dynt yt was both sad and sar,
    That he of Mongon-byrry sete;
The swane-fethars, that his arrowe bar,
    With his hart blood the wear wete.

Ther was never a freake wone foot wolde fle,
    But still in stour dyd stand,
Heawyng on yche othar, whyll the myght dre,
    With many a bal-ful brande.

This battell begane in Chyviat
    An owar befor the none,
And when even-song bell was rang
    The battell was nat half done.

The tooke 'on' on ethar hand
    Be the lyght off the mone;
Many hade no strenght for to stande,
    In Chyviat the hyllys aboun.

Of fifteen hondrith archars of Ynglonde
    Went away but fifti and thre;
Of twenty hondrith spear-men of Skotlonde,
    But even five and fifti:

But all wear slayne Cheviat within:
    The hade no strengthe to stand on hie;
The chylde may rue that ys un-borne,
    It was the mor pittè.

Thear was slayne with the lord Persè
    Sir John of Agerstone,
Sir Roger the hinde Hartly,
    Sir Wyllyam the bolde Hearone.

Sir Jorg the worthè Lovele
    A knyght of great renowen,
Sir Raff the ryche Rugbè
    With dyntes wear beaten dowene.

For Wetharryngton my harte was wo,
    That ever he slayne shulde be;
For when both his leggis wear hewyne in to,
    Yet he knyled and fought on hys kne.

Ther was slayne with the dougheti Douglas
    Sir Hewe the Mongon-byrry,
Sir Davye Lwdale, that worthè was,
    His sistars son was he:

Sir Charles a Murrè, in that place,
    That never a foot wolde fle;
Sir Hewe Maxwell, a lorde he was,
    With the Duglas dyd he dey.

So on the morrowe the mayde them byears
    Off byrch, and hasell so 'gray;'
Many wedous with wepyng tears,
    Cam to fach ther makys a-way.

Tivydale may carpe off care,
    Northombarlond may mayk grat mone,
For towe such captayns, as slayne wear thear,
    On the march perti shall never be none.

Word ys commen to Edden-burrowe,
    To Jamy the Skottishe kyng,
That dougheti Duglas, lyff-tenant of the Merches,
    He lay slean Chyviot with-in.

His handdes dyd he weal and wryng,
    He sayd, Alas, and woe ys me!
Such another captayn Skotland within,
    He sayd, y-feth shuld never be.

Worde ys commyn to lovly Londone
  Till the fourth Harry our kyng,
That lord Persè, leyff-tennante of the Merchis,
  He lay slayne Chyviat within.

God have merci on his soll, sayd kyng Harry,
  Good lord, yf thy will it be!
I have a hondrith captayns in Yynglonde, he sayd,
  As good as ever was hee:
But Persè, and I brook my lyffe,
  Thy deth well quyte shall be.

As our noble kyng made his a-vowe,
  Lyke a noble prince of renowen,
For the deth of the lord Persè,
  He dyd the battel of Hombyll-down:

Wher syx and thritte Skottish knyghtes
  On a day wear beaten down:
Glendale glytteryde on ther armor bryght,
  Over castill, towar, and town.

This was the hontynge off the Cheviat;
  That tear begane this spurn:
Old men that knowen the grownde well yenoughe,
  Call it the Battell of Otterburn.

At Otterburn began this spurne
  Uppon a monnyn day:
Ther was the dougghté Doglas slean,
  The Persè never went away.

Ther was never a tym on the march partes
  Sen the Doglas and the Persè met,
But yt was marvele, and the redde blude ronne not,
  As the reane doys in the stret.

Jhesue Christ our balys bete,
  And to the blys us brynge!
Thus was the hountynge of the Chevyat:
  God send us all good ending!

The old song of Chevy-Chase is the favourite ballad of the common people of England, and Ben Jonson used to say he had rather have been the author of it than of all his works. Sir Philip Sidney in his Discourse of Poetry speaks of it in the following words: 'I never heard the old song of Piercy and Douglas, that I found not my heart more moved than with a trumpet; and yet it is sung but by some blind crowder with no rougher voice than rude style; which being so evil apparelled in the dust and cobwebs of that uncivil age, what would it work trimmed in the gorgeous eloquence of Pindar?'

JOSEPH ADDISON
The Spectator (May 21, 1711)

ANONYMOUS

FIFTEENTH CENTURY

LAWYER PATELIN

Patelin.

Or vien çà, et parles. Qu'es tu?
Ou demandeur ou defendeur?

Le Bergier.

J'ay afaire à un entendeur,
Entendez vous bien, mon doulx maistre,
A qui j'ay long temps mené paistre
Ses brebis, et les (y) gardoye.
Par mon serment, je regardoye
Qu'il me payoit petitement. . . .
Diray je tout?

Patelin.

Dea, seurement
A son conseil doit on tout dire.

Le Bergier.

Il est vray et vérité, sire,
Que je les y'ay assommées,
Tant que plusieurs se sont pasmées
Maintesfois et sont cheutes mortes
Tant feussent elles saines et fortes.
Et puis je luy fesoie entendre,
Affin qu'il ne m'en peust reprendre,

500

Qu'ilz mouroient de la clavelée.
Ha! fait il, ne soit plus meslée
Avec les aultres: jette la!
Volentiers, fais-je. Mais cela
Se faisoit par une autre voye,
Car, par saint Jehan, je les mengeoye,
Qui sçavoye bien la maladie!
Que voulez vous que je vous die?
J'ay cecy tant continué,
J'en ai assommé et tué
Tant qu'il s'en est bien apperceu;
Et quant il s'est trouvé deceu,
M'aist dieu! il m'a fait espier,
Car on les oyt bien hault crier,
Entendez vous, quant on le fait.
Or ay je esté prins sur le fait,
Je ne le puis jamais nier.
Si vous voudroy je bien prier
(Pour du mien j'ay assez finance)
Que nous deux luy baillons l'avance.
Je sçay bien qu'il a bonne cause:
Mais vous trouverez bien tel clause,
Se voulez, qu'il l'aura mauvaise.

Patelin.

Par ta foy, seras tu bien aise?
Que donras tu se je renverse
Le droit de ta partie adverse,
Et se l'en t'en envoye assoulz?

Le Bergier.

Je ne vous paieray point en solz,
Mais en bel or à la couronne.

Patelin.

Donc auras tu ta cause bonne. . . .
Se tu parles, on te prendra
Coup à coup aux positions;
Et en telz cas, confessions
Sont si tres prejudiciables
Et nuysent tant que ce sont diables!
Et pour ce vecy qu'il fauldra:
Ja tost quant on t'appellera

Pour comparoir en jugement,
Tu ne respondras nullement
Fors Bê, pour rien que l'en te die.

Patelin

Come here and speak. What are you? Plaintiff or defendant?

The Shepherd

I am talking to an expert; listen well! My gentle master, whose sheep I have pastured and kept for a long time—on my oath, I considered my pay too small—shall I tell everything?

Patelin

Surely, you must tell everything to your lawyer.

The Shepherd

It is true and the truth, sir, that I knocked them on the head, so that many a time several fainted and dropped dead, however healthy and strong they might have been. And then I made him believe (so he would not blame me) that they died of the sheep-pox. "Ha!" says he, "don't let it get mixed up with the others; throw it away!" "Gladly," says I. But I did it differently, for, by George, I ate them, knowing well of what they died. What shall I tell you? I continued at it until I slaughtered so many of them that my master noticed it; and when he found out he'd been fooled, so help me God, he got someone to spy on me. For, as you understand, they can be heard bleating very loudly when one does the job. Now, I was caught in the act, I cannot deny it. I would like to propose (as for me, I have enough money) that both of us should post a bond against loss of the case. I know well that he has a good case; but you'll devise such a trick, if you want, that the plaintiff will have a bad one.

Patelin

By God, won't you be glad if I should do that! What will you give me if I succeed in turning the tables on your adversary, and obtain you an acquittal?

The Shepherd

I will not pay you in coin, but in beautiful crowned gold.

Patelin

Then your case will be good! . . . If you speak, they'll catch you every time you make a statement, and in such cases, confessions are so tre-

mendously prejudicial, and harmful like the devil! Therefore, let me
suggest what you should do: as soon as they call you to appear at trial,
you will answer nothing except *ba-aa-h*, however much they might
question you!

L'Avocat Patelin (c. 1470)

A little prodigy of art.

JEAN FRANÇOIS MARMONTEL
Éléments de littérature (1787)

ANONYMOUS

FIFTEENTH CENTURY

OF THE VIRGIN AND CHILD

'Lullay, myn lykyng, my dere sone, myn swetyng,
Lullay, my dere herte, myn owyn dere derlyng.'

I saw a fayr maydyn syttyn and synge;
Sche lullyd a lytyl chyld, a swete lordyng.

That eche Lord is that that made alle thinge;
Of alle lordis he is Lord, of alle kynges Kyng.

Ther was mekyl melody at that chyldes berthe;
Alle tho wern in heuene blys, thei made mekyl merth.

Aungele bryght, thei song that nyght and seydyn to that chyld,
'Blyssid be thou, and so be sche that is bothe mek and myld.'

Prey we now to that chyld, and to his moder dere,
Grawnt hem his blyssyng that now makyn chere.

The masterpiece of the lullaby carols.

RICHARD L. GREENE
The Early English Carols (1935)

ANONYMOUS

FIFTEENTH CENTURY

ON THE VIRGIN

I syng a of a mayden
    that is makeles,
Kyng of alle kynges
    to here sone che ches.
He cam also stylle
    ther his moder was,
As dew in Aprylle
    that fallyt on the gras.
He cam also stylle
    to his moderes bowr,
As dew in Aprille
    that fallyt on the flour.
He cam also stylle
    ther his moder lay,
As dew in Aprille
    that fallyt on the spray.
Moder and maydyn
    was never non but che;
Wel may swych a lady
    Godes moder be.

ADAM

Adam lay i-bowndyn,
    bowndyn in a bond,
Fowre thowsand wynter
    thowt he not to long;
And al was for an appil,
    an appil that he tok,
As clerkes fyndyn wretyn
    in here book.
Ne hadde the appil take ben,
    the appil taken ben,
Ne hadde never our lady
    a ben hevene quen.
Blyssid be the tyme
    that appil take was!
Therfore we mown syngyn
    Deo gracias.

504

The highest level of lyrical beauty of which medieval poetry was capable.

English Literature at the Close of the Middle Ages (1945)

ANONYMOUS

FIFTEENTH CENTURY?

QUIA AMORE LANGUEO

In the vaile of restles mynd
  I sowght in mownteyn & in mede,
trustyng a treulofe for to fynd:
  vpon an hyll than toke I hede;
  a voise I herd (and nere I yede)
    in gret dolour complaynyng tho,
  "see, derë soule, my sydës blede
    Quia amore langueo."

Vpon thys mownt I fand a tree;
  vndir thys tree a man sittyng;
from hede to fote wowndyd was he,
  hys hert blode I saw bledyng;
  A semely man to be a kyng,
    A graciose face to loke vnto.
  I askyd hym how he had paynyng,
    he said, "*Quia amore langueo.*"

I am treulove that fals was neuer:
  my sistur, mannys soule, I loued hyr thus;
By-cause I wold on no wyse disseuere,
  I left my kyngdome gloriouse;
  I purueyd hyr a place full preciouse;
    she flytt I folowyd I luffed her soo;
  that I suffred thes paynès piteuouse
    Quia amore langueo.

My faire love and my spousë bryght,
  I saued hyr fro betyng and she hath me bett;
I clothed hyr in grace and heuenly lyght,
  this blody surcote she hath on me sett;

for langyng love, I will not lett,
    swetë strokys be thes, loo;
I haf loued euer als I hett,
    Quia amore langueo.

I crownyd hyr with blysse and she me with thorne,
I led hyr to chambre and she me to dye;
I browght hyr to worship and she me to skorne,
    I dyd hyr reuerence and she me velanye.
to love that loueth is no maistrye,
    hyr hate made neuer my love hyr foo;
ask than no moo questions whye,
    but *Quia amore langueo.*

loke vnto myn handys, man!
thes gloues were geuen me whan I hyr sowght;
they be nat white but rede and wan,
    embrodred with blode my spouse them bowght;
they wyll not of I lefe them nowght,
    I wowe hyr with them where euer she goo;
thes handes full frendly for hyr fowght,
    Quia amore langueo.

Maruell not, man, thof I sitt styll,
    my love hath shod me wondyr strayte;
she boklyd my fete as was hyr wyll
    with sharp nailes well thow maist waite!
in my love was neuer dissaite,
    for all my membres I haf opynd hyr to;
my body I made hyr hertys baite,
    Quia amore langueo.

In my syde I haf made hyr nest,
    loke in me how wyde a wound is here!
this is hyr chambre here shall she rest,
    that she and I may slepe in fere.
here may she wasshe if any filth were;
    here is socour for all hyr woo;
cum if she will she shall haf chere,
    Quia amore langueo.

I will abide till she be redy,
    I will to hyr send or she sey nay;
If she be rechelesse I will be redy,
    If she be dawngerouse I will hyr pray.

If she do wepe than byd I nay;
    myn armes ben spred to clypp hyr to;
crye onys, "I cum!" now, soule, assaye!
    Qui amore langueo.

I sitt on an hille for to se farre,
I loke to the vayle my spouse I see;
now rynne she awayward, now cummyth she narre,
    yet fro myn eye syght she may nat be;
sum waite ther pray to make hyr flee,
    I rynne tofore to chastise hyr foo;
recouer my soule agayne to me,
    Quia amore langueo.

My swete spouse will we goo play;
    apples ben rype in my gardine;
I shall clothe the in new array,
    thy mete shall be mylk honye & wyne;
now, dere soule, latt us go dyne,
    thy sustenance is in my skrypp, loo!
tary not now fayre spousë myne,
    Quia amore langueo.

yf thow be fowle I shall make [thee] clene,
    if thow be seke, I shall the hele;
yf thow owght morne I shall be-mene,
    spouse, why will thow nowght with me dele?
thow fowndyst neuer love so lele;
    what wilt thow, sowle that I shall do?
I may of vnkyndnes the appele,
    Quia amore langueo.

What shall I do now with my spouse?
    abyde I will hyre iantilnesse,
wold she loke onys owt of hyr howse
    of flesshely affeccions and vnclennesse;
hyr bed is made hyr bolstar is in blysse,
    hyr chambre is chosen, suche ar no moo;
loke owt at the wyndows of kyndnesse,
    Quia amore langueo.

Long and love thow neuer so hygh,
    yit is my love more than thyn may be;
thow gladdyst thou wepist I sitt the bygh,
    yit myght thow, spouse loke onys at me!

507

spouse, shuld I alway fedë the
with childys mete? nay, love, nat so!
I pray the, love, with aduersite,
Quia amore langueo.

My spouse is in chambre, hald your pease!
make no noyse but lat hyr slepe;
my babe shall sofre noo disease,
I may not here my dere childe wepe,
for with my pappe I shall hyr kepe;
no wondyr thowgh I tend hyr to,
thys hoole in my side had neuer ben so depe,
but *Quia amore langueo.*

Wax not wery, myn owne dere wyfe,
what mede is aye to lyffe in comfort?
for in tribulacion, I ryñ more ryfe
ofter tymes than in disport;
In welth, in woo, euer I support;
than, derë soule, go neuer me fro!
thy mede is markyd, whan thow art mort,
in blysse; *Quia amore langueo.*

*The finest mystical poem written in English before the great age of
English mystical poetry, the seventeenth century.*

T. EARLE WELBY
A Popular History of English Poetry (1933)

MAURICE SCÈVE

C. 1 5 0 0 — 1 5 6 4

FROM LA DELIE

Au Caucasus de mon souffrir lyé
Dedans l'Enfer de ma peine eternelle,
Ce grand desir de mon bien oblyé,
Comme l'Aultour de ma mort immortelle,
Ronge l'esprit par une fureur telle,
Que consommé d'un si ardent poursuyvre,
Espoir le fait, non pour mon bien, revivre:

Mais pour au mal renaistre incessamment,
Affin qu'en moy ce mien malheureux vivre
Prometheus tourmente innocemment.

Bound to the Caucasus of my suffering, within the Hell of my eternal punishment, the great desire of my forgotten happiness, vulture of my everlasting death, gnaws my soul with such fury that, consumed by so fiery a pursuit, hope makes my spirit live again, to my loss; I am reborn constantly to suffering so that this unhappy life of mine tortures me like an innocent Prometheus.

Délie, Objet de plus haute vertu (1544)

Without doubt LA DÉLIE *is the most powerful and masterly of poetic meditations.*

THIERRY MAULNIER
Introduction à la poésie française (1939)

JOACHIM DU BELLAY

C . 1 5 2 2 — 1 5 6 0

THE POET

O combien je desire voir secher ces *Printemps,* chastier ces *Petites jeunesses,* rabattre ces *Coups d'essay,* tarir ces *Fontaines,* bref, abolir tous ces beaux titres assez suffisans pour degouster tout lecteur sçavant d'en lire davantage. Je ne souhaite moins, que ces *Despourveus,* ces humbles *Esperans,* ces *Bannis de lyesse,* ces *Esclaves,* ces *Traverseurs* soient renvoyez à la table ronde, et ces belles petites devises aux gentils hommes et damoiselles, d'où on les a empruntées. Que diray plus? Je supplie à Phœbus Apollon, que la France, après avoir esté si longtemps sterile, grosse de luy, enfante bientost un poëte, dont le luc bien resonant fasse taire ces enrouées cornemuses, non autrement que les grenouilles, quand on jette une pierre en leurs marais. Et si, nonobstant cela, cette fievre chaude d'escrire les tourmentoit encores, je leur conseilleroy' ou d'aller prendre medecine en Anticyre, ou, pour le mieux, se remettre à l'etude, et sans honte, à l'exemple de Caton, qui en sa vieillesse apprit les lettres grecques. Je pense bien qu'en parlant ainsi de nos rymeurs, je sembleray à beaucoup trop mordant et satyrique: mais veritable à ceux qui ont sçavoir et jugement et qui desirent la santé de nostre langue, où

509

cet ulcere et chair corrompue de mauvaises poësies est si inveterée, qu'elle ne se peut oster qu'avec le fer et le cautere. Pour conclure ce propos, sçache, lecteur, que celui sera veritablement le poëte que je cerche en nostre langue, qui me fera indigner, appaiser, ejouir, douloir, aimer, haïr, admirer, estonner: bref, qui tiendra la bride de mes affections, me tournant çà et là à son plaisir. Voyla la vraye pierre de touche où il faut que tu esprouves tous poëmes et en toutes langues.

Oh, how greatly do I desire to see dried up these springs, chastised these little youths, and destroyed these experimental verses, running dry these fountains, in short, abolished all these fine titles, sufficient to disgust any learned reader from reading further.

I hope no less that these *deprived ones*, these humble *hopefuls*, these *exiles from joy*, these *slaves*, and these *travellers* may be sent back to the round table, and these pretty little devices to the gentlemen and damosels from whom they were borrowed. What shall I say more? I beg Phoebus Apollo, that France, having been so long sterile, big with child through him may soon bring forth a poet, whose well resounding lute may silence these hoarse bagpipes, none otherwise than the frogs when a stone is thrown into their marsh. And if, notwithstanding this, the hot fever of writing torment them still, I would advise them either to go take medicine in Anticyra, or, better, to return to their studies: and without shame, after the example of Cato, who in his old age, learnt Greek letters.

I well believe that in thus speaking of our rhymesters I shall appear to many too biting and satirical, but veridical to those who have learning and judgment, and who desire the health of our language, wherein that ulcer and corrupt flesh of bad poetry is so inveterate, that it can be removed only with iron and cauterizing. To conclude this question, know, reader, that he will be veritably the poet whom I seek in our language, who will make me to be angry, to be appeased, to rejoice, to be grieved, to love, to hate, to admire, to wonder, in short, who will hold the reins of my emotions, turning me this way and that at his pleasure. That is the true touchstone whereby thou shouldst test all poems in every language.

La Deffense et illustration de la langue française (1549)
Translated by Gladys M. Turquet

One of the noblest descriptions of the true poet ever penned.

WARNER FORREST PATTERSON
Three Centuries of French Poetic Theory (1935)

EPISODE OF ADAMASTOR OFF THE CAPE OF GOOD HOPE

Porem já cinco soes erão passados,
Que d'ali nos partiramos, cortando
Os mares nunca de outrem navegados,
Prosperamente os ventos assoprando,
Quando hũa noite, estando descuidados
Na cortadora proa vigiando,
Hũa nuvem, que os ares escurece,
Sobre nossas cabeças aparece.

Tão temerosa vinha e carregada,
Que pôs nos corações hum grande medo;
Bramindo o negro mar de longe brada
Como se désse em vão nalgum rochedo.
"O' Potestade" disse "sublimada,
Que ameaço divino ou que segredo
Este clima e este mar nos apresenta,
Que mór cousa parece que tormenta!"

Não acabava, quando hũa figura
Se nos mostra no ar, robusta e valida,
De disforme e grandissima estatura,
O rosto carregado, a barba esqualida,
Os olhos encovados, e a postura
Medonha e má, e a côr terrena e pallida,
Cheios de terra e crespos os cabellos,
A boca negra, os dentes amarellos.

Tão grande era de membros, que bem posso
Certificar-te que este era o segundo
De Rhodes estranhissimo Colosso,
Que hum dos sete milagres foi do mundo.
Cum tom de voz nos falla horrendo e grosso,
Que pareceo sair do mar profundo:
Arrepião-se as carnes e o cabello
A mi e a todos só de ouvi-lo e ve-lo.

E disse: "O' gente ousada, mais que quantas
No mundo cometêrão grandes cousas,

511

Tu, que por guerras cruas, taes e tantas,
E por trabalhos vãos nunca repousas,
Pois os vedados terminos quebrantas
E navegar meus longos mares ousas,
Que eu tanto tempo ha já que guardo e tenho,
Nunca arados de estranho ou proprio lenho,

Pois vens ver os segredos escondidos
Da natureza e do humido elemento,
A nenhum grande humano concedidos
De nobre ou de immortal merecimento,
Ouve os damnos de mi, que apercebidos
Estão a teu sobejo atrevimento
Por todo o largo mar e pola terra
Que inda has-de sojugar com dura guerra.

Sabe que quantas naos esta viagem,
Que tu fazes, fizerem de atrevidas,
Inimiga terão esta paragem
Com ventos e tormentas desmedidas;
E na primeira armada que passagem
Fizer por estas ondas insoffridas,
Eu farei de improviso tal castigo,
Que seja mór o damno que o perigo.

Aqui espero tomar, se não me engano,
De quem me descobrio, summa vingança.
E não se acabará só nisto o damno
De vossa pertinace confiança;
Antes em vossas naos vereis cada anno,
Se he verdade o que meu juizo alcança,
Naufragios, perdições de toda sorte,
Que o menor mal de todos seja a morte.

E do primeiro illustre que a ventura
Com fama alta fizer tocar os ceos,
Serei eterna e nova sepultura
Por juizos incognitos de Deos.
Aqui porá da Turca armada dura
Os soberbos e prosperos tropheos;
Comigo de seus damnos o ameaça
A destruida Quiloa com Mombaça.

Outro tambem virá de honrada fama,
Liberal, cavalleiro e namorado,
E comsigo trará a fermosa dama

Que Amor por grão mercê lhe terá dado.
Triste ventura e negro fado os chama
Neste terreno meu, que duro e irado
Os deixará de hum crú naufragio vivos
Pera verem trabalhos excessivos.

Verão morrer com fome os filhos caros,
Em tanto amor gèrados e nacidos;
Verão os Cafres asperos e avaros
Tirar á linda dama seus vestidos;
Os crystallinos membros e perclaros
A' calma, ao frio, ao ar verão despidos,
Despois de ter pisada longamente
Cos delicados pés a areia ardente.

E verão mais os olhos que escaparem
De tanto mal, de tanta desventura,
Os dous amantes miseros ficarem
Na férvida e implacabil espessura;
Ali, despois que as pedras abrandarem
Com lagrimas de dor, de magoa pura,
Abraçados as almas soltarão
Da fermosa e miserrima prisão."

Mais hia por diante o monstro horrendo
Dizendo nossos fados, quando alçado
Lhe disse eu: "Quem és tu? que esse estupendo
Corpo certo me tem maravilhado."
A boca e os olhos negros retorcendo
E dando hum espantoso e grande brado,
Me respondeo com voz pesada e amara,
Como quem da pergunta lhe pesara:

"Eu sou aquelle occulto e grande cabo
A quem chamais vós outros Tormentorio,
Que nunca a Ptolomeu, Pomponio, Estrabo,
Plinio, e quantos passárão, fui notorio.
Aqui toda a Africana costa acabo
Neste meu nunca visto promontorio,
Que pera o pólo Antarctico se estende;
A quem vossa ousadia tanto offende.

Fui dos filhos asperrimos da Terra,
Qual Encelado, Egeo e o Centimano;
Chamei-me Adamastor, e fui na guerra
Contra o que vibra os raios de Vulcano;

Não que posesse serra sobre serra,
Mas conquistando as ondas do Oceano
Fui capitão do mar, por onde andava
A armada de Neptuno, que eu buscava.

Amores da alta esposa de Peleo
Me fizerão tomar tamanha empresa;
Todas as Deosas desprezei do ceo
Só por amar das agoas a Princesa.
Hum dia a vi, co as filhas de Nereo
Sair nua na praia, e logo presa
A vontade senti de tal maneira,
Que inda não sinto cousa que mais queira.

Como fosse impossibil alcançá-la
Pola grandeza feia de meu gesto,
Determinei por armas de tomá-la,
E a Doris este caso manifesto.
De medo a Deosa então por mi lhe falla;
Mas ella cum fermoso riso honesto
Respondeo: "Qual será o amor bastante
De Nympha que sustente o de hum Gigante?

Com tudo por livrarmos o Oceano
De tanta guerra, eu buscarei maneira
Com que, com minha honra, escuse o damno."
Tal resposta me torna a mensageira.
Eu que cair não pude neste engano
—Que he grande dos amantes a cegueira—
Enchêrão-me com grandes abondanças
O peito de desejos e esperanças.

Já nescio, já da guerra desistindo,
Hūa noite de Doris prometida
Me aparece de longe o gesto lindo
Da branca Thetis, unica, despida.
Como doudo corri, de longe abrindo
Os braços, pera aquella que era vida
D'este corpo, e começo os olhos bellos
A lhe beijar, as faces e os cabellos.

O' que não sei de nojo como o conte!
Que crendo ter nos braços quem amava,
Abraçado me achei cum duro monte
De aspero mato e de espessura brava.

Estando cum penedo fronte a fronte,
Que eu polo rosto angelico apertava,
Não fiquei homem, não, mas mudo e quedo,
E junto de hum penedo outro penedo.

O' Nympha, a mais fermosa do Oceano,
Já que minha presença não te agrada,
Que te custava ter-me neste engano,
Ou fosse monte, nuvem, sonho, ou nada?
D'aqui me parto, irado e quasi insano
Da magoa e da deshonra ali passada,
A buscar outro mundo onde não visse
Quem de meu pranto e de meu mal se risse.

Erão já neste tempo meus irmãos
Vencidos e em miseria estrema postos,
E por mais segurar-se os Deoses vãos,
Alguns a varios montes sottopostos.
E como contra o Ceo não valem mãos,
Eu que chorando andava meus desgostos,
Comecei a sentir do fado immigo
Por meus atrevimentos o castigo.

Converte-se-me a carne em terra dura,
Em penedos os ossos se fizerão,
Estes membros que vês e esta figura
Por estas longas agoas se estendêrão;
Em fim minha grandissima estatura
Neste remoto cabo convertêrão
Os Deoses, e por mais dobradas magoas
Me anda Thetis cercando d'estas agoas."

Assi contava, e cum medonho choro
Subito de ante os olhos se apartou;
Desfez-se a nuvem negra, e cum sonoro
Bramido muito longe o mar soou.
Eu levantando as mãos ao sancto coro
Dos Anjos, que tão longe nos guiou,
A Deos pedi que removesse os duros
Casos que Adamastor contou futuros.

The *Sun* five times the *Earth* had compassed
Since *We* (from thence departed) *Seas* did plough
Where never Canvas wing before was spred,

515

A prosp'rous Gale making the *top-yards* bow:
When on a *night* (without suspect, or dred,
Chatting together in the cutting *Prow*)
        Over our Heads appear'd a sable *Clowd,*
        Which in thick darkness did the *Welkin* shrowd.

So big it lookt, such stern *Grimaces* made,
As fill'd our Hearts with horror, and appall,
Black was the *Sea,* and at long distance brayd
As if it roar'd *through* Rocks, *down* Rocks did fall.
O *Pow'r* inhabiting the *Heav'ns,* I said!
What divine threat is? What *mystical*
        Imparting of thy will in so *new form,*
        For this is a Thing greater than a *Storm?*

I had not ended, when a *humane* Feature
Appear'd to us ith' *Ayre,* Robustious, ralli'd
Of *Heterogeneal* parts, of *boundless* Stature,
A *Clowd* in's *Face,* a *Beard* prolix and squallid:
Cave-Eyes, a *gesture* that betray'd ill *nature,*
And a worse mood, a clay *complexion* pallid:
        His crispt *Hayre* fill'd with *earth,* and hard as *Wyre,*
        A *mouth* cole-black, of *Teeth* two yellow Tyre.

Of such *portentous* Bulk was this Colosse,
That I may tell thee (and not tell amiss)
Of that of Rhodes it might supply the loss
(One of the World's *Seav'n Wonders*) out of this
A *Voyce* speaks to us: so profound, and grosse,
It seems ev'n torn out of the vast Abyss.
        The *Hayre* with horror stands on end, of *mee*
        And all of us, at what we *hear,* and *see.*

And *this* it spake. O *you,* the boldest Folke
That ever in the world great things assayd;
Whom such dire *Wars,* and infinite, the *smoke*
And *Toyle* of Glory have not weary made;
Since these *forbidden* bounds by *you* are broke,
And *my* large Seas *your* daring *keeles* invade,
        Which I so long injoy'd, and kept *alone,*
        Unplough'd by *forreign* Vessel, or our *owne.*

Since the hid secrets you are come to spye
Of Nature and the *humid* Element;
Never reveal'd to any Mortal's Eye
Noble, or *Heroes,* that before you went:

Hear from *my* mouth, for your presumption high
What *losses* are in store, what *Plagues* are meant,
    All the wide OCEAN over, and the LAND,
    Which with hard *War* shall *bow* to your command.

This know; As many *Ships* as shall persever
Boldly to make the Voyage *you* make now,
Shall find this POYNT their enemie for ever
With *winds* and *tempests* that no bound shall know:
And the first FLEET OF WAR that shall indeaver
Through these inextricable Waves to go,
    So fearful an *example* will I make,
    That men shall say I *did* more than I *spake*.

Here I expect (unless my hopes have ly'de)
On my *discov'rer* full Revenge to have;
Nor shall *He* (onely) *all* the Ills abide,
Your *pertinacious* confidences crave:
But to your Vessels *yearly* shall betide
(Unless, provoked, I in vain do rave)
    Shipwracks, and *losses* of each kinde and Race;
    Amongst which, *death* shall have the lowest place.

And of the first that comes this way (in whom
With heighth of *Fortune*, heighth of *Fame* shall meet)
I'll be a new, and everlasting Tomb,
Through GOD's unfathom'd judgement. At these Feet
He shall drop *all* his *Glories*, and inhume
The glitt'ring *Trophies* of a *Turkish* Fleet.
    With *me* conspire his Ruine, and his Fall,
    Destroyd QUILOA, and MOMBASSA's Wall.

Another shall come after, of good *fame*,
A *Knight*, a *Lover*, and a *lib'ral Hand;*
And with him bring a fair and gentle *dame*,
Knit *his* by LOVE, and HYMEN's sacred Band.
In an ill hour, and to your loss and shame,
Ye come within the *Purlews* of *my* land;
    Which (kindly cruel) from the *sea* shall free you,
    Drown'd in a *sea* of miseries to see you.

Sterv'd shall they see to death their *Children* deare;
Begot, and rear'd, in so great *love*. The black
Rude CAFRES (out of *Avarice*) shall teare
The *Cloathes* from the *Angellick Lady's* back.

517

Her dainty limbs of *Alablaster* cleare
To *Heate,* to *Cold,* to *Storm,* to *Eyes's* worse *Rack*
    Shall be laid *naked;* after she hath trod
    (Long time) with her soft Feet the burning Clod.

Besides all this; *Their Eyes* (whose happier lot
Will be to scape from so much miserie)
This *Yoake* of LOVERS, out into the hot
And unrelenting *Thickets* turn'd shall see.
Ev'n *there* (when *Teares* they shall have squeez'd and got
From *Rocks* and *Desarts,* vvhere no *waters* be)
    Embracing *(kind)* their *souls* they shall exhale
    Out of the faire, but miserable, *Iayle.*

The ugly *Monster* vvent to rake into
More, of our *Fate;* vvhen, starting on my feet,
I ask him, *Who art Thou?* (for to say true
Thy hideous Bulk amazes me to see't.)
HEE (vvreathing his black mouth) about him threvv
His savvcer-Eyes: And (as his soul vvould fleet)
    Fetching a dismal groan, *replide* (as *sory,*
    Or *vext,* or *Both,* at the *Intergatory.*)

I am that great and secret HEAD of LAND,
Which *you* the CAPE OF TEMPESTS well did call;
From STRABO, PTOLOMEE, POMPONIUS, And
Grave PLINY hid, and from the ANTIENTS all.
I the *but-end,* that knits wide AFFRICK's strand;
My *Promontory* is her *Moun'd* and *Wall,*
    To the ANTARTICK POLE: which (neverthelesse)
    You, only, have the boldness to transgresse.

Of the rough *sons* oth' EARTH, was *I:* and *Twin,*
Brother to *Him,* that had an hundred Hands,
I was call'd ADAMASTOR, and was in
The *Warr* 'gainst *Him,* That hurls hot VULCAN's Brands.
Yet Hills on Hills *I* heapt not: but (to win
That *Empire,* which the SECOND JOVE commands)
    Was GENERALL at *Sea;* on which did sayle
    The *Fleet* of NEPTUNE, which *I* was to quayle.

The *love* I bare to PELEUS's spouse divine
Imbarqu'd mee in so wild an *Enterprize.*
The fayrest GODDESSE that the *Heav'ns* inshrine
I, for the *Princesse* of the *Waves* despise.

Vpon a day when *out* the *Sun* did shine,
With Nereus's daughters (on the Beach) these eyes
    Beheld her *naked:* streight I felt a *dart*
    Which *Time,* nor *scorns,* can pull out of my *Heart.*

I knew't impossible to gain her *Love*
By reason of my great deformitie
What *force* can doe I purpose then to prove:
And, Doris call'd, let *Her* my purpose see.
The *Goddess* (out of feare) did Thetys move
On my behalfe: but with a chaste smile *shee*
    (As *vertuous* full, as she is *fayre*) replide,
    What Nymph can such a heavy love abide?

How ever *Wee* (to save the *sea* a part
In so dire *War*) will take it into thought
How with our *honour* we may cure his smart.
My *Messenger* to *mee* thus answer brought.
I, That suspect no *stratagem,* no *Art,*
(How easily are purblind *Lovers* caught)
    Feel my selfe wondrous light with this Return;
    And fann'd with *Hopes,* with fresh *desire* doe burn.

Thus fool'd, thus cheated from the warr begun,
On a time (Doris pointing where to meet)
I spy the glitt'ring forme, ith' *evening* dun,
Of snowy Thetys with the silver feet.
With open Armes (farr off) like mad I run
To clip therein my *Ioy,* my *Life,* my *Sweet:*
    And (*clipt*) begin those orient *Eyes* to kis,
    That Face, *that* Hayre, *that* Neck, *that* All that is.

O, how I choake in utt'ring my disgrace!
Thinking I *Her* embrac'd whom I did seek,
A *Mountain* hard I found I did embrace
O'regrown with Trees and Bushes nothing sleek.
Thus (grapling with a *Mountain* face to face,
Which I stood pressing for her *Angel's* cheek)
    I was no *Man:* No but a stupid *Block*
    And *grew* unto a *Rock* another *Rock.*

O *Nymph* (the fayrest of the Ocean's Brood)!
Since with my *Features* thou could'st not be caught,
What had it cost to spare me that *false* good,
Were it a *Hill,* a *Clowd,* a *Dreame,* or *Thought?*

Away fling I (with *Anger* almost *wood*,
Nor lesse with *shame* of the *Affront* distraught)
    To seek *another* World: That I might live,
    Where *none* might *laugh*, to see me *weep*, and *grieve*.

By this my *Brethren* on their Backs were cast,
Reduc'd unto the depth of misery:
And the *vain Gods* (all hopes to put them past)
On *Those*, That *Mountayns* pyl'd, pyl'd *Mountains* high.
Nor I, that mourn'd farr off my deep distast,
"(HEAU'N, HANDS in vain *resist*, in vain FEET *fly*.
    For my *design'd* Rebellion, and Rape,
    The vengeance of pursuing *Fate* could scape.

My *solid flesh* converteth to *tough Clay*:
My *Bones* to *Rocks* are metamorphosed:
These *leggs*, these *thighs* (behold how large are *they*!)
O're the long *sea* extended were and spred.
In fine into this CAPE out of the way
My monstrous *Trunk*, and high-erected *Head*,
    The GODS did turn: where (for my greater payn)
    THETYS doth *Tantalize* me with the MAYN.

Here ends. And (gushing out into a *Well*
Of *Tears*) forthwith he vanish from our sight.
The black *Clowd* melting, with a hideous yell
The OCEAN sounded a long way forthright.
I (in *their* presence, who by *miracle*
Had thus far brought us, ev'n the ANGELLS bright)
    Besought the LORD to shield his *Heritage*
    From *all* that ADAMASTOR did presage.

Os Lusiadas (1571), v, 37–60
Translated by Richard Fanshaw

Our minds are entranced, infused with a feeling of admiration; we experience at the same time sublime emotions and a heightened interest in a picture that, without either physical or moral being, justifiably enjoys all the noblest, boldest and most sublime privileges that ever existed in the most fanciful universe of the most supreme poetry. Such is the sovereign marvel of the never sufficiently to be praised episode of Adamastor in the Lusiads, the first epopee that appeared in Europe written in octave rhyme.

FRANCISCO DIAS GOMES
Analyse (1790)

PIERRE DE RONSARD

1 5 2 4 — 1 5 8 5

ODE

Mignonne, allons voir si la rose
Qui ce matin avoit desclose
Sa robe de pourpre au Soleil,
A point perdu ceste vesprée
Les plis de sa robe pourprée
Et son teint au vostre pareil.

Las! voyez comme en peu d'espace,
Mignonne, elle a dessus la place
Las, las, ses beautez laissé cheoir!
O vrayment marastre Nature,
Puis qu'une telle fleur ne dure
Que du matin jusques au soir!

Donc, si vous me croyez mignonne,
Tandis que vostre âge fleuronne
En sa plus verte nouveauté,
Cueillez, cueillez vostre jeunesse:
Comme à ceste fleur la vieillesse
Fera ternir vostre beauté.

See, Mignonne, hath not the rose,
That this morning did unclose
  Her purple mantle to the light,
Lost, before the day be dead,
The glory of her raiment red,
  Her color, bright as yours is bright?

Ah, Mignonne, in how few hours
The petals of her purple flowers
  All have faded, fallen, died;
Sad Nature, mother ruinous,
That seest thy fair child perish thus
  'Twixt matin song and even-tide.

Hear me, darling, speaking sooth,
Gather the fleet flower of your youth,
  Take ye your pleasure at the best;

Be merry ere your beauty flit,
For length of days will tarnish it
Like roses that were loveliest.

Translated by Andrew Lang

It is the perfection of his tongue. Its rhythm reaches the exact limit of change which a simple metre will tolerate: where it saddens, a lengthy hesitation at the opening of the seventh line introduces a new cadence, a lengthy lingering upon the last syllables of the tenth, eleventh and twelfth closes a grave complaint. So, also by an effect of quantities, the last six lines rise out of melancholy into their proper character of appeal and vivacity: an exhortation.

Certainly those who are so unfamiliar with French poetry as not to know that its whole power depends upon an extreme subtlety of rhythm, may find here the principal example of the quality they have missed. Something much less weighty than the stress of English lines, a just perceptible difference between nearly equal syllables, marks the excellent from the intolerable in French prosody: and to feel this truth in the eighteen lines . . . it is necessary to read them virtually in the modern manner—for the "s" in "vesprée" or "vostre" were pedantries in the sixteenth century—but one must give the mute "e's" throughout as full a value as they have in singing. Indeed, reading this poem, one sees how it must have been composed to some good and simple air in the man's head.

If the limits of a page permitted it, I would also show how worthy the thing was of fame from its pure and careful choice of verb— "Tandis que vostre age FLEURONNE"—*but space prevents me, luckily, for all this is like splitting a diamond.*

HILAIRE BELLOC
Avril (1904)

PIERRE DE RONSARD

1 5 2 4 — 1 5 8 5

SONNET

Je fuy les pas frayez du meschant populaire,
Et les villes où sont les peuples amassez:
Les rochers, les forests desja sçavent assez
Quelle trampe a ma vie estrange et solitaire.
    Si ne suis-je si seul, qu'Amour mon secretaire

N'accompagne mes pieds debiles et cassez:
Qu'il ne conte mes maux et presens et passez
A ceste voix sans corps, qui rien ne sçauroit taire.
 Souvent plein de discours, pour flatter mon esmoy,
Je m'arreste, et je dy: Se pourroit-il bien faire
Qu'elle pensast, parlast, ou se souvint de moy?
 Qu'à sa pitié mon mal commençast à desplaire?
Encor que je me trompe, abusé du contraire,
Pour me faire plaisir, Helene, je le croy.

I fly the crowded roads where thousands hurry,
 and fly the populous town for rock and wood,
those friends, who know how well their natures marry
 with my strange temper and my solitude.
Am I alone, when love, my secretary,
 follows my halting steps, as though he could
with his immortal voice bid Time to tarry
 while he repeats the pains I have withstood?
Often indeed, when most my sorrows fret me,
 I stop to wonder, "Does she speak, my pretty,
or think of him who loves her—or forget me
 because my agony outruns her pity?"
And thus, though knowing it is false, I feign
to dream of pleasure while I live in pain.

Translated by Humbert Wolfe

He has the right to wear the purple in the Olympia of the poets.

THÉODORE DE BANVILLE
Les Poëtes français (1861)

PIERRE DE RONSARD

1 5 2 4 — 1 5 8 5

MY GOLDEN HELEN

Ma douce Hélène, non, mais bien ma douce haleine,
 Qui froide rafraischis la chaleur de mon cœur,
Je prens de ta vertu cognoissance et vigueur,
 Et ton œil, comme il veut, à son plaisir me meine:
Heureux celuy qui souffre une amoureuse peine

Pour un nom si fatal! heureuse la douleur,
Bienheureux le tourment qui vient pour la valeur
Des yeux, non, pas des yeux, mais de l'astre d'Hélène!
   Nom malheur des Troyens, sujet de mon soucy,
Ma sage Penelope et mon Hélène aussi,
Qui d'un soin amoureux tout le cœur m'envelope:
   Nom qui m'a jusqu'au Ciel de la terre enlevé,
Qui eust jamais pensé que j'eusse retrouvé
   En une mesme Hélène une autre Penelope?

L'autre jour que j'estois sur le haut d'un degré
   Passant tu m'advisas, et, me tournant la veue,
Tu m'esblouis les yeux, tant j'avois l'ame esmeue
De me voir en sursaut de tes yeux rencontré.
   Ton regard dans le cœur, dans le sang m'est rentré,
Comme un esclat de foudre alors qu'il fend la nue
J'eus de froid et de chaud la fievre continue
D'un si poignant regard mortellement outré.
   Et si ta belle main passant ne m'eust faict signe,
Main blanche qui se vante d'estre celle d'un cygne,
Je fusse mort, Hélène, aux rayons de tes yeux:
   Mais ton signe retint l'ame presque ravie,
Ton œil se contenta d'estre victorieux,
Ta main se réjouit de me donner la vie.

Ma Dame se levoit un beau matin d'esté,
   Quand le Soleil attache à ses chevaux la bride:
Amour estoit present avecq sa trousse vuide,
Venu pour la remplir des traicts de sa clarté.
   J'entre-vy dans son sein deux pommes de beauté,
Telles qu'on ne void point au verger Hesperide:
Telles ne porte point la deësse de Cnide,
Ny celle qui a Mars des siennes allaicté.
   Telle enflure d'yvoire en sa voute arrondie,
Tel relief de porphyre, ouvrage de Phidie,
Eut Andromede alors que Persée passa,
   Quand il la vid liée à des roches marines,
Et quand la peur de mort tout le corps luy glaça,
Transformant ses tetins en deux boules marbrines.

Je ne veux comparer tes beautez à la Lune:
   La Lune est inconstante, et ton vouloir n'est qu'un:
Encor moins au Soleil; le Soleil est commun,
Commune est sa lumiere, et tu n'est pas commune.
   Tu forces par vertu l'envie et la rancune,

Je ne suis, te louant, un flateur importun;
Tu sembles à toymesme, et n'as pourtraict aucun,
Tu es toute ton Dieu, ton astre et ta fortune.

    Ceux qui font de leur dame à toy comparaison
Sont ou presomptueux, ou perclus de raison;
D'esprit et de sçavoir de bien loin tu les passes.

    Ou bien quelque demon de ton corps s'est vestu,
Ou bien tu es pourtraict de la mesme Vertu,
Ou bien tu es Pallas, ou bien l'une des Graces.

Vous estes le bouquet de vostre bouquet mesme,
    Et la fleur de sa fleur, sa grace et sa verdeur:
De vostre douce haleine il a pris son odeur,
Il est, comme je suis, de vostre amour tout blesme.

    Madame, voyez donc, puis qu'un bouquet vous aime,
Indigne de juger que peut vostre valeur,
Combien doy-je sentir l'ame de douleur
Qui sers par jugement vostre excellence extresme.

    Mais ainsi qu'un bouquet se flestrit en un jour,
J'ay peur qu'un mesme jour flestrisse vostre amour:
    Toute amitié de femme est soudain effacée.

    Advienne le Destin comme il pourra venir,
Il ne peut de vos yeux m'oster le souvenir:
Il faudroit m'arracher le cœur et la pensée.

A fin qu'à tout jamais de siecle en siecle vive
    La parfaicte amitié que Ronsard vous portoit,
    Comme vostre beauté la raison luy ostoit,
Comme vous enchaisniez sa liberté captive,

    A fin que d'âge en âge à nos nepveux arrive
Que toute dans mon sang vostre figure estoit,
Et que rien sinon vous mon cœur ne souhaittoit,
Je vous fais un present de ceste sempervive.

    Elle vit longuement en sa jeune verdeur;
    Long temps aprez la mort je vous feray revivre,
Tant peut le docte soin d'un gentil serviteur,

    Qui veut en vous servant toutes vertus ensuivre.
Vous vivrez, croyez-moy, comme Laure en grandeur,
Au moins tant que vivront les plumes et le livre.

    My golden Helen, nay my gold inhaling
        that tempers my hot heart with its cool air,
        your eyes at will mislead me everywhere

slave to your virtue noted and prevailing.
Thrice happy he, whose stricken heart is ailing
　　for Helen's fatal name, enchanted care,
　　exquisite pain for eyelids that outwear
earthlight to shine in heaven a star unveiling.
Anguish of Troy, name! ensign of my grief,
　　my wise Penelope, my Helen splendid
　　whose lovely torment holds the heart of me,
name, that enskied a lover beyond belief,
　　who could have guessed I'd find when all was ended
　　in the same Helen a new Penelope.

Lately as dreaming on a stair I stood
　　you passed me by, and, looking on my face,
　　blinded my eyes with the immediate grace
of unanticipated neighbourhood.
As lightning splits the clouds, my heart and blood
　　split with your beauty, and began to race,
　　now ice, now fever, shattered in their place
by that unparalleled beatitude.
And, if your hand, in passing, had not beckoned—
　　your whiter hand than is the swan's white daughter,
　　Helen, your eyes had wounded me to death.
But your hand saved me in the mortal second,
　　and your triumphant eyes the moment after
　　revived their captive with an alms of breath.

When the sun yoked his horses of the air
　　Helen one summer morning took the breeze,
while love, with empty quiver, did repair
　　for arrows to his lucid armouries.
I saw the apples of her breast as fair
　　as orchard fruit of the Hesperides,
outshining what the Cnidian laid bare,
　　or hers who suckled Mars upon her knees.
The swelling ivories in their rounded arches
　　were such as Pheidias fashioned in relief
　　for his Andromeda, when her young Greek
found her rock-fastened by the sea's cold marches,
　　her breasts by mortal terror changed and grief
　　into the marbled globe of Verd Antique.

Shall I your beauties with the moon compare?
　　She's faithless, you a single purpose own.
Or to the general sun, who everywhere
　　goes common with his light; You walk alone?

And you are such that envy must despair
    of finding in my praise aught to condone,
who have no likeness since there's naught as fair,
    yourself your god, your star, Fate's overtone.
Those mad or rash, who make some other woman
    your rival, hurt themselves when they would hurt you,
    so far your excellence their dearth outpaces.
Either your body shields some noble demon,
    or mortal you image immortal virtue,
    Or Pallas you or first among the Graces.

You are the scent wherewith your posy's scented,
    bloom of its bloom, the wherefore and the whence
of all its sweet, that with your love acquainted
    suffers, like me, passion's pale decadence.
And if these flowers are by love demented,
    adoring what so far exceeds their sense,
judge if I am divinely discontented
    who know by heart your perfect excellence!
But, as the flower's beauty is diurnal
    may not, as is the way with woman's kindness,
    a single day bring all your love to naught?
Fate, do your worst! My love will be eternal,
    unless you overwhelm my eyes with blindness,
    and pluck my heart out and uproot all thought.

Let all men know reborn from age to age
    the perfect love love-perfect Ronsard bore you,
so that within your beauty, as in a cage,
    his mind's sole liberty was to adore you.
And let these be our children's heritage—
    this evergreen that I have woven for you,
bright with your face, immortal in the page,
    long as the love for which I did implore you.
Nor ever will its verdant youth be withered,
    unless to death your lover must surrender
    his utmost skill through which you live again
with all your graces in their blossom gathered.
    No! but with Laura you shall share love's splendour
    as long as there is life in book and pen.
                    Translated by Humbert Wolfe

The perfection and quintessence of high love-poetry.
                    D. B. WYNDHAM LEWIS
                    Ronsard (1944)

527

PIERRE DE RONSARD

1 5 2 4 — 1 5 8 5

MAGIC

Quand vous serez bien vieille, au soir, à la chandelle.

When you grow old, at evening, in the candle-light.

Is there any single line in all English poetry more subdued to magic?
. . . That single line has sounded in the ears of the poets down the
centuries. Supreme in itself, it has begotten children of the divine race.
And when W. B. Yeats wrote his version:

'*When you are old and gray and full of sleep*'

he was on behalf of English poetry paying the ultimate tribute to the
great Frenchman, whom he could imitate but could not equal.

HUMBERT WOLFE
Pierre de Ronsard: Sonnets pour Helene (1934)

———————

PIERRE DE RONSARD

1 5 2 4 — 1 5 8 5

DE L'ELECTION DE SON SEPULCRE

Antres, & vous fontaines
De ces roches hautaines
Devallans contre bas
D'un glissant pas:

Et vous forests, & ondes
Par ces prez vagabondes,
Et vous rives, & bois
Oiez ma vois.

Quand le ciel, & mon heure
Jugeront que je meure,
Ravi du dous sejour
Du commun jour,

Je veil, j'enten, j'ordonne,
Qu'un sepulcre on me donne,
Non pres des Rois levé,
    Ne d'or gravé,

Mais en cette isle verte,
Où la course entrouverte
Du Loir, autour coulant,
    Est accolant'.

Là où Braie s'amie
D'une eau non endormie,
Murmure à l'environ
    De son giron.

Je deffen qu'on ne rompe
Le marbre pour la pompe
De vouloir mon tumbeau
    Bâtir plus beau,

Mais bien je veil qu'un arbre
M'ombrage en lieu d'un marbre:
Arbre qui soit couvert
    Tousjours de vert.

De moi puisse la terre
Engendrer un l'hierre,
M'embrassant en maint tour
    Tout alentour.

Et la vigne tortisse
Mon sepulcre embellisse,
Faisant de toutes pars
    Un ombre épars.

Là viendront chaque année
A ma feste ordonnée,
Les pastoureaus estans
    Prés habitans.

Puis aiant fait l'office
De leur beau sacrifice,
Parlans à l'isle ainsi
    Diront ceci.

Que tu es renommée
D'estre tumbeau nommée

D'un de qui l'univers
    Ouira les vers!

Et qui onc en sa vie
Ne fut brulé d'envie
Mendiant les honneurs
    Des grans seigneurs!

Ni ne r'apprist l'usage
De l'amoureus breuvage,
Ni l'art des anciens
    Magiciens!

Mais bien à nos campaignes,
Feist voir les seurs compaignes
Foulantes l'herbe aus sons
    De ses chansons.

Car il sçeut sur sa lire
Si bons acords élire,
Qu'il orna de ses chants
    Nous, & nos champs.

La douce manne tumbe
A jamais sur sa tumbe,
Et l'humeur que produit
    En Mai, la nuit.

Tout alentour l'emmure
L'herbe, & l'eau qui murmure,
L'un d'eus i verdoiant,
    L'autre ondoiant.

Et nous aians memoire
Du renom de sa gloire,
Lui ferons comme à Pan
    Honneur chaque an.

Ainsi dira la troupe,
Versant de mainte coupe
Le sang d'un agnelet
    Avec du laict

Desus moi, qui à l'heure
Serai par la demeure
Où les heureus espris
    Ont leurs pourpris.

La gresle, ne la nége,
N'ont tels lieus pour leur siege,
Ne la foudre onque là
    Ne devala.

Mais bien constante i dure
L'immortelle verdure,
Et constant en tout tens
    Le beau printens.

Et Zephire i alaine
Les mirtes, & la plaine
Qui porte les couleurs
    De mile fleurs.

Le soin qui solicite
Les Rois, ne les incite
Le monde ruiner
    Pour dominer.

Ains comme freres vivent,
Et morts encore suivent
Les métiers qu'ils avoient
    Quand ils vivoient.

Là, là, j'oirai d'Alcée
La lire courroucée,
Et Saphon qui sur tous
    Sonne plus dous.

Combien ceus qui entendent
Les odes qu'ils rependent,
Se doivent réjouir
    De les ouir!

Quand la peine receue
Du rocher, est deceue
Sous les acords divers
    De leurs beaus vers!

La seule lire douce
L'ennui des cueurs repousse,
Et va l'esprit flattant
    De l'écoutant.

Caverns and you, cascades,
From yonder steep arcades
That downward, valeward, fleet,
    With gliding feet;

And forests you and hills,
Runnels and wandering rills,
That through these meadows stray,
    Hark what I say!

Whenever death to me
Heaven and my hour decree,
Bidding me take my flight
    From kindly light,

I do forbid them hew
Out marble, so to view
My tomb may statelier show
    And fairer. No;

No, I will have a tree,
For marble, shadow me,
A tree that shall be seen
    Still full of green.

Yea, let an ivy birth
Have from my mouldering earth
And clip me, as I lie,
    With many a ply;

And let the trellised vine
About my tomb entwine,
Shedding, on every side,
    Its shadow wide.

So, on my festal day,
Each year, the shepherds gay
Shall to this grave of mine
    Come with their kine;

And having offered there
Their due of praise and prayer,
To th' eyot on this wise
    Shall they devise;

"How art thou high-renowned,
Being his burial-ground,
Of whom the universe
    Chanteth the verse!

Who in his lifetime ne'er
Consumed was with the care
Of honours nor chagrin
    Worship to win,

Who ne'er professed t'impart
The necromantic art
Nor eke the philtres sold
    Of usance old;

But to our lands, in fine,
He showed the Sisters Nine,
Following his tuneful song,
    The meads along:

For from his lyre he drew
Such sweet accords and true,
Us and our fields elect
    With songs he decked.

Be heaven's manna shed
For ever on his head
And those sweet dews that still
    May-nights distil!

Green grasses wall him round
And waters' murmuring sound,
These ever fresh and sweet,
    Those live and fleet!

Whilst we, still holding dear
His glory, every year,
To him, as Pan unto,
    Will honour do."

Thus shall the pastoral band
Discourse, with lavish hand,
Lambs' blood and milk, withal,
    Outpouring all

Upon my grave, who, then,
Beyond the abodes of men,
Shall be where spirits blest
    Forever rest.

There neither hail nor snow
The happy regions know,
Nor ever on them broke
    The thunderstroke;

But still on fields and woods
Immortal verdure broods
And constant ever there
    Is Springtide fair.

The care, that harries kings,
These happy never stings,
For empire's sake, to work
    Their neighbours' irk.

They dwell in brotherhood
And that which they ensued,
Whilst life on earth they led,
    Still follow, dead.

Alcæus' angry lyre
Shall greet me in that choir
And Sappho's, that o'er all
    Doth sweetliest fall.

How those, whose ears partake
The music that they make,
Must joy with glad amaze
    To hear their lays!

Since Sisyphus his toil
Their sweetness doth assoil
and Tantalus forgets
    His torment's frets.

The dulcet Lyre's sole air
Doth purge the heart of care
And healeth of despite
    The heark'ner's spright.

Odes, iv, 5
Translated by John Payne

All merits are united in this delectable work. . . . Above all its execu-tion is perfect.

C. - A. S A I N T E - B E U V E
Tableau historique et critique de la poésie française (1842)

ÉTIENNE JODELLE

1 5 3 2 — 1 5 7 3

AUX CENDRES DE CLAUDE COLET

Si ma voix, qui me doit bien tost pousser au nombre
  Des Immortels, pouuoit aller iusqu'à ton ombre,
    COLET, à qui la mort
  Se monstra trop ialouse & dépite d'attendre
  Que tu eusses parfait ce qui te peut deffendre
    De son auare port:

Si tu pouuois encor sous la cadence saincte
  D'vn Lut, qui gemiroit & ta mort, & ma plainte,
    Tout ainsi te rauir,
  Que tu te rauissois dessous tant de merueilles,
  Lors que durant tes iours ie faisois tes oreilles
    Sous mes loix s'asseruir:

Tu ferois escouter à la trouppe sacree
  Des Manes bien heureux, qui seule se recree
    Entre les lauriers verds,
  Les mots que maintenant deuôt en mon office
  Ie rediray neuf fois, pour l'heureux sacrifice,
    Que te doiuent mes vers.

Mais pource que ma voix, aduersaire aux tenebres,
  Ne pourroit pas passer par les fleuues funebres,
    Qui de bras tortillez
  Vous serrent à l'entour, & dont, peut estre, l'onde
  Pourroit souiller mes vers, qui dedans nostre monde
    Ne seront point souillez:

Il me faut contenter, pour mon deuoir te rendre,
  De tesmoigner tout bas à ta muette cendre,
    Bien que ce soit en vain,
  Que ceste horrible Sœur qui a tranché ta vie,
  Ne trancha point alors l'amitié qui me lie,
    Où rien ne peut sa main.

Que les fardez amis, dont l'amitié chancelle
  Sous le vouloir du fort, euitent vn IODELLE,
    Obstiné pour vanger
  Toute amitié rompue, amoindrie, & volage,
  Autant qu'il est ami des bons amis, que l'age
    Ne peut iamais changer.

Sois moy donc vn tesmoin, ô toy Tumbe poudreuse,
Sois moy donc vn tesmoin, ô toy Fosse cendreuse,
Qui t'anoblis des os
Desia pourris en toy, sois tesmoin que i'arrache
Maugré l'iniuste mort ce beau nom, qui se cache
Dedans ta poudre enclos.

Vous qui m'accompagnez, ô trois fois trois pucelles,
Qu'on donne à ce beau nom des ailes immortelles,
Pour voler de ce lieu,
Iusqu'à l'autel que tient vostre mere Memoire,
Qui regaignant sans fin sus la mort la victoire,
D'vn homme fait vn Dieu.

Pour accomplir mon vœu, ie vois trois fois espandre
Trois gouttes de ce laict dessus la seiche cendre,
Et tout autant de vin,
Tien, reçoy le cyprés, l'amaranthe, & la rose,
O Cendre bien heureuse, & mollement repose
Icy iusqu'à la fin.

TO THE ASHES OF CLAUDE COLET

If only my song, that soon must exalt me to the band of Immortals, could reach your shade, Colet, for which death showed itself too jealous and spiteful to wait till you had fulfilled the work that would have saved you from oblivion; if only you could again hear the holy cadence of a lute which would lament your death with my sorrow, and enchant you just as you were transported by spells of magic in the days when I enslaved your ears to my will; then you would impel the sacred band of the blessed Shades, who alone rejoice among the green laurels, to listen to the words that now I shall repeat nine times in devout fulfillment of the happy sacrifice that my verses owe you.

But because my song, enemy of darkness, can not cross the funereal rivers that enclose you with tortuous arms, and because those waves might defile my verses, which in our world shall never be defiled, I must be content, in fulfilling my duty to honor you, to testify vainly in a soft voice to your silent ashes. The awesome Fate which has cut short your life did not sever, and has no power over, the friendship that binds me. Let the false friends, whose friendship slackens under the will of the strong, avoid Jodelle, who, as a friend of true friends whom time can never change, is determined to revenge all broken, weakened, and fickle friendships.

Be to me then a witness, O dusty Tomb! Be to me a witness, O ashy Grave, ennobled by bones already mouldered in you! Be witness that, in spite of unjust death, I snatch from you Colet's beautiful name that is concealed and enclosed in your dust. You that accompany me, O three times three maidens, give to Colet's beautiful name immortal wings to fly from this place as far as the altar held by your mother, Memory, who, gaining forever victory over death, changes a man into a god.

To accomplish my vow, three times I shall scatter three drops of milk over the dry ashes, and as much wine. Therefore receive the cypress, the amaranth, and the rose, O blessed Shade, and gently rest here till the end.

An incontestable masterpiece of French poetry.

THIERRY MAULNIER
Introduction à la poésie française (1939)

JEAN-ANTOINE DE BAÏF

1 5 3 2 — 1 5 8 9

LOVES

O doux plaisir plein de doux pensement,
   Quand la douceur de la douce meslee,
   Etreint & ioint, l'ame en l'ame meslee,
   Le corps au corps d'vn mol embrassement,

O douce vie! ô doux trepassement!
   Mon ame alors de grand' ioye troublee,
   De moy dans toy cherche d'aller emblee,
   Puis haut, puis bas s'écoulant doucement.

Quand nous ardants, Meline, d'amour forte,
   Moy d'estre en toy, toy d'en toy tout me prendre,
   Par cela mien, qui dans toy entre plus,

Tu la reçois, me laissant masse morte:
   Puis vient ta bouche en ma bouche la rendre,
   Me ranimant tous mes membres perclus.

Oh, the sweet pleasure full of sweet thought, when the sweetness of the sweet love struggle, clasps and joins, soul in soul mingled, body to body with a soft embrace. Oh, sweet life! Oh, sweet death! My soul then stirred with great joy, seeks at once to transfuse itself into you, now high, now low and sweetly flowing. When both of us, Meline, ardent with strong desire, I being part of you, and you fully receptive, I being wholly myself the more I become part of you; you receive my life, leaving me a dead mass, then your lips restore life into my lips, reviving all my lifeless limbs.

A sonnet of a unique voluptuous sweetness which is perhaps the master-piece of French erotic poetry.

THIERRY MAULNIER
Introduction à la poésie française (1939)

JEAN PASSERAT

1 5 3 4 — 1 6 0 2

VILLANELLE

J'ai perdu ma tourterelle;
Est-ce point celle que j'oy?
Je veux aller après elle.

Tu regrettes ta femelle,
Hélas! aussi fais-je moy.
J'ai perdu ma tourterelle.

Si ton amour est fidelle,
Aussi est ferme ma foy;
Je veux aller après elle.

Ta plainte se renouvelle,
Toujours plaindre je me doy;
J'ai perdu ma tourterelle.

En ne voyant plus la belle,
Plus rien de beau je ne voy;
Je veux aller après elle.

Mort, que tant de fois j'appelle,
Prends ce qui se donne à toy!
J'ai perdu ma tourterelle;
Je veux aller après elle.

I have lost my turtle-doo.
Is't not she I hear hard by?
After her I'd fain ensue.

Thou thy mate regrettest **too.**
Wellaway! And so do I.
I have lost my turtle-doo.

If thy love, indeed, is true,
So my faith is firm and high;
After her I'd fain ensue.

Thy complaint is ever new;
I too still must weep and sigh;
I have lost my turtle-doo.

Since I bade my fair adieu,
Nought of pleasance I espy;
After her I'd fain ensue.

Death, to whom so oft I sue,
Take thine own and let me die.
I have lost my turtle-doo;
After her I'd fain ensue.

Translated by John Payne

*It has given its exact character to the subsequent history of the villanelle.
. . . This exquisite lyric has continued to be the type of its class.*

EDMUND GOSSE
in Encyclopædia Britannica (1911)

ST. JOHN OF THE CROSS

1 5 4 2 — 1 5 9 1

CANCIONES ENTRE EL ALMA Y EL ESPOSO

ESPOSA

1.—¿A dónde te escondiste,
    Amado, y me dejaste con gemido?
    Como el ciervo huiste,
    Habiéndome herido;
    Salí tras tí clamando, y eras ido.

2.—Pastores, los que fuerdes
   Allá por las majadas al Otero,
   Si por ventura vierdes
   Aquel que yo más quiero,
   Decilde que adolezco, peno y muero.

3.—Buscando mis amores,
   Iré por esos montes y riberas,
   Ni cogeré las flores,
   Ni temeré las fieras,
   Y pasaré los fuertes y fronteras.

PREGUNTA A LAS CRIATURAS

4.—¡Oh, bosques y espesuras,
   Plantadas por la mano del Amado!
   ¡Oh, prado de verduras,
   De flores esmaltado,
   Decid si por vosotros ha pasado!

RESPUESTA DE LAS CRIATURAS

5.—Mil gracias derramando,
   Pasó por estos sotos con presura,
   Y yéndolos mirando,
   Con sola su figura
   Vestidos los dejó de hermosura.

ESPOSA

6.—¡Ay, quién podrá sanarme!
   Acaba de entregarte ya de vero,
   No quieras enviarme
   De hoy más ya mensajero,
   Que no saben decirme lo que quiero.

7.—Y todos cuantos vagan,
   De ti me van mil gracias refiriendo,
   Y todos más me llagan,
   Y déjame muriendo
   Un no sé qué que quedan balbuciendo.

8.—Mas, ¿cómo perseveras,
   Oh vida, no viviendo donde vives,
   Y haciendo porque mueras,
   Las flechas que recibes,
   De lo que del Amado en ti concibes?

9.—¿Por qué, pues has llagado
    Aqueste corazón, no le sanaste?
    Y pues me le has robado,
    ¿Por qué así le dejaste,
    Y no tomas el robo que robaste?

10.—Apaga mis enojos,
    Pues que ninguno basta a deshacellos,
    Y véante mis ojos,
    Pues eres lumbre dellos,
    Y sólo para ti quiero tenellos.

11.—¡Oh, cristalina fuente,
    Si en esos tus semblantes plateados,
    Formases de repente
    Los ojos deseados,
    Que tengo en mis entrañas dibujados!

12.—Apártalos, Amado,
    Que voy de vuelo.

EL ESPOSO

                Vuélvete, paloma,
    Que el ciervo vulnerado
    Por el otero asoma,
    Al aire de tu vuelo, y fresco toma.

LA ESPOSA

13.—Mi Amado las montañas,
    Los valles solitarios nemorosos,
    Las ínsulas extrañas,
    Los ríos sonorosos,
    El silbo de los aires amorosos.

14.—La noche sosegada
    En par de los levantes de la aurora,
    La música callada,
    La soledad sonora,
    La cena que recrea y enamora.

15.—Nuestro lecho florido
    De cuevas de leones enlazado,
    En púrpura tendido,
    De paz edificado,
    De mil escudos de oro coronado

16.—A zaga de tu huella
Las jóvenes discurren al camino
Al toque de centella,
Al adobado vino,
Emisiones de bálsamo divino.

17.—En la interior bodega
De mi Amado bebí, y cuando salía
Por toda aquesta vega,
Ya cosa no sabía,
Y el ganado perdí que antes seguía.

18.—Allí me dió su pecho,
Allí me enseñó ciencia muy sabrosa,
Y yo le di de hecho
A mí, sin dejar cosa,
Allí le prometí de ser su esposa.

19.—Mi alma se ha empleado,
Y todo mi caudal en su servicio;
Ya no guardo ganado,
Ni ya tengo otro oficio,
Que ya sólo en amar es mi ejercicio.

20.—Pues ya si en el ejido
De hoy más no fuere vista ni hallada,
Diréis que me he perdido;
Que andando enamorada,
Me hice perdidiza, y fuí ganada.

21.—De flores y esmeraldas,
En las frescas mañanas escogidas,
Haremos las guirnaldas
En tu amor florecidas,
Y en un cabello mío entretejidas.

22.—En sólo aquel cabello
Que en mi cuello volar consideraste,
Mirástele en mi cuello,
Y en él preso quedaste,
Y en uno de mis ojos te llagaste.

23.—Cuando tú me mirabas,
Tu gracia en mí tus ojos imprimían;
Por eso me adamabas,
Y en eso merecían
Los míos adorar lo que en ti vían.

24.—No quieras despreciarme,
   Que si color moreno en mí hallaste,
   Ya bien puedes mirarme,
   Después que me miraste,
   Que gracia y hermosura en mí dejaste.

25.—Cogednos las raposas,
   Que está ya florecida nuestra viña,
   En tanto que de rosas
   Hacemos una piña,
   Y no parezca nadie en la montiña.

26.—Detente, Cierzo muerto,
   Ven, Austro, que recuerdas los amores,
   Aspira por mi huerto,
   Y corran sus olores,
   Y pacerá el Amado entre las flores.

ESPOSO

27.—Entrado se ha la Esposa
   En el ameno huerto deseado,
   Y a su sabor reposa,
   El cuello reclinado
   Sobre los dulces brazos del Amado.

28.—Debajo del manzano,
   Allí conmigo fuiste desposada,
   Allí te dí la mano,
   Y fuiste reparada
   Donde tu madre fuera violada.

29.—A las aves ligeras,
   Leones, ciervos, gamos saltadores,
   Montes, valles, riberas,
   Aguas, aires, ardores
   Y miedos de las noches veladores.

30.—Por las amenas liras,
   Y canto de serenas os conjuro,
   Que cesen vuestras iras,
   Y no toquéis al muro,
   Porque la Esposa duerma más seguro.

543

ESPOSA

31.—Oh, ninfas de Judea,
En tanto que en las flores y rosales
El ámbar perfumea,
Morá en los arrabales,
Y no queráis tocar nuestros umbrales.

32.—Escóndete, Carillo,
Y mira con tu haz a las montañas,
Y no quieras decillo;
Mas mira las compañas
De la que va por ínsulas extrañas.

ESPOSO

33.—La blanca palomica
Al arca con el ramo se ha tornado,
Y ya la tortolica
Al socio deseado
En las riberas verdes ha hallado.

34.—En soledad vivía,
Y en soledad ha puesto ya su nido,
Y en soledad la guía
A solas su querido,
También en soledad de amor herido.

ESPOSA

35.—Gocémonos, Amado,
Y vámonos a ver en tu hermosura
Al monte o al collado,
Do mana el agua pura,
Entremos más adentro en la espesura.

36.—Y luego a las subidas
Cavernas de la piedra nos iremos,
Que están bien escondidas,
Y allí nos entraremos,
Y el mosto de granadas gustaremos.

37.—Allí me mostrarías
Aquello que mi alma pretendía,
Y luego me darías
Allí tú, vida mía,
Aquello que me diste el otro día.

38.—El aspirar del aire,
   El canto de la dulce filomena,
   El soto y su donaire,
   En la noche serena
   Con llama que consume y no da pena.

39.—Que nadie lo miraba,
   Aminadab tampoco parecía,
   Y el cerco sosegaba,
   Y la caballería
   A vista de las aguas descendía.

SONG OF THE SOUL
AND THE BRIDEGROOM

THE BRIDE

1. Where hast Thou hidden Thyself,
   And abandoned me in my groaning, O my Beloved?
   Thou hast fled like the hart,
   Having wounded me.
   I ran after Thee, crying; but Thou wert gone.

2. O shepherds, you who go
   Through the sheepcots up the hill,
   If you shall see Him
   Whom I love the most,
   Tell Him I languish, suffer, and die.

3. In search of my Love
   I will go over mountains and strands;
   I will gather no flowers,
   I will fear no wild beasts;
   And pass by the mighty and the frontiers.

QUESTION TO THE CREATURES

4. O groves and thickets
   Planted by the hand of the Beloved;
   O verdant meads
   Enamelled with flowers,
   Tell me, has He passed by you?

5. A thousand graces diffusing
   He passed through the groves in haste,
   And merely regarding them
   As He passed
   Clothed them with His beauty.

THE BRIDE

6. Oh! who can heal me?
   Give me at once Thyself,
   Send me no more
   A messenger
   Who cannot tell me what I wish.

7. All they who serve are telling me
   Of Thy unnumbered graces;
   And all wound me more and more,
   And something leaves me dying,
   I know not what, of which they are darkly speaking.

8. But how thou perseverest, O life,
   Not living where thou livest;
   The arrows bring death
   Which thou receivest
   From thy conceptions of the Beloved.

9. Why, after wounding
   This heart, hast Thou not healed it?
   And why, after stealing it,
   Has Thou thus abandoned it.
   And not carried away the stolen prey?

10. Quench Thou my troubles,
    For no one else can soothe them;
    And let mine eyes behold Thee,
    For thou art their light,
    And I will keep them for Thee alone.

11. O crystal well!
    Oh that on Thy silvered surface
    Thou wouldest mirror forth at once
    Those eyes desired
    Which are outlined in my heart!

12. Turn them away, O my Beloved!
    I am on the wing:

THE BRIDEGROOM

Return, My Dove!
The wounded hart
Looms on the hill
In the air of thy flight and is refreshed.

THE BRIDE

13. My Beloved is the mountains,
    The solitary wooded valleys,
    The strange islands,
    The roaring torrents,
    The whisper of the amorous gales;

14. The tranquil night
    At the approaches of the dawn,
    The silent music,
    The murmuring solitude,
    The supper which revives, and enkindles love.

15. Our bed is of flowers
    By dens of lions encompassed,
    Hung with purple,
    Made in peace,
    And crowned with a thousand shields of gold.

16. In Thy footsteps
    The young ones run Thy way;
    At the touch of the fire
    And by the spiced wine,
    The divine balsam flows.

17. In the inner cellar
    Of my Beloved have I drunk; and when I went forth
    Over all the plain
    I knew nothing,
    And lost the flock I followed before.

18. There He gave me His breasts,
    There He taught me the science full of sweetness.
    And there I gave to Him
    Myself without reserve;
    There I promised to be His bride.

19. My soul is occupied,
    And all my substance in His service;
    Now I guard no flock,
    Nor have I any other employment:
    My sole occupation is love.

20. If, then, on the common land
    I am no longer seen or found,
    You will say that I am lost;
    That, being enamoured,
    I lost myself; and yet was found.

21. Of emeralds, and of flowers
    In the early morning gathered,
    We will make the garlands,
    Flowering in Thy love,
    And bound together with one hair of my head.

22. By that one hair
    Thou hast observed fluttering on my neck,
    And on my neck regarded,
    Thou wert captivated;
    And wounded by one of my eyes.

23. When Thou didst regard me,
    Thine eyes imprinted in me Thy grace:
    For this didst Thou love me again,
    And thereby mine eyes did merit
    To adore what in Thee they saw

24. Despise me not,
    For if I was swarthy once
    Thou canst regard me now;
    Since Thou hast regarded me,
    Grace and beauty hast Thou given me.

25. Catch us the foxes,
    For our vineyard hath flourished;
    While of roses
    We make a nosegay,
    And let no one appear on the hill.

26. O killing north wind, cease!
    Come, south wind, that awakenest love!
    Blow through my garden,
    And let its odours flow,
    And the Beloved shall feed among the flowers.

THE BRIDEGROOM

27. The bride has entered
The pleasant and desirable garden,
And there reposes to her heart's content;
Her neck reclining
On the sweet arms of the Beloved.

28. Beneath the apple-tree
There wert thou betrothed;
There I gave thee My hand,
And thou wert redeemed
Where thy mother was corrupted.

29. Light-wingèd birds,
Lions, fawns, bounding does,
Mountains, valleys, strands,
Waters, winds, heat,
And the terrors that keep watch by night;

30. By the soft lyres
And the siren strains, I adjure you,
Let your fury cease,
And touch not the wall,
That the bride may sleep in greater security.

THE BRIDE

31. O nymphs of Judea!
While amid the flowers and the rose-trees
The amber sends forth its perfume,
Tarry in the suburbs,
And touch not our thresholds.

32. Hide thyself, O my Beloved!
Turn Thy face to the mountains.
Do not speak,
But regard the companions
Of her who is travelling amidst strange islands.

THE BRIDEGROOM

33. The little white dove
Has returned to the ark with the bough;
And now the turtle-dove
Its desired mate
On the green banks has found.

549

34. In solitude she lived,
    And in solitude built her nest;
    And in solitude, alone
    Hath the Beloved guided her,
    In solitude also wounded with love.

THE BRIDE

35. Let us rejoice, O my Beloved!
    Let us go forth to see ourselves in Thy beauty.
    To the mountain and the hill,
    Where the pure water flows:
    Let us enter into the heart of the thicket.

36. We shall go at once
    To the deep caverns of the rock
    Which are all secret,
    There we shall enter in
    And taste of the new wine of the pomegranate.

37. There thou wilt show me
    That which my soul desired;
    And there Thou wilt give at once,
    O Thou, my life!
    That which Thou gavest me the other day.

38. The breathing of the air,
    The song of the sweet nightingale,
    The grove and its beauty
    In the serene night,
    With the flame that consumes, and gives no pains.

39. None saw it;
    Neither did Aminadab appear.
    The siege was intermitted,
    And the cavalry dismounted
    At the sight of the waters.

                                    Translated by David Lewis

We exclaim, as Dante exclaimed of Virgil: 'Onorate l'altissimo poeta.'
                                    E. ALLISON PEERS
        The Complete Works of Saint John of the Cross (1934)

TORQUATO TASSO

1 5 4 4 — 1 5 9 5

ERMINIA WANDERS IN THE FIELDS
AND DREAMS OF LOVE

Fuggí tutta la notte, e tutto il giorno
Errò senza consiglio e senza guida,
Non udendo o vedendo altro d' intorno,
Che le lagrime sue, che le sue strida.
Ma ne l' ora che 'l sol dal carro adorno
Scioglie i corsieri, e in grembo al mar s' annida,
Giunse del bel Giordano a le chiare acque,
E scese in riva al fiume, e qui si giacque. . . .

La fanciulla regal di rozze spoglie
S' ammanta, e cinge al crin ruvido velo;
Ma nel moto de gli occhi e de le membra
Non già di boschi abitatrice sembra.

Non copre abito vil la nobil luce,
E quanto è in lei d' altero e di gentile;
E fuor la mäestà regia traluce
Per gli atti ancor de l' esercizio umíle.
Guida la greggia a i paschi e la riduce
Con la povera verga al chiuso ovile;
E da l' irsute mamme il latte preme,
E 'n giro accolto poi lo stringe insieme.

Sovente, allor che su gli estivi ardori
Giacean le pecorelle a l' ombra assise,
Ne la scorza de' faggi e de gli allori
Segnò l' amato nome in mille guise:
E de' suoi strani ed infelici amori
Gli aspri successi in mille piante incise;
E in rileggendo poi le proprie note
Rigò di belle lagrime le gote.

Indi dicea piangendo: In voi serbate
Questa dolente istoria, amiche piante;
Perché, se fia ch' a le vostr' ombre grate
Giammai soggiorni alcun fedele amante,
Senta svegliarsi al cor dolce pietate
De le sventure mie sí varie e tante;

E dica: Ah troppo ingiusta empia mercede
Diè fortuna ed amore a sí gran fede!

Forse avverrà, se 'l Ciel benigno ascolta
Affettüoso alcun prego mortale,
Che venga in queste selve anco tal volta
Quegli a cui di me forse or nulla cale;
E, rivolgendo gli occhi ove sepolta
Giacerà questa spoglia inferma e frale,
Tardo premio conceda a' miei martíri
Di poche lacrimette e di sospiri:

Onde, se in vita il cor misero fue,
Sia lo spirito in morte almen felice,
E 'l cener freddo de le fiamme sue
Goda quel ch' or godere a me non lice.

Through thicke and thin, all night, all day, she driued,
Withouten comfort, company or guide,
Her plaints and teares with euery thought reuiued,
She heard and saw her griefes, but nought beside:
But when the sun his burning chariot diued
In *Thetis* waue, and weary teame vntide,
    On Iordans sandy bankes her course she staid
    At last, there downe she light, and downe she laid. . . .

The Princesse dond a poore pastoraes geare,
A kerchiefe course vpon her head she tide;
    But yet her gestures and her lookes (I gesse)
    Were such, as ill beseem'd a shepherdesse.

Not those rude garments could obscure and hide,
The heau'nly beauty of her angels face,
Nor was her princely off-spring damnifide,
Or ought disparag'd by those labours base;
Her little flocks to pasture would she guide,
And milke her goats, and in their folds them place,
    Both cheese and butter could she make, and frame
    Her selfe to please the shepherd and his dame.

But oft, when vnderneath the greene-wood shade
Her flocks lay hid from *Phœbus* scorching raies,
Vnto her Knight she songs and sonnets made,
And them engrau'd in barke of beech and baies;

She told how *Cupid* did her first inuade,
How conquer'd her, and ends with *Tancreds* praise:
    And when her passions writ she ouer read,
    Againe she mourn'd, againe salt teares she shed.

You happy trees for euer keepe (quoth shee)
This wofull story in your tender rinde,
Another day vnder your shade may bee,
Will come to rest againe some louer kinde;
Who if these trophies of my griefes he see,
Shall feele deare pitie pearce his gentle minde;
    With that she sigh'd and said, too late I proue
    There is no troath in fortune, trust in loue.

Yet may it be (if gracious heau'ns attend
The earnest suit of a distressed wight)
At my entreat they will vouchsafe to send
To these huge desarts that vnthankfull Knight,
That when to earth the man his eyes shall bend,
And sees my graue, my tombe, and ashes light,
    My wofull death, his stubborne heart may moue,
    With teares and sorrowes to reward my loue.

So, though my life hath most vnhappy beene,
At least yet shall my spirit dead be blest,
My ashes cold shall buried on this greene,
Enioy that good this bodie nere possest.

                Gerusalemme Liberata (1581), vii
                Translated by Edward Fairefax

Erminia abandoned to love has exquisite moments of lyricism. . . . Her soul has the melancholy and thoughtful imprint of Tasso: a sort of sweetness and delicacy of fibre that keeps her far from despair, and attunes her heart to the peace and solitude of the country, the picture of which is one of the most finished in Italian poetry.

                FRANCESCO DE SANCTIS
                Storia della letteratura italiana (1870)
                Translated by Joan Redfern

ROBERT GARNIER

C . 1 5 4 5 — C . 1 6 0 0

ŒDIPUS

Je me veux séparer moymesme de mon corps.
Je me fuiray moymesme aux plutoniques bords.
Je fuiray ces deux mains, ces deux mains parricides,
Ce cœur, cet estomac, ces entrailles humides,
Horribles de forfaits. J'esloigneray les cieux,
L'air, la mer et la terre, édifices des dieux.
Puis-je encore fouler les campagnes fécondes
Que Cérès embellist de chevelures blondes?
Puis-je respirer l'air, boire l'eau qui refuit,
Et me paistre du bien que la terre produit?
Puis-je encore, polu des baisers d'Iocaste,
De ma dextre toucher la tienne qui est chaste?
Puis-je entendre le son, qui le cœur me refend,
Des sacrez noms de père et de mère et d'enfant?
Las! dequoy m'a servy qu'en la nuict éternelle
J'aye fait amortir ma lumière jumelle,
Si tous mes autres sens également touchez
De mes crimes ne sont, comme mes yeux, bouchez?
Il faut que tout mon corps pourrisse sous la terre,
Et que mon âme triste aux noirs rivages erre,
Victime de Pluton. Que fay-je plus ici,
Qu'infecter de mon corps l'air et la terre aussi?
Je ne voyois encor la clairté vagabonde
Du jour, et je n'estois encores en ce monde,
Les doux flancs maternels me retenoyent contraint,
Qu'on me craignoit desjà, que j'estois desjà craint.

I wish to cast off my body. On the Plutonic shores I will flee from myself. I will flee from these hands, these two parricidal hands, this heart, this stomach, these blood-dripping entrails, horrible in crime. I will thrust away the heavens, the air, the sea and the land, abodes of the gods. Can I again tread upon the fruitful fields that Ceres embellishes with golden grain? Can I breathe the air, drink the elusive water, and feed on the bounty of the land? Can I again, polluted with the kisses of Jocasta, with my right hand touch your chaste one. Can I hear the heart-rending sound of the sacred names of father, mother and child? Alas! what profits it me that in the eternal night I have quenched the twin lights of my eyes, if all my other senses, equally touched by my crimes, are not closed like my eyes? All my body must rot under the earth, and

554

my sad soul must wander along the black shores, a victim of Pluto. Nothing is left for me here now but to pollute with my body both the air and the earth. When I had not yet seen the wandering light of day, before I had seen this world, the sweet maternal flanks held me enclosed; even then they already feared me; I even then was feared.

Antigone (1579)
Act i, Scene i

He has no equal in our literature. His equivalent is found only in Shakespeare and in the ancient writers. . . . He is the incomparable poet of invocation, imprecation and malediction.

THIERRY MAULNIER
Introduction à la poésie française (1939)

MIGUEL DE CERVANTES

1 5 4 7 — 1 6 1 6

FIRST AND LAST

En un lugar de la Mancha, de cuyo nombre no quiero acordarme, no há mucho tiempo que vivía un hidalgo de los de lanza en astillero, adarga antigua, rocín flaco, y galgo corredor.

In a certain village in La Mancha, of which I cannot remember the name, there lived not long ago one of those old-fashioned gentlemen, who are never without a lance upon a rack, an old target, a lean horse, and a greyhound.

❋   ❋   ❋   ❋

Yo, señores, siento que me voy muriendo a toda priesa: déjense burlas aparte, y tráiganme un confesor que me confiese, y un escribano que haga mi testamento, que en tales trances como éste no se ha de burlar el hombre con el alma.

I find it comes fast upon me; therefore pray, gentlemen, let us be serious. I want a priest to receive my confession, and a scrivener to draw up my will. There is no trifling at a time like this.

Don Quixote (1605–15)
Translated by Peter Anthony Motteux

No book has such a good beginning as DON QUIXOTE. *. . . . No book has a finer end.*

MAURICE BARING
Have You Anything to Declare? (1936)

Of all the books I have read, DON QUIXOTE *is the one I would desire most to have written.*

CHARLES DE SAINT-ÉVREMOND
De Quelques Livres espagnols, italiens et français (1705)

GILLES DURANT

1 5 5 0 ? — 1 6 0 5 ?

ODE

Charlotte, si ton ame
Se sent ore allumer
De cette douce flâme
Qui nous force d'aimer,
    Allons contens,
Allons sur la verdure,
Allons, tandis que dure
Notre jeune printemps.

Avant que la journée
De notre âge qui fuit,
Se trouve environnée
Des ombres de la nuit,
    Prenons loisir
De vivre notre vie;
Et, sans craindre l'envie,
Donnons-nous du plaisir.

Du soleil la lumiere
Vers le soir se déteint,
Puis à l'aube premiere
Elle reprend son teint;
    Mais notre jour,
Quand une fois il tombe,
Demeure sous la tombe,
Sans espoir de retour.

Et puis les ombres saintes,
Hotesses de là-bas,
Ne démennent qu'en feintes
Les amoureux ébats:

Entre elles, plus
Amour n'a de puissance,
Et plus n'ont connoissance
Des plaisirs de Vénus.

Mais, tristement couchées
Sous les myrthes pressés,
Elles pleurent fâchées
Leurs âges mal passés;
    Se lamentant
Que n'ayant plus de vie,
Encore cette envie
Les aille tourmentant.

En vain elles desirent
De quitter leur séjour;
En vain elles soupirent
De revoir notre jour:
    Jamais un mort,
Ayant passé le fleuve
Qui les ombres abreuve,
Ne revoit notre bord.

Aimons donc à notre aise,
Baisons-nous bien et beau,
Puisque plus on ne baise
Là-bas sous le tombeau.
    Sentons-nous pas
Comme jà la jeunesse,
Des plaisirs larronnesse,
Fuit de nous à grands pas?

Çà, finette affinée,
Çà, trompons le destin,
Qui clôt notre journée
Souvent dès le matin.

TO HIS MISTRESS

If, fairest, through thy heart
Anon thou feelest course
The fire of that sweet smart,
That makes us love perforce,

On the sward sooth
Come let us take our fill
Of ease, whilst dureth still
The Springtide of our youth.

Or e'er the dulcet day
Of this our age in flight
Be given for a prey
Unto the shades of night,
    Let's leisure take
Our life at ease to live
Nor heed to envy give,
But love and merry make.

The sun, indeed, is shorn
Of all his rays at e'en;
Yet, with the break of morn,
He hath again his sheen:
    But this our day,
When once 't hath lost its bloom,
Descendeth to the tomb
Nor thence returneth aye.

Yea, and the shadows blest,
That fill the realms below,
But counterfeit, at best,
Love's sports in empty show:
    Among these sprights,
He hath no puissance more;
The taste the dead ignore
Of Venus's delights.

Nay, lying sad and prone,
Among the myrtles pale,
Their sweet days they bemoan,
Forspent without avail,
    Lamenting shrill
That, though they're quit of life,
The wish thereof to strife
And sorrow stirs them still.

In vain and still in vain
To quit their stead they sigh;
In vain they yearn, again
To see the day on high:

The dead ne'ermore,
Once past the river's brink,
Whereof the shadows drink,
Set eyes upon Life's shore.

Then let us kiss and share
Our fill of love and mirth.
There is no kissing, fair,
Beneath the graveyard earth.
Do we not feel
How Time, with hurrying feet,
That thief of pleasance sweet,
Our youth from us doth steal?

Come, then, coquettish maid,
Let's steal a march on Fate,
That doth our day o'ershade,
Oft ere the morn wax late.
On the sward sooth
Come let us take our fill
Of ease, whilst dureth still
The Springtide of our youth.

Translated by John Payne

*Neither Passerat, nor Ronsard nor any other poet of the century ex-
pressed better than he that sensation of sadness which is born even in
the midst of gaiety, and those thoughts of death eternally linked with
experiences of pleasure.*

C.-A. SAINTE-BEUVE
La Poésie française (1843)

THÉODORE AGRIPPA D'AUBIGNÉ

1 5 5 2 — 1 6 3 0

CAIN

Ainsi Abel offroit en pure conscience
Sacrifices à Dieu, Caïn offroit aussi:
L'un offroit un cœur doux, l'autre un cœur endurci,
L'un fut au gré de Dieu, l'autre non agreable.
Caïn grinça les dents, palit, espouvantable,

Il massacra son frere, & de cet agneau doux
Il fit un sacrifice à son amer courroux.
Le sang fuit de son front, & honteux se retire
Sentant son frere sang que l'aveugle main tire;
Mais, quand le coup fut fait, sa premiere pasleur
Au prix de la seconde estoit vive couleur:
Ses cheveux vers le ciel herissés en furie,
Le grincement de dents en sa bouche flestrie,
L'œil sourcillant de peur descouvroit son ennuy.
Il avoit peur de tout, tout avoit peur de luy:
Car le ciel s'affeubloit du manteau d'une nue
Si tost que le transi au ciel tournoit la veuë;
S'il fuyoit au desert, les rochers & les bois
Effrayés abbayoyent au son de ses abois.
Sa mort ne peut avoir de mort pour recompense,
L'enfer n'eut point de morts à punir cette offense,
Mais autant que de jours il sentit de trespas:
Vif il ne vescut point, mort il ne mourut pas.
Il fuit d'effroi transi, troublé, tremblant et blesme,
Il fuit de tout le monde, il s'enfuit de soy-mesme.
Les lieux plus asseurés luy estoyent des hazards,
Les fueilles, les rameaux & les fleurs des poignards,
Les plumes de son lict des esguilles piquantes,
Ses habits plus aisez des tenailles serrantes,
Son eau jus de ciguë, & son pain des poisons;
Ses mains le menaçoyent de fines trahisons:
Tout image de mort, & le pis de sa rage
C'est qu'il cerche la mort & n'en voit que l'image.
De quelqu'autre Caïn il craignoit la fureur,
Il fut sans compagnon & non pas sans frayeur,
Il possedoit le monde et non une asseurance,
Il estoit seul par tout, hors mis sa conscience:
Et fut marqué au front afin qu'en s'enfuyant
Aucun n'osast tuer ses maux en le tuant.

Just as Abel offered sacrifices to God, with a pure conscience, Cain offered them as well. The one offered a gentle, the other a hardened heart; the one was acceptable to God, but not the other. Cain gnashed his teeth, grew pale, full of dread; he slaughtered his brother, and of that gentle lamb he made a sacrifice to his bitter wrath. The blood leaves his face, shamefully withdraws as it feels the brotherly blood drawn by the murderous blind hand; but, when the deed was done, its first pallor was vivid in comparison with the one which followed it. His hair bristled in fury towards heaven; the gnashing of teeth in his withered mouth, his eyes frowning with fear, disclosed his distress. He dreaded everything, and everything dreaded him; whenever the trembling Cain turned his eyes towards the sky, it appeared wrapped in a cloak of clouds. When he ran towards the desert, the crags and woods shouted back with fright at the sound of his cries. His deadly crime cannot be atoned for by death. Hell contained no deaths adequate to punish his crime. But he suffered as many deaths as the days of his life; alive he did not live, dead he died not. He flees distressed with fright, troubled, trembling and pale; he flees from everyone, he flees from himself. The most secure places were menacing for him; the leaves, the branches and the flowers were daggers, the feathers of his bed were as pricking needles, his most comfortable clothing was like a tightening vice, his water the juice of hemlock, his bread poison. His hands threaten him with subtle treason; everything to him was an image of death; and his greatest grief was that he sought for death and found only its image. He feared the fury of some other Cain, he walked alone but not without fright, he possessed the world but no self-trust. He was alone everywhere except within his conscience, and was branded on his forehead, so that, while fleeing, none dared kill his agony by killing him.

Les Tragiques (c. 1577)

Since the beginnings of French literature there has never been a page with such sustained and truly eloquent power.

ÉMILE FAGUET
Histoire de la poésie française (1923)

THÉODORE AGRIPPA D'AUBIGNÉ

1 5 5 2 — 1 6 3 0

PSEAUME HUICTANTE HUICT

Sauveur Eternel, nuict & jour devant toi
Mes soupirs s'en vont relevés de leur foi.
Sus, soupirs, montez de ce creux & bas lieu
 Jusques à mon Dieu!

Au milieu des vifs demi-mort je transis:
Au milieu des morts demi-vif je languis.
C'est mourir sans mort, & ne rien avancer,
 Qu'ainsi balancer.

Dans le ventre obscur du mal-heur reserré,
Ainsi qu'au tombeau je me sens atterré,

Sans amis, sans jour qui me luise & sans voir
    L'aube de l'espoir.

Qui se souviendra de loüer ta grandeur
Dans le profond creux d'oubliance & d'horreur?
Pourroit aux Enfers tenebreux ta bonté
    Rendre sa clarté.

Quand le jour s'enfuit, le serain brunissant,
Quand la nuict s'en va, le matin renaissant,
Au silence obscur, à l'esclair des hauts jours
    J'invoque toujours.

Mais voulant chanter je ne rends que sanglots,
En joignant les mains je ne joins que des os:
Il ne sort nul feu, nulle humeur de mes yeux
    Pour lever aux Cieux.

Veux-tu donc, ô Dieu, que mon ombre sans corps
Serve pour chanter ton ire entre les morts,
Et que ton grand Nom venerable & tant beau
    Sorte du tombeau?

Ou que les vieux tests à la fosse rangés
Soyent rejoincts des nerfs que la mort a rongés,
Pour crier tes coups, & glacer de leurs cris
    Nos foibles esprits?

N'est-ce plus au Ciel que triomphent tes faits?
N'as tu plus d'autels que sepulchres infects?
Donc ne faut-il plus d'holocaustes chauffer
    Temple que l'Enfer?

Mes amis s'en vont devenus mes bourreaux,
Tel flattoit mes biens qui se rit de mes maux,
Mon lict est un cep, ce qui fut ma maison
    M'est une prison.

Si jadis forclos de ton œil, le berceau
Dur me fut, moins dur ne sera le tombeau.
Or coulez, mes jours orageux, & mes nuicts
    Fertiles d'ennuis.

Pour jamais as-tu ravi d'entre mes bras
Ma moitié, mon tout, & ma compaigne? helas!
Las! ce dur penser de regrets va tranchant
    Mon cœur & mon chant.

PSALM EIGHTY-EIGHT

Savior Eternal, night and day before Thee my sighs ascend, uplifted by their faith. Courage, sighs, rise from this empty, wretched place unto my God! Half dead, in the midst of the living, I am numbed; half alive, in the midst of the dead, I languish. To waver thus is to die without death, and to move not. Hemmed about by the gloomy maw of misfortune, I feel as if I were buried in a tomb, without friends, without day to light me, and unable to see the dawn of hope. Who will remember to praise Thy grandeur in the profound depths of forgetfulness and misery? Only Thy goodness could restore light to darkest Hell. When the day departs at darkling evening, when the night passes with the coming of morning, in obscure silence, in the light of full day, I invoke Thee ever. Wishing to sing I do but sigh; in joining my hands, I join but bones; no fire, no moisture issues from my eyes when I raise them to Heaven. Oh, God, dost Thou desire that my bodiless shadow may sing Thy wrath only among the dead, and that Thy great, venerable, and so beautiful Name issue out of a tomb? Or that the ancient skulls ranged in the grave be rejoined to the nerves that death has gnawed away, to cry out at Thy blows, and to chill by their cries our weak spirits? Do Thy deeds no longer triumph in Heaven? Hast Thou no more altars but contaminated sepulchers? Is there no other temple but Hell to warm with holocausts? My friends depart, having become my executioners; he who formerly fawned on my riches laughs at my evils; my bed is a manacle; what formerly was my house is but a prison. Formerly, when I was shut out of Thy glance, the cradle was hard to me; my grave will be hard no less. Flow on my stormy days, my nights rife with grief! For ever hast Thou snatched from my arms my half, my all, my mate? Alas! Alas! my heart and song are torn with regrets at this cruel thought.

His great procession of stanzas maintains the highest flight without a fault.

THIERRY MAULNIER
Introduction à la poésie française (1939)

ASTROPHEL

Shepheards that wont on pipes of oaten reed,
Oft times to plaine your loues concealed smart:
And with your piteous layes haue learnd to breed
Compassion in a countrey lasses hart.
Hearken ye gentle shepheards to my song,
And place my dolefull plaint your plaints emong.

To you alone I sing this mournfull verse,
The mournfulst verse that euer man heard tell:
To you whose softened hearts it may empierse,
With dolours dart for death of Astrophel.
To you I sing and to none other wight,
For well I wot my rymes bene rudely dight.

Yet as they been, if any nycer wit
Shall hap to heare, or couet them to read:
Thinke he, that such are for such ones most fit,
Made not to please the liuing but the dead.
And if in him found pity euer place,
Let him be moov'd to pity such a case.

A Gentle Shepheard borne in *Arcady*,
Of gentlest race that euer shepheard bore:
About the grassie bancks of *Hæmony*,
Did keepe his sheep, his litle stock and store.
Full carefully he kept them day and night,
In fairest fields, and *Astrophel* he hight.

Young *Astrophel* the pride of shepheards praise,
Young *Astrophel* the rusticke lasses loue:
Far passing all the pastors of his daies,
In all that seemly shepheard might behoue.
In one thing onely fayling of the best,
That he was not so happie as the rest.

For from the time that first the Nymph his mother
Him forth did bring, and taught her lambs to feed,
A sclender swaine excelling far each other,
In comely shape, like her that did him breed,
He grew vp fast in goodnesse and in grace,
And doubly faire wox both in mynd and face.

Which daily more and more he did augment,
With gentle vsage and demeanure myld:
That all mens hearts with secret rauishment
He stole away, and weetingly beguyld.
Ne spight it selfe that all good things doth spill,
Found ought in him, that she could say was ill.

His sports were faire, his ioyance innocent,
Sweet without sowre, and honny without gall:
And he himselfe seemd made for meriment,
Merily masking both in bowre and hall.
There was no pleasure nor delightfull play,
When *Astrophel* so euer was away.

For he could pipe and daunce, and caroll sweet,
Emongst the shepheards in their shearing feast:
As Somers larke that with her song doth greet
The dawning day forth comming from the East.
And layes of loue he also could compose.
Thrise happie she, whom he to praise did chose.

Full many Maydens often did him woo,
Them to vouchsafe emongst his rimes to name,
Or make for them as he was wont to doo,
For her that did his heart with loue inflame.
For which they promised to dight, for him,
Gay chapelets of flowers and gyrlonds trim.

And many a Nymph both of the wood and brooke,
Soone as his oaten pipe began to shrill:
Both christall wells and shadie groues forsooke,
To heare the charmes of his enchanting skill.
And brought him presents, flowers if it were prime,
Or mellow fruit if it were haruest time.

But he for none of them did care a whit,
Yet wood Gods for them often sighed sore:
Ne for their gifts vnworthie of his wit,
Yet not vnworthie of the countries store.
For one alone he cared, for one he sight,
His lifes desire, and his deare loues delight.

Stella the faire, the fairest star in skie,
As faire as *Venus* or the fairest faire:
A fairer star saw neuer liuing eie,
Shot her sharp pointed beames through purest aire.
Her he did loue, her he alone did honor,
His thoughts, his rimes, his songs were all vpon her.

To her he vowd the seruice of his daies,
On her he spent the riches of his wit:
For her he made hymnes of immortall praise,
Of onely her he sung, he thought, he writ.
Her, and but her, of loue he worthie deemed,
For all the rest but litle he esteemed.

Ne her with ydle words alone he wowed,
And verses vaine (yet verses are not vaine)
But with braue deeds to her sole seruice vowed,
And bold atchieuements her did entertaine.
For both in deeds and words he nourtred was,
Both wise and hardie (too hardie alas).

In wrestling nimble, and in renning swift,
In shooting steddie, and in swimming strong:
Well made to strike, to throw, to leape, to lift,
And all the sports that shepheards are emong.
In euery one he vanquisht euery one,
He vanquisht all, and vanquisht was of none.

Besides, in hunting, such felicitie,
Or rather infelicitie he found:
That euery field and forest far away,
He sought, where saluage beasts do most abound.
No beast so saluage but he could it kill,
No chace so hard, but he therein had skill.

Such skill matcht with such courage as he had,
Did prick him foorth with proud desire of praise:
To seek abroad, of daunger nought y'drad,
His mistresse name, and his owne fame to raise.
What needeth perill to be sought abroad,
Since round about vs, it doth make aboad?

It fortuned, as he that perilous game
In forreine soyle pursued far away:
Into a forest wide and waste he came
Where store he heard to be of saluage pray.
So wide a forest and so waste as this,
Nor famous *Ardeyn*, nor fowle *Arlo* is.

There his welwouen toyles and subtil traines
He laid, the brutish nation to enwrap:
So well he wrought with practise and with paines,
That he of them great troups did soone entrap.
Full happie man (misweening much) was hee,
So rich a spoile within his power to see.

Eftsoones all heedlesse of his dearest hale,
Full greedily into the heard he thrust:
To slaughter them, and worke their finall bale,
Least that his toyle should of their troups be brust.
Wide wounds emongst them many one he made,
Now with his sharp borespear, now with his blade.

His care was all how he them all might kill,
That none might scape (so partiall vnto none)
Ill mynd so much to mynd anothers ill,
As to become vnmyndfull of his owne.
But pardon that vnto the cruell skies,
That from himselfe to them withdrew his eies.

So as he rag'd emongst that beastly rout,
A cruell beast of most accursed brood
Vpon him turnd (despeyre makes cowards stout)
And with fell tooth accustomed to blood,
Launched his thigh with so mischieuous might,
That it both bone and muscles ryued quight.

So deadly was the dint and deep the wound,
And so huge streames of blood thereout did flow,
That he endured not the direfull stound,
But on the cold deare earth himselfe did throw.
The whiles the captiue heard his nets did rend,
And hauing none to let, to wood did wend.

Ah where were ye this while his shepheard peares,
To whom aliue was nought so deare as hee:
And ye faire Mayds the matches of his yeares,
Which in his grace did boast you most to bee?
Ah where were ye, when he of you had need,
To stop his wound that wondrously did bleed?

Ah wretched boy the shape of dreryhead,
And sad ensample of mans suddein end:
Full litle faileth but thou shalt be dead,
Vnpitied, vnplaynd, of foe or frend.
Whilest none is nigh, thine eylids vp to close,
And kisse thy lips like faded leaues of rose.

A sort of shepheards sewing of the chace,
As they the forest raunged on a day:
By fate or fortune came vnto the place,
Where as the lucklesse boy yet bleeding lay.
Yet bleeding lay, and yet would still haue bled,
Had not good hap those shepheards thether led.

They stopt his wound (too late to stop it was)
And in their armes then softly did him reare:
Tho (as he wild) vnto his loued lasse,
His dearest loue him dolefully did beare.
The dolefulst beare that euer man did see,
Was *Astrophel,* but dearest vnto mee.

She when she saw her loue in such a plight,
With crudled blood and filthie gore deformed:
That wont to be with flowers and gyrlonds dight,
And her deare fauours dearly well adorned,
Her face, the fairest face, that eye mote see,
She likewise did deforme like him to bee.

Her yellow locks that shone so bright and long,
As Sunny beames in fairest somers day
She fiersly tore, and with outragious wrong
From her red cheeks the roses rent away.
And her faire brest the threasury of ioy,
She spoyld thereof, and filled with annoy.

His palled face impictured with death,
She bathed oft with teares and dried oft:
And with sweet kisses suckt the wasting breath,
Out of his lips like lillies pale and soft.
And oft she cald to him, who answerd nought,
But onely by his lookes did tell his thought.

The rest of her impatient regret,
And piteous mone the which she for him made,
No toong can tell, nor any forth can set,
But he whose heart like sorrow did inuade.
At last when paine his vitall powres had spent,
His wasted life her weary lodge forwent.

Which when she saw, she staied not a whit,
But after him did make vntimely haste:
Forth with her ghost out of her corps did flit,
And followed her make like Turtle chaste.
To proue that death their hearts cannot diuide,
Which liuing were in loue so firmly tide.

The Gods which all things see, this same beheld,
And pittying this paire of louers trew,
Transformed them there lying on the field,
Into one flowre that is both red and blew.
It first growes red, and then to blew doth fade,
Like *Astrophel,* which thereinto was made.

And in the midst thereof a star appeares,
As fairly formd as any star in skyes:
Resembling *Stella* in her freshest yeares,
Forth darting beames of beautie from her eyes,
And all the day it standeth full of deow,
Which is the teares, that from her eyes did flow.

That hearbe of some, Starlight is cald by name,
Of others *Penthia*, though not so well
But thou where euer thou doest finde the same,
From this day forth do call it *Astrophel*.
And when so euer thou it vp doest take,
Do pluck it softly for that shepheards sake.

Hereof when tydings far abroad did passe,
The shepheards all which loued him full deare,
And sure full deare of all he loued was,
Did thether flock to see what they did heare.
And when that pitteous spectacle they vewed.
The same with bitter teares they all bedewed.

And euery one did make exceeding mone,
With inward anguish and great griefe opprest:
And euery one did weep and waile, and mone,
And meanes deviz'd to shew his sorrow best.
That from that houre since first on grassie greene
Shepheards kept sheep, was not like mourning seen.

But first his sister that *Clorinda* hight,
The gentlest shepheardesse that liues this day:
And most resembling both in shape and spright
Her brother deare, began this dolefull lay.
Which least I marre the sweetnesse of the vearse,
In sort as she it sung, I will rehearse.

Ay me, to whom shall I my case complaine,
That may compassion my impatient griefe?
Or where shall I enfold my inward paine,
That my enriuen heart may find reliefe?
Shall I vnto the heauenly powres it show?
Or vnto earthly men that dwell below?

To heauens? ah they alas the authors were,
And workers of my vnremedied wo:
For they foresee what to vs happens here,
And they foresaw, yet suffred this be so.
  From them comes good, from them comes also il,
  That which they made, who can them warne to spill.

To men? ah they alas like wretched bee,
And subiect to the heauens ordinance:
Bound to abide what euer they decree,
Their best redresse, is their best sufferance.
  How then can they, like wretched, comfort mee,
  The which no lesse, need comforted to bee?

Then to my selfe will I my sorrow mourne,
Sith none aliue like sorrowfull remaines:
And to my selfe my plaints shall back retourne,
To pay their vsury with doubled paines.
  The woods, the hills, the riuers shall resound
  The mournfull accent of my sorrowes ground.

Woods, hills and riuers, now are desolate,
Sith he is gone the which them all did grace:
And all the fields do waile their widow state,
Sith death their fairest flowre did late deface.
  The fairest flowre in field that euer grew,
  Was *Astrophel;* that was, we all may rew,

What cruell hand of cursed foe vnknowne,
Hath cropt the stalke which bore so faire a flowre?
Vntimely cropt, before it well were growne,
And cleane defaced in vntimely howre.
  Great losse to all that euer him did see,
  Great losse to all, but greatest losse to mee.

Breake now your gyrlonds, O ye shepheards lasses,
Sith the faire flowre, which them adornd, is gon:
The flowre, which them adornd, is gone to ashes,
Neuer againe let lasse put gyrlond on.
  In stead of gyrlond, weare sad Cypres nowe,
  And bitter Elder, broken from the bowe.

Ne euer sing the loue-layes which he made,
Who euer made such layes of loue as hee?
Ne euer read the riddles, which he sayd
Vnto your selues, to make you mery glee.
  Your mery glee is now laid all abed,
  Your mery maker now alasse is dead.

Death the deuourer of all worlds delight,
Hath robbed you and reft fro me my ioy:
Both you and me, and all the world he quight
Hath robd of ioyance, and left sad annoy.
  Ioy of the world, and shepheards pride was hee,
  Shepheards hope neuer like againe to see.

Oh death that hast vs of such riches reft,
Tell vs at least, what hast thou with it done?
What is become of him whose flowre here left
Is but the shadow of his likenesse gone.
  Scarse like the shadow of that which he was,
  Nought like, but that he like a shade did pas.

But that immortall spirit, which was deckt
With all the dowries of celestiall grace:
By soueraine choyce from th'heuenly quires select,
And lineally deriv'd from Angels race,
  O what is now of it become, aread.
  Ay me, can so diuine a thing be dead?

Ah no: it is not dead, ne can it die,
But liues for aie, in blisfull Paradise:
Where like a new-borne babe it soft doth lie.
In bed of lillies wrapt in tender wise.
  And compast all about with roses sweet,
  And daintie violets from head to feet.

There thousand birds all of celestiall brood,
To him do sweetly caroll day and night:
And with straunge notes, of him well vnderstood,
Lull him a sleep in Angelick delight;
  Whilest in sweet dreame to him presented bee
  Immortall beauties, which no eye may see.

But he them sees and takes exceeding pleasure
Of their diuine aspects, appearing plaine,
And kindling loue in him aboue all measure,
Sweet loue still ioyous, neuer feeling paine.
  For what so goodly forme he there doth see,
  He may enioy from iealous rancor free.

There liueth he in euerlasting blis,
Sweet spirit neuer fearing more to die:
Ne dreading harme from any foes of his,
Ne fearing saluage beasts more crueltie.
  Whilest we here wretches waile his priuate lack,
  And with vaine vowes do often call him back.

But liue thou there still happie, happie spirit,
And giue vs leaue thee here thus to lament:
Not thee that doest thy heauens ioy inherit,
But our owne selues that here in dole are drent.
  Thus do we weep and waile, and wear our eies,
  Mourning in others, our owne miseries.

Which when she ended had, another swaine
Of gentle wit and daintie sweet deuice:
Whom *Astrophel* full deare did entertaine,
Whilest here he liv'd, and held in passing price,
Hight *Thestylis*, began his mournfull tourne,
And made the *Muses* in his song to mourne.

And after him full many other moe,
As euerie one in order lov'd him best,
Gan dight themselues t'expresse their inward woe,
With dolefull layes vnto the time addrest.
The which I here in order will rehearse,
As fittest flowres to deck his mournfull hearse.

(1586)

One of the most finished and beautiful elegies in the English language.
PATRICK FRASER TYTLER
Life of Sir Walter Raleigh (1833)

EDMUND SPENSER

1 5 5 2 ? — 1 5 9 9

VNWORTHY WRETCHEDNESSE

Nought is there vnder heau'ns wide hollownesse,
That moues more deare compassion of mind,
Then beautie brought t'vnworthy wretchednesse.
The Faerie Queene (1590–96), i

The mournful sweetness of those lines is insurpassable; and they are quintessential Spenser. Yet it is unluckily characteristic of him, too, that he mars half the effect of this perfect passage by not stopping with its completion, but following it with a line which makes an anti-climax, and is too manifestly inserted for rhyme's sake:

Through envy's snares, or fortune's freaks unkind.

One might almost take that little passage as a text for one's whole disquisition on Spenser. For, after all, it is not in the richly luxuriant descriptive embroidery, or the pictures brushed in with words as with line and colour, which are traditionally quoted by this poet's critics, that the highest Spenser lies. The secret of him is shut in those three lines.

Wherein lies their power? The language is so utterly plain that an uninspired poet would have fallen upon baldness. Yet Spenser is a mine of diction (as was remarked to us by a poet who had worked in that mine). But here he had no need for his gorgeous opulence of diction: a few commonest words, and the spell was worked. It is all a matter of relation: the words take life from each other, and become an organism, as with Coleridge. And it is a matter of music; an integral element in the magic of the passage is its sound. In this necromancy, by which the most elementary words, entering into a secret relation of sense and sound, acquire occult property, Spenser is a master. And that which gives electric life to their relation is the Spenserian subtlety of emotion. Here it is specifically pathos, at another time it is joyous exultation, or again the pleasure of beauty. But behind and underneath all these emotional forms, the central and abiding quality, the essence of his emotion, is peace, and the radiance of peace. The final effect of all, in this and kindred passages, is lyrical.

FRANCIS THOMPSON
The Poets' Poet (1913)

EDMUND SPENSER

1 5 5 2 ? — 1 5 9 9

THE CAVE OF MAMMON

That houses forme within was rude and strong,
 Like an huge caue, hewne out of rocky clift,
 From whose rough vaut the ragged breaches hong,
 Embost with massy gold of glorious gift,
 And with rich metall loaded euery rift,
 That heauy ruine they did seeme to threat;
 And ouer them *Arachne* high did lift
 Her cunning web, and spred her subtile net,
Enwrapped in fowle smoke and clouds more blacke then Iet.

Both roofe, and floore, and wals were all of gold,
 But ouergrowne with dust and old decay,
 And hid in darkenesse, that none could behold
 The hew thereof: for vew of chearefull day
 Did neuer in that house it selfe display,

573

But a faint shadow of vncertain light;
  Such as a lamp, whose life does fade away:
  Or as the Moone cloathed with clowdy night,
Does shew to him, that walkes in feare and sad affright.

❋   ❋   ❋   ❋

And ouer them sad Horrour with grim hew,
  Did alwayes sore, beating his yron wings;
  And after him Owles and Night-rauens flew,
  The hatefull messengers of heauy things,
  Of death and dolour telling sad tidings;
  Whiles sad *Celeno*, sitting on a clift,
  A song of bale and bitter sorrow sings,
  That hart of flint a sunder could haue rift:
Which hauing ended, after him she flyeth swift.

The Faerie Queene (1590–96), ii

*Unrivalled for the portentous massiness of the forms, the splendid
chiaro-scuro, and shadowy horror.*

WILLIAM HAZLITT
Lectures on the English Poets (1818)

EDMUND SPENSER

1 5 5 2 ? — 1 5 9 9

THE WANTON MAIDEN

Withall she laughed, and she blusht withall,
  That blushing to her laughter gaue more grace,
  And laughter to her blushing.

The Faerie Queene (1590–96), ii

*Perhaps this is the loveliest thing of the kind, mixing the sensual with
the graceful, that ever was painted.*

JAMES HENRY LEIGH HUNT
Imagination and Fancy (1844)

574

EPITHALAMION

Ye learned sisters which haue oftentimes
Beene to me ayding, others to adorne:
Whom ye thought worthy of your gracefull rymes,
That euen the greatest did not greatly scorne
To heare theyr names sung in your simple layes,
But ioyed in theyr prayse.
And when ye list your owne mishaps to mourne,
Which death, or loue, or fortunes wreck did rayse,
Your string could soone to sadder tenor turne,
And teach the woods and waters to lament
Your dolefull dreriment.
Now lay those sorrowfull complaints aside,
And hauing all your heads with girland crownd,
Helpe me mine owne loues prayses to resound,
Ne let the same of any be enuide:
So Orpheus did for his owne bride,
So I vnto my selfe alone will sing,
The woods shall to me answer and my Eccho ring.

Early before the worlds light giuing lampe,
His golden beame vpon the hils doth spred,
Hauing disperst the nights vnchearefull dampe,
Doe ye awake, and with fresh lusty hed,
Go to the bowre of my beloued loue,
My truest turtle doue,
Bid her awake; for Hymen is awake,
And long since ready forth his maske to moue,
With his bright Tead that flames with many a flake,
And many a bachelor to waite on him,
In theyr fresh garments trim.
Bid her awake therefore and soone her dight,
For lo the wished day is come at last,
That shall for al the paynes and sorrowes past,
Pay to her vsury of long delight:
And whylest she doth her dight,
Doe ye to her of ioy and solace sing,
That all the woods may answer and your eccho ring.

Bring with you all the Nymphes that you can heare
Both of the riuers and the forrests greene:
And of the sea that neighbours to her neare,
Al with gay girlands goodly wel beseene.
And let them also with them bring in hand,
Another gay girland
For my fayre loue of lillyes and of roses,
Bound trueloue wize with a blew silke riband.
And let them make great store of bridale poses,
And let them eeke bring store of other flowers
To deck the bridale bowers.
And let the ground whereas her foot shall tread,
For feare the stones her tender foot should wrong
Be strewed with fragrant flowers all along,
And diapred lyke the discolored mead.
Which done, doe at her chamber dore awayt,
For she will waken strayt,
The whiles doe ye this song vnto her sing,
The woods shall to you answer and your Eccho ring.

Ye Nymphes of Mulla which with carefull heed,
The siluer scaly trouts doe tend full well,
And greedy pikes which vse therein to feed,
(Those trouts and pikes all others doo excell)
And ye likewise which keepe the rushy lake,
Where none doo fishes take,
Bynd vp the locks the which hang scatterd light,
And in his waters which your mirror make,
Behold your faces as the christall bright,
That when you come whereas my loue doth lie,
No blemish she may spie.
And eke ye lightfoot mayds which keepe the deere,
That on the hoary mountayne vse to towre,
And the wylde wolues which seeke them to deuoure,
With your steele darts doo chace from comming neer
Be also present heere,
To helpe to decke her and to help to sing,
That all the woods may answer and your eccho ring.

Wake, now my loue, awake; for it is time,
The Rosy Morne long since left Tithones bed,
All ready to her siluer coche to clyme,
And Phœbus gins to shew his glorious hed.
Hark how the cheerefull birds do chaunt theyr laies
And carroll of loues praise.

The merry Larke hir mattins sings aloft,
The thrush replyes, the Mauis descant playes,
The Ouzell shrills, the Ruddock warbles soft,
So goodly all agree with sweet consent,
To this dayes merriment.
Ah my deere loue why doe ye sleepe thus long,
When meeter were that ye should now awake,
T'awayt the comming of your ioyous make,
And hearken to the birds louelearned song,
The deawy leaues among.
For they of ioy and pleasance to you sing,
That all the woods them answer and theyr eccho ring.

My loue is now awake out of her dreame,
And her fayre eyes like stars that dimmed were
With darksome cloud, now shew theyr goodly beams
More bright then Hesperus his head doth rere.
Come now ye damzels, daughters of delight,
Helpe quickly her to dight,
But first come ye fayre houres which were begot
In Loues sweet paradice, of Day and Night,
Which doe the seasons of the yeare allot,
And al that euer in this world is fayre
Doe make and still repayre.
And ye three handmayds of the Cyprian Queene,
The which doe still adorne her beauties pride,
Helpe to addorne my beautifullest bride:
And as ye her array, still throw betweene
Some graces to be seene,
And as ye vse to Venus, to her sing,
The whiles the woods shal answer and your eccho ring.

Now is my loue all ready forth to come,
Let all the virgins therefore well awayt,
And ye fresh boyes that tend vpon her groome
Prepare your selues; for he is comming strayt.
Set all your things in seemely good aray
Fit for so ioyfull day,
The ioyfulst day that euer sunne did see.
Faire Sun, shew forth thy fauourable ray,
And let thy lifull heat not feruent be
For feare of burning her sunshyny face,
Her beauty to disgrace.
O fayrest Phœbus, father of the Muse,
If euer I did honour thee aright,
Or sing the thing, that mote thy mind delight,

577

Doe not thy seruants simple boone refuse,
But let this day let this one day be myne,
Let all the rest be thine.
Then I thy souerayne prayses loud wil sing,
That all the woods shal answer and theyr eccho ring.

Harke how the Minstrels gin to shrill aloud
Their merry Musick that resounds from far,
The pipe, the tabor, and the trembling Croud,
That well agree withouten breach or iar.
But most of all the Damzels doe delite,
When they their tymbrels smyte,
And thereunto doe daunce and carrol sweet,
That all the sences they doe rauish quite,
The whyles the boyes run vp and downe the street,
Crying aloud with strong confused noyce,
As if it were one voyce.
Hymen io Hymen, Hymen they do shout,
That euen to the heauens theyr shouting shrill
Doth reach, and all the firmament doth fill,
To which the people standing all about,
As in approuance doe thereto applaud
And loud aduaunce her laud,
And euermore they Hymen Hymen sing,
That al the woods them answer and theyr eccho ring.

Loe where she comes along with portly pace
Lyke Phœbe from her chamber of the East,
Arysing forth to run her mighty race,
Clad all in white, that seemes a virgin best.
So well it her beseemes that ye would weene
Some angell she had beene.
Her long loos yellow locks lyke golden wyre,
Sprinckled with perle, and perling flowres a tweene,
Doe lyke a golden mantle her attyre,
And being crowned with a girland greene,
Seeme lyke some mayden Queene.
Her modest eyes abashed to behold
So many gazers, as on her do stare,
Vpon the lowly ground affixed are.
Ne dare lift vp her countenance too bold,
But blush to heare her prayses sung so loud,
So farre from being proud.
Nathlesse doe ye still loud her prayses sing.
That all the woods may answer and your eccho ring.

Tell me ye merchants daughters did ye see
So fayre a creature in your towne before,
So sweet, so louely, and so mild as she,
Adornd with beautyes grace and vertues store,
Her goodly eyes lyke Saphyres shining bright,
Her forehead yuory white,
Her cheekes lyke apples which the sun hath rudded,
Her lips lyke cherryes charming men to byte,
Her brest like to a bowle of creame vncrudded,
Her paps lyke lyllies budded,
Her snowie necke lyke to a marble towre,
And all her body like a pallace fayre,
Ascending vppe with many a stately stayre,
To honors seat and chastities sweet bowre.
Why stand ye still ye virgins in amaze,
Vpon her so to gaze,
Whiles ye forget your former lay to sing,
To which the woods did answer and your eccho ring.

But if ye saw that which no eyes can see,
The inward beauty of her liuely spright,
Garnisht with heauenly guifts of high degree,
Much more then would ye wonder at that sight,
And stand astonisht lyke to those which red
Medusaes mazeful hed.
There dwels sweet loue and constant chastity,
Vnspotted fayth and comely womanhood,
Regard of honour and mild modesty,
There vertue raynes as Queene in royal throne,
And giueth lawes alone.
The which the base affections doe obay,
And yeeld theyr seruices vnto her will,
Ne thought of thing vncomely euer may
Thereto approch to tempt her mind to ill.
Had ye once seene these her celestial threasures,
And vnreuealed pleasures,
Then would ye wonder and her prayses sing,
That al the woods should answer and your echo ring.

Open the temple gates vnto my loue,
Open them wide that she may enter in,
And all the postes adorne as doth behoue,
And all the pillours deck with girlands trim,
For to recyue this Saynt with honour dew,
That commeth in to you.

With trembling steps and humble reuerence,
She commeth in, before th'almighties vew,
Of her ye virgins learne obedience,
When so ye come into those holy places,
To humble your proud faces:
Bring her vp to th'high altar, that she may
The sacred ceremonies there partake,
The which do endlesse matrimony make,
And let the roring Organs loudly play
The praises of the Lord in liuely notes,
The whiles with hollow throates
The Choristers the ioyous Antheme sing,
That al the woods may answere and their eccho ring.

Behold whiles she before the altar stands
Hearing the holy priest that to her speakes
And blesseth her with his two happy hands,
How the red roses flush vp in her cheekes,
And the pure snow with goodly vermill stayne,
Like crimsin dyde in grayne,
That euen th'Angels which continually,
About the sacred Altare doe remaine,
Forget their seruice and about her fly,
Ofte peeping in her face that seemes more fayre,
The more they on it stare.
But her sad eyes still fastened on the ground,
Are gouerned with goodly modesty,
That suffers not one looke to glaunce awry,
Which may let in a little thought vnsownd.
Why blush ye loue to giue to me your hand,
The pledge of all our band?
Sing ye sweet Angels, Alleluya sing,
That all the woods may answere and your eccho ring.

Now al is done; bring home the bride againe,
Bring home the triumph of our victory,
Bring home with you the glory of her gaine,
With ioyance bring her and with iollity.
Neuer had man more ioyfull day then this,
Whom heauen would heape with blis.
Make feast therefore now all this liue long day,
This day for euer to me holy is,
Poure out the wine without restraint or stay,
Poure not by cups, but by the belly full,
Poure out to all that wull,

And sprinkle all the postes and wals with wine,
That they may sweat, and drunken be withall.
Crowne ye God Bacchus with a coronall,
And Hymen also crowne with wreathes of vine,
And let the Graces daunce vnto the rest;
For they can doo it best:
The whiles the maydens doe theyr carroll sing,
To which the woods shal answer and theyr eccho ring.

Ring ye the bels, ye yong men of the towne,
And leaue your wonted labors for this day:
This day is holy; doe ye write it downe,
That ye for euer it remember may.
This day the sunne is in his chiefest hight,
With Barnaby the bright,
From whence declining daily by degrees,
He somewhat loseth of his heat and light,
When once the Crab behind his back he sees.
But for this time it ill ordained was,
To chose the longest day in all the yeare,
And shortest night, when longest fitter weare:
Yet neuer day so long, but late would passe.
Ring ye the bels, to make it weare away,
And bonefiers make all day,
And daunce about them, and about them sing:
That all the woods may answer, and your eccho ring.

Ah when will this long weary day haue end,
And lende me leaue to come vnto my loue?
How slowly do the houres theyr numbers spend?
How slowly does sad Time his feathers moue?
Hast thee O fayrest Planet to thy home
Within the Westerne fome:
Thy tyred steedes long since haue need of rest.
Long though it be, at last I see it gloome,
And the bright euening star with golden creast
Appeare out of the East.
Fayre childe of beauty, glorious lampe of loue
That all the host of heauen in rankes doost lead,
And guydest louers through the nightes dread,
How chearefully thou lookest from aboue,
And seemst to laugh atweene thy twinkling light
As ioying in the sight
Of these glad many which for ioy doe sing,
That all the woods them answer and their echo ring.

Now ceasse ye damsels your delights forepast;
Enough is it, that all the day was youres:
Now day is doen, and night is nighing fast:
Now bring the Bryde into the brydall boures.
Now night is come, now soone her disaray,
And in her bed her lay;
Lay her in lillies and in violets,
And silken courteins ouer her display,
And odourd sheetes, and Arras couerlets.
Behold how goodly my faire loue does ly
In proud humility;
Like vnto Maia, when as Ioue her tooke,
In Tempe, lying on the flowry gras,
Twixt sleepe and wake, after she weary was,
With bathing in the Acidalian brooke.
Now it is night, ye damsels may be gon,
And leaue my loue alone,
And leaue likewise your former lay to sing:
The woods no more shal answere, nor your echo ring.

Now welcome night, thou night so long expected,
That long daies labour doest at last defray,
And all my cares, which cruell loue collected,
Hast sumd in one, and cancelled for aye:
Spread thy broad wing ouer my loue and me,
That no man may vs see,
And in thy sable mantle vs enwrap,
From feare of perrill and foule horror free.
Let no false treason seeke vs to entrap,
Nor any dread disquiet once annoy
The safety of our ioy:
But let the night be calme and quietsome,
Without tempestuous storms or sad afray:
Lyke as when Ioue with fayre Alcmena lay,
When he begot the great Tirynthian groome:
Or lyke as when he with thy selfe did lie,
And begot Maiesty.
And let the mayds and yongmen cease to sing:
Ne let the woods them answer, nor theyr eccho ring.

Let no lamenting cryes, nor dolefull teares,
Be heard all night within nor yet without:
Ne let false whispers, breeding hidden feares,
Breake gentle sleepe with misconceiued dout.
Let no deluding dreames, nor dreadful sights
Make sudden sad affrights;

Ne let housefyres, nor lightnings helpelesse harmes,
Ne let the Pouke, nor other euill sprights,
Ne let mischiuous witches with theyr charmes,
Ne let hob Goblins, names whose sence we see not,
Fray vs with things that be not.
Let not the shriech Oule, nor the Storke be heard:
Nor the night Rauen that still deadly yels,
Nor damned ghosts cald vp with mighty spels,
Nor griesly vultures make vs once affeard:
Ne let th'unpleasant Quyre of Frogs still croking
Make vs to wish theyr choking.
Let none of these theyr drery accents sing;
Ne let the woods them answer, nor theyr eccho ring.

But let stil Silence trew night watches keepe,
That sacred peace may in assurance rayne,
And tymely sleep, when it is tyme to sleepe,
May poure his limbs forth on your pleasant playne,
The whiles an hundred little winged loues,
Like diuers fethered doues,
Shall fly and flutter round about your bed,
And in the secret darke, that none reproues,
Their prety stealthes shal worke, and snares shal spread
To filch away sweet snatches of delight,
Conceald through couert night.
Ye sonnes of Venus, play your sports at will,
For greedy pleasure, carelesse of your toyes,
Thinks more vpon her paradise of ioyes,
Then what ye do, albe it good or ill.
All night therefore attend your merry play,
For it will soone be day:
Now none doth hinder you, that say or sing,
Ne will the woods now answer, nor your Eccho ring.

Who is the same, which at my window peepes?
Or whose is that faire face, that shines so bright,
Is it not Cinthia, she that neuer sleepes,
But walkes about high heauen al the night?
O fayrest goddesse, do thou not enuy
My loue with me to spy:
For thou likewise didst loue, though now vnthought,
And for a fleece of woll, which priuily,
The Latmian shephard once vnto thee brought,
His pleasures with thee wrought.
Therefore to vs be fauorable now;

And sith of wemens labours thou hast charge,
And generation goodly dost enlarge,
Encline thy will t'effect our wishfull vow,
And the chast wombe informe with timely seed,
That may our comfort breed:
Till which we cease our hopefull hap to sing,
Ne let the woods vs answere, nor our Eccho ring.

And thou great Iuno, which with awful might
The lawes of wedlock still dost patronize,
And the religion of the faith first plight
With sacred rites hast taught to solemnize:
And eeke for comfort often called art
Of women in their smart,
Eternally bind thou this louely band,
And all thy blessings vnto vs impart.
And thou glad Genius, in whose gentle hand,
The bridale bowre and geniall bed remaine,
Without blemish or staine,
And the sweet pleasures of theyr loues delight
With secret ayde doest succour and supply,
Till they bring forth the fruitfull progeny,
Send vs the timely fruit of this same night.
And thou fayre Hebe, and thou Hymen free,
Grant that it may so be.
Til which we cease your further prayse to sing,
Ne any woods shal answer, nor your Eccho ring.

And ye high heauens, the temple of the gods,
In which a thousand torches flaming bright
Doe burne, that to vs wretched earthly clods,
In dreadful darknesse lend desired light;
And all ye powers which in the same remayne,
More then we men can fayne,
Poure out your blessing on vs plentiously,
And happy influence vpon vs raine,
That we may raise a large posterity,
Which from the earth, which they may long possesse,
With lasting happinesse,
Vp to your haughty pallaces may mount,
And for the guerdon of theyr glorious merit
May heauenly tabernacles there inherit,
Of blessed Saints for to increase the count.
So let vs rest, sweet loue, in hope of this,
And cease till then our tymely ioyes to sing,
The woods no more vs answer, nor our eccho ring.

Song made in lieu of many ornaments,
With which my loue should duly haue bene dect,
Which cutting off through hasty accidents,
Ye would not stay your dew time to expect,
But promist both to recompens,
Be vnto her a goodly ornament,
And for short time an endlesse moniment.

(1595)

The most pure and exalted love-poem that was ever written.

COVENTRY PATMORE
Religio Poetæ (1898)

SIR WALTER RALEIGH

1 5 5 2 ? — 1 6 1 8

DEATH

O eloquent, just, and mighty Death! whom none could advise, **thou hast** perswaded; what none have dared, thou hast done; and whom **all the** world hath flattered, thou only hast cast out of the world and despised: thou hast drawn together all the far stretched greatness, all the **pride,** cruelty, and ambition of man, and covered it all over with these **two** narrow words, *Hic jacet.*

A History of the World (1614)

I sometimes like to make clear to myself what are the great sentences in English that appeal to me most. As to Raleigh's invocation of Death, as the most magnificent, I seldom vary. It may not be a perfect sentence, one touch more to its grandiosity and it might topple over into absurdity. But the most magnificent it still remains.

HAVELOCK ELLIS
Impressions and Comments, Second Series (1921)

IMITATION DU PSEAUME

N'esperons plus, mon ame, aux promesses du monde:
Sa lumiere est un verre, et sa faveur une onde,
Que tousjours quelque vent empesche de calmer;
Quittons ces vanitez, lassons-nous de les suivre:
  C'est Dieu qui nous faict vivre,
  C'est Dieu qu'il faut aimer.

En vain, pour satisfaire à nos lasches envies,
Nous passons pres des rois tout le temps de nos vies,
A souffrir des mespris et ployer les genoux;
Ce qu'ils peuvent n'est rien: ils sont comme nous sommes,
  Veritablement hommes,
  Et meurent comme nous.

Ont-ils rendu l'esprit, ce n'est plus que poussiere
Que cette majesté si pompeuse et si fiere
Dont l'esclat orgueilleux estonne l'univers;
Et dans ces grands tombeaux où leurs ames hautaines
  Font encore les vaines,
  Ils sont mangez des vers.

Là se perdent ces noms de maistres de la terre,
D'arbitres de la paix, de foudres de la guerre:
Comme ils n'ont plus de sceptre, ils n'ont plus de flatteurs,
Et tombent avecque eux d'une cheute commune
  Tous ceux que leur fortune
  Faisoit leurs serviteurs.

IMITATION OF A PSALM

Let us trust no longer, my soul, in the promises of the world; its light is like a glass, and its favor a wave, that some wind always prevents from subsiding. Let us leave these vanities, let us weary of following them; it is God who makes us live, it is God whom we must love. Vainly, to gratify our base desires, we pass all the days of our lives near kings, suffering their contempt, and bending our knee. What they can do is nothing; they are as we are, only men, and die like us. When they die their proud and pompous majesty, whose showy glitter impresses the world, is only dust. And in the great tombs, where their arrogant souls still flaunt vanity, they are eaten by worms. The names of masters of the earth, arbiters of peace, thunderbolts of war, are lost there. As they no longer have the scepter, they no longer have the flatterers; and there fall with them, altogether, those whom fortune compelled to be their servants.

The four stanzas in which he has paraphrased a section of Psalm CXLV are perfect. . . . Stanzas of this type suffice to restore a language, and are worthy of a lyre.

C.-A. SAINTE-BEUVE
Causeries du lundi (1853)

FRANÇOIS DE MALHERBE

1 5 5 5 — 1 6 2 8

ON THE DEATH OF MLLE. DE CONTY

N'égalons point cette petite
Aux déesses que nous récite
L'histoire des siècles passés:
Tout cela n'est qu'une chimère;
Il faut dire, pour dire assez,
Elle est belle comme sa mère.

This little child do not compare
With goddesses however fair
Who lived, we're told, in days of yore;
These are but fancies woven in space.
Say this, and you need say no more:
She has her mother's lovely face.

Translated by J. G. Legge

His short poem on the death in infancy of Mlle de Conty. . . . shows how high within his range was Malherbe's poetic sense, and how the union of grace, finesse, and tact makes a French compliment the most exquisite in the world.

J. G. LEGGE
Chanticleer (1935)

GEORGE PEELE

1 5 5 8 ? — 1 5 9 7 ?

CUPID'S CURSE

INCIPIT OENONE
Faire and fayre and twise so faire,
    As fayre as any may be:

OENONE
The fayrest sheepeherd on our grene,
    A loue for anie Ladie.

PARIS
Faire and faire and twise so fayre,
    As fayre as anie may bee:
Thy loue is fayre for thee alone,
    And for no other Ladie.

OENONE
My loue is faire, my loue is gaie,
    As fresh as bine the flowers in May,
And of my loue my roundylaye,
My merrie merrie merrie roundelaie
Concludes with Cupids curse:
They that do chaunge olde loue for newe,
Pray Gods they chaunge for worse.

AMBO (*Simul.*)
They that do chaunge, &c.

OENONE
Faire and faire, &c,

PARIS
Faire and faire, &c. Thy loue is faire &c.

OENONE
My loue can pype, my loue can sing,
My loue can manie a pretie thing,
And of his louelie prayses ring
My merry merry roundelayes: Amen to Cupids curse:
They that do chaunge, &c.

PARIS
They that do chaunge, &c.

AMBO
Faire and fayre, &c.

The Araygnement of Paris (1584)
Act i, Scene v

TO MY ESTEEMED FRIEND, AND EXCELLENT MUSICIAN, V. N., ESQ.

Dear Sir,

I conjure you, in the name of all the sylvan deities, and of the Muses, whom you honour, and they reciprocally love and honour you,—rescue this old and passionate DITTY—*the very flower of an old* FORGOTTEN PASTORAL, *which had it been in all parts equal, the Faithful Shepherdess of Fletcher had been but a second name in this sort of writing—rescue it from the profane hands of every common composer; and in one of your tranquillest moods, when you have most leisure from those sad thoughts, which sometimes unworthily beset you; yet a mood, in itself not unallied to the better sort of melancholy; laying by for once the lofty organ, with which you shake the Temples; attune, as to the pipe of Paris himself, to some milder and more love-according instrument, this pretty courtship between Paris and his (then-not as yet-forsaken) Œnone. Oblige me, and all more knowing judges of music and of poesy by the adaptation of fit musical numbers, which it only wants to be the rarest love dialogue in our language.*

Your implorer,
C. L.

CHARLES LAMB
Specimens of English Dramatic Poets (1808)

GEORGE CHAPMAN

1 5 5 9 ? — 1 6 3 4

FROM HOMER'S ILIADS

For *Hectors* glorie still he stood; and euer went about,
To make him cast the fleet such fire, as neuer should go out;
Heard *Thetis* foule petition; and wisht, in any wise,
The splendor of the burning ships, might satiate his eyes.
From him yet, the repulse was then, to be on *Troy* conferd,
The honor of it giuen the *Greeks;* which (thinking on) he stird
(With such addition of his spirit) the spirit *Hector* bore,
To burne the fleet; that of it selfe, was hote enough before.
But now he far'd like *Mars* himselfe, so brandishing his lance;
As through the deepe shades of a hill, a raging fire should glance;
Held vp to all eyes by a hill; about his lips, a fome
Stood; as when th' *Ocean* is enrag'd; his eyes were ouercome
With feruour, and resembl'd flames; set off, by his darke browes:
And from his temples, his bright helme, abhorred lightnings throwes.

For *Ioue,* from foorth the sphere of starres, to his state, put his owne;
And all the blaze of both the hosts, confin'd, in him alone.
And all this was, since after this, he had not long to liue;
This lightning flew before his death: which *Pallas* was to giue,
(A small time thence, and now prepar'd) beneath the violence
Of great *Pelides.* In meane time, his present eminence,
Thought all things vnder it: and he, still where he saw the stands
Of greatest strength, and brauest arm'd, there he would proue his hands:
Or no where; offering to breake through. But that past all his powre,
Although his will, were past all theirs; they stood him like a towre
Conioynd so firme: that as a rocke, exceeding high and great;
And standing neare the hoarie sea, beares many a boisterous threate
Of high-voic't winds, and billowes huge, belcht on it by the stormes;
So stood the *Greeks* great *Hectors* charge, nor stird their battellous
    formes.

Ἕκτορι γάρ οἱ θυμὸς ἐβούλετο κῦδος ὀρέξαι,
Πριαμίδῃ, ἵνα νηυσὶ κορωνίσι θεσπιδαὲς πῦρ
ἐμβάλῃ ἀκάματον, Θέτιδος δ' ἐξαίσιον ἀρὴν
πᾶσαν ἐπικρήνειε· τὸ γὰρ μένε μητίετα Ζεύς,
νηὸς καιομένης σέλας ὀφθαλμοῖσιν ἰδέσθαι.
ἐκ γὰρ δὴ τοῦ ἔμελλε παλίωξιν παρὰ νηῶν
θησέμεναι Τρώων, Δαναοῖσι δὲ κῦδος ὀρέξαι.
τὰ φρονέων, νήεσσιν ἔπι γλαφυρῇσιν ἔγειρεν
Ἕκτορα Πριαμίδην, μάλα περ μεμαῶτα καὶ αὐτόν.
μαίνετο δ', ὡς ὅτ' Ἄρης ἐγχέσπαλος, ἢ ὀλοὸν πῦρ
οὔρεσι μαίνηται, βαθέης ἐν τάρφεσιν ὕλης·
ἀφλοισμὸς δὲ περὶ στόμα γίγνετο, τὼ δέ οἱ ὄσσε
λαμπέσθην βλοσυρῇσιν ὑπ' ὀφρύσιν· ἀμφὶ δὲ πήληξ
σμερδαλέον κροτάφοισι τινάσσετο μαρναμένοιο.
[Ἕκτορος· αὐτὸς γάρ οἱ ἀπ' αἰθέρος ἦεν ἀμύντωρ
Ζεύς, ὅς μιν πλεόνεσσι μετ' ἀνδράσι μοῦνον ἐόντα
τίμα καὶ κύδαινε. μινυνθάδιος γὰρ ἔμελλεν
ἔσσεσθ'· ἤδη γάρ οἱ ἐπώρνυε μόρσιμον ἦμαρ
Παλλὰς Ἀθηναίη ὑπὸ Πηλείδαο βίηφιν.]
καί ῥ' ἔθελεν ῥῆξαι στίχας ἀνδρῶν, πειρητίζων,
ᾗ δὴ πλεῖστον ὅμιλον ὅρα καὶ τεύχε' ἄριστα·
ἀλλ' οὐδ' ὣς δύνατο ῥῆξαι, μάλα περ μενεαίνων.
ἴσχον· γὰρ πυργηδὸν ἀρηρότες, ἠΰτε πέτρη
ἠλίβατος, μεγάλη, πολιῆς ἁλὸς ἐγγὺς ἐοῦσα,
ἥτε μένει λιγέων ἀνέμων λαιψηρὰ κέλευθα,
κύματά τε τροφόεντα, τάτε προσερεύγεται αὐτήν·
ὣς Δαναοὶ Τρῶας μένον ἔμπεδον, οὐδ' ἐφέβοντο.

Iliad, xv, 596–622

590

He himself spoke of his Homeric translations (he rendered the whole works, doing also Hesiod, a satire of Juvenal, and some minor fragments, Pseudo-Virgilian, Petrarchian and others) as "the work that he was born to do." His version, with all its faults, outlived the popularity even of Pope, was for more than two centuries the resort of all who, unable to read Greek, wished to know what the Greek was, and, despite the finical scholarship of the present day, is likely to survive all the attempts made with us. I speak with all humility, but as having learnt Homer from Homer himself, and not from any translation, prose or verse. I am perfectly aware of Chapman's outrageous liberties, of his occasional unfaithfulness (for a libertine need not necessarily be unfaithful in translation), and of the condescension to his own fancies and the fancies of his age, which obscures not more perhaps than some condescensions which nearness and contemporary influences prevent some of us from seeing the character of the original. But at the same time, either I have no skill in criticism, and have been reading Greek for thirty years to none effect, or Chapman is far nearer Homer than any modern translator in any modern language.

GEORGE SAINTSBURY
A History of Elizabethan Literature (1887)

GEORGE CHAPMAN

1 5 5 9 ? — 1 6 3 4

INVOCATION TO SPIRIT

I long to know
How my deare mistresse fares; and be informd
What hand she now holds on the troubled bloud
Of her incensed Lord: me thought the Spirit,
(When he had vtterd his perplext presage)
Threw his chang'd countenance headlong into clowdes;
His forehead bent, as it would hide his face;
He knockt his chin against his darkned breast,
And struck a churlish silence through his powrs;
Terror of darknesse: O thou King of flames,
That with thy Musique-footed horse dost strike
The cleere light out of chrystall, on darke earth;
And hurlst instructiue fire about the world:
Wake, wake, the drowsie and enchanted night;
That sleepes with dead eies in this heauy riddle:

591

Or thou great Prince of shades where neuer sunne
Stickes his far-darted beames: whose eies are made,
To shine in darknesse: and see euer best
Where men are blindest: open now the heart
Of thy abashed oracle: that for feare,
Of some ill it includes, would faine lie hid,
And rise thou with it in thy greater light.

Bussy D'Ambois (1613)

*This calling upon Light and Darkness for information, but, above all,
the description of the spirit—"Threw his changed countenance headlong
into clouds"—is tremendous, to the curdling of the blood. I know nothing
in poetry like it.*

CHARLES LAMB
Specimens of English Dramatic Poets (1808)

LOPE DE VEGA

1 5 6 2 — 1 6 3 5

ESTRELLA LEARNS THAT HER LOVER
HAS KILLED HER BROTHER

(Sala en casa de Busto. Estrella y Teodora.)

ESTRELLA

No sé si me vestí bien,
como me vestí de prisa.
Dame, Teodora, ese espejo.

TEODORA

Verte, Señora, en tí misma
puedes, porque no hay cristal
que tantas verdades diga,
ni de hermosura tan grande
haga verdadera cifra.

ESTRELLA

Alterado tengo el rostro
y la color encendida.

TEODORA

Es, Señora, que la sangre
se ha asomado á las mejillas

entre temor y vergüenza,
sólo á celebrar tus dichas.

ESTRELLA

Ya me parece que llega,
el rostro bañado de risa,
mi esposo á darme la mano
entre mil tiernas caricias.
Ya me parece que dice,
mil ternezas y que oídas,
sale el alma por los ojos,
disimulando las niñas.
¡Ay venturoso día!
Esta ha sido, Teodora, estrella mía.

TEODORA

Parece que gente suena.
Cayó el espejo. De envidia,   (*Álzale*)
el cristal, dentro la hoja,
de una luna hizo infinitas.

ESTRELLA

¿Quebróse?

TEODORA

                              Señora, sí.

ESTRELLA

Bien hizo, porque imagina
que aguardo el cristal, Teodora,
en que mis ojos se miran.
Y pues tal espejo aguardo,
quiébrese el espejo, amiga;
que no quiero que con él,
este de espejo me sirva.

(*Clarindo, muy galán.—Dichas.*)

CLARINDO

Ya aquesto suena, Señora,
á gusto y volatería;
que las plumas del sombrero
los casamientos publican.
Á mi dueño dí el papel,
y dióme aquesta sortija
en albricias.

ESTRELLA

                      Pues yo quiero
feriarte aquesas albricias.
Dámela, y toma por ella
este diamante.

CLARINDO
    Partida
está por medio la piedra:
será de melancolía;
que los jacintos padecen
de ese mal, aunque le quitan.
Partida por medio está.

ESTRELLA
No importa que esté partida;
que es bien que las piedras sientan
mis contentos y alegrías.
¡Ay, venturoso día!
Esta, amigos, ha sido estrella mía!

TEODORA
Gran tropel suena en los patios.

CLARINDO
Y ya la escalera arriba
parece que sube gente.

ESTRELLA
¿Qué valor hay que resista
al placer?

*(Los dos Alcaldes mayores, con gente que
trae el cadáver de Busto.—Dichos.)*

ESTRELLA
    Pero. . . . ¿qué es esto?

DON PEDRO
Los desastres y desdichas
se hicieron para los hombres;
que es mar de llanto esta vida.
El Señor Busto Tabera
es muerto.

ESTRELLA
    ¡Suerte enemiga!

DON PEDRO
El consuelo que aquí os queda,
es que está el fiero homicida,
Sancho Ortiz de las Roelas,
preso, y dél se hará justicia
mañana sin falta . . .

ESTRELLA
Dejadme, gente enemiga;
que en vuestras lenguas traéis
de los infiernos las iras.
¡Mi hermano es muerto, y le ha muerto

594

Sancho Ortiz! ¿Hay quien lo diga?
¿Hay quien lo escuche y no muera?
Píedra soy, pues estoy viva.
¡Ay riguroso día!
Esta, amigos, ha sido estrella mía.
Pero si hay piedad humana,
matadme.

DON PEDRO

El dolor la priva,
y con razón.

ESTRELLA

¡Desdichada
ha sido la estrella mía!
¡Mi hermano es muerto, y le ha muerto
Sancho Ortiz! ¡Él quien divida
tres almas de un corazón! . . .
Dejadme que estoy perdida.

DON PEDRO

Ella está desesperada.

FARFÁN

¡Infeliz beldad!

DON PEDRO

Seguidla.

CLARINDO

Señora . . .

ESTRELLA

Déjame, ingrato,
sangre de aquel fratricida.
Y pues acabo con todo,
quiero acabar con la vida.
¡Ay riguroso día!
Esta ha sido, Teodora, estrella mía.

A Room in Busto Tabera's House.
Enter Estrella and Theodora.

ESTRELLA

I know not, Theodora, if this robe
Becomes me, for I dressed in such glad haste.
Give me the glass.

THEODORA

Madam, you are yourself
Beauty's own mirror, nor can any glass
Declare such sweet perfection, nor resume
In its small sphere so many dazzling charms.

ESTRELLA

See how my looks are changed, my cheeks how flushed.

THEODORA

Why, 'tis the blood mounts to your cheeks, and there,
Mocking reserve and maiden modesty,
Betrays your happiness.

ESTRELLA

Methinks he comes,
My well-beloved, his eyes lit with love's joy,
To take my hand with many a soft caress.
And now methinks he whispers in my ear
A thousand tender messages of love,
And from the rapture of my swooning eyes
Calls forth my willing soul. Ah, happy day!
This, Theodora, is my kindly star.

THEODORA

Hark, hear you not the sound of merriment?
Alas! the mirror's fallen. The envious glass
Within its frame has formed of one smooth face
A thousand facets.

ESTRELLA

What? 'Tis broken then?

THEODORA

Ay, madam.

ESTRELLA

'Tis well done; poor glass, it knows
I have a mirror in whose loving eyes
My own shall see themselves reflected. So,
Let your glass break, since I await my own,
Which having, I shall need no other glass.

Enter Clarindo, dressed in his best.

CLARINDO

Madam, here is a wind that blows you fair—
And foul. These feathered furnishings proclaim
Your wedding day. I to my master gave
The letter you gave me, and he in turn
Gave me this ring for a reward.

ESTRELLA

Why then,
I will outbid him. Come, give me the ring,
And take this diamond in exchange.

CLARINDO

The stone
Is cleft in twain. A sign, they say, of sadness.

Your jacinth suffers from the self-same ill
It takes away. The stone is cleft in twain.

ESTRELLA

What matter? It is right that stones should feel
My joy, my sweet content. Ah, happy day!
Dear friends, this is my charitable star.

THEODORA

A noisy throng fills the courtyard below.

CLARINDO

And now it seems that footsteps mount the stair.

ESTRELLA

Who can resist such joy?

*Enter the two Chief Magistrates,
with others carrying the dead body.*

But . . . what is this?

PEDRO

Misfortunes and disasters were ordained
For mortal men. This life is but a sea
Of tears. Busto Tabera's slain.

ESTRELLA

O cruel,
Cruel fate!

PEDRO

Lady, this comfort still
Remains: the bloody murderer, Sancho Ortiz,
Is taken, and tomorrow without fail
Shall pay the penalty.

ESTRELLA

Ah God! Avaunt,
Ye fiends that bear Hell's fury in your tongues,
Away! My brother slain, and by the hand
Of Sancho Ortiz! How can I utter it,
How hear it and still live? I am a stone,
That still I am alive. Unhappy day!
This, friends, is my unfriendly star. But if
One spark of human pity linger yet,
Come, slay me now.

PEDRO

Alas, she's crazed with grief!

ESTRELLA

Unhappy destiny! My brother dead,
And by the hand of Sancho Ortiz! That he
Should sever three souls from one bleeding heart!
Leave me; I am undone.

PEDRO

She is distraught.

FARFÁN

Alas, unhappy woman!

PEDRO, TO CLARINDO

Go with her.

CLARINDO

Lady . . . ?

ESTRELLA

Begone, thou art contaminate
With that false fratricide. All, all is lost,
All but the hope of death. Unhappy day!
This, Theodora, is my cruel star.
          Exeunt

La Estrella de Sevilla
Translated by Henry Thomas

No finer example of a fearful peripeteia exists on any stage.

RUDOLPH SCHEVILL
The Dramatic Art of Lope de Vega (1918)

SAMUEL DANIEL

1 5 6 2 — 1 6 1 9

ULYSSES AND THE SIREN

Come worthy Greeke, *Vlisses* come
Possesse these shores with me:
The windes and Seas are troublesome,
And heere we may be free.
     Here may we sit, and view their toile
That trauaile in the deepe,
And ioy the day in mirth the while,
And spend the night in sleepe.

Certaine Small Poems (1605)

*A promising young poetaster could not do better than lay up that stanza
in his memory, not necessarily as a pattern to set before him, but as a
touchstone to keep at his side. Diction and movement alike, it is perfect.
It is made out of the most ordinary words, yet it is pure from the least*

598

alloy of prose; and however much nearer heaven the art of poetry may have mounted, it has never flown on a surer or a lighter wing.

A. E. HOUSMAN
The Name and Nature of Poetry (1933)

SAMUEL DANIEL

1 5 6 2 — 1 6 1 9

THE WRITER'S TRAGEDY

And therefore since I haue out-liu'd the date
Of former grace, acceptance and delight,
I would my lines late-borne beyond the fate
Of her spent line, had neuer come to light.
So had I not beene tax'd for wishing well,
Nor now mistaken by the censuring Stage,
Nor, in my fame and reputation fell,
Which I esteeme more then what all the age
Or th'earth can giue. But yeeres hath done this wrong,
To make me write too much, and liue too long.

The Tragedie of Philotas (1605)

These words—perhaps the most pathetic ever uttered by an artist upon his work.

SIR ARTHUR QUILLER-COUCH
Adventures in Criticism (1925)

CHRISTOPHER MARLOWE

1 5 6 4 — 1 5 9 3

HELEN OF TROY

FAUSTUS
Was this the face that lancht a thousand shippes?
And burnt the toplesse Towres of *Ilium?*
Sweete *Helen,* make me immortall with a kisse: (*Kisses her.*)
Her lips suckes forth my soule, see where it flies:

599

Come *Helen,* come giue mee my soule againe.
Here wil I dwel, for heauen be in these lips,
And all is drosse that is not *Helena:*   *Enter old man.*
I wil be *Paris,* and for loue of thee,
Insteede of *Troy* shal *Wertenberge* be sackt,
And I wil combate with weake *Menelaus,*
And weare thy colours on my plumed Crest:
Yea I wil wound *Achillis* in the heele,
And then returne to *Helen* for a kisse.
O thou art fairer then the euening aire,
Clad in the beauty of a thousand starres,
Brighter art thou then flaming *Iupiter,*
When he appeard to haplesse *Semele,*
More louely then the monarke of the skie
In wanton *Arethusaes* azurde armes,
And none but thou shalt be my paramour.

The tragicall History of Doctor Faustus (1601)
Scene xiv

O LENTE, LENTE, CURITE NOCTIS EQUI

FAUSTUS

Ah Faustus,
Now hast thou but one bare hower to liue,
And then thou must be damnd perpetually:
Stand stil you euer moouing spheres of heauen,
That time may cease, and midnight neuer come:
Faire Natures eie, rise, rise againe, and make
Perpetuall day, or let this houre be but
A yeere, a moneth, a weeke, a naturall day,
That Faustus may repent, and saue his soule,
O lente, lente curite noctis equi:
The starres mooue stil, time runs, the clocke wil strike,
The diuel wil come, and Faustus must be damnd.
O Ile leape vp to my God: who pulles me downe?
See see where Christs blood streames in the firmament.
One drop would saue my soule, halfe a drop, ah my Christ.
Ah rend not my heart for naming of my Christ,
Yet wil I call on him: oh spare me *Lucifer!*
Where is it now? tis gone: And see where God
Stretcheth out his arme, and bends his irefull browes:
Mountaines and hilles, come, come, and fall on me,
And hide me from the heauy wrath of God.
No, no.

Then wil I headlong runne into the earth:
Earth gape. O no, it wil not harbour me:
You starres that raignd at my natiuitie,
Whose influence hath alotted death and hel,
Now draw vp Faustus like a foggy mist,
Into the intrailes of yon labring cloude,
That when you vomite foorth into the ayre,
My limbes may issue from your smoaky mouthes,
So that my soule may but ascend to heauen:
Ah, halfe the houre is past: *The watch strikes.*
Twil all be past anone:
Oh God,
If thou wilt not haue mercy on my soule,
Yet for Christs sake, whose bloud hath ransomd me,
Impose some end to my incessant paine.
Let Faustus liue in hel a thousand yeeres,
A hundred thousand, and at last be sau'd.
O no end is limited to damned soules,
Why wert thou not a creature wanting soule?
Or, why is this immortall that thou hast?
Ah *Pythagoras metemsucosis,* were that true,
This soule should flie from me, and I be changde
Vnto some brutish beast: al beasts are happy,
For when they die,
Their soules are soone dissolud in elements,
But mine must liue still to be plagde in hel:
Curst be the parents that ingendred me:
No Faustus, curse thy selfe, curse *Lucifer,*
That hath depriude thee of the ioyes of heauen:

              The clocke striketh twelue.

O it strikes, it strikes: now body turne to ayre,
Or *Lucifer* wil beare thee quicke to hel:

              Thunder and lightning.

O soule, be changde into little water drops,
And fal into the *Ocean,* nere be found:
My God, my God, looke not so fierce on me:

              Enter diuels.

Adders, and Serpents, let me breathe a while:
Vgly hell gape not, come not *Lucifer,*
Ile burne my bookes, ah *Mephastophilis.*

              Exeunt with him.

The tragicall History of Doctor Faustus (1601)

Scene xvi

601

TAMBURLAINE

If all the pens that euer poets held,
Had fed the feeling of their maisters thoughts,
And euery sweetnes that inspir'd their harts,
Their minds, and muses on admyred theames:
If all the heauenly Quintessence they still
From their immortall flowers of Poesy,
Wherein as in a myrrour we perceiue
The highest reaches of a humaine wit.
If these had made one Poems period
And all combin'd in Beauties worthinesse,
Yet should ther houer in their restlesse heads,
One thought, one grace, one woonder at the least,
Which into words no vertue can digest:
But how vnseemly is it for my Sex
My discipline of armes and Chiualrie,
My nature and the terrour of my name,
To harbour thoughts effeminate and faint?
Saue onely that in Beauties iust applause,
With whose instinct the soule of man is toucht,
And euery warriour that is rapt with loue,
Of fame, of valour, and of victory
Must needs haue beauty beat on his conceites,
I thus conceiuing and subduing both
That which hath st(o)opt the tempest of the Gods,
Euen from the fiery spangled vaile of heauen,
To feele the louely warmth of shepheards flames,
And martch in cottages of strowed weeds,
Shal giue the world to note for all my byrth,
That Vertue solely is the sum of glorie,
And fashions men with true nobility.

Tamburlaine the Great (1590)
Part i, Act v, Scene ii

Shakespere himself has not surpassed, which is equivalent to saying that no other writer has equalled, the famous and wonderful passages in "Tamburlaine" and "Faustus," which are familiar to every student of English literature as examples of the NE PLUS ULTRA *of the poetic powers, not of the language but of language.*

GEORGE SAINTSBURY
A History of Elizabethan Literature (1887)

CHRISTOPHER MARLOWE

1 5 6 4 — 1 5 9 3

EDWARD'S DEATH

EDWARD

    Whose there, what light is that, wherefore comes thou?

LIGHTBORNE

    To comfort you, and bring you ioyfull newes.

EDWARD

    Small comfort findes poore *Edward* in thy lookes,
    Villaine, I know thou comst to murther me.

LIGHTBORNE

    To murther you my most gratious lorde?
    Farre is it from my hart to do you harme.
    The Queene sent me, to see how you were vsed,
    For she relents at this your miserie.
    And what eyes can refraine from shedding teares,
    To see a king in this most pittious state?

EDWARD

    Weepst thou already? list a while to me,
    And then thy heart, were it as *Gurneys* is,
    Or as *Matreuis*, hewne from the *Caucasus*,
    Yet will it melt, ere I haue done my tale.
    This dungeon where they keepe me, is the sincke,
    Wherein the filthe of all the castell falles.

LIGHTBORNE

    O villaines!

EDWARD

    And there in mire and puddle haue I stood,
    This ten dayes space, and least that I should sleepe,
    One plaies continually vpon a Drum,
    They giue me bread and water being a king,
    So that for want of sleepe and sustenance,
    My mindes distempered, and my bodies numde,
    And whether I haue limmes or no, I know not.
    O would my bloud dropt out from euery vaine,
    As doth this water from my tattered robes:
    Tell *Isabell* the Queene, I lookt not thus,
    When for her sake I ran at tilt in Fraunce,
    And there vnhorste the duke of *Cleremont*.

LIGHTBORNE

    O speake no more my lorde, this breakes my heart.
    Lie on this bed, and rest your selfe a while.

EDWARD

These lookes of thine can harbor nought but death.
I see my tragedie written in thy browes,
Yet stay a while, forbeare thy bloudie hande,
And let me see the stroke before it comes,
That euen then when I shall lose my life,
My minde may be more stedfast on my God.

LIGHTBORNE

What meanes your highnesse to mistrust me thus?

EDWARD

What meanes thou to dissemble with me thus?

LIGHTBORNE

These handes were neuer stainde with innocent bloud,
Nor shall they now be tainted with a kings.

EDWARD

Forgiue my thought, for hauing such a thought
One iewell haue I left, receiue thou this.
Still feare I, and I know not whats the cause,
But euerie iointe shakes as I giue it thee:
O if thou harborst murther in thy hart,
Let this gift change thy minde, and saue thy soule,
Know that I am a king, oh at that name,
I feele a hell of greefe: where is my crowne?
Gone, gone, and doe I remaine aliue?

LIGHTBORNE

Your ouerwatchde my lord, lie downe and rest.

EDWARD

But that greefe keepes me waking, I shoulde sleepe,
For not these ten daies haue these eyes lids closd.
Now as I speake they fall, and yet with feare
Open againe. O wherefore sits thou heare?

LIGHTBORNE

If you mistrust me, ile be gon my lord.

EDWARD

No, no, for if thou meanst to murther me,
Thou wilt returne againe, and therefore stay.

LIGHTBORNE

He sleepes.

EDWARD

O let me not die yet, stay, O stay a while.

LIGHTBORNE

How now my Lorde.

EDWARD

Something still busseth in mine eares,
And tels me, if I sleepe I neuer wake,

604

This feare is that which makes me tremble thus,
And therefore tell me, wherefore art thou come?

LIGHTBORNE

To rid thee of thy life. *Matreuis* come.

EDWARD

I am too weake and feeble to resist,
Assist me sweete God, and receiue my soule.

The Tragedie of Edward the second (1594)

Act v, Scene v

The death-scene of Marlowe's king moves pity and terror beyond any scene ancient or modern with which I am acquainted.

CHARLES LAMB

Specimens of English Dramatic Poets (1808)

WILLIAM SHAKESPEARE

1 5 6 4 — 1 6 1 6

THE GRAND STYLE

Our Reuels now are ended: These our actors,
(As I foretold you) were all Spirits, and
Are melted into Ayre, into thin Ayre,
And like the baselesse fabricke of this vision
The Clowd-capt Towres, the gorgeous Pallaces.
The solemne Temples, the great Globe it selfe,
Yea, all which it inherit, shall dissolue,
And like this insubstantiall Pageant faded
Leaue not a racke behinde: we are such stuffe
As dreames are made on; and our little life
Is rounded with a sleepe.

The Tempest (1623)

Act iv, Scene i

My definition of the Grand Style is certainly wider than Mr. Arnold's, whose own seems to have been framed to insist upon that "high serious-ness" of his which is no doubt a grand thing. Mine would, I think, come nearer to the Longinian "Sublime"—the perfection of expression in every direction and kind, the commonly called great and the commonly called small, the tragic and the comic, the serious, the ironic, and even to some extent the trivial (not in the worst sense, of course). Whenever this perfection of expression acquires such force that it transmutes the

subject and transports the hearer or reader, then and there the Grand
Style exists, for so long, and in such a degree, as the transmutation
of the one and the transportation of the other lasts. It may persist, or
cease, or disappear and reappear, like a fixed or a revolving light, but
there it is IN ESSENTIA or IN POTENTIA. . . . It comes sometimes, as it
were, "promiscuously" in the vulgar sense of that term. It would, for
instance, be exceedingly difficult for the most expert, or the most futile,
ingenuity of the commentator to assign an exact reason for the occur-
rence, where it occurs, of what is perhaps the grandest example of the
Grand Style in all literature—the words of Prospero to Ferdinand, when
the revels are ended. An excuse is wanted to break off the pretty
"vanity of his art"; to get rid of the lovers; and to punish, in defeating
it, the intentionally murderous but practically idle plot of Caliban and
his mates. Anything would do; and the actual pretext is anything or
nothing. But Shakespeare chooses to accompany it with a "criticism of
life"—and of more than life—so all-embracing, couched in expression
of such magnificence, that one knows not where to look for its like as
form and matter combined. An ordinary man, if, PER IMPOSSIBLE, he
could have written it, would have put it at the end; an extraordinary
one might have substituted it for, or added it to, the more definite an-
nouncement of abdication and change which now comes later with "Ye
elves," etc. Shakespeare puts it here.

GEORGE SAINTSBURY
Collected Essays (1923)

WILLIAM SHAKESPEARE

1 5 6 4 — 1 6 1 6

LET ME LIVE

ISABELLA

What saies my brother?

CLAUDIO

Death is a fearefull thing.

ISABELLA

And shamed life, a hatefull.

CLAUDIO

I, but to die, and go we know not where,
To lie in cold obstruction, and to rot,
This sensible warme motion, to become
A kneaded clod; And the delighted spirit
To bath in fierie floods, or to recide
In thrilling Region of thicke-ribbed Ice,

To be imprison'd in the viewlesse windes
And blowne with restlesse violence round about
The pendant world: or to be worse than worst
Of those, that lawlesse and incertaine thought,
Imagine howling, 'tis too horrible.
The weariest, and most loathed worldly life
That Age, Ache, penury, and imprisonment
Can lay on nature, is a Paradise
To what we feare of death.

ISABELLA

Alas, alas.

CLAUDIO

Sweet Sister, let me liue.
What sinne you do, to saue a brothers life,
Nature dispenses with the deede so farre,
That it becomes a vertue.

ISABELLA

Oh you beast,
Oh faithlesse Coward, oh dishonest wretch,
Wilt thou be made a man, out of my vice?
Is't not a kinde of Incest, to take life
From thine owne sisters shame? What should I thinke,
Heauen shield my Mother plaid my Father faire:
For such a warped slip of wildernesse
Nere issu'd from his blood. Take my defiance,
Die, perish: Might but my bending downe
Repreeue thee from thy fate, it should proceede.
Ile pray a thousand praiers for thy death,
No word to saue thee.

CLAUDIO

Nay heare me *Isabell*.

ISABELLA

Oh fie, fie, fie:
Thy sinn's not accidentall, but a Trade;
Mercy to thee would proue it selfe a Bawd,
'Tis best that thou diest quickly.

CLAUDIO

Oh heare me *Isabella*.

Measure for Measure (1623)
Act iii, Scene i

The very perfection of poetic diction.

HERBERT READ
Phases of English Poetry (1929)

WILLIAM SHAKESPEARE

1 5 6 4 — 1 6 1 6

IN SUCH A NIGHT

LORENZO

The moone shines bright. In such a night as this,
When the sweet winde did gently kisse the trees,
And they did make no noyse, in such a night
Troylus me thinkes mounted the Troian walls,
And sigh'd his soule toward the Grecian tents
Where *Cressed* lay that night.

JESSICA

In such a night
Did *Thisbie* fearefully ore-trip the dewe,
And saw the Lyons shadow ere himselfe,
And ranne dismayed away.

LORENZO

In such a night
Stood *Dido* with a Willow in her hand
Vpon the wilde sea bankes, and waft her Loue
To come againe to Carthage.

JESSICA

In such a night
Medea gathered the inchanted hearbs
That did renew old *Eson.*

LORENZO

In such a night
Did *Jessica* steale from the wealthy Jewe,
And with an Vnthrift Loue did runne from Venice,
As farre as Belmont.

JESSICA

In such a night
Did young *Lorenzo* sweare he lou'd her well,
Stealing her soule with many vowes of faith,
And nere a true one.

LORENZO

In such a night
Did pretty *Jessica* (like a little shrow)
Slander her Loue, and he forgaue it her.

JESSICA

I would out-night you did no body come:
But harke, I heare the footing of a man.

The Merchant of Venice (1623)
Act v, Scene i

The Elizabethan was an open-air theatre, and plays were presented in the afternoon by the light of the sun; it was therefore necessary for Shakespeare in writing the Merchant of Venice, Act V. i. to invoke before the eyes of his audience such a picture of the night as would be forever memorable in the literature of the world.

GEORGE GORDON
Airy Nothings or What You Will (1917)

WILLIAM SHAKESPEARE

1 5 6 4 — 1 6 1 6

MOONLIGHT

How sweet the moone-light sleepes vpon this banke.

The Merchant of Venice (1623)
Act v, Scene i

The happiest instance I remember of imaginative metaphor.

JAMES HENRY LEIGH HUNT
Imagination and Fancy (1844)

WILLIAM SHAKESPEARE

1 5 6 4 — 1 6 1 6

THIS ENGLAND

This royall Throne of Kings, this sceptred Isle,
This earth of Maiesty, this seate of Mars,
This other Eden, demy paradise,
This Fortresse built by Nature for her selfe,
Against infection, and the hand of warre:
This happy breed of men, this little world,
This precious stone set in the siluer sea,
Which serues it in the office of a wall,
Or as a Moate defensiue to a house,
Against the enuy of lesse happier Lands,
This blessed plot, this earth, this Realme, this England.

King Richard the Second (1597)
Act ii, Scene i

WILLIAM SHAKESPEARE

1 5 6 4 — 1 6 1 6

GENTLE RICHARD

As in a Theater, the eyes of men
After a well graced Actor leaues the Stage,
Are idely bent on him that enters next,
Thinking his prattle to be tedious:
Euen so, or with much more contempt, mens eyes
Did scowle on gentle *Richard:* no man cried, God saue him:
No ioyfull tongue gaue him his welcome home,
But dust was throwne vpon his Sacred head,
Which with such gentle sorrow he shooke off,
His face still combating with teares and smiles
(The badges of his greefe and patience)
That had not God for some strong purpose steel'd
The hearts of men, they must perforce haue melted,
And Barbarisme it selfe haue pittied him.

King Richard the Second (1597)
Act v, Scene ii

WILLIAM SHAKESPEARE

1 5 6 4 — 1 6 1 6

THE KING'S ARMY

All furnisht, all in Armes:
All plum'd like Estridges that with the wind
Baited like Eagles hauing lately bathd,
Glittering in golden coates like images,

As ful of spirit as the month of May,
And gorgeous as the sunne at Midsummer:
Wanton as youthful goates, wild as young buls,
I saw yong Harry with his Beuer on,
His cushes on his thighs, gallantly armde,
Rise from the ground like feathered Mercury,
And vaulted with such ease into his seat,
As if an Angel dropt down from the clouds,
To turne and wind a fiery Pegasus,
And witch the world with noble horsemanship.

> King Henry the Fourth, Part One (1598)
> Act iv, Scene i

There are also many descriptions in the poets and orators which owe their sublimity to a richness and profusion of images in which the mind is so dazzled as to make it impossible to attend to that exact coherence and agreement of the illusions which we should require on every other occasion. I do not now remember a more striking example of this than the description which is given of the King's army in the play of HENRY THE FOURTH.

> EDMUND BURKE
> On the Sublime and Beautiful (1756)

WILLIAM SHAKESPEARE

1 5 6 4 — 1 6 1 6

THE TAVERN

A Room in the Boar's-head Tavern in EAST-CHEAP.

1 DRAWER

What the diuel hast thou brought there? Apple-Iohns? Thou know'st Sir *Iohn* cannot endure an Apple-Iohn.

2 DRAWER

Mas thou say'st true: the Prince once set a Dish of Apple-Iohns before him, and told him there were fiue more Sir *Iohns*: and, putting off his Hat, said, I will now take my leaue of these six drie, round, old-wither'd Knights. It anger'd him to the heart: but hee hath forgot that.

1 DRAWER

Why then couer, and set them downe: and see if thou canst finde out *Sneakes* Noyse; Mistris *Teare-sheet* would faine heare some Musique.

Dispatch! The roome where they supt is too hot, theile come in straight.

2 DRAWER

Sirrha, heere will be the Prince, and Master *Points,* anon: and they will put on two of our Ierkins, and Aprons, and Sir *Iohn* must not know of it: *Bardolph* hath brought word.

1 DRAWER

By the mas here will be old Vtis: it will be an excellent strategem.

2 DRAWER

Ile see if I can finde out *Sneake.*

Exit.

Enter Hostesse, and Dol.

HOSTESSE

Yfaith sweet-heart, me thinkes now you are in an excellent good temperalitie: your Pulsidge beates as extraordinarily, as heart would desire; and your Colour (I warrant you) is as red as any Rose, in good truth la! but yfaith you haue drunke too much Canaries, and that's a maruellous searching Wine; and it perfumes the blood, ere one can say what's this. How doe you now?

DOL

Better then I was: Hem.

HOSTESSE

Why thats well said: A good heart's worth Gold. Loe, here comes Sir *Iohn.*

Enter Falstaffe.

FALSTAFFE

When Arthur first in Court—   *Sings.*
       (Emptie the Iordan)   *Exit 1 Drawer.*
And was a worthy King:
How now Mistris *Dol*?

HOSTESSE

Sick of a Calme: yea, good faith.

FALSTAFFE

So is all her Sect: and they be once in a Calme, they are sick.

DOᵀ

A pox damne you, you muddie Rascall, is that all the comfort you giue me?

FALSTAFFE

You make fat Rascalls, Mistris *Dol.*

DOL

I make them? Gluttonie and Diseases make them, I make them not.

FALSTAFFE

If the Cooke help to make the Gluttonie, you helpe to make the

Diseases (*Dol*) we catch of you (*Dol*) we catch of you: Grant that, my poore Vertue, grant that.

DOL

Yea ioy, our Chaynes, and our Iewels.

FALSTAFFE

Your Brooches, Pearles, and Owches: For to serue brauely, is to come halting off: you know, to come off the Breach, with his Pike bent brauely, and to Surgerie brauely; to venture vpon the charg'd-Chambers brauely.

DOL

Hang your selfe, you muddie Cunger, hang your selfe.

HOSTESSE

By my troth this is the olde fashion: you two neuer meete, but you fall to some discord: you are both (in good truth) as Rheumatike as two drie Tostes, you cannot one beare with anothers Confirmities. What the good-yere? One must beare, and that must bee you: you are the weaker Vessell; as they say, the emptier Vessell.

DOL

Can a weake emptie Vessell beare such a huge full Hogs-head? There's a whole Marchants Venture of Burdeux-Stuffe in him: you haue not seene a Hulke better stufft in the Hold. Come, Ile be friends with thee *Iacke:* Thou art going to the Warres, and whether I shall euer see thee againe, or no, there is no body cares.

Enter Drawer.

DRAWER

Sir, Ancient *Pistoll* is below, and would speake with you.

DOL

Hang him, swaggering Rascall, let him not come hither: it is the foule-mouth'dst Rogue in England.

HOSTESSE

If hee swagger, let him not come here: no by my faith I must liue among my Neighbors, Ile no Swaggerers: I am in good name, and fame, with the very best: shut the doore, there comes no Swaggerers heere: I haue not liu'd all this while, to haue swaggering now: shut the doore, I pray you.

FALSTAFFE

Do'st thou heare, Hostesse?

HOSTESSE

'Pray you pacifie your selfe (Sir *Iohn*) there comes no Swaggerers heere.

FALSTAFFE

Do'st thou heare? it is mine Ancient.

HOSTESSE

Tilly-fally (Sir *Iohn*) nere tell me, your ancient Swaggerer comes not in my doores. I was before Master *Tisick* the Debuty, tother day: and as hee said to me, twas no longer agoe then Wednesday last: I' good faith, Neighbour *Quickly* (sayes hee;) Master *Dumbe,* our Minister, was by then: Neighbour *Quickly* (sayes hee) receiue those that are Ciuill; for (saide hee) you are in an ill Name: now a saide so, I can tell whereupon: for (sayes hee) you are an honest Woman, and well thought on; therefore take heede what Guests you receiue: Receiue (sayes hee) no swaggering Companions. There comes none heere. You would blesse you to heare what hee said. No, Ile no Swaggerers.

FALSTAFFE

Hee's no Swaggerer (Hostesse:) a tame Cheater, yfaith: you may stroake him as gently, as a Puppie Greyhound: heele not swagger with a Barbarie Henne, if her feathers turne backe in any shew of resistance. Call him vp (Drawer.) *Exit Drawer.*

HOSTESSE

Cheater, call you him? I will barre no honest man my house, nor no Cheater: but I doe not loue swaggering. By my troth, I am the worse when one sayes, swagger: Feele Masters, how I shake: looke you, I warrant you.

DOL

So you doe, Hostesse.

HOSTESSE

Doe I? yea, in very truth doe I, and twere an Aspen Leafe: I cannot abide Swaggerers.

Enter Pistol, and Bardolph and his Boy.

PISTOL

God saue you, Sir *Iohn.*

FALSTAFFE

Welcome Ancient *Pistol.* Here (*Pistol*) I charge you with a Cup of Sacke: doe you discharge vpon mine Hostesse.

PISTOL

I will discharge vpon her (Sir *Iohn*) with two Bullets.

FALSTAFFE

She is Pistoll-proofe (Sir) you shall hardly offend her.

HOSTESSE

Come, Ile drinke no Proofes, nor no Bullets: Ile drinke no more then will doe me good, for no mans pleasure, I.

PISTOL

Then to you (Mistris *Dorothie*) I will charge you.

DOL

Charge me? I scorne you (scuruie Companion) what? you poore, base, rascally, cheating, lacke-Linnen-Mate: away you mouldie Rogue, away; I am meat for your master.

614

PISTOL

I know you, Mistris *Dorothie.*

DOL

Away you Cut-purse Rascall, you filthy Bung, away: By this Wine,
Ile thrust my Knife in your mouldie Chappes, and you play the
sawcie Cuttle with me. Away you Bottle-Ale Rascall, you Basket-hilt
stale Iugler, you. Since when, I pray you, Sir? Gods light, with two
Points on your shoulder? much.

PISTOL

God let me not liue, but I will murther your Ruffe, for this.

FALSTAFFE

No more *Pistol,* I would not haue you go off here, discharge your
selfe of our company, *Pistoll.*

HOSTESSE

No, good Captaine *Pistol:* not heere, sweete Captaine.

DOL

Captaine? thou abhominable damn'd Cheater, art thou not asham'd
to be call'd Captaine? And Captaines were of my minde, they would
trunchion you out, for taking their Names vpon you, before you haue
earn'd them. You a Captaine? you slaue, for what? for tearing a poore
Whores Ruffe in a Bawdy-house? Hee a Captaine? hang him Rogue,
hee liues vpon mouldie stew'd-Pruines, and dry'de Cakes. A Captaine? Gods light these Villaines will make the word as odious as the
word occupy, which was an excellent good worde before it was il
sorted, therefore Captaines had neede looke too't.

BARDOLPH

'Pray thee goe downe, good Ancient.

FALSTAFFE

Hearke thee hither, Mistris *Dol.*

PISTOL

Not I: I tell thee what, Corporall *Bardolph,* I could teare her: Ile be
reueng'd of her.

PAGE

'Pray thee goe downe.

PISTOL

Ile see her damn'd first: to *Pluto's* damn'd Lake, by this hand to the
Infernall Deepe, with *Erebus* and Tortures vile also. Hold Hooke and
Line, say I: Downe: downe Dogges, downe Faters: haue wee not
Hiren here?

HOSTESSE

Good Captaine *Peesel* be quiet, tis very late yfaith: I beseeke you
now, aggrauate your Choler.

PISTOL

These be good Humors indeede. Shall Pack-Horses,
And hollow-pamper'd Iades of Asia,

Which cannot goe but thirtie mile a day,
Compare with *Cæsars,* and with Caniballs,
And Troian Greekes? nay, rather damne them with
King *Cerberus,* and let the Welkin roare:
Shall wee fall foule for Toyes?

HOSTESSE

By my troth Captaine, these are very bitter words.

BARDOLPH

Be gone, good Ancient: this will grow to a Brawle anon.

PISTOL

Die men, like Dogges; giue Crownes like Pinnes: Haue we not
Hiren here?

HOSTESSE

O' my word (Captaine) there's none such here. What the good-yere,
doe you thinke I would denye her? for Gods sake be quiet.

PISTOL

Then feed, and be fat (My faire *Calipolis.*)
Come, giue's some Sack.
Si fortune me tormente, sperato me contento.
Feare wee broad-sides? No, let the Fiend giue fire:
Giue me some Sack: and Sweet-heart lye thou there.

Layes down his sword.

Come wee to full Points here, and are *et cetera's* nothing?

FALSTAFFE

Pistol, I would be quiet.

PISTOL

Sweet Knight, I kisse thy Neaffe: what? wee haue seene the seuen
Starres.

DOL

For Gods sake thrust him downe stayres, I cannot endure such a
Fustian Rascall.

PISTOL

Thrust him downe stayres? know we not *Galloway* Nagges?

FALSTAFFE

Quoit him downe (*Bardolph*) like a shoue-groat shilling: nay, and a
doe nothing but speake nothing, a shall be nothing here.

BARDOLPH

Come, get you downe stayres.

PISTOL

What? shall wee haue Incision? shall wee embrew?

Snatches up his sword.

Then Death rocke me asleepe, abridge my dolefull dayes:
Why then let grieuous, gastly, gaping Wounds,
Vntwin'd the Sisters three: Come *Atropos,* I say.

HOSTESSE

Here's goodly stuffe toward.

FALSTAFFE

Giue me my Rapier, Boy.

DOL

I pray thee *Iack*, I pray thee doe not draw.

FALSTAFFE

Get you downe stayres.

Drawing and driving Pistol out.

HOSTESSE

Here's a goodly tumult: Ile forsweare keeping house, afore Ile be in these tirrits, and frights. So: Murther I warrant now. Alas, alas, put vp your naked Weapons, put vp your naked Weapons.

Exeunt Pistol and Bardolph.

DOL

I pray thee *Iack* be quiet, the Rascall's gone: ah, you whorson little valiant Villaine, you.

HOSTESSE

Are you not hurt i'th'Groyne? me thought a made a shrewd Thrust at your Belly.

Enter Bardolph.

FALSTAFFE

Haue you turn'd him out o' doores?

BARDOLPH

Yea Sir: the Rascall's drunke: you haue hurt him (Sir) i'th shoulder.

FALSTAFFE

A Rascall to braue me.

DOL

Ah, you sweet little Rogue, you: alas, poore Ape, how thou sweat'st? Come, let me wipe thy Face: Come on, you whorson Chops: Ah Rogue, yfaith I loue thee: Thou art as valorous as *Hector* of Troy, worth fiue of *Agamemnon*, and tenne times better then the nine Worthies: ah Villaine.

FALSTAFFE

A rascally Slaue, I will tosse the Rogue in a Blanket.

DOL

Doe, and thou dar'st for thy heart: and thou doo'st, Ile canuas thee betweene a paire of Sheetes.

Enter Musique.

PAGE

The Musique is come, Sir.

FALSTAFFE

Let them play: play Sirs. Sit on my Knee, *Dol*. A Rascall, bragging Slaue: the Rogue fled from me like Quick-siluer.

DOL

Yfaith and thou follow'd'st him like a Church: thou whorson little tydie *Bartholmew* Bore-pigge, when wilt thou leaue fighting a dayes, and foyning a nights, and begin to patch vp thine old Body for Heauen?

Enter the Prince and Poines disguis'd.

FALSTAFFE

Peace (good *Dol*) doe not speake like a Deaths-head: doe not bid me remember mine end.

DOL

Sirrha, what humor's the Prince of?

FALSTAFFE

A good shallow young fellow: a would haue made a good Pantler, a would a chipp'd Bread well.

DOL

They say *Poines* has a good Wit.

FALSTAFFE

Hee a good Wit? hang him Baboone, his Wit's as thicke as Tewksburie Mustard: theres no more conceit in him, then is in a Mallet.

DOL

Why does the Prince loue him so then?

FALSTAFFE

Because their Legges are both of a bignesse: and a playes at Quoits well, and eates Conger and Fennell, and drinkes off Candles ends for Flap-dragons, and rides the wilde-Mare with the Boyes, and iumpes vpon Ioyn'd-stooles, and sweares with a good grace, and weares his Bootes very smooth, like vnto the Signe of the Legge; and breedes no bate with telling of discreete stories: and such other Gamboll Faculties a has, that shew a weake Minde, and an able Body, for the which the Prince admits him; for the Prince himselfe is such another: the weight of a hayre will turne the Scales betweene their *Haber-de-pois*.

PRINCE

Would not this Naue of a Wheele haue his Eares cut off?

POINES

Lets beat him before his Whore.

PRINCE

Looke, where the wither'd Elder hath not his Poll claw'd like a Parrot.

POINES

Is it not strange, that Desire should so many yeeres out-liue performance?

FALSTAFFE

Kisse me *Dol.*

618

PRINCE

Saturne and *Venus* this yeere in Coniunction? What sayes the Almanack to that?

POINES

And looke whether the fierie *Trigon*, his Man, be not lisping to his Masters old Tables, his Note-Booke, his Councell-keeper?

FALSTAFFE

Thou do'st giue me flatt'ring Busses.

DOL

By my troth, I kisse thee with a most constant heart.

FALSTAFFE

I am olde, I am olde.

DOL

I loue thee better, then I loue ere a scuruie young Boy of them all.

FALSTAFFE

What Stuffe wilt haue a Kirtle of? I shall receiue Money a Thursday: shalt haue a Cappe to morrow. A merrie Song, come: it growes late, weele to bed. Thou't forget me, when I am gone.

DOL

By my troth thou't set me a weeping, and thou say'st so: proue that euer I dresse my selfe handsome, till thy returne: well, hearken a'th end.

FALSTAFFE

Some Sack, *Francis.*

PRINCE, POINES

Anon, anon, Sir.

FALSTAFFE

Ha? a Bastard Sonne of the Kings? And art not thou *Poines* his Brother?

PRINCE

Why thou Globe of sinfull Continents, what a Life do'st thou lead?

FALSTAFFE

A better then thou: I am a Gentleman, thou art a Drawer.

PRINCE

Very true, Sir: and I come to draw you out by the Eares.

HOSTESSE

Oh, the Lord preserue thy good Grace: by my troth welcom to London. Now the Lord blesse that sweete Face of thine: O *Iesu,* are you come from Wales?

FALSTAFFE

Thou whorson mad Compound of Maiestie: by this light Flesh, and corrupt Blood, thou art welcome.

DOL

How? you fat Foole, I scorne you.

POINES

My Lord, hee will driue you out of your reuenge, and turne all to a merryment, if you take not the heat.

PRINCE

You whorson Candle-myne you, how vilely did you speake of me euen now, before this honest, vertuous, ciuill Gentlewoman?

HOSTESSE

Gods blessing of your good heart, and so shee is by my troth.

FALSTAFFE

Didst thou heare me?

PRINCE

Yea: and you knew me, as you did when you ranne away by *Gadshill*: you knew I was at your back, and spoke it on purpose, to trie my patience.

FALSTAFFE

No, no, no: not so: I did not thinke, thou wast within hearing.

PRINCE

I shall driue you then to confesse the wilfull abuse, and then I know how to handle you.

FALSTAFFE

No abuse (*Hall*) a mine Honor, no abuse.

PRINCE

Not to disprayse me? and call me Pantler, and Bread-chipper, and I know not what?

FALSTAFFE

No abuse (*Hal.*)

POINES

No abuse?

FALSTAFFE

No abuse (*Ned*) i'th World: honest *Ned* none. I disprays'd him before the Wicked, that the Wicked might not fall in loue with him: In which doing, I haue done the part of a carefull Friend, and a true Subiect, and thy Father is to giue me thankes for it. No abuse (*Hal:*) none (*Ned*) none; no faith Boyes, none.

PRINCE

See now whether pure Feare, and entire Cowardise, doth not make thee wrong this vertuous Gentlewoman, to close with vs? Is shee of the Wicked? Is thine Hostesse heere, of the Wicked? Or is thy Boy of the Wicked? Or honest *Bardolph* (whose Zeale burnes in his Nose) of the Wicked?

POINES

Answere thou dead Elme, answere.

FALSTAFFE

The Fiend hath prickt downe *Bardolph* irrecouerable, and his Face is *Lucifers* Priuy-Kitchin, where hee doth nothing but rost Mault-Wormes: for the Boy, there is a good Angell about him, but the Deuill outbids him too.

PRINCE

For the Women?

FALSTAFFE

For one of them, shees in Hell alreadie, and burnes poore Soules: for the other, I owe her Money; and whether shee bee damn'd for that, I know not.

HOSTESSE

No, I warrant you.

FALSTAFFE

No, I thinke thou art not: I thinke thou art quit for that. Marry, there is another Indictment vpon thee, for suffering flesh to bee eaten in thy house, contrary to the Law, for the which I thinke thou wilt howle.

HOSTESSE

All Victuallers doe so: Whats a Ioynt of Mutton, or two, in a whole Lent?

PRINCE

You, Gentlewoman.

DOL

What sayes your Grace?

FALSTAFFE

His Grace sayes that, which his flesh rebells against.

Peto knockes at doore.

HOSTESSE

Who knocks so lowd at doore? Looke to the doore there, *Francis*.

Enter Peto.

PRINCE

Peto, how now? what newes?

PETO

The King, your Father, is at Westminster,
And there are twentie weake and wearied Postes,
Come from the North: and as I came along,
I met, and ouer-tooke a dozen Captaines,
Bare-headed, sweating, knocking at the Tauernes,
And asking euery one for Sir *Iohn Falstaffe*.

PRINCE

By Heauen (*Poines*) I feele me much to blame,
So idly to prophane the precious time,
When Tempest of Commotion, like the South,
Borne with black Vapour, doth begin to melt,

And drop vpon our bare vnarmed heads.
Giue me my Sword, and Cloake: *Falstaffe*, good night.

Exeunt Prince, Poines, [Peto, and Bardolph.]

FALSTAFFE

Now comes in the sweetest Morsell of the night, and wee must hence, and leaue it vnpickt. More knocking at the doore?

Enter Bardolph.

How now? what's the matter?

BARDOLPH

You must away to Court, Sir, presently,
A dozen Captaines stay at doore for you.

FALSTAFFE [*to the Page*]

Pay the Musitians, Sirrha.

Farewell Hostesse, farewell *Dol*. You see (my good Wenches) how men of Merit are sought after: the vndeseruer may sleepe, when the man of Action is call'd on. Farewell good Wenches: if I be not sent away poste, I will see you againe, ere I goe.

DOL

I cannot speake: if my heart bee not readie to burst— Well (sweete *Iacke*) haue a care of thy selfe.

FALSTAFFE

Farewell, farewell. *Exit [with Bardolph].*

HOSTESSE

Well, fare thee well: I haue knowne thee these twentie nine yeeres, come Pescod-time: but an honester, and truer-hearted man— Well, fare thee well.

BARDOLPH [*within*]

Mistris *Teare-sheet.*

HOSTESSE

What's the matter?

BARDOLPH

Bid Mistris *Teare-sheet* come to my Master.

HOSTESSE

Oh runne *Dol*, runne: runne, good *Dol*, come. (*She comes blubbered.*)
Yea! will you come *Doll*? *Exeunt.*

King Henry the Fourth, Part Two (1600)
Act ii, Scene iv

The finest tavern scene ever written.

JOHN MASEFIELD
Shakespeare (1911)

MORTALITY

SHALLOW

Come-on, come-on, come-on sir: giue mee your Hand, Sir; giue mee your Hand, Sir: an early stirrer, by the Rood. And how doth my good Cousin *Silence*?

SILENCE

Good-morrow, good Cousin *Shallow*.

SHALLOW

And how doth my Cousin, your Bed-fellow? and your fairest Daughter, and mine, my God-daughter *Ellen*?

SILENCE

Alas, a blacke Woosel (Cousin *Shallow*.)

SHALLOW

By yea and no, Sir, I dare say my Cousin *William* is become a good Scholler? hee is at Oxford still, is hee not?

SILENCE

Indeede Sir, to my cost.

SHALLOW

A must then to the Innes a Court shortly: I was once of *Clements* Inne; where (I thinke) they will talke of mad *Shallow* yet.

SILENCE

You were call'd lustie *Shallow* then (Cousin.)

SHALLOW

By the masse I was call'd any thing: and I would haue done any thing indeede too, and roundly too. There was I, and little *Iohn Doit* of Staffordshire, and blacke *George Barnes*, and *Francis Pick-bone*, and *Will Squele* a Cotsole-man, you had not foure such Swindge-bucklers in all the Innes a Court againe: And I may say to you, wee knew where the *Bona-Roba's* were, and had the best of them all at commandement. Then was *Iacke Falstaffe* (now Sir *Iohn*) a Boy, and Page to *Thomas Mowbray*, Duke of Norfolke.

SILENCE

This Sir *Iohn* (Cousin) that comes hither anon about Souldiers?

SHALLOW

The same Sir *Iohn*, the very same: I see him breake *Scoggan's* Head at the Court-Gate, when a was a Crack, not thus high: and the very same day did I fight with one *Sampson Stock-fish*, a Fruiterer, be-hinde Greyes-Inne. *Iesu, Iesu*, the mad dayes that I haue spent! and to see how many of my olde Acquaintance are dead?

SILENCE

Wee shall all follow (Cousin.)

SHALLOW

Certaine: 'tis certaine: very sure, very sure: Death (as the Psalmist saith) is certaine to all, all shall dye. How a good Yoke of Bullocks at Stamford Fayre?

SILENCE

By my troth, I was not there.

SHALLOW

Death is certaine. Is old *Double* of your Towne liuing yet?

SILENCE

Dead, Sir.

SHALLOW

Iesu, Iesu, dead! a drew a good Bow: and dead? a shot a fine shoote. *Iohn* a Gaunt loued him well, and betted much Money on his head. Dead? a would haue clapt ith Clowt at Twelue-score, and carryed you a fore-hand Shaft a foureteene, and foureteene and a halfe, that it would haue done a mans heart good to see. How a score of Ewes now?

SILENCE

Thereafter as they be: a score of good Ewes may be worth tenne pounds.

SHALLOW

And is olde *Double* dead?

King Henry the Fourth, Part Two (1600)
Act iii, Scene ii

A finer sermon on mortality was never preached.

WILLIAM HAZLITT
Lectures on the English Comic Writers (1819)

WILLIAM SHAKESPEARE

1 5 6 4 — 1 6 1 6

THE DEATH OF FALSTAFF

PISTOLL

Bardolph, be blythe: *Nim,* rowse thy vaunting Veines:
Boy, brissle thy Courage vp: for *Falstaffe* hee is dead,
And wee must erne therefore.

Would I were with him, wheresomere hee is, eyther in Heauen, or in Hell.

HOSTESSE

Nay sure, hee's not in Hell: hee's in *Arthurs* Bosome, if euer man went to *Arthurs* Bosome: a made a finer end, and went away an it had beene any Christome Child: a parted eu'n iust betweene Twelue and One, eu'n at the turning o'th'Tyde: for after I saw him fumble with the Sheets, and play with Flowers, and smile vpon his fingers ends, I knew there was but one way: for his Nose was as sharpe as a Pen, and a babled of greene fields. How now Sir *Iohn* (quoth I?) what man? be a good cheare: so a cryed out, God, God, God, three or foure times: now I, to comfort him, bid him a should not thinke of God; I hop'd there was no neede to trouble himselfe with any such thoughts yet: so a bad me lay more Clothes on his feet: I put my hand into the Bed, and felt them, and they were as cold as any stone: then I felt to his knees, and so vpward, and vpward, and all was as cold as any stone.

King Henry the Fifth (1623)
Act ii, Scene iii

It is wonderful. There is nothing remotely like it in all the literature of the world. How should there be? It is Shakespeare's requiem over the darling of his imagination.

JOHN MIDDLETON MURRY
Shakespeare (1936)

WILLIAM SHAKESPEARE

1 5 6 4 — 1 6 1 6

WINTER OF OUR DISCONTENT

Now is the Winter of our Discontent,
Made glorious Summer by this Son of Yorke:
And all the clouds that lowr'd vpon our house
In the deepe bosome of the Ocean buried.
Now are our browes bound with Victorious Wreathes,
Our bruised armes hung vp for Monuments;
Our sterne Alarums chang'd to merry Meetings;
Our dreadfull Marches, to delightfull Measures.
Grim-visag'd Warre, hath smooth'd his wrinkled Front:
And now, in stead of mounting Barbed Steeds,
To fright the Soules of fearfull Aduersaries,

He capers nimbly in a Lady's Chamber,
To the lasciuious pleasing of a Lute.
But I, that am not shap'd for sportiue trickes,
Nor made to court an amorous Looking-glasse:
I, that am Rudely stampt, and want loue's Maiesty,
To strut before a wanton ambling Nymph:
I, that am curtail'd of this faire Proportion,
Cheated of Feature by dissembling Nature,
Deform'd, vn-finish'd, sent before my time
Into this breathing World, scarse halfe made vp,
And that so lamely and vnfashionable,
That dogges barke at me, as I halt by them.
Why I (in this weake piping time of Peace)
Haue no delight to passe away the time,
Vnlesse to see my Shadow in the Sunne,
And descant on mine owne Deformity.

King Richard the Third (1623)
Act i, Scene i

No poet in history opens a play with a more magnificent certainty.

JOHN MASEFIELD
William Shakespeare (1931)

WILLIAM SHAKESPEARE

1 5 6 4 — 1 6 1 6

LOVE'S LIGHT WINGS

With Loue's light wings did I o'er-perch these Walls,
For stony limits cannot hold Loue out.

       ◦   ◦   ◦   ◦

It is my soule that calls vpon my name;
How siluer sweet sound Louers' tongues by night,
Like softest Musicke to attending eares!

Romeo and Juliet (1599)
Act ii, Scene ii

The most exquisite words of love that ever were penned.

GEORG BRANDES
William Shakespeare (1898)

---

1 5 6 4 — 1 6 1 6

THE VISION

Enter Katharine Dowager, sicke, lead betweene Griffith, her
Gentleman Vsher, and Patience her Woman.

GRIFFITH

How do's your Grace?

KATHARINE

     O *Griffith*, sicke to death:
My Legges like loaden Branches bow to'th'Earth,
Willing to leaue their burthen: Reach a Chaire,
So now (me thinkes) I feele a little ease.
Did'st thou not tell me *Griffith*, as thou lead'st mee,
That the great Childe of Honor, Cardinall *Wolsey*
Was dead?

GRIFFITH

    Yes Madam: but I thinke your Grace
Out of the paine you suffer'd, gaue no eare too't.

KATHARINE

Pre'thee good *Griffith*, tell me how he dy'de.
If well, he stept before me happily
For my example.

GRIFFITH

     Well, the voyce goes Madam,
For after the stout Earle Northumberland
Arrested him at Yorke, and brought him forward
As a man sorely tainted, to his Answer,
He fell sicke sodainly, and grew so ill
He could not sit his Mule.

KATHARINE

     Alas poore man.

GRIFFITH

At last, with easie Rodes, he came to Leicester,
Lodg'd in the Abbey; where the reuerend Abbot
With all his Couent, honourably receiu'd him;
To whom he gaue these words. O Father Abbot,
An old man, broken with the stormes of State,
Is come to lay his weary bones among ye:
Giue him a little earth for Charity.
So went to bed; where eagerly his sicknesse
Pursu'd him still, and three nights after this,
About the houre of eight, which he himselfe

627

Foretold should be his last, full of Repentance,
Continuall Meditations, Teares, and Sorrowes,
He gaue his Honors to the world agen,
His blessed part to Heauen, and slept in peace.

KATHARINE

So may he rest, his Faults lye gently on him:
Yet thus farre *Griffith*, giue me leaue to speake him,
And yet with Charity. He was a man
Of an vnbounded stomacke, euer ranking
Himselfe with Princes. One that by suggestion
Ty'de all the Kingdome. Symonie, was faire play,
His owne Opinion was his Law. I'th'presence
He would say vntruths, and be euer double
Both in his words, and meaning. He was neuer
(But where he meant to Ruine) pittifull.
His Promises, were as he then was, Mighty:
But his performance, as he is now, Nothing:
Of his owne body he was ill, and gaue
The Clergy ill example.

GRIFFITH

Noble Madam:
Mens euill manners liue in Brasse, their Vertues
We write in Water. May it please your Highnesse
To heare me speake his good now?

KATHARINE

Yes good *Griffith*,
I were malicious else.

GRIFFITH

This Cardinall,
Though from an humble Stocke, vndoubtedly
Was fashion'd to much Honor from his Cradle.
He was a Scholler, and a ripe, and good one:
Exceeding wise, faire spoken, and perswading:
Lofty, and sowre to them that lou'd him not:
But, to those men that sought him, sweet as Summer.
And though he were vnsatisfied in getting,
(Which was a sinne) yet in bestowing, Madam,
He was most Princely: Euer witnesse for him
Those twinnes of Learning, that he rais'd in you,
Ipswich and Oxford: one of which, fell with him,
Vnwilling to out-liue the good that did it.
The other (though vnfinish'd) yet so Famous,
So excellent in Art, and still so rising,
That Christendome shall euer speake his Vertue.

628

His Ouerthrow, heap'd Happinesse vpon him:
For then, and not till then, he felt himselfe,
And found the Blessednesse of being little.
And to adde greater Honors to his Age
Then man could giue him; he dy'de, fearing God.

KATHARINE

After my death, I wish no other Herald,
No other speaker of my liuing Actions,
To keepe mine Honor, from Corruption,
But such an honest Chronicler as *Griffith*.
Whom I most hated Liuing, thou hast made mee
With thy Religious Truth, and Modestie,
(Now in his Ashes) Honor: Peace be with him.
Patience, be neere me still, and set me lower.
I haue not long to trouble thee. Good *Griffith*,
Cause the Musitians play me that sad note
I nam'd my Knell; whil'st I sit meditating
On that Cœlestiall Harmony I go too.

Sad and solemne Musicke.

GRIFFITH

She is asleep: Good wench, let's sit down quiet,
For feare we wake her. Softly, gentle *Patience*.

The Uision.

*Enter solemnely tripping one after another, sixe Personages,
clad in white Robes, wearing on their heades Garlands of
Bayes, and golden Vizards on their faces, Branches of
Bayes or Palme in their hands. They first Conge vnto her,
then Dance: and at certaine Changes, the first two hold a
spare Garland ouer her Head, at which the other foure
make reuerend Curtsies. Then the two that held the Garland, deliuer the same to the other next two, who obserue the
same order in their Changes, and holding the Garland ouer
her head. Which done, they deliuer the same Garland to
the last two: who likewise obserue the same Order. At which
(as it were by inspiration) she makes (in her sleepe) signes
of reioycing, and holdeth vp her hands to heauen. And so,
in their Dancing vanish, carrying the Garland with them.
The Musicke continues.*

KATHARINE

Spirits of peace, where are ye? Are ye all gone?
And leaue me heere in wretchednesse, behind ye?

GRIFFITH

Madam, we are heere.

629

KATHARINE

It is not you I call for,
Saw ye none enter since I slept?

GRIFFITH

None Madam.

KATHARINE

No? Saw you not euen now a blessed Troope
Inuite me to a Banquet, whose bright faces
Cast thousand beames vpon me, like the Sun?
They promis'd me eternall Happinesse,
And brought me Garlands (*Griffith*) which I feele
I am not worthy yet to weare: I shall assuredly.

GRIFFITH

I am most ioyfull Madam, such good dreames
Possesse your Fancy.

KATHARINE

Bid the Musicke leaue,
They are harsh and heauy to me.

Musicke ceases.

PATIENCE

Do you note
How much her Grace is alter'd on the sodaine?
How long her face is drawne? How pale she lookes,
And of an earthy cold? Marke her eyes?

GRIFFITH

She is going Wench. Pray, pray.

PATIENCE

Heauen comfort her.

Enter a Messenger.

MESSENGER

And't like your Grace—

KATHARINE

You are a sawcy Fellow,
Deserue we no more Reuerence?

GRIFFITH

You are too blame,
Knowing she will not loose her wonted Greatnesse
To vse so rude behauiour. Go too, kneele.

MESSENGER

I humbly do entreat your Highnesse pardon,
My hast made me vnmannerly. There is staying
A Gentleman sent from the King, to see you.

KATHARINE

    Admit him entrance *Griffith*. But this Fellow
    Let me ne're see againe.

                                  Exit Messenger.

       Enter Lord Capuchius.

                 If my sight faile not,
  You should be Lord Ambassador from the Emperor,
  My Royall Nephew, and your name *Capuchius*.

CAPUCHIUS

  Madam the same. Your Seruant.

KATHARINE

                O my Lord,
  The Times and Titles now are alter'd strangely
  With me, since first you knew me. But I pray you,
  What is your pleasure with me?

CAPUCHIUS

              Noble Lady,
  First mine owne seruice to your Grace, the next
  The Kings request, that I would visit you,
  Who greeues much for your weaknesse, and by me
  Sends you his Princely Commendations,
  And heartily entreats you take good comfort.

KATHARINE

  O my good Lord, that comfort comes too late,
  'Tis like a Pardon after Execution;
  That gentle Physicke giuen in time, had cur'd me:
  But now I am past all Comforts heere, but Prayers.
  How does his Highnesse?

CAPUCHIUS

           Madam, in good health.

KATHARINE

  So may he euer do, and euer flourish,
  When I shall dwell with Wormes, and my poore name
  Banish'd the Kingdome. *Patience*, is that Letter
  I caus'd you write, yet sent away?

PATIENCE

              No Madam.

KATHARINE

  Sir, I most humbly pray you to deliuer
  This to my Lord the King.

CAPUCHIUS

          Most willing Madam.

KATHARINE

In which I haue commended to his goodnesse
The Modell of our chaste loues: his yong daughter,
The dewes of Heauen fall thicke in Blessings on her,
Beseeching him to giue her vertuous breeding.
She is yong, and of a Noble modest Nature,
I hope she will deserue well; and a little
To loue her for her Mothers sake, that lou'd him,
Heauen knowes how deerely. My next poore Petition,
Is, that his Noble Grace would haue some pittie
Vpon my wretched women, that so long
Haue follow'd both my Fortunes, faithfully,
Of which there is not one, I dare auow
(And now I should not lye) but will deserue
For Vertue, and true Beautie of the Soule,
For honestie, and decent Carriage
A right good Husband (let him be a Noble)
And sure those men are happy that shall haue'em.
The last is for my men, they are the poorest,
(But pouerty could neuer draw'em from me)
That they may haue their wages, duly paid'em,
And something ouer to remember me by.
If Heauen had pleas'd to haue giuen me longer life
And able meanes, we had not parted thus.
These are the whole Contents, and good my Lord,
By that you loue the deerest in this world,
As you wish Christian peace to soules departed,
Stand these poore peoples Friend, and vrge the King
To do me this last right.

CAPUCHIUS

By Heauen I will,
Or let me loose the fashion of a man.

KATHARINE

I thanke you honest Lord. Remember me
In all humilitie vnto his Highnesse:
Say his long trouble now is passing
Out of this world. Tell him in death I blest him
(For so I will) mine eyes grow dimme. Farewell
My Lord. *Griffith* farewell. Nay *Patience*,
You must not leaue me yet. I must to bed,
Call in more women. When I am dead, good Wench,
Let me be vs'd with Honor; strew me ouer
With Maiden Flowers, that all the world may know
I was a chaste Wife, to my Graue: Embalme me,

632

Then lay me forth (Although vnqueen'd) yet like
A queene, and Daughter to a King enterre me.
I can no more.   *Exeunt leading Katharine.*

King Henry the Eighth (1623)
Act iv, Scene ii

This scene is, above any other part of SHAKESPEARE'S *tragedies, and
perhaps above any scene of any other poet, tender and pathetick, without gods, or furies, or poisons, or precipices, without the help of roman-
tick circumstances, without improbable sallies of poetical lamentation,
and without any throes of tumultuous misery.*

SAMUEL JOHNSON
The Plays of William Shakespeare (1765)

WILLIAM SHAKESPEARE

1 5 6 4 — 1 6 1 6

GOOD DEEDS PAST

Time hath (my Lord) a wallet at his backe,
Wherein he puts almes for obliuion:
A great siz'd monster of ingratitudes:
Those scraps are good deedes past, which are deuour'd
As fast as they are made, forgot as soone
As done: perseuerance, deere my Lord,
Keepes honour bright, to haue done, is to hang
Quite out of fashion, like a rustie mail,
In monumentall mockrie: take the instant way,
For honour trauels in a straight so narrow,
Where one but goes a breast, keepe then the path:
For emulation hath a thousand Sonnes,
That one by one pursue; if you giue way,
Or hedge aside from the direct forth right,
Like to an entred Tyde they all rush by,
And leaue you hindmost:
Or like a gallant Horse falne in first ranke,
Lye there for pauement to the abiect rear,
Ore-run and trampled on.

Troilus and Cressida (1609)
Act iii, Scene iii

When Shakespeare's petulant Achilles asks, "What, are my deeds forgot?"—his Ulysses has an answer for him which is one of the greatest things in the world. Yet it could all be reduced to the merest commonplaces of proverbial wisdom. But this worldly lore has come to new and individual life in Shakespeare's mind; it is being experienced there like a keenly appreciated event. It is something vividly happening, and all the powers of imagination come trooping together to join in. Common sense, without ceasing to be thought, turns also to a pomp of things seen and felt; and the language of the poet gives us a rich and instantaneous harmony of imaginative experience which is thought, sensation, and feeling all at once.

LASCELLES ABERCROMBIE
The Theory of Poetry (1926)

WILLIAM SHAKESPEARE

1 5 6 4 — 1 6 1 6

NIGHT

MACBETH

Is this a Dagger, which I see before me,
The Handle toward my Hand? Come, let me clutch thee:
I haue thee not, and yet I see thee still.
Art thou not fatall Vision, sensible
To feeling, as to sight? or art thou but
A Dagger of the Minde, a false Creation,
Proceeding from the heat-oppressed Braine?
I see thee yet, in forme as palpable,
As this which now I draw.
Thou marshall'st me the way that I was going,
And such an Instrument I was to vse.
Mine Eyes are made the fooles o'th'other Sences,
Or else worth all the rest: I see thee still;
And on thy Blade, and Dudgeon, Gouts of Blood,
Which was not so before. There's no such thing:
It is the bloody Businesse, which informes
Thus to mine Eyes. Now o're the one halfe World
Nature seemes dead, and wicked Dreames abuse
The Curtain'd sleepe: Witchcraft celebrates
Pale *Heccats* Offrings: and wither'd Murther,
Alarum'd by his Centinell, the Wolfe,

Whose howle's his Watch, thus with his stealthy pace,
With *Tarquins* rauishing strides, towards his designe
Moues like a Ghost. Thou sure and firme-set Earth
Heare not my steps, which way they walke, for feare
Thy very stones prate of my where-about,
And take the present horror from the time,
Which now sutes with it. Whiles I threat, he liues:
Words to the heat of deedes too cold breath giues.

A Bell rings

I goe, and it is done: the Bell inuites me.
Heare it not, *Duncan,* for it is a Knell,
That summons thee to Heauen, or to Hell.

Macbeth (1623)
Act ii, Scene i

  ——Now o'er one half the world
 Nature seems dead,—

*That is, over our hemisphere all action and motion seem to have ceased.
This image, which is perhaps the most striking that poetry can produce,
has been adopted by* DRYDEN *in his* CONQUEST OF *Mexico.*

 All things are hush'd as Nature's self lay dead,
 The mountains seem to nod their drowsy head;
 The little birds in dreams their songs repeat,
 And sleeping flow'rs beneath the night dews sweat.
 Even lust and envy sleep!

*These lines, though so well known, I have transcribed, that the contrast
between them and this passage of* SHAKESPEARE *may be more accurately
observed.*

 *Night is described by two great poets, but one describes a night of
quiet, the other of perturbation. In the night of Dryden, all the disturbers
of the world are laid asleep; in that of* SHAKESPEARE, *nothing but sorcery,
lust and murder, is awake. He that reads* DRYDEN, *finds himself lull'd
with serenity, and disposed to solitude and contemplation. He that
peruses* SHAKESPEARE, *looks round alarmed, and starts to find himself
alone. One is the night of a lover, the other, of a murderer.*

SAMUEL JOHNSON
The Plays of William Shakespeare (1765)

WILLIAM SHAKESPEARE

1 5 6 4 — 1 6 1 6

MULTITUDINOUS SEAS INCARNADINE

MACBETH

I haue done the deed: Didst thou not heare a noyse?

LADY MACBETH

I heard the Owle schreame, and the Crickets cry.
Did not you speake?

MACBETH

When?

LADY MACBETH

Now.

MACBETH

As I descended?

LADY MACBETH

I.

MACBETH

Hearke,
Who lyes i'th'second Chamber?

LADY MACBETH

Donalbaine.

MACBETH

This is a sorry sight.   *Looks on his hand.*

LADY MACBETH

A foolish thought, to say a sorry sight.

MACBETH

There's one did laugh in's sleepe, and one cry'd Murther,
That they did wake each other: I stood, and heard them:
But they did say their Prayers, and addrest them
Againe to sleepe.

LADY MACBETH

There are two lodg'd together.

MACBETH

One cry'd God blesse vs, and Amen the other,
As they had seene me with these Hangmans hands:
Listning their feare, I could not say Amen,
When they did say God blesse vs.

LADY MACBETH

Consider it not so deepely.

MACBETH

But wherefore could not I pronounce Amen?

I had most need of Blessing, and Amen
Stuck in my throat.

LADY MACBETH
                These deeds must not be thought
After these wayes: so, it will make vs mad.

MACBETH
Me thought I heard a voyce cry, Sleep no more:
Macbeth does murther Sleepe, the innocent Sleepe,
Sleepe that knits vp the rauel'd Sleeue of Care,
The death of each dayes Life, sore Labors Bath,
Balme of hurt Mindes, great Natures second Course,
Chiefe nourisher in Life's Feast.

LADY MACBETH
                        What doe you meane?

MACBETH
Still it cry'd, Sleepe no more to all the House:
Glamis hath murther'd Sleepe, and therefore *Cawdor*
Shall sleepe no more: *Macbeth* shall sleepe no more.

LADY MACBETH
Who was it, that thus cry'd? why worthy Thane,
You doe vnbend your Noble strength, to thinke
So braine-sickly of things: Goe get some Water,
And wash this filthie Witnesse from your Hand.
Why did you bring these Daggers from the place?
They must lye there: goe carry them, and smeare
The sleepie Groomes with blood.

MACBETH
                    Ile goe no more:
I am afraid, to thinke what I haue done:
Looke on't againe, I dare not.

LADY MACBETH
                      Infirme of purpose:
Giue me the Daggers: the sleeping, and the dead,
Are but as Pictures: 'tis the Eye of Child-hood,
That feares a painted Deuill. If he doe bleed,
Ile guild the Faces of the Groomes withall,
For it must seeme their Guilt.   *Exit.*
                         Knocke within.

MACBETH
                Whence is that knocking?
How is't with me, when euery noyse appalls me?
What Hands are here? hah: they pluck out mine Eyes.
Will all great *Neptunes* Ocean wash this blood
Cleane from my Hand? no: this my Hand will rather

The multitudinous Seas incarnadine,
Making the Greene one, Red.

Enter Lady Macbeth.

LADY MACBETH

My Hands are of your colour: but I shame
To weare a Heart so white.

Knocke.

                    I heare a knocking
At the South entry: retyre we to our Chamber:
A little Water cleares vs of this deed.
How easie is it then? your Constancie
Hath left you vnattended.

Knocke.

            Hearke, more knocking.
Get on your Night-Gowne, lest occasion call vs,
And shew vs to be Watchers: be not lost
So poorely in your thoughts.

MACBETH

To know my deed,

Knocke.

        'Twere best not know my selfe.
Wake *Duncan* with thy knocking: I would thou could'st.

Exeunt.

Macbeth (1623)
Act ii, Scene ii

*It was my custom to study my characters at night, when all the domestic
cares and business of the day were over. On the night preceding that in
which I was to appear in this part for the first time, I shut myself up, as
usual, when all the family were retired, and commenced my study of
LADY MACBETH. As the character is very short, I thought I should soon
accomplish it. Being then only twenty years of age, I believed, as many
others do believe, that little more was necessary than to get the words
into my head; for the necessity of discrimination, and the development
of character, at that time of my life, had scarcely entered into my imagination. But, to proceed. I went on with tolerable composure, in the silence
of the night, (a night I never can forget,) till I came to the assassination
scene, when the horrors of the scene rose to a degree that made it impossible for me to get farther. I snatched up my candle, and hurried out
of the room, in a paroxysm of terror. My dress was of silk, and the rustling
of it, as I ascended the stairs to go to bed, seemed to my panic-struck
fancy like the movement of a spectre pursuing me. At last I reached my
chamber, where I found my husband fast asleep. I clapt my candlestick*

down upon the table, without the power of putting the candle out; and I threw myself on my bed, without daring to stay even to take off my clothes.

SARAH SIDDONS
Life of Mrs. Siddons, by Thomas Campbell (1834)

WILLIAM SHAKESPEARE

1 5 6 4 — 1 6 1 6

LIFE'S FITFUL FEVER

After Lifes fitfull Feuer, he sleepes well.
Macbeth (1623)
Act iii, Scene ii

THEOCRITUS

THIRD CENTURY B.C.

NOT FOR ME

μή μοι γᾶν Πέλοπος, μή μοι Κροίσεια τάλαντα

O, not for me the land of Pelops' pride;
The golden hoard of Croesus not for me.
Idylls, viii, 53
Translated by Henry Harmon Chamberlin

LUCRETIUS

96? — 55 B.C.

LORD OF LIGHTNING

Altitonans Volturnus et Auster fulmine pollens.

Volturnus thundering on high and Auster lord of lightning.
De Natura Rerum, v, 745
Translated by W. H. D. Rouse

I have heard good critics say that the most musical verse in English poetry is

> After life's fitful fever he sleeps well.

Evidently they are counting as elements in the music not merely the sounds but the associations of the various words, and probably also the contrast of rhythm between this line and the other blank verse lines round about it. In that sense one may value the music of Shakespeare's line more highly than that of

> Μή μοι γᾶν Πέλοπος, μή μοι χρυσειὰ τάλαντα,

or

> Altitonans Volturnus et Auster fulmine pollens.

I only suggest that the classical verses are, first, more sonorous, and, secondly, far nearer to dancing and music and more remote from the rhythm of common speech.

GILBERT MURRAY
The Classical Tradition in Poetry (1927)

WILLIAM SHAKESPEARE

1 5 6 4 — 1 6 1 6

FRAILTY, THY NAME IS WOMAN

HAMLET

Oh that this too too solid Flesh, would melt,
Thaw, and resolue it selfe into a Dew:
Or that the Euerlasting had not fixt
His Cannon 'gainst Selfe-slaughter. O God, O God!
How weary, stale, flat, and vnprofitable
Seeme to me all the vses of this world!
Fie on't! Ah fie, 'tis an vnweeded Garden
That growes to Seed: Things rank, and grosse in Nature
Possesse it meerely. That it should come to this:
But two months dead: Nay, not so much; not two,
So excellent a King, that was to this
Hiperion to a Satyre: so louing to my Mother,
That he might not beteeme the windes of heauen
Visit her face too roughly. Heauen and Earth!
Must I remember? why she would hang on him,

As if encrease of Appetite had growne
By what it fed on; and yet within a month,—
Let me not thinke on't: Frailty, thy name is woman.
A little Month, or ere those shooes were old,
With which she followed my poore Fathers body
Like *Niobe,* all teares, why she, euen she
(O God! a beast that wants discourse of Reason
Would haue mourn'd longer) married with my Vnkle,
My Fathers Brother: but no more like my Father,
Than I to *Hercules.* Within a Moneth?
Ere yet the salt of most vnrighteous Teares
Had left the flushing in her gauled eyes,
She married. O most wicked speed, to post
With such dexterity to Incestuous sheets:
It is not, nor it cannot come to good.
But breake my heart, for I must hold my tongue.

Hamlet (1604)
Act i, Scene ii

WHAT I AM, I CANNOT AVOIDE

FORD

Hum: ha? Is this a vision? Is this a dreame? doe I sleepe? Master
Ford awake, awake Master *Ford:* ther's a hole made in your best
coate (Master *Ford:*) this 'tis to be married; this 'tis to haue Lynnen,
and Buck-baskets: Well, I will proclaime my selfe what I am: I will
now take the Leacher: hee is at my house: hee cannot scape me: 'tis
impossible hee should: hee cannot creepe into a halfe-penny purse,
nor into a Pepper-Boxe: But least the Diuell that guides him, should
aide him, I will search impossible places: though what I am, I cannot
auoide; yet to be what I would not, shall not make me tame: If I
haue hornes, to make one mad, let the prouerbe goe with me, Ile be
horne-mad.

The Merry Wives of Windsor (1623)
Act iii, Scene v

*Shakespeare's soliloquies may justly be established as a model; for it is
not easy to conceive any model more perfect.*

HENRY HOME OF KAMES
Elements of Criticism (1762)

WILLIAM SHAKESPEARE

1 5 6 4 — 1 6 1 6

TO BE OR NOT TO BE

HAMLET

To be, or not to be, that is the Question:
Whether 'tis Nobler in the minde to suffer
The Slings and Arrowes of outragious Fortune,
Or to take Armes against a Sea of troubles,
And by opposing end them: to dye, to sleepe:
No more; and by a sleepe, to say we end
The Heart-ake, and the thousand Naturall shockes
That Flesh is heyre to. 'Tis a consummation
Deuoutly to be wish'd. To dye, to sleepe,
To sleepe, perchance to Dreame; I, there's the rub,
For in that sleepe of death, what dreames may come,
When we haue shuffled off this mortall coile,
Must giue vs pawse. There's the respect
That makes Calamity of so long life:
For who would beare the Whips and Scornes of time,
Th' Oppressor's wrong, the proude man's Contumely,
The pangs of despiz'd Loue, the Lawes delay,
The insolence of Office, and the Spurnes
That patient merit of the vnworthy takes,
When he himselfe might his *Quietus* make
With a bare Bodkin? Who would these Fardles beare
To grunt and sweat vnder a weary life,
But that the dread of something after death,
The vndiscouer'd Countrey, from whose Borne
No Traueller returnes, Puzels the will,
And makes vs rather beare those illes we haue,
Than flye to others that we know not of.
Thus Conscience does make Cowards of vs all,
And thus the Natiue hew of Resolution
Is sicklied o're, with the pale cast of Thought,
And enterprizes of great pith and moment,
With this regard their Currants turne awry,
And loose the name of Action.

Hamlet (1604)
Act iii, Scene i

The supreme soliloquy.

ALGERNON CHARLES SWINBURNE
A Study of Shakespeare (1880)

WILLIAM SHAKESPEARE

1 5 6 4 — 1 6 1 6

O FOOLE, I SHALL GO MAD

Enter Cornewall, Regan, Gloster, Seruants

LEAR

Good morrow to you both.

CORNEWALL

Haile to your Grace.

Kent here set at liberty.

REGAN

I am glad to see your Highnesse.

LEAR

Regan, I thinke you are. I know what reason
I haue to thinke so, if thou should'st not be glad,
I would diuorce me from thy Mothers Tombe,
Sepulchring an Adultresse. O are you free?

To Kent.

Some other time for that. Beloued *Regan,*
Thy Sisters naught: oh *Regan,* she hath tied
Sharpe tooth'd vnkindnesse, like a vulture, heere,

[Lays his hand on his heart.]

I can scarce speake to thee, thou'lt not beleeue
With how deprau'd a quality. Oh *Regan.*

REGAN

I pray you Sir, take patience, I haue hope
You lesse know how to value her desert,
Then she to scant her dutie.

LEAR

Say? How is that?

REGAN

I cannot thinke my Sister in the least
Would faile her Obligation. If Sir perchance
She haue restrained the Riots of your Followres,
'Tis on such ground, and to such wholesome end,
As cleeres her from all blame.

LEAR

My curses on her.

REGAN

O Sir, you are old,
Nature in you stands on the very Verge
Of her confine: you should be rul'd, and led
By some discretion, that discernes your state

Better then you your selfe: therefore I pray you,
That to our Sister, you do make returne,
Say you haue wrong'd her sir.

LEAR

Aske her forgiuenesse?
Do you but marke how this becomes the house?
Deere daughter, I confesse that I am old;
Age is vnnecessary: on my knees I begge,
That you'l vouchsafe me Rayment, Bed and Food.

REGAN

Good Sir, no more: these are vnsightly trickes:
Returne you to my Sister.

LEAR

Neuer *Regan:*
She hath abated me of halfe my Traine;
Look'd blacke vpon me, strooke me with her Tongue
Most Serpent-like, vpon the very Heart.
All the stor'd Vengeances of Heauen, fall
On her ingratefull top: strike her yong bones
You taking Ayres, with Lamenesse.

CORNEWALL

Fye sir, fie.

LEAR

You nimble Lightnings, dart your blinding flames
Into her scornfull eyes: Infect her Beauty,
You Fen-suck'd Fogges, drawne by the powrfull Sunne,
To fall, and blast her pride.

REGAN

O the blest Gods! so will you wish on me,
When the rash moode is on.

LEAR

No *Regan,* thou shalt neuer haue my curse:
Thy tender-hefted Nature shall not giue
Thee o're to harshnesse: Her eyes are fierce, but thine
Do comfort, and not burne. 'Tis not in thee
To grudge my pleasures, to cut off my Traine,
To bandy hasty words, to scant my sizes,
And in conclusion, to oppose the bolt
Against my comming in. Thou better know'st
The Offices of Nature, bond of Childhood,
Effects of Curtesie, dues of Gratitude:
Thy halfe o' th' Kingdome hast thou not forgot,
Wherein I thee endow'd.

REGAN

Good Sir, to th' purpose.

644

LEAR

Who put my man i'th'Stockes? _Tucket within._

CORNEWALL

What Trumpet's that?

REGAN

I know't, my Sisters: this approues her Letter,
That she would soone be heere.

Enter Steward.

Is your Lady come?

LEAR

This is a Slaue, whose easie borrowed pride
Dwels in the fickle grace of her he followes.
Out Varlet, from my sight.

CORNEWALL

What meanes your Grace?

Enter Gonerill.

LEAR

Who stockt my Seruant? _Regan_, I haue good hope
Thou did'st not know on't. Who comes here?
O Heauens!

If you do loue old men, if your sweet sway
Allow Obedience; if your selues are old,
Make it your cause: Send downe, and take my part.

To Gonerill.

Art not asham'd to looke vpon this Beard?
O _Regan_, will you take her by the hand?

GONERILL

Why not by th' hand Sir? How haue I offended?
All's not offence that indiscretion findes,
And dotage termes so.

LEAR

O sides, you are too tough!
Will you yet hold? How came my man i'th' Stockes?

CORNEWALL

I set him there, Sir: but his owne Disorders
Deseru'd much lesse aduancement.

LEAR

You? Did you?

REGAN

I pray you Father being weake, seeme so.
If till the expiration of your Moneth
You will returne and soiourne with my Sister,
Dismissing halfe your traine, come then to me,

645

I am now from home, and out of that prouision
Which shall be needfull for your entertainment.

LEAR

Returne to her? and fifty men dismiss'd?
No, rather I abiure all roofes, and chuse
To wage against the enmity o' th' ayre,
To be a Comrade with the Wolfe, and Owle,
Necessities sharpe pinch. Returne with her?
Why the hot-bloodied *France,* that dowerlesse tooke
Our yongest borne, I could as well be brought
To knee his Throne, and Squire-like pension beg,
To keepe base life a foote; returne with her?
Perswade me rather to be slaue and sumpter
To this detested groome.

GONERILL

At your choice Sir.

LEAR

I prythee Daughter do not make me mad,
I will not trouble thee my Child; farewell:
Wee'l no more meete, no more see one another.
But yet thou art my flesh, my blood, my Daughter,
Or rather a disease that's in my flesh,
Which I must needs call mine. Thou art a Byle,
A plague sore, an imbossed Carbuncle
In my corrupted blood. But Ile not chide thee,
Let shame come when it will, I do not call it,
I do not bid the Thunder-bearer shoote,
Nor tell tales of thee to high-iudging *Ioue,*
Mend when thou can'st, be better at thy leisure,
I can be patient, I can stay with *Regan,*
I and my hundred Knights.

REGAN

Not altogether so,
I look'd not for you yet, nor am prouided
For your fit welcome, giue eare Sir to my Sister,
For those that mingle reason with your passion,
Must be content to thinke you old, and so—
But she knowes what she doe's.

LEAR

Is this well spoken?

REGAN

I dare auouch it, Sir. What, fifty Followers?
Is it not well? What should you need of more?
Yea, or so many? Sith that both charge and danger,
Speake 'gainst so great a number? How in one house

Should many people, vnder two commands
Hold amity? 'Tis hard, almost impossible.

GONERILL

Why might not you my Lord, receiue attendance
From those that she cals Seruants, or from mine?

REGAN

Why not my Lord? If then they chanc'd to slacke ye,
We could comptroll them; if you will come to me,
(For now I spie a danger) I entreate you
To bring but fiue and twentie, to no more
Will I giue place or notice.

LEAR

I gaue you all.

REGAN

                    And in good time you gaue it.

LEAR

Made you my Guardians, my Depositaries,
But kept a reseruation to be followed
With such a number. What, must I come to you
With fiue and twenty? *Regan,* said you so?

REGAN

And speak't againe my Lord, no more with me.

LEAR

Those wicked Creatures yet do look wel fauor'd
When others are more wicked, not being the worst
Stands in some ranke of praise. [*To Gonerill.*] Ile go with thee,
Thy fifty yet doth double fiue and twenty,
And thou art twice her Loue.

GONERILL

                    Heare me my Lord;
What need you fiue and twenty? Ten? or fiue?
To follow in a house, where twice so many
Haue a command to tend you?

REGAN

                    What need one?

LEAR

O reason not the need: our basest Beggers
Are in the poorest thing superfluous,
Allow not Nature, more then Nature needs:
Mans life is cheape as Beastes. Thou art a Lady;
If onely to go warme were gorgeous,
Why Nature needs not what thou gorgeous wear'st,
Which scarcely keepes thee warme. But for true need—
You Heauens, giue me that patience, patience I need,
You see me heere (you Gods) a poore old man,

As full of griefe as age, wretched in both,
If it be you that stirres these Daughters hearts
Against their Father, foole me not so much,
To beare it tamely: touch me with Noble anger,
And let not womens weapons, water drops,
Staine my mans cheekes. No you vnnaturall Hags,
I will haue such reuenges on you both,
That all the world shall—I will do such things,
What they are yet, I know not, but they shalbe
The terrors of the earth! you thinke Ile weepe,
No, Ile not weepe, I haue full cause of weeping,

Storm and Tempest.

But this heart shal break into a hundred thousand flawes
Or ere Ile weepe; O Foole, I shall go mad.

Exeunt.

King Lear (1623)
Act ii, Scene iv

*If there is anything in any author like this yearning of the heart, these
throes of tenderness, this profound expression of all that can be thought
and felt in the most heart-rending situations, we are glad of it; but it
is in some author that we have not read.*

WILLIAM HAZLITT
Characters of Shakespeare's Plays (1817)

WILLIAM SHAKESPEARE

1 5 6 4 — 1 6 1 6

LEAR AND CORDELIA

CORDELIA
How does my Royall Lord? How fares your Maiesty?
LEAR
You do me wrong to take me out o'th'graue,
Thou art a Soule in blisse, but I am bound
Vpon a wheele of fire, that mine owne teares
Do scal'd, like molten Lead.

648

CORDELIA

Sir, do you know me?

LEAR

You are a spirit I know, when did you dye?

CORDELIA

Still, still, farre wide.

DOCTOR

He's scarse awake, let him alone a while.

LEAR

Where haue I bin? Where am I? Faire day light?
I am mightily abus'd; I should eu'n dye with pitty
To see another thus. I know not what to say:
I will not sweare these are my hands: let's see,
I feele this pin pricke, would I were assur'd
Of my condition.

CORDELIA

O looke vpon me Sir,
And hold your hands in benediction o're me,
No Sir, you must not kneele.

LEAR

Pray do not mocke me:
I am a very foolish fond old man,
Fourescore and vpward, not an houre more, nor lesse:
And to deale plainely,
I feare I am not in my perfect mind.
Me thinkes I should know you, and know this man;
Yet I am doubtfull: For I am mainely ignorant
What place this is: and all the skill I haue
Remembers not these garments: nor I know not
Where I did lodge last night. Do not laugh at me,
For (as I am a man) I thinke this Lady
To be my childe *Cordelia*.

CORDELIA

And so I am: I am.

LEAR

Be your teares wet? Yes faith: I pray weepe not,
If you haue poyson for me, I will drinke it:
I know you do not loue me, for your Sisters
Haue (as I do remember) done me wrong.
You haue some cause, they haue not.

CORDELIA

No cause, no cause.

King Lear (1623)
Act iv, Scene vii

649

One is loth to analyse its perfection; but we are talking of mere technique, of the means to the end, not trying to explain in what the great poet is great—and possibly at his greatest when he can achieve such pregnant simplicity. What are the means? The contrast with the Lear that was; the homeliness of the speech, given its one enhancing touch of richness in that 'wheel of fire'; the quiet cadence of the lines, kept from monotony by a short line here and there; the descent from 'You are a spirit, I know' through 'I should e'en die with pity to see another thus' (this from Lear!) to the deliberately commonplace 'Would I were assured of my condition!' Then, for an answer to the gracious beauty of '. . . hold your hands in benediction o'er me', the sudden sight instead of the old king falling humbly on his knees to her, and Cordelia's compassionate horror at the sight; this picture informing her suspense and ours with the silent question: Will he come to his right senses now? His passing from darkness back to light is told in the opposition of two words: I think this LADY *to be my* CHILD *Cordelia. And at that she falls on her knees, too. We may be as sure she is meant to as if Shakespeare had written the direction; for this was the poignant moment in the old play, and no false pride would stop him taking for his own such a thing of beauty— the two there together, contending in humility as they had contended in pride—when he found it. A daring and unmatchable picture, for it is upon the extreme edge of beauty.*

HARLEY GRANVILLE-BARKER
Shakespeare's Dramatic Art (1934)

WILLIAM SHAKESPEARE

1 5 6 4 — 1 6 1 6

MY POORE FOOLE

LEAR

And my poore Foole is hang'd: no, no, no life?
Why should a Dog, a Horse, a Rat haue life,
And thou no breath at all? Thou'lt come no more,
Neuer, neuer, neuer, neuer, neuer.
Pray you vndo this Button. Thanke you Sir,
Do you see this? Looke on her! Looke, her lips!
Looke there, looke there.

King Lear (1623)
Act v, Scene iii

*Lear's five-times repeated 'Never', in which the simplest and most un-
answerable cry of anguish rises note by note till the heart breaks, is
romantic in its naturalism; and to make a verse out of this one word
required the boldness as well as the inspiration which came infallibly to
Shakespeare at the greatest moments. But the familiarity, boldness and
inspiration are surpassed (if that can be) by the next line, which shows
the bodily oppression asking for bodily relief. The imagination that produced Lear's curse or his defiance of the storm may be paralleled in its
kind, but where else are we to seek the imagination that could venture
to follow that cry of 'Never' with such a phrase as 'undo this button',
and yet could leave us on the topmost peaks of poetry?*

A. C. BRADLEY
Shakespearean Tragedy (1904)

WILLIAM SHAKESPEARE

1 5 6 4 — 1 6 1 6

JEALOUSY

Not Poppy, nor Mandragora,
Nor all the drowsie Syrrups of the world
Shall euer medicine thee to that sweete sleepe
Which thou owd'st yesterday.

Othello (1623)
Act iii, Scene iii

The effect is stupendous. The passage assaults and benumbs the faculties.

H. L. MENCKEN
Prejudices Third Series (1922)

WILLIAM SHAKESPEARE

1 5 6 4 — 1 6 1 6

OTHELLO'S DEATH

OTHELLO

Soft you; a word or two before you goe:
I haue done the State some seruice, and they know't:
No more of that. I pray you in your Letters,
When you shall these vnluckie deeds relate,
Speake of me, as I am. Nothing extenuate,
Nor set downe ought in malice. Then must you speake,
Of one that lou'd not wisely, but too well:
Of one, not easily Iealious, but being wrought,
Perplexed in the extreame: Of one, whose hand
(Like the base Indean) threw a Pearle away
Richer than all his Tribe: Of one, whose subdu'd Eyes,
Albeit vn-vsed to the melting moode,
Drops teares as fast as the Arabian Trees
Their medicinall gumme. Set you downe this:
And say besides, that in *Aleppo* once,
Where a malignant, and a Turbond-Turke
Beate a Venetian, and traduc'd the State,
I tooke by th'throat the circumcised Dogge,
And smoate him, thus.

Othello (1623)
Act v, Scene ii

There is a kind of criticism that would see in all these allusions, figures of speech, and wandering reflections, an unnatural rendering of suicide. The man, we might be told, should have muttered a few broken phrases, and killed himself without this pomp of declamation, like the jealous husbands in the daily papers. But the conventions of the tragic stage are more favourable to psychological truth than the conventions of real life. If we may trust the imagination (and in imagination lies, as we have seen, the test of propriety), this is what Othello would have felt. If he had not expressed it, his dumbness would have been due to external hindrances, not to the failure in his mind of just such complex and rhetorical thoughts as the poet has put into his mouth. The height of passion is naturally complex and rhetorical. Love makes us poets, and the approach of death should make us philosophers. When a man knows that his life is over, he can look back upon it from a universal standpoint. He has nothing more to live for, but if the energy of his mind remains unimpaired, he will still wish to live, and, being cut off from his personal ambitions, he will impute to himself a kind of vicarious immortality by identifying himself with what is eternal. He speaks of himself as he is, or rather as he was. He sums himself up, and points to his achievement. This I have been, says he, this I have done.

This comprehensive and impartial view, this synthesis and objectification of experience, constitutes the liberation of the soul and the essence of sublimity.

GEORGE SANTAYANA
The Sense of Beauty (1896)

WILLIAM SHAKESPEARE

1 5 6 4 — 1 6 1 6

THE ETERNAL FEMININE

Enter Cleopatra, Charmian, Iras, and Alexas

CLEOPATRA

Giue me some Musicke: Musicke, moody foode
Of vs that trade in Loue.

OMNES

              The Musicke, hoa.

Enter Mardian the Eunuch

CLEOPATRA

Let it alone, let's to Billiards: come *Charmian*.

CHARMIAN

My arme is sore, best play with *Mardian*.

CLEOPATRA

As well a woman with an Eunuch plaide,
As with a woman. Come you'le play with me Sir?

MARDIAN

As well as I can Madam.

CLEOPATRA

And when good will is shewed, though't come to short
The Actor may pleade pardon. Ile none now,
Giue me mine Angle, weele to'th'Riuer there
My Musicke playing farre off, I will betray
Tawny-finn'd fishes, my bended hooke shall pierce
Their slimy iawes: and as I draw them vp,
Ile thinke them euery one an *Anthony*,
And say, ah ha; y'are caught.

CHARMIAN

'Twas merry when
You wager'd on your Angling, when your diuer
Did hang a salt fish on his hooke which he
With feruencie drew vp.

CLEOPATRA

That time? Oh times:
I laught him out of patience: and that night
I laught him into patience, and next morne,
Ere the ninth houre, I drunke him to his bed:
Then put my Tires and Mantles on him, whilst
I wore his Sword Phillippan. Oh from Italie,

Enter a Messenger

Ramme thou thy fruitefull tidings in mine eares,
That long time haue bin barren.

MESSENGER

Madam, Madam.

CLEOPATRA

Anthony's dead. If thou say so Villaine,
Thou kil'st thy Mistris: but well and free,
If thou so yield him, there is Gold, and heere
My blewest vaines to kisse: a hand that Kings
Haue lipt, and trembled kissing.

MESSENGER

First Madam, he is well.

CLEOPATRA

Why there's more Gold.
But sirrah marke, we vse
To say, the dead are well: bring it to that,
The Gold I giue thee, will I melt and powr
Downe thy ill vttering throate.

MESSENGER

Good Madam heare me.

CLEOPATRA

Well, go too I will:
But there's no goodnesse in thy face; if *Anthony*
Be free and healthfull; why so tart a fauour
To trumpet such good tidings? If not well,
Thou shouldst come like a Furie crown'd with Snakes,
Not like a formall man.

MESSENGER

Wilt please you heare me?

CLEOPATRA

I haue a mind to strike thee ere thou speak'st:

654

Yet if thou say *Anthony* liues, 'tis well,
Or friends with *Cæsar,* or not Captiue to him,
Ile set thee in a shower of Gold, and haile
Rich Pearles vpon thee.

MESSENGER

Madam, he's well.

CLEOPATRA

Well said.

MESSENGER

And Friends with *Cæsar.*

CLEOPATRA

Th'art an honest man.

MESSENGER

Cæsar, and he, are greater Friends than euer.

CLEOPATRA

Make thee a Fortune from me.

MESSENGER

But yet Madam.

CLEOPATRA

I do not like but yet, it does alay
The good precedence, fie vpon but yet,
But yet is as a Iaylor to bring foorth
Some monstrous Malefactor. Prythee Friend,
Powre out the packe of matter to mine eare,
The good and bad together: he's friends with *Cæsar,*
In state of health thou saist, and thou saist, free.

MESSENGER

Free Madam, no: I made no such report,
He's bound vnto *Octauia.*

CLEOPATRA

For what good turne?

MESSENGER

For the best turne i'th'bed.

CLEOPATRA

I am pale *Charmian.*

MESSENGER

Madam, he's married to *Octauia.*

CLEOPATRA

The most infectious Pestilence vpon thee.

Strikes him downe.

MESSENGER

Good Madam patience.

CLEOPATRA

What say you? Hence

Strikes him.

655

Horrible Villaine, or Ile spurne thine eyes
Like balls before me: Ile vnhaire thy head,

She hales him vp and downe.

Thou shalt be whipt with Wyer, and stew'd in brine,
Smarting in lingring pickle.

MESSENGER

Gratious Madam,
I that do bring the newes, made not the match.

CLEOPATRA

Say 'tis not so, a Prouince I will giue thee,
And make thy Fortunes proud: the blow thou had'st
Shall make thy peace, for mouing me to rage,
And I will boot thee with what guift beside
Thy modestie can begge.

MESSENGER

He's married Madam.

CLEOPATRA

Rogue, thou hast liu'd too long.

Draw a knife.

MESSENGER

Nay then Ile runne:
What meane you Madam, I haue made no fault.

Exit.

CHARMIAN

Good Madam keepe your selfe within your selfe,
The man is innocent.

CLEOPATRA

Some Innocents scape not the thunderbolt:
Melt Egypt into Nyle: and kindly creatures
Turne all to Serpents. Call the slaue againe,
Though I am mad, I will not byte him: Call!

CHARMIAN

He is afeared to come.

CLEOPATRA

I will not hurt him.   *Exit Charmian.*
These hands do lacke Nobility, that they strike
A meaner then my selfe: since I my selfe
Haue giuen my selfe the cause. Come hither Sir.

Enter Charmian and the Messenger againe.

Though it be honest, it is neuer good
To bring bad newes: giue to a gratious Message
An host of tongues, but let ill tydings tell
Themselues, when they be felt.

656

MESSENGER

I haue done my duty.

CLEOPATRA

Is he married?
I cannot hate thee worser then I do,
If thou againe say yes.

MESSENGER

He's married Madam.

CLEOPATRA

The Gods confound thee, dost thou hold there still?

MESSENGER

Should I lye Madame?

CLEOPATRA

Oh, I would thou didst:
So halfe my Egypt were submerg'd and made
A Cesterne for scal'd Snakes. Go get thee hence,
Had'st thou *Narcissus* in thy face, to me
Thou would'st appeere most vgly: He is married?

MESSENGER

I craue your Highnesse pardon.

CLEOPATRA

He is married?

MESSENGER

Take no offence, that I would not offend you,
To punnish me for what you make me do
Seemes much vnequall, he's married to *Octauia*.

CLEOPATRA

Oh that his fault should make a knaue of thee,
That art not what th'art sure of. Get thee hence,
The Marchandize which thou hast brought from Rome
Are all too deere for me: lye they vpon thy hand,
And be vndone by 'em.

Exit Messenger.

CHARMIAN

Good your Highnesse patience.

CLEOPATRA

In praysing *Anthony*, I haue disprais'd *Cæsar*.

CHARMIAN

Many times Madam.

CLEOPATRA

I am paid for't now:
Lead me from hence,
I faint, oh *Iras, Charmian:* 'tis no matter.
Go to the Fellow, good *Alexas* bid him
Report the feature of *Octauia:* her yeares,

Her inclination, let him not leaue out
The colour of her haire. Bring me word quickly,

Exit Alexas.

Let him for euer go: let him not! *Charmian!*
Though he be painted one way like a Gorgon,
The other wayes a Mars. [*To Mardian.*] Bid you *Alexas*
Bring me word, how tall she is: pitty me *Charmian*,
But do not speake to me. Lead me to my Chamber.   *Exeunt.*

Antony and Cleopatra (1623)
Act ii, Scene v

*Perhaps the most wonderful revelation that literature gives us of the
essentially feminine; not necessarily of woman in the general, but of that
which radically, in looking at human nature, seems to differentiate the
woman from the man.*

ARTHUR SYMONS
Studies in the Elizabethan Drama (1919)

WILLIAM SHAKESPEARE

1 5 6 4 — 1 6 1 6

ANTONY'S FAREWELL TO CLEOPATRA

I am dying, Egypt, dying.

Antony and Cleopatra (1623)
Act iv, Scene xv

*Those ineffable penultimate words . . . . which attain the absolute per-
fection of pathos in verbal music.*

GEORGE SAINTSBURY
George Saintsbury: The Memorial Volume (1945)

WILLIAM SHAKESPEARE

1 5 6 4 — 1 6 1 6

EASTERNE STARRE

IRAS
> Finish good Lady, the bright day is done,
> And we are for the darke.

    ❖   ❖   ❖   ❖

CHARMIAN
> Oh Easterne Starre.

CLEOPATRA
>   Peace, peace:
> Dost thou not see my Baby at my breast,
> That suckes the Nurse asleepe.

> Antony and Cleopatra (1623)
> Act v, Scene ii

Among the most beautiful things ever written by man.
> JOHN MASEFIELD
> William Shakespeare (1911)

WILLIAM SHAKESPEARE

1 5 6 4 — 1 6 1 6

I AM FIRE, AND AYRE

CLEOPATRA
> Giue me my Robe, put on my Crowne, I haue
> Immortall longings in me. Now no more
> The iuyce of Egypt's Grape shall moyst this lip.
> Yare, yare, good *Iras;* quicke: Me thinkes I heare
> *Anthony* call: I see him rowse himselfe
> To praise by Noble Act. I heare him mock
> The lucke of *Cæsar,* which the Gods giue men
> To excuse their after wrath. Husband, I come:
> Now to that name, my Courage proue my Title.
> I am Fire, and Ayre; my other Elements

I giue to baser life. So, haue you done?
Come then, and take the last warmth of my Lippes.
Farewell kinde *Charmian, Iras,* long farewell
Haue I the Aspicke in my lippes? Dost fall?
If thou, and Nature can so gently part,
The stroke of death is as a Louer's pinch,
Which hurts, and is desir'd. Dost thou lye still?
If thus thou vanishest, thou tell'st the world,
It is not worth leaue-taking.

Antony and Cleopatra (1623)
Act v, Scene ii

*A passage surpassed in poetry, if at all, only by the final speech of Othello.**

A. C. BRADLEY
Oxford Lectures on Poetry (1923)

WILLIAM SHAKESPEARE

1 5 6 4 — 1 6 1 6

FUNERAL SONG

Feare no more the heate o'th'Sun,
Nor the furious Winters rages,
Thou thy worldly task hast don,
Home art gon, and tane thy wages.
　Golden Lads, and Girles all must,
　As Chimney-Sweepers come to dust.

Feare no more the frowne o'th'Great,
Thou art past the Tirants stroake,
Care no more to cloath and eate,
To thee the Reede is as the Oake:
　The Scepter, Learning, Physicke must,
　All follow this and come to dust.

Feare no more the Lightning flash.
Nor th'all-dreaded Thunderstone.
Feare not Slander, Censure rash.
Thou hast finish'd Ioy and mone.

---

* For Othello's speech, see page 652.

All Louers young, all Louers must,
Consigne to thee and come to dust.

No Exorcisor harme thee,
Nor no witch-craft charme thee.
Ghost vnlaid forbeare thee.
Nothing ill come neere thee.
    Quiet consumation haue,
    And renowned be thy graue.

Cymbeline (1623)
Act iv, Scene ii

O MISTRIS MINE

O Mistris mine where are you roming?
O stay and heare, your true loues coming,
That can sing both high and low.
Trip no further prettie sweeting:
Iourneys end in louers meeting,
Euery wise mans sonne doth know.

What is loue? tis not heereafter,
Present mirth, hath present laughter:
What's to come, is still vnsure.
In delay there lies no plentie,
Then come kisse me sweet and twentie:
Youth's a stuffe will not endure.

Twelfth Night (1623)
Act ii, Scene iii

The very summits of lyrical achievement.

A. E. HOUSMAN
The Name and Nature of Poetry (1933)

WILLIAM SHAKESPEARE

1 5 6 4 — 1 6 1 6

CRABBED AGE AND YOUTH

Crabbed age and youth cannot liue together,
Youth is full of pleasance, Age is full of care,
Youth like summer morne, Age like winter weather,
Youth like summer braue, Age like winter bare.

Youth is full of sport, Age's breath is short,
Youth is nimble, Age is lame
Youth is hot and bold, Age is weake and cold,
Youth is wild, and Age is tame.
  Age I doe abhor thee, Youth I doe adore thee,
    O my loue my loue is young:
  Age I doe defie thee. Oh sweet Shepheard hie thee:
    For me thinks thou staies too long.

The Passionate Pilgrim (1599), xii

One of the loveliest lyrics in the language.

SIR ARTHUR QUILLER-COUCH
Adventures in Criticism (1925)

WILLIAM SHAKESPEARE

1 5 6 4 — 1 6 1 6

DEUOURING TIME

Deuouring time blunt thou the Lyons pawes,
And make the earth deuoure her owne sweet brood,
Plucke the keene teeth from the fierce Tygers yawes,
And burne the long liu'd Phænix in her blood,
Make glad and sorry seasons as thou fleet'st,
And do what ere thou wilt swift-footed time,
To the wide world and all her fading sweets:
But I forbid thee one most hainous crime,
O carue not with thy howers my loues faire brow,
Nor draw noe lines there with thine antique pen,
Him in thy course vntainted doe allow,
For beauties patterne to succeding men.
  Yet doe thy worst ould Time dispight thy wrong,
  My loue shall in my verse euer liue young.

Sonnets (1609), xix

*This is, in all probability, the greatest sonnet in the English language,
with its tremendous first lines. . . . The huge, fiery, and majestic double
vowels contained in 'deuouring' and 'Lyons' (those in 'Lyons' rear themselves up and then bring down their splendid and terrible weight)—
these make the line stretch onward and outward until it is overwhelmed,
as it were, by the dust of death, by darkness, with the muffling sounds,*

first of 'blunt', than of the far thicker, more muffling sound of 'pawes'.

This gigantic system of stretching double vowels, long single vowels muffled by the earth, continues through the first three lines:

> And make the earth deuoure her owne sweet brood;
> Plucke the keene teeth from the fierce Tygers yawes,
> And burne the long-liu'd Phœnix in her blood.

The thick P of 'pawes' muffles us with the dust, the dark hollow sound of 'yawes' covers us with the eternal night.

The music is made more vast still by the fact that, in the third line, two long stretching double vowels are placed close together ('keene teeth'), and that in the fourth there are two alliterative B's,—'burne' and 'blood', these giving an added majesty, a gigantic balance.

EDITH SITWELL
A Poet's Notebook (1943)

WILLIAM SHAKESPEARE

1 5 6 4 — 1 6 1 6

HEAUENLY ALCUMY

Guilding pale streames with heauenly alcumy.
Sonnets (1609), xxxiii

When to the Sessions of sweet silent thought.
Sonnets (1609), xxx

The perfection of human utterance.

SIDNEY LEE
Shakespeares Sonnets (1905)

WILLIAM SHAKESPEARE

1 5 6 4 — 1 6 1 6

BEING YOUR SLAUE

Being your slaue what should I doe but tend,
Vpon the houres, and times of your desire?
I haue no precious time at al to spend;
Nor seruices to doe til you require.
Nor dare I chide the world without end houre,
Whilst I (my soueraine) watch the clock for you,
Nor thinke the bitternesse of absence sowre,
When you haue bid your seruant once adieue.
Nor dare I question with my iealious thought,
Where you may be, or your affaires suppose,
But like a sad slaue stay and thinke of nought
Saue where you are, how happy you make those.
　So true a foole is loue, that in your Will,
　(Though you doe any thing) he thinkes no ill.

Sonnets (1609), lvii

Technically perfect and altogether admirable.

JOHN CROWE RANSOM
The World's Body (1938)

WILLIAM SHAKESPEARE

1 5 6 4 — 1 6 1 6

THE SPIGHT OF FORTUNE

Then hate me when thou wilt, if euer, now,
Now while the world is bent my deeds to crosse,
Ioyne with the spight of fortune, make me bow,
And doe not drop in for an after losse:
Ah doe not, when my heart hath scapte this sorrow,
Come in the rereward of a conquerd woe,
Giue not a windy night a rainie morrow,
To linger out a purposd ouer-throw.
If thou wilt leaue me, do not leaue me last,
When other pettie griefes haue done their spight,

664

But in the onset come, so shall I taste
At first the very worst of fortunes might.
And other straines of woe, which now seeme woe,
Compar'd with losse of thee, will not seeme so.

Sonnets (1609), xc

*I doubt if in all recorded speech such faultless perfection may be found,
so sustained through fourteen consecutive lines.*

GEORGE WYNDHAM
The Poems of Shakespeare (1898)

WILLIAM SHAKESPEARE

1 5 6 4 — 1 6 1 6

THE MARRIAGE OF TRUE MINDES

Let me not to the marriage of true mindes
Admit impediments, loue is not loue
Which alters when it alteration findes,
Or bends with the remouer to remoue.
O no, it is an euer fixed marke
That lookes on tempests and is neuer shaken;
It is the star to euery wandring barke,
Whose worths vnknowne, although his higth be taken.
Lou's not Times foole, though rosie lips and cheeks
Within his bending sickles compasse come,
Loue alters not with his breefe houres and weekes,
But beares it out euen to the edge of doome:
If this be error and vpon me proued,
I neuer writ, nor no man euer loued.

Sonnets (1609), cxvi

*It consists of three separate quatrains, each concluded by a full stop,
and a summarizing couplet. The chief pause in sense is after the twelfth
line. Seventy-five per cent of the words are monosyllables; only three
contain more syllables than two; none belongs in any degree to the
vocabulary of 'poetic' diction. There is nothing recondite, exotic, or
'metaphysical' in the thought. There are three run-on lines, one pair of
double endings. There is nothing to remark about the riming except the
happy blending of open and closed vowels, and of liquids, nasals, and
stops; nothing to say about the harmony except to point out how the*

fluttering accents in the quatrains give place in the couplet to the em-
phatic march of ten almost unrelieved iambic feet. In short, the poet has
employed one hundred and ten of the simplest words in the language,
and the two simplest rime-schemes, to produce a poem which has about
it no strangeness whatever except the strangeness of perfection.

TUCKER BROOKE
Shakespeare's Sonnets (1936)

WILLIAM SHAKESPEARE

1 5 6 4 — 1 6 1 6

PAST REASON HUNTED

Th' expence of Spirit in a waste of shame
Is lust in action, and till action, lust
Is periurd, murdrous, blouddy full of blame,
Sauage, extreame, rude, cruell, not to trust,
Inioyd no sooner but dispised straight,
Past reason hunted, and no sooner had
Past reason hated as a swollowed bayt,
On purpose layd to make the taker mad.
Made In pursut and in possession so,
Had, hauing, and in quest, to haue extreame,
A blisse in proofe and proud and very wo,
Before a ioy proposd behind a dreame,
    All this the world well knowes yet none knowes well,
    To shun the heauen that leads men to this hell.

Sonnets (1609), cxxix

The greatest in the world.

THEODORE WATTS-DUNTON
Quoted, William Sharp, The Songs, Poems, and
Sonnets of William Shakespeare (1880)

JEAN OGIER DE GOMBAUL

C. 1570 — 1666

SONNET

La voix qui retentit de l'vn à l'autre Pole,
  La terreur & l'espoir des viuans & des morts,
  Qui du rien sçait tirer les esprits & les corps,
  Et qui fit l'Vniuers, d'vne seule parole.

La voix du Souuerain, qui les cedres desole,
  Cependant que l'espine estale ses tresors;
  Qui contre la cabane espargne ses efforts,
  Et reduit à neant l'orgueil du Capitole.

Ce tonnerre esclatant, cette diuine voix,
  A qui sçavent respondre & les monts, & les bois,
  Et qui fait qu'à leur fin toutes choses se rendent.

Que les Cieux les plus hauts, que les lieux les plus bas,
  Que ceux qui ne sont point, & que les morts entendent,
  Mon ame, elle t'appelle, & tu ne l'entens pas.

The Voice that resounds from pole to pole, the terror and hope of the living and dead, that Voice which can evoke spirits and bodies from nothingness, and that created the Universe, with a single word. The Voice of the Lord, that ravages the cedars, while the thorn flaunts its treasures; that spares the hut and reduces to nothingness the pride of the capital. The resounding thunder, the divine Voice, to which the mountains and the woods respond, and that directs all things to their end. The Voice that is heard by the highest heavens, and the lowest depths, by those that are not, and by those that are dead, beseeches Thee, my soul, and Thou hearest it not.

The best ode in your language is in the form of a sonnet by Gombaud.
WALTER SAVAGE LANDOR
Imaginary Conversations, Abbé Delille and Landor (1824-9)

JOHN DONNE

1 5 7 3 — 1 6 3 1

OF THE PROGRESSE OF THE SOULE

So long,
As till Gods great *Venite* change the song.

The Second Anniversary (1612)

The finest line in English sacred poetry . . . a DIES IRAE *and a* VENITE
itself combined in ten English syllables.

GEORGE SAINTSBURY
Introduction, Poems of Donne (1896)

JOHN DONNE

1 5 7 3 — 1 6 3 1

THE WILL

Before I sigh my last gaspe, let me breath,
Great love, some Legacies; Here I bequeath
Mine eyes to *Argus*, if mine eyes can see,
If they be blinde, then Love, I give them thee;
My tongue to Fame; to'Embassadours mine eares;
      To women or the sea, my teares.
Thou, Love, hast taught mee heretofore
By making mee serve her who'had twenty more,
That I should give to none, but such, as had too much before.

My constancie I to the planets give;
My truth to them, who at the Court doe live;
Mine ingenuity and opennesse,
To Jesuites; to Buffones my pensivenesse;
My silence to'any, who abroad hath beene;
      My mony to a Capuchin.
Thou Love taught'st me, by appointing mee
To love there, where no love receiv'd can be,
Onely to give to such as have an incapacitie.

My faith I give to Roman Catholiques;
All my good works unto the Schismaticks

668

Of Amsterdam: my best civility
And Courtship, to an Universitie;
My modesty I give to souldiers bare,
    My patience let gamesters share.
Thou Love taughtst mee, by making mee
Love her that holds my love disparity,
Onely to give to those that count my gifts indignity.

I give my reputation to those
Which were my friends; Mine industrie to foes;
To Schoolemen I bequeath my doubtfulnesse;
My sicknesse to Physitians, or excesse;
To Nature, all that I in Ryme have writ;
    And to my company my wit.
Thou Love, by making mee adore
Her, who begot this love in mee before,
Taughtst me to make, as though I gave, when I did but restore.

To him for whom the passing bell next tolls,
I give my physick bookes; my writen rowles
Of Morall counsels, I to Bedlam give;
My brazen medals, unto them which live
In want of bread; To them which passe among
    All forrainers, mine English tongue.
Thou, Love, by making mee love one
Who thinkes her friendship a fit portion
For yonger lovers, dost my gifts thus disproportion.

Therefore I'll give no more; But I'll undoe
The world by dying; because love dies too.
Then all your beauties will bee no more worth
Then gold in Mines, where none doth draw it forth;
And all your graces no more use shall have
    Then a Sun dyall in a grave.
Thou Love taughtst mee, by making mee
Love her, who doth neglect both mee and thee,
To'invent, and practise this one way, to'annihilate all three.

(1633)

THE WILL OF JOHN DONNE *is probably the wittiest and the bitterest lyric in our language.*

OSWALD CRAWFURD
Lyrical Verse (1896)

669

JOHN DONNE

1 5 7 3 — 1 6 3 1

GOD'S MERCIES

If some King of the earth have so large an extent of Dominion, in North, and South, as that he hath Winter and Summer together in his Dominions, so large an extent East and West, as that he hath day and night together in his Dominions, much more hath God mercy and judgement together: He brought light out of darknesse, not out of a lesser light; he can bring thy Summer out of Winter, though thou have no Spring; though in the wayes of fortune, or understanding, or conscience, thou have been benighted till now, wintred and frozen, clouded and eclypsed, damped and benummed, smothered and stupefied till now, now God comes to thee, not as in the dawning of the day, not as in the bud of the spring, but as the Sun at noon to illustrate all shadowes, as the sheaves in harvest, to fill all penuries, all occasions invite his mercies, and all times are his seasons.

LXXX Sermons (1640)

And now for Donne; in a passage than which I hardly know anything more exquisitely rhythmed in the whole range of English from Ælfric to Pater. . . . Here there could be no change without disaster, except in the possible substitution of some other word for the thrice-repeated "dominion[s]," which to our ears (though apparently neither to French nor to English ones of the seventeenth century) make a disagreeable jingle without emphasis to excuse it. "Now," as repeated, is in a very different position, and makes one of the appeals of the piece. The Shakespearian magnificence of the diction, such as the throng of kindred but never tautological phrase in "wintered and frozen," etc., and the absolute perfection of rhythmical——never metrical——movement, could not be better wedded. It has, I have said, never been surpassed. I sometimes doubt whether it has ever been equalled.

GEORGE SAINTSBURY
A History of English Prose Rhythm (1912)

JOHN DONNE

1 5 7 3 — 1 6 3 1

ETERNITY

A state but of one Day, because no Night shall over-take, or determine it, but such a Day, as is not of a thousand yeares, which is the longest measure in the Scriptures, but of a thousand millions of millions of gener-ations: *Qui nec præceditur hesterno, nec excluditur crastino,* A day that hath no *pridie,* nor *postridie,* yesterday doth not usher it in, nor to morrow shall not drive it out. *Methusalem,* with all his hundreds of yeares, was but a Mushrome of a nights growth, to this day, And all the foure Monarchies, with all their thousands of yeares, And all the power-full Kings, and all the beautifull Queenes of this world, were but as a bed of flowers, some gathered at six, some at seaven, some at eight, All in one Morning, in respect of this Day. In all the two thousand yeares of Nature, before the Law given by *Moses,* And the two thousand yeares of Law, before the Gospel given by Christ, And the two thousand of Grace, which are running now, (of which last houre we have heard three quarters strike, more than fifteen hundred of this last two thou-sand spent) In all this six thousand, and in all those, which God may be pleased to adde, *In domo patris,* In this House of his Fathers, there was never heard quarter clock to strike, never seen minute glasse to turne.

LXXX Sermons (1640)

A description of the unending day of eternity unsurpassed in our literature.

LOGAN PEARSALL SMITH
Donne's Sermons (1919)

BEN JONSON

1 5 7 3 ? — 1 6 3 7

HERE'S THE RICH PERU

MAMMON, SVRLY

MAMMON
    Come on, sir. Now, you set your foot on shore
    In *nouo orbe;* Here's the rich *Peru:*
    And there within, sir, are the golden mines,

Great SALOMON's *Ophir!* He was sayling to't,
Three yeeres, but we haue reach'd it in ten months.
This is the day, wherein, to all my friends,
I will pronounce the happy word, *be rich.*
This day, you shall be *spectatissimi.*
You shall no more deale with the hollow die,
Or the fraile card. No more be at charge of keeping
The liuery-punke, for the yong heire, that must
Seale, at all houres, in his shirt. No more
If he denie, ha'him beaten to't, as he is
That brings him the commoditie. No more
Shall thirst of satten, or the couetous hunger
Of veluet entrailes, for a rude-spun cloke,
To be displaid at *Madame* AVGVSTA's, make
The sonnes of *sword,* and *hazzard* fall before
The golden calfe, and on their knees, whole nights,
Commit idolatrie with wine, and trumpets:
Or goe a feasting, after drum and ensigne.
No more of this. You shall start vp yong *Vice-royes,*
And haue your punques, and punquettees, my SVRLY.
And vnto thee, I speake it first, *be rich.*
Where is my SVBTLE, there? Within hough?

FACE

(*Within*) Sir. Hee'll come to you, by and by.

MAMMON

                                    That's his fire-drake,
His lungs, his *Zephyrus,* he that puffes his coales,
Till he firke nature vp, in her owne center.
You are not faithfull, sir. This night, I'll change
All, that is mettall, in thy house, to gold.
And, early in the morning, will I send
To all the plumbers, and the pewterers,
And buy their tin, and lead vp: and to *Lothbury,*
For all the copper.

SVRLY

               What, and turne that too?

MAMMON

Yes, and I'll purchase *Deuonshire,* and *Cornwaile,*
And make them perfect *Indies!* You admire now?

SVRLY

No, faith.

MAMMON

But when you see th' effects of the great med'cine!
Of which one part proiected on a hundred
Of *Mercurie,* or *Venus,* or the *Moone,*

Shall turne it to as many of the *Sunne;*
Nay, to a thousand, so *ad infinitum:*
You will beleeue me.

SVRLY

                    Yes, when I see't, I will.
But, if my eyes doe cossen me so (and I
Giuing'hem no occasion) sure, I'll haue
A whore, shall pisse'hem out, next day.

MAMMON

                         Ha! Why?
Doe you thinke, I fable with you? I assure you,
He that has once the *flower of the sunne,*
The perfect *ruby,* which we call *elixir,*
Not onely can doe that, but by it's vertue,
Can confer honour, loue, respect, long life,
Giue safety, valure: yea, and victorie,
To whom he will. In eight, and twentie dayes,
I'll make an old man, of fourescore, a childe.

SVRLY

No doubt, hee's that alreadie.

MAMMON

                    Nay, I meane,
Restore his yeeres, renew him, like an eagle,
To the fifth age; make him get sonnes, and daughters,
Yong giants; as our *Philosophers* haue done
(The antient *Patriarkes* afore the floud)
But taking, once a weeke, on a kniues point,
The quantitie of a graine of mustard, of it:
Become stout MARSES, and beget yong CVPIDS.

SVRLY

The decay'd V*estalls* of *Pickt-hatch* would thanke you,
That keepe the fire a-liue, there.

MAMMON

                         'Tis the secret
Of nature, naturiz'd 'gainst all infections,
Cures all diseases, comming of all causes,
A month's griefe, in a day; a yeeres, in twelue:
And, of what age soeuer, in a month.
Past all the doses of your drugging Doctors.
I'll vndertake, withall, to fright the plague
Out o' the kingdome, in three months.

SVRLY

                         And I'll
Be bound the players shall sing your praises, then,
Without their poets.

MAMMON

                    Sir, I'll doo't. Meane time,
I'll giue away so much, vnto my man,
Shall serue th'whole citie, with preseruatiue,
Weekely, each house his dose, and at the rate—

SVRLY

    As he that built the water-worke, do's with water?

MAMMON

    You are incredulous.

SVRLY

                   Faith, I haue a humor,
I would not willingly be gull'd. Your *stone*
Cannot transmute me.

MAMMON

                PERTINAX, SVRLY,
Will you beleeue antiquitie? recordes?
I'll shew you a booke, where MOSES, and his sister,
And SALOMON haue written, of the art;
I, and a treatise penn'd by ADAM.

SVRLY

                      How!

MAMMON

    O' the *Philosophers stone*, and in high-*Dutch*.

SVRLY

    Did ADAM write, sir, in high-*Dutch?*

MAMMON

                   He did:
Which proues it was the primitiue tongue.

SVRLY

                    What paper?

MAMMON

    On cedar board.

SVRLY

           O that, indeed (they say)
Will last 'gainst wormes.

MAMMON

              'Tis like your *Irish* wood,
'Gainst cob-webs. I haue a peece of IASONS fleece, too,
Which was no other, then a booke of *alchemie*,
Writ in large sheepe-skin, a good fat ram-vellam.
Such was PYTHAGORA's thigh, PANDORA's tub;
And, all that fable of MEDEAS charmes,
The manner of our worke: The Bulls, our fornace,
Still breathing fire; our *argent-viue*, the Dragon:
The Dragons teeth, *mercury* sublimate,

That keepes the whitenesse, hardnesse, and the biting;
And they are gather'd, into IASON's helme,
(Th'*alembeke*) and then sow'd in MARS his field,
And, thence, sublim'd so often, till they are fix'd.
Both this, th'*Hesperian* garden, CADMVS storie,
IOVE's shower, the boone of MIDAS, ARGVS eyes,
BOCCACE his *Demogorgon*, thousands more,
All abstract riddles of our *stone*. How now?

    (*Enter Face*)

Doe we succeed? Is our day come? and holds it?
FACE
  The euening will set red, vpon you, sir;
  You haue colour for it, crimson: the red *ferment*
  Has done his office. Three houres hence, prepare you
  To see proiection.
MAMMON
                 PERTINAX, my SVRLY,
  Againe, I say to thee, aloud: *be rich*.
  This day, thou shalt haue ingots: and, to morrow,
  Giue lords th'affront. Is it, my ZEPHYRVS, right?
  Blushes the *bolts-head?*
FACE
              Like a wench with child, sir,
  That were, but now, discouer'd to her master.
MAMMON
  Excellent wittie *Lungs!* My onely care is,
  Where to get stuffe, inough now, to proiect on,
  This towne will not halfe serue me.
FACE
                 No, sir? Buy
  The couering of o'churches.
MAMMON
           That's true.
FACE
              Yes.
  Let'hem stand bare, as doe their auditorie.
  Or cap 'hem, new, with shingles.
MAMMON
            No, good thatch:
  Thatch will lie light vpo'the rafters, *Lungs*.
  Lungs, I will manumit thee, from the fornace;
  I will restore thee thy complexion, *Puffe*,
  Lost in the embers; and repaire this braine,
  Hurt wi'the fume o'the mettalls.

FACE

I haue blowne, sir,
Hard, for your worship; throwne by many a coale,
When 'twas not beech; weigh'd those I put in, iust,
To keepe your heat, still euen; These bleard-eyes
Haue wak'd, to reade your seuerall colours, sir,
Of the *pale citron*, the *greene lyon*, the *crow*,
The *peacocks taile*, the *plumed swan*.

MAMMON

And lastly,
Thou hast descryed the *flower*, the *sanguis agni?*

FACE

Yes, sir.

MAMMON

Where's master?

FACE

At's praiers, sir, he,
Good man, hee's doing his deuotions,
For the successe.

MAMMON

Lungs, I will set a period,
To all thy labours: Thou shalt be the master
Of my *seraglia.*

FACE

Good, sir.

MAMMON

But doe you heare?
I'll geld you, *Lungs.*

FACE

Yes, sir.

MAMMON

For I doe meane
To haue a list of wiues, and concubines,
Equall with Salomon; who had the *stone*
Alike, with me: and I will make me, a back
With the *elixir*, that shall be as tough
As Hercvles, to encounter fiftie a night.
Th'art sure, thou saw'st it *bloud?*

FACE

Both *bloud, and spirit,* sir.

MAMMON

I will haue all my beds, blowne vp; not stuft:
Downe is too hard. And then, mine oual roome,
Fill'd with such pictures, as Tiberivs tooke

676

From ELEPHANTIS: and dull ARETINE
But coldly imitated. Then, my glasses,
Cut in more subtill angles, to disperse,
And multiply the figures, as I walke
Naked betweene my *succubæ*. My mists
I'le haue of perfume, vapor'd 'bout the roome,
To loose our selues in; and my baths, like pits
To fall into: from whence, we will come forth,
And rowle vs drie in gossamour, and roses.
(Is it arriu'd at *ruby*?)—Where I spie
A wealthy citizen, or rich lawyer,
Haue a sublim'd pure wife, vnto that fellow
I'll send a thousand pound, to be my cuckold.

FACE

And I shall carry it?

MAMMON

                       No. I'll ha'no bawds,
But fathers, and mothers. They will doe it best.
Best of all others. And, my flatterers
Shall be the pure, and grauest of Diuines,
That I can get for money. My mere fooles,
Eloquent burgesses, and then my poets
The fame that writ so subtly of the *fart,*
Whom I will entertaine, still, for that subiect.
The few, that would giue out themselues, to be
Court, and towne-stallions, and, each where, belye
Ladies, who are knowne most innocent, for them;
Those will I begge, to make me *eunuchs* of:
And they shall fan me with ten estrich tailes
A piece, made in a plume, to gather wind.
We will be braue, *Puffe*, now we ha'the *med'cine.*
My meat, shall all come in, in *Indian* shells,
Dishes of agate, set in gold, and studded,
With emeralds, saphyres, hiacynths, and rubies.
The tongues of carpes, dormise, and camels heeles,
Boil'd i'the spirit of SOL, and dissolu'd pearle,
(APICIVS diet, 'gainst the *epilepsie*)
And I will eate these broaths, with spoones of amber,
Headed with diamant, and carbuncle.
My foot-boy shall eate phesants, calured salmons,
Knots, godwits, lampreys: I my selfe will haue
The beards of barbels, seru'd, in stead of sallades;
Oild mushromes; and the swelling vnctuous paps
Of a fat pregnant sow, newly cut off
Drest with an exquisite, and poynant sauce;

For which, Ile say vnto my cooke, there's gold,
Goe forth, and be a knight.

FACE

Sir, I'll goe looke
A little, how it heightens.

MAMMON

Doe. My shirts
I'll haue of taffata-sarsnet, soft, and light
As cob-webs; and for all my other rayment
It shall be such, as might prouoke the *Persian;*
Were he to teach the world riot, a new.
My gloues of fishes, and birds-skins, perfum'd
With gummes of *paradise,* and easterne aire—

SVRLY

And do'you thinke to haue the *stone,* with this?

MAMMON

No, I doe thinke, t'haue all this, with the *stone.*

SVRLY

Why, I haue heard, he must be *homo frugi,*
A pious, holy, and religious man,
One free from mortall sinne, a very virgin.

MAMMON

That makes it, sir, he is so. But I buy it.
My venter brings it me. He, honest wretch,
A notable, superstitious, good soule,
Has worne his knees bare, and his slippers bald,
With prayer, and fasting for it: and, sir, let him
Do'it alone, for me, still. Here he comes,
Not a prophane word, afore him: 'Tis poyson.

The Alchemist (1612)
Act ii, Scenes i, ii

*The judgement is perfectly overwhelmed by the torrent of images,
words, and book-knowledge with which Mammon confounds and stuns
his incredulous hearer. They come pouring out like the successive strokes
of Nilus. They "doubly redouble strokes upon the foe." Description out-
strides proof. We are made to believe effects before we have testimony
for their causes; as a lively description of the joys of heaven sometimes
passes for an argument to prove the existence of such a place. If there
be no one image which rises to the height of the sublime, yet the con-
fluence and assemblage of them all produces an effect equal to the
grandest poetry. Xerxes' army that drank up whole rivers from their
numbers may stand for single Achilles. Epicure Mammon is the most
determined offspring of the author. It has the whole "matter and copy of
the father, eye, nose, lip, the trick of his frown." It is just such a swag-*

gerer as contemporaries have described old Ben to be. Meercraft, Boba-
dil, the Host of the New Inn, have all his "image and superscription;"
but Mammon is arrogant pretension personified. Sir Sampson Legend,
in Love for Love, is such another lying overbearing character, but he
does not come up to Epicure Mammon. What a "towering bravery"
there is in his sensuality! He affects no pleasure under a sultan. It is as if
"Egypt with Assyria strove in luxury."

CHARLES LAMB
Specimens of English Dramatic Poets (1808)

BEN JONSON

1 5 7 3 ? — 1 6 3 7

SONG. TO CELIA

Drinke to me, onely, with thine eyes,
    And I will pledge with mine;
Or leave a kisse but in the cup,
    And Ile not looke for wine.
The thirst, that from the soule doth rise,
    Doth aske a drinke divine:
But might I of Jove's *Nectar* sup,
    I would not change for thine.
I sent thee, late, a rosie wreath,
    Not so much honoring thee,
As giving it a hope, that there
    It could not withered bee.
But thou thereon did'st onely breath,
    And sent'st it backe to mee:
Since when it growes, and smells, I sweare,
    Not of it selfe, but thee.

The Forrest (1616), ix

*One of those perfect poems which somehow seem to have always
existed.*

DOUGLAS BUSH
English Literature in the Earlier Seventeenth Century (1945)

BEN JONSON

1 5 7 3 ? — 1 6 3 7

INJURIES

Injuries doe not extinguish courtesies: they only suffer them not to appeare faire. For a man that doth me an injury after a courtesie, takes not away the courtesie, but defaces it: As he that writes other verses upon my verses, takes not away the first Letters, but hides them.

Timber: or, Discoveries; Made Vpon Men and Matter (1641)

No sentence more high-minded and generous than that was ever written.

ALGERNON CHARLES SWINBURNE
A Study of Ben Jonson (1889)

CYRIL TOURNEUR

1 5 7 5 ? — 1 6 2 6

CASTIZA REBUKES HER MOTHER

I haue endur'd you with an eare of fire,
Your Tongues haue struck hotte yrons on my face;
Mother, come from that poysonous woman there.

The Revengers Tragædie (1607)
Act ii, Scene i

In 'The Revenger's Tragedy' there is an imaginative stroke which the greatest of poets might envy, when Castiza cries out to her mother, who has been swayed by her brother's cynical pretence to the idea of traffic in her honour. . . . That appeal to the mother to stand forth from her false self is beyond praise.

T. EARLE WELBY
A Popular History of English Poetry (1933)

I WAS THE MAN

Enter VINDICE *and* HIPPOLITO, *bringing out their Mother one by one shoulder, and the other by the other, with daggers in their hands.*

VINDICE

O thou? for whom no name is bad ynough.

MOTHER

What meanes my sonnes? what will you murder me?

VINDICE

Wicked, vnnaturall Parent.

HIPPOLITO

Feend of women.

MOTHER

Oh! are sonnes turnd monsters? helpe.

VINDICE

In vaine.

MOTHER

Are you so barbarous to set Iron nipples
Vpon the brest that gaue you suck?

VINDICE

That brest,
Is turnd to Quarled poyson.

MOTHER

Cut not your daies for't, am not I your mother?

VINDICE

Thou dost vsurpe that title now by fraud
For in that shell of mother breeds a bawde.

MOTHER

A bawde? O name far loathsomer then hell.

HIPPOLITO

It should be so knewst thou thy Office well.

MOTHER

I hate it.

VINDICE

Ah ist possible, you [heavenly] powers on hie,
That women should dissemble when they die.

MOTHER

Dissemble.

VINDICE

Did not the Dukes sonne direct

A fellow, of the worlds condition, hither,
That did corrupt all that was good in thee:
Made the vnciuilly forget thy selfe,
And worke our sister to his lust?

MOTHER

Who I?
That had beene monstrous. I defie that man
For any such intent; none liues so pure,
But shall be soild with slander,—good sonne beleiue it not.

VINDICE

Oh I'me in doubt,
Whether I'me my selfe, or no.
Stay, let me looke agen vpon this face.
Who shall be sau'd when mothers haue no grace?

HIPPOLITO

Twould make one halfe dispaire.

VINDICE

I was the man,
Defie me, now? lets see, do't modestly.

MOTHER

O hell vnto my soule.

VINDICE

In that disguize, I sent from the Dukes sonne,
Tryed you, and found you base mettell,
As any villaine might haue donne.

MOTHER

O no, no tongue but yours could haue bewitcht me so.

VINDICE

O nimble in damnation, quick in tune,
There is no diuill could strike fire so soone:
I am confuted in a word.

MOTHER

Oh sonnes, forgiue me, to my selfe ile proue more true,
You that should honor me, I kneele to you.

VINDICE

A mother to giue ayme to her owne daughter.

HIPPOLITO

True brother, how far beyond nature 'tis,
Tho many Mothers do't.

VINDICE

Nay and you draw teares once, go you to bed,
Wet will make yron blush and change to red:
Brother it raines, twill spoile your dagger, house it.

HIPPOLITO

Tis done.

VINDICE

Yfaith tis a sweete shower, it dos much good.

The fruitfull grounds, and meadowes of her soule,

Has beene long dry: powre downe thou blessed dew;

Rise Mother, troth this shower has made you higher.

MOTHER

O you heauens! take this infectious spot out of my soule,

Ile rence it in seauen waters of mine eyes.

Make my teares salt ynough to tast of grace.

To weepe, is to our sexe naturally giuen:

But to weepe truely thats a gift from heauen.

VINDICE

Nay Ile kisse you now: kisse her brother.

Lets marry her to our soules, wherein's no lust,

And honorably loue her.

HIPPOLITO

Let it be.

VINDICE

For honest women are so sild and rare,

Tis good to cherish those poore few that are.

Oh you of easie waxe, do but imagine

Now the disease has left you, how leprously

That Office would haue cling'd vnto your forehead.

All mothers that had any gracefull hue,

Would haue worne maskes to hide their face at you:

It would haue growne to this, at your foule name

Greene-collour'd maides would haue turnd red with shame.

HIPPOLITO

And then our sister full of hire, and bassenesse.

VINDICE

There has beene boyling lead agen,

The dukes sonnes great Concubine:

A drab of State, a cloath a siluer slut,

To haue her traine borne vp, and her soule traile i'th durt; great.

HIPPOLITO

To be miserably great, rich to be eternally wretched.

VINDICE

O common madnesse:

Aske but the thriuingst harlot in cold bloud,

Sheed giue the world to make her honour good,

Perhaps youle say but onely to th' Dukes sonne,

In priuate; why, shee first begins with one,

Who afterward to thousand prooues a whore:

Breake Ice in one place, it will crack in more.

MOTHER

Most certainly applyed.

HIPPOLITO

Oh Brother, you forget our businesse.

VINDICE

And well remembred, ioye's a subtill elfe,
I thinke man's happiest, when he forgets himselfe:
Farewell once dryed, now holy-watred Meade,
Our hearts weare Feathers, that before wore Lead.

MOTHER

Ile giue you this, that one I neuer knew
Plead better, for, and gainst the Diuill, then you.

VINDICE

You make me proud ont.

HIPPOLITO

Commend vs in all vertue to our Sister.

VINDICE

I for the loue of heauen, to that true maide.

MOTHER

With my best words.

VINDICE

Why that was motherly sayd.   *Exeunt.*

The Revengers Tragædie (1607)
Act iv, Scene iv

The reality and life of this dialogue passes any scenical illusion I ever felt. I never read it but my ears tingle, and I feel a hot blush spread my cheeks, as if I were presently about to "proclaim" some such "malefactions" of myself, as the brothers here rebuke in their unnatural parent; in words more keen and dagger-like than those which Hamlet speaks to his mother. Such power has the passion of shame truly personated, not only to "strike guilty creatures unto the soul," but to "appal" even those that are "free."

CHARLES LAMB
Specimens of English Dramatic Poets (1808)

JOHN FLETCHER

1 5 7 9 — 1 6 2 5

SWEETEST MELANCHOLY

Hence all you vain Delights,
As short as are the nights,
    Wherein you spend your folly,
There's nought in this life sweet,
If man were wise to see't,
    But only melancholly,
    Oh sweetest melancholly.
Welcome folded Arms, and fixed Eyes,
A sigh that piercing mortifies,
A look that's fast'ned to the ground,
A tongue chain'd up without a sound.

Fountain heads, and pathless Groves,
Places which pale passion loves:
Moon-light walks, when all the Fowls
Are warmly hous'd, save Bats and Owls;
    A mid-night Bell, a parting groan,
    These are the sounds we feed upon;
Then stretch our bones in a still gloomy valley,
Nothing's so dainty sweet, as lovely melancholly.

The Nice Valour (1647)

Act iii, Scene i

The perfection of this kind of writing.

WILLIAM HAZLITT

Lectures on the Dramatic Literature of the Age of Elizabeth (1820)

JOHN WEBSTER

1 5 8 0 ? — 1 6 2 5 ?

DIRGE

CORNELIA

Call for the Robin-Red-brest and the wren,
Since ore shadie groves they hover,
And with leaves and flowres doe cover
The friendlesse bodies of unburied men.
Call unto his funerall Dole
The Ante, the field-mouse, and the mole
To reare him hillockes, that shall keepe him warme,
And (when gay tombes are rob'd) sustaine no harme,
But keepe the wolfe far thence, that's foe to men,
For with his nailes hee'l dig them up agen.

The White Divel (1612)
Act v, Scene iv

WILLIAM SHAKESPEARE

1 5 6 4 — 1 6 1 6

DITTY

Full fadom fiue thy Father lies,
Of his bones are Corrall made:
Those are pearles that were his eies,
Nothing of him that doth fade,
But doth suffer a Sea-change
Into something rich, and strange.
Sea Nymphs hourly ring his knell.

Burthen: ding dong
Harke now I heare them, ding-dong bell.

The Tempest (1623)
Act i, Scene ii

I never saw anything like this Dirge, except the Ditty which reminds
Ferdinand of his drowned father in the Tempest. As that is of the water,
watery; so this is of the earth, earthy. Both have that intenseness of
feeling, which seems to resolve itself into the elements which it con-
templates.

CHARLES LAMB
Specimens of English Dramatic Poets (1808)

JOHN FORD

1 5 8 6 — 1 6 3 9 ?

ROYALL LADY

An Altar couered with white.

*Two lights of Virgin wax, during which musicke of Recorders,
enter foure bearing Ithocles on a hease, or in a chaire, in
a rich robe, and a Crowne on his head; place him on one side
of the Altar, after him enter Calantha in a white robe, and
crown'd Euphranea; Philema, Christalla in white, Nearchus,
Armostes, Crotolon, Prophilus, Amelus, Bassanes, Lemophil,
and Groneas. Calantha goes and kneeles before the Altar,
the rest stand off, the women kneeling behind; cease
Recorders during her deuotions. Sofe musicke. Calantha
and the rest rise doing obeysance to the Altar.*

CALANTHA
Our Orisons are heard, the gods are mercifull:
Now tell me, you whose loyalties payes tribute
To vs your lawfull Soueraigne, how vnskilfull
Your duties or obedience is, to render
Subiection to the Scepter of a Virgin,
Who haue beene euer fortunate in Princes
Of masculine and stirring composition?
A woman has enough to gouerne wisely
Her owne demeanours, passions, and diuisions.
A Nation warlike and inur'd to practice
Of policy and labour, cannot brooke
A feminate authority: we therefore
Command your counsaile, how you may aduise vs
In choosing of a husband whose abilities
Can better guide this kingdome.

NEARCHUS
                          Royall Lady,
Your law is in your will.

ARMOSTES
                    We haue seene tokens
Of constancy too lately to mistrust it.

CROTOLON
Yet if your highnesse settle on a choice
By your owne iudgement both allow'd and lik'd of,
Sparta may grow in power, and proceed
To an increasing height.

687

CALANTHA

Hold you the same minde.

BASSANES

Alas great mistris, reason is so clouded
With the thicke darkenesse of my infinites woes
That I forecast, nor dangers, hopes, or safety:
Give me some corner of the world to weare out
The remnant of the minutes I must number,
Where I may heare no sounds, but sad complaints
Of Virgins who have lost contracted partners;
Of husbands howling that their wives were ravisht
By some untimely fate; of friends divided
By churlish opposition, or of fathers
Weeping upon their childrens slaughtered carcasses;
Or daughters groaning ore their fathers hearses,
And I can dwell there, and with these keepe consort
As musicall as theirs: what can you looke for
From an old foolish peevish doting man, .
But crasinesse of age?

CALANTHA

Cozen of *Argos*.

NEARCHUS

Madam.

CALANTHA

Were I presently
To choose you for my Lord, Ile open freely
What articles I would propose to treat on
Before our marriage.

NEARCHUS

Name them vertuous Lady.

CALANTHA

I would presume you would retaine the royalty
Of *Sparta* in her owne bounds: then in *Argos*
Armostes might be Viceroy; in *Messene*
Might *Crotolon* beare sway, and *Bassanes*—

BASSANES

I, Queene? alas! what I?

CALANTHA

Be *Sparta's* Marshall:
The multitudes of high imployments could not
But set a peace to priuate griefes: these Gentlemen,
Groneas and *Lemophil,* with worthy pen ons
Should wait vpon your person in your Chamber:
I would bestow *Christalla* on *Amelus,*

Shee'll proue a constant wife, and *Philema*
Should into *Vesta's* Temple.

BASSANES

This is a Testament,
It sounds not like conditions on a marriage.

NEARCHUS

All this should be perform'd.

CALANTHA

Lastly, for *Prophilus*,
He should be (Cozen) solemnly inuested
In all those honors, titles, and preferments
Which his deare friend, and my neglected husband
Too short a time enioy'd.

PROPHILUS

I am vnworthy
To liue in your remembrance.

EUPHRANEA

Excellent Lady!

NEARCHUS

Madam, what meanes that word neglected husband?

CALANTHA

Forgiue me: now I turne to thee thou shadow
Of my contracted Lord: beare witnesse all,
I put my mother wedding Ring vpon
His finger, 'twas my fathers last bequest:
Thus I new marry him whose wife I am;
Death shall not separate vs: ô my Lords,
I but deceiu'd your eyes with Anticke gesture,
When one newes straight came hudling on another,
Of death, and death, and death, still I danc'd forward,
But it strooke home, and here, and in an instant,
Be such meere women, who with shreeks and out-cries
Can vow a present end to all their sorrowes,
Yet liue to vow new pleasures, and out-liue them:
They are the silent griefes which cut the hart-strings;
Let me dye smiling.

NEARCHUS

'Tis a truth too ominous.

CALANTHA

One kisse on these cold lips, my last; cracke, cracke.
Argos now's *Sparta's* King.

The Broken Heart (1633)
Act v, Scene ii

I do not know where to find in any play a catastrophe so grand, so solemn, and so surprising as this. This in indeed, according to Milton, to "describe high passions and high actions." The fortitude of the Spartan boy who let a beast gnaw out his bowels till he died without expressing a groan, is a faint bodily image of this dilaceration of the spirit and exenteration of the inmost mind, which Calantha with a holy violence against her nature keeps closely covered, till the last duties of a wife and a queen are fulfilled. Stories of martyrdom are but of chains and the stake; a little bodily suffering; these torments

> On the purest spirits prey
> As on entrails, joints, and limbs,
> With answerable pains, but more intense.

What a noble thing is the soul in its strengths and in its weaknesses! who would be less weak than Calantha? who can be so strong? the expression of this transcendent scene almost bears me in imagination to Calvary and the Cross; and I seem to perceive some analogy between the scenical sufferings which I am here contemplating, and the real agonies of that final completion to which I dare no more than hint a reference.

Ford was of the first order of poets. He sought for sublimity, not by parcels in metaphors or visible images, but directly where she has her full residence in the heart of man; in the actions and sufferings of the greatest minds. There is a grandeur of the soul above mountains, seas, and the elements.

CHARLES LAMB
Specimens of English Dramatic Poets (1808)

—————

ROBERT HERRICK

1 5 9 1 — 1 6 7 4

CORINNA'S *GOING A MAYING*

Get up, get up for shame, the Blooming Morne
Upon her wings presents the god unshorne.
    See how *Aurora* throwes her faire
    Fresh-quilted colours through the aire:
    Get up, sweet-Slug-a-bed, and see
    The Dew-bespangling Herbe and Tree.

Each Flower has wept, and bow'd toward the East,
Above an houre since; yet you not drest,
  Nay! not so much as out of bed?
  When all the Birds have Mattens seyd,
  And sung their thankfull Hymnes: 'tis sin,
  Nay, profanation to keep in,
When as a thousand Virgins on this day,
Spring, sooner then the Lark, to fetch in May.

Rise; and put on your Foliage, and be seene
To come forth, like the Spring-time, fresh and greene;
  And sweet as *Flora*. Take no care
  For Jewels for your Gowne, or Haire:
  Feare not; the leaves will strew
  Gemms in abundance upon you:
Besides, the childhood of the Day has kept,
Against you come, some *Orient Pearls* unwept:
  Come, and receive them while the light
  Hangs on the Dew-locks of the night:
  And *Titan* on the Eastern hill
  Retires himselfe, or else stand still
Till you come forth. Wash, dresse, be briefe in praying:
Few Beads are best, when once we goe a Maying.

Come, my *Corinna*, come; and comming, marke
How each field turns a street; each street a Parke
  Made green, and trimm'd with trees: see how
  Devotion gives each House a Bough,
  Or Branch: Each Porch, each doore, ere this,
  An Arke a Tabernacle is
Made up of white-thorn neatly enterwove;
As if here were those cooler shades of love.
  Can such delights be in the street,
  And open fields, and we not see't?
  Come, we'll abroad; and let's obay
  The Proclamation made for May:
And sin no more, as we have done, by staying;
But my *Corinna*, come, let's goe a Maying.

There's not a budding Boy, or Girle, this day,
But is got up, and gone to bring in May.
  A deale of Youth, ere this, is come
  Back, and with *White-thorn* laden home.
  Some have dispatcht their Cakes and Creame,
  Before that we have left to dreame:

And some have wept, and woo'd, and plighted Troth,
And chose their Priest, ere we can cast off sloth:
    Many a green-gown has been given;
    Many a kisse, both odde and even:
    Many a glance too has been sent
    From out the eye, Loves Firmament:
Many a jest told of the Keyes betraying
This night, and Locks pickt, yet w'are not a Maying.

Come, let us goe, while we are in our prime;
And take the harmlesse follie of the time.
    We shall grow old apace, and die
    Before we know our liberty.
    Our life is short; and our dayes run
    As fast away as do's the Sunne:
And as a vapour, or a drop of raine
Once lost, can ne'r be found againe:
    So when or you or I are made
    A fable, song, or fleeting shade;
    All love, all liking, all delight
    Lies drown'd with us in endlesse night.
Then while time serves, and we are but decaying;
Come, my *Corinna,* come, let's goe a Maying.

Hesperides (1648)

One of the most perfect studies of idealized village life in the language.

J. H. B. MASTERMAN

The Age of Milton (1897)

THE BIBLE,
SIXTINE-CLEMENTINE EDITION

1 5 9 2

BEING

Ego sum qui sum.

I am that I am.

Exodus, iii, 14

*The author of Exodus often surpasses Homer in loftiness of expression;
and, at the same time, he has hidden meanings that in the sublimity of
their significance surpass all metaphysics, as in that phrase with which*

God describes himself to Moses: SUM QUI SUM, *admired by Dionysius Longinus, prince of critics, as reaching complete grandeur of poetic style.*

GIAMBATTISTA VICO
La Scienza Nuova Prima (1725)

VINCENT VOITURE

1 5 9 8 — 1 6 4 8

RONDEAU

Ma foi, c'est fait de moi; car Isabeau
M'a conjuré de lui faire un rondeau,
Cela me met en une peine extrême.
Quoi! treize vers, huit en eau, cinq en ème!
Je lui ferais aussitôt un bateau.

En voilà cinq pourtant en un monceau,
Faisons en huit, en invoquant Brodeau,
Et puis mettons par quelque stratagème:
    Ma foi, c'est fait!

Si je pouvais encor de mon cerveau
Tirer cinq vers, l'ouvrage serait beau.
Mais cependant je suis dedans l'onzième,
Et ci je crois que je fais le douzième,
En voilà treize ajustés au niveau:
    Ma foi, c'est fait!

By Jove, 'tis done with me, for Isabeau
Conjures me straight a Rondeau to bestow,
   Which puts me in perplexity extreme!
   Verses thirteen, in 'eau' eight, five in 'eme'—
As well attempt to build a boat I trow.

But here at least are five, I'd have you know,
To make them eight I here invoke Brédeau;
   Next will squeeze in by some ingenious scheme.
    By Jove, 'tis done!

Now from my labouring brain if yet would flow
Five more, 'twould make indeed a goodly show;
   And now the twelfth is added to my team;
And here at last the thirteenth joins the row.
   By Jove, 'tis done.

Translated by H. Carrington

Above all he is the king and the master of the rondeau. In this little poem which is so spirited, airy, fleet and sprightly in its pace, and at the same time so clean and incisive, none has surpassed or equaled Voiture. Here is his absolute triumph.

THÉODORE DE BANVILLE
Les Poëtes français (1861)

PEDRO CALDERÓN DE LA BARCA

1 6 0 0 — 1 6 8 1

THE CROSS

Arbol, donde el cielo quiso
Dar el fruto verdadero
Contra el bocado primero,
Flor del nuevo paraiso,
Arco de luz, cuyo aviso
En piélago mas profundo
La paz publicó del mundo,
Planta hermosa, fértil vid,
Harpa del nuevo David,
Tabla del Moises segundo:
Pecador soy, tus favores
Pido por justicia yo:
Pues Dios en tí padeció
Solo por los pecadores.
A mí me debes tus loores;
Que por mí solo muriera
Dios, si mas mundo no hubiera.

Tree, which heaven has willed to dower
With that true fruit whence we live,
As that other, death did give;
Of new Eden loveliest flower;

694

Bow of light, that in worst hour
Of the worst flood signal true
O'er the world, of mercy threw;
Fair plant, yielding sweetest wine;
Of our David harp divine;
Of our Moses tables new;
Sinner am I, therefore I
Claim upon thy mercies make,
Since alone for sinners' sake
God on thee endured to die;
And for me would God have died
Had there been no world beside.

La Devocion de la Cruz
Translated by Richard Chenevix Trench

Perfect finish and completeness in itself.

RICHARD CHENEVIX TRENCH
Life's a Dream: The Great Theatre of the World (1856)

SIR THOMAS BROWNE

1 6 0 5 — 1 6 8 2

URNE-BURIALL

Now since these dead bones have already out-lasted the living ones of Methuselah, and in a yard under ground, and thin walls of clay, outworn all the strong and specious buildings above it; and quietly rested under the drums and tramplings of three conquests; What Prince can promise such diuturnity unto his Reliques, or might not gladly say,

Sic ego componi versus in ossa velim.

Time which antiquates Antiquities, and hath an art to make dust of all things, hath yet spared these minor monuments. In vain we hope to be known by open and visible conservatories, when to be unknown was the means of their continuation, and obscurity their protection: If they dyed by violent hands, and were thrust into their Urnes, these bones become considerable, and some old Philosophers would honour them, whose soules they conceived most pure, which were thus snatched from their bodies; and to retain a stronger propension unto them: whereas they weariedly left a languishing corps, and with faint desires of reunion. If they fell by long and aged decay, yet wrapt up in the bundle of time, they fall into indistinction, and make but one blot with infants. If we begin to die when we live, and long life be but a prolongation of death; our life is a sad composition; we live with death, and die not in a moment. How many pulses made up the life of Methuselah, were work for Archimedes: Common Counters sum up the life of Moses his name. Our dayes become considerable like petty sums by minute accumulations; where numerous fractions make up but small round numbers; and our dayes of a span long make not one little finger.

If the nearnesse of our last necessity, brought a nearer conformity unto it, there were a happinesse in hoary hairs, and no calamity in half senses. But the long habit of living indisposeth us for dying; When Avarice makes us the sport of death; When even David grew politickly cruel; and Solomon could hardly be said to be the wisest of men. But many are too early old, and before the date of age. Adversity stretcheth our dayes, misery makes Alcmena's nights, and time hath no wings unto it. But the most tedious being is that which can unwish it self, content to be nothing, or never to have been, which was beyond the *male*-content of Job, who cursed not the day of his life, but his nativity: Content to have so far been, as to have a title to future being; Although he had lived here but in an hidden state of life, and as it were an abortion.

What Song the Syrens sang, or what name Achilles assumed when he hid himself among women, though puzling questions are not beyond all conjecture. What time the persons of these Ossuaries entred the famous Nations of the dead, and slept with Princes and Counsellors, might admit a wide solution. But who were the proprietaries of these bones, or what bodies these ashes made up, were a question above Antiquarism; not to be resolved by man, nor easily perhaps by spirits, except we consult the Provincial Guardians, or tutelary observators. Had they made as good provision for their names, as they have done for their Reliques, they had not so grosly erred in the art of perpetuation. But to subsist in bones, and be but Pyramidally extant, is a fallacy in duration. Vain ashes, which in the oblivion of names, persons, times and sexes, have found unto themselves, a fruitlesse continuation, and onely arise unto late posterity, as Emblemes of mortal vanities; Antidotes against pride, vainglory, and madding vices. Pagan vainglories which thought the world might last for ever, had encouragement for ambition, and finding an *Atropos* unto the immortality of their names, were never dampt with the necessity of oblivion. Even old ambitions had the advantage of ours, in the attempts of their vainglories, who acting early, and before the probable Meridian of time, have by this time found great accomplishment of their designes, whereby the ancient Heroes have already outlasted their Monuments, and Mechanical preservations. But in this latter Scene of time we cannot expect such Mummies unto our memories, when ambition may fear the Prophecy of Elias, and Charles the fift can never hope to live within two Methusela's of Hector.

And therefore restlesse inquietude for the diuturnity of our memories unto present considerations, seemes a vanity almost out of date, and superannuated peece of folly. We cannot hope to live so long in our names, as some have done in their persons, one face of Janus holds no proportion to the other. 'Tis too late to be ambitious. The great mutations of the world are acted, or time may be too short for our designes. To extend our memories by Monuments, whose death we dayly pray for, and whose duration we cannot hope, without injury to our expectations, in the advent of the last day, were a contradiction to our beliefs. We whose generations are ordained in this setting part of time, are providentially taken off from such imaginations. And being necessitated to eye the remaining particle of futurity, are naturally constituted unto thoughts of the next world, and cannot excusably decline the consideration of that duration, which maketh Pyramids pillars of snow, and all that's past a moment.

Circles and right lines limit and close all bodies, and the mortal right-lined-circle must conclude and shut up all. There is no antidote against the Opium of time, which temporally considereth all things; Our fathers finde their graves in our short memories, and sadly tell us how we may be buried in our Survivors. Grave-stones tell truth scarce fourty yeers: Generations passe while some trees stand, and old Families last not three Oakes. To be read by bare inscriptions like many in Gruter, to hope for Eternity by Ænigmatical Epithetes, or first letters of our names, to be studied by Antiquaries, who we were, and have new Names given us like many of the Mummies, are cold consolations unto the Students of perpetuity, even by everlasting Languages.

To be content that times to come should onely know there was such a man, not caring whether they knew more of him, was a frigid ambition in Cardan: disparaging his horoscopal inclination and judgement of himself, who cares to subsist like Hippocrates' Patients, or Achilles' horses in Homer, under naked nominations, without deserts and noble acts, which are the balsame of our memories, the Entelechia and soul of our subsistences. To be namelesse in worthy deeds exceeds an infamous history. The Canaanitish woman lives more happily without a name, then Herodias with one. And who had not rather have been the good theef, then Pilate?

But the iniquity of oblivion blindly scattereth her poppy, and deals with the memory of men without distinction to merit of perpetuity. Who can but pity the founder of the Pyramids? Herostratus lives that burnt the Temple of Diana, he is almost lost that built it. Time hath spared the Epitaph of Adrian's horse, confounded that of himself. In vain we compute our felicities by the advantage of our good names, since bad have equal durations; and Thersites is like to live as long as Agamemnon.

Who knows whether the best of men be known? or whether there be not more remarkable persons forgot, then any that stand remembred in the known account of time? Without the favour of the everlasting register the first man had been as unknown as the last, and Methuselah's long life had been his only Chronicle.

Oblivion is not to be hired: The greater part must be content to be as though they had not been, to be found in the register of God, not in the record of man. Twenty seven names make up the first story, and the recorded names ever since contain not one living Century. The number of the dead long exceedeth all that shall live. The night of time far sur-passeth the day, and who knows when was the Æquinox? Every houre addes unto that current Arithmetique, which scarce stands one moment. And since death must be the Lucina of life, and even Pagans could doubt whether thus to live, were to die; Since our longest Sun sets at right descensions, and makes but winter arches, and therefore it cannot be long before we lie down in darknesse, and have our light in ashes; Since the brother of death daily haunts us with dying *memento's,* and time that grows old it self, bids us hope no long duration: Diuturnity is a dream and folly of expectation.

Darknesse and light divide the course of time, and oblivion shares with memory, a great part even of our living beings; we slightly re-member our felicities, and the smartest stroaks of affliction leave but short smart upon us. Sense endureth no extremities, and sorrows destroy us or themselves. To weep into stones are fables. Afflictions induce calosi-ties; miseries are slippery, or fall like snow upon us, which notwith-standing is no unhappy stupidity. To be ignorant of evils to come, and forgetful of evils past, is merciful provision in nature, whereby we digest the mixture of our few and evil dayes, and, our delivered senses not relapsing into cutting remembrances, our sorrows are not kept raw by the edge of repetitions. A great part of Antiquity contented their hopes of subsistency with a transmigration of their souls: a good way to con-tinue their memories, while having the advantage of plural successions, they could not but act something remarkable in such variety of beings, and enjoyning the fame of their passed selves, make accumulation of glory unto their last durations. Others rather then be lost in the uncom-fortable night of nothing, were content to recede into the common being, and made one particle of the publick soul of all things, which was no more then to return into their unknown and divine Original again. Ægyptian ingenuity was more unsatisfied, contriving their bodies in sweet consistences, to attend the return of their souls. But all was vanity, feeding the winde, and folly. The Ægyptian Mummies, which Cambyses or time hath spared, avarice now consumeth. Mummie is become Mer-chandise, Mizraim cures wounds, and Pharoah is sold for balsams.

In vain do individuals hope for immortality, or any patent from oblivion, in preservations below the Moon: Men have been deceived even in their flatteries above the Sun, and studied conceits to perpetuate their names in heaven. The various Cosmography of that part hath already varied the names of contrived constellations; Nimrod is lost in Orion, and Osyris in the Dogge-star. While we look for incorruption in the heavens, we finde they are but like the Earth; Durable in their main bodies, alterable in their parts: whereof beside Comets and new Stars, perspectives begin to tell tales. And the spots that wander about the Sun, with Phaeton's favour, would make clear conviction.

There is nothing strictly immortal, but immortality; whatever hath no beginning may be confident of no end (all others have a dependent being, and within the reach of destruction); which is the peculiar of that necessary essence that cannot destroy it self; And the highest strain of omnipotency to be so powerfully constituted, as not to suffer even from the power of it self. But the sufficiency of Christian Immortality frustrates all earthly glory, and the quality of either state after death makes a folly of posthumous memory. God who can onely destroy our souls, and hath assured our resurrection, either of our bodies or names hath directly promised no duration. Wherein there is so much of chance that the boldest expectants have found unhappy frustration; and to hold long subsistence, seems but a scape in oblivion. But man is a noble Animal, splendid in ashes, and pompous in the grave, solemnizing Nativities and Deaths with equal lustre, nor omitting Ceremonies of bravery, in the infamy of his nature.

Life is a pure flame, and we live by an invisible Sun within us. A small fire sufficeth for life, great flames seemed too little after death, while men vainly affected precious pyres, and to burn like Sardanapalus; but the wisdom of funeral Laws found the folly of prodigal blazes, and reduced undoing fires unto the rule of sober obsequies, wherein few could be so mean as not to provide wood, pitch, a mourner, and an Urne.

Five Languages secured not the Epitaph of Gordianus. The man of God lives longer without a Tomb then any by one, invisibly interred by Angels, and adjudged to obscurity, though not without some marks directing humane discovery. Enoch and Elias without either tomb or burial, in an anomalous state of being, are the great examples of perpetuity, in their long and living memory, in strict account being still on this side death, and having a late part yet to act upon this stage of earth. If in the decretory term of the world we shall not all die but be changed, according to received translation; the last day will make but few graves; at least quick Resurrections will anticipate lasting Sepultures; Some graves will be opened before they be quite closed, and Lazarus be no wonder. When many that feared to die shall groan that they can die but once, the dismal state is the second and living death, when life puts despair on the damned; when men shall wish the coverings of Mountains, not of Monuments, and annihilation shall be courted.

While some have studied Monuments, others have studiously declined them: and some have been so vainly boisterous, that they durst not acknowledge their Graves; wherein Alaricus seems most subtle, who had a River turned to hide his bones at the bottome. Even Sylla that thought himself safe in his Urne, could not prevent revenging tongues, and stones thrown at his Monument. Happy are they whom privacy makes innocent, who deal so with men in this world, that they are not afraid to meet them in the next, who when they die, make no commotion among the dead, and are not toucht with that poeticall taunt of Isaiah.

Pyramids, Arches, Obelisks, were but the irregularities of vain-glory, and wilde enormities of ancient magnanimity. But the most magnanimous resolution rests in the Christian Religion, which trampleth upon pride, and sets on the neck of ambition, humbly pursuing that infallible perpetuity, unto which all others must diminish their diameters and be poorly seen in Angles of contingency.

Pious spirits who passed their dayes in raptures of futurity, made little more of this world, then the world that was before it, while they lay obscure in the Chaos of preordination, and night of their fore-beings. And if any have been so happy as truely to understand Christian annihilation, extasis, exolution, liquefaction, transformation, the kisse of the Spouse, gustation of God, and ingression into the divine shadow, they have already had an handsome anticipation of heaven; the glory of the world is surely over, and the earth in ashes unto them.

To subsist in lasting Monuments, to live in their productions, to exist in their names, and prædicament of Chymera's, was large satisfaction unto old expectations and made one part of their Elyziums. But all this is nothing in the Metaphysicks of true belief. To live indeed is to be again our selves, which being not onely an hope but an evidence in noble beleevers, 'tis all one to lie in St. Innocent's Church-yard, as in the Sands of Ægypt: Ready to be anything, in the extasie of being ever, and as content with six foot as the Moles of Adrianus.

Hydriotaphia (1658)

One of the greatest poems in our language . . . the famous fifth chapter, which to have written, brief as it is, were sufficient for eternal fame.

CHARLES WHIBLEY
Essays in Biography (1913)

EDMUND WALLER

1 6 0 6 — 1 6 8 7

THREE WORDS

Goe lovely Rose.

Poems (1645)

Most of all I envy the octogenarian poet who joined three words—

'Go, lovely Rose'—

so happily together, that he left his name to float down through time on the wings of a phrase and a flower.

LOGAN PEARSALL SMITH
Afterthoughts (1931)

PIERRE CORNEILLE

1 6 0 6 — 1 6 8 4

STANCES À LA MARQUISE

Marquise, si mon visage
A quelques traits un peu vieux,
Souvenez-vous qu'à mon âge
Vous ne vaudrez guère mieux.

Le temps aux plus belles choses
Se plaît à faire un affront,
Et saura faner vos roses
Comme il a ridé mon front.

Le même cours des planètes
Règle nos jours et nos nuits,
On m'a vu ce que vous êtes;
Vous serez ce que je suis.

Cependant j'ai quelques charmes
Qui sont assez éclatants
Pour n'avoir pas trop d'alarmes
De ces ravages du temps.

701

Vous en avez qu'on adore,
Mais ceux que vous méprisez
Pourraient bien durer encore
Quand ceux-là seront usés.

Ils pourront sauver la gloire
Des yeux qui me semblent doux,
Et dans mille ans faire croire
Ce qu'il me plaira de vous.

Chez cette race nouvelle
Où j'aurai quelque crédit,
Vous ne passerez pour belle
Qu'autant que je l'aurai dit.

Pensez-y, belle Marquise:
Quoiqu'un grison fasse effroi,
Il vaut bien qu'on le courtise,
Quand il est fait comme moi.

STANZAS

Lady fair, if on the page
Of my face traits elderly
Show, remember, at my age,
Yours will little better be.

Time to all that is most fair
Loves to offer his affront;
He your roses will not spare,
As he furrowed hath my front.

The same course of star and star
Rules the days of you and me:
Folk have seen me what you are;
And what I am you will be.

None the less, I have some charm,
Enough puissant, anydele,
For me not o'er much alarm
At Time's ravages to feel.

Charms you have, that men adore;
But this other, that you scorn,
Well may last, when yours of yore
Have been long ago outworn.

702

I the glory of your eyes
Can preserve for ages new
And cause races yet to rise
What I choose believe of you.

'Midst the newborn nations, where
I shall in some credit be,
You will only pass for fair,
Inasmuch as pleases me.

So bethink you, fair Marquise:
Though a greybeard fright the eye,
He is worth the pains to please,
When he fashioned is as I.

Translated by John Payne

The masterpiece of its kind.

EUGÈNE NOEL
Les Poëtes français (1861)

THOMAS HEYWOOD

? — C. 1650

THE ANGRY KYNGES

Goe hurtles soules, whom mischiefe hath opprest
Even in first porch of life but lately had,
And fathers fury goe unhappy kind
O litle children, by the way ful sad
    Of journey knowen.
    Goe see the angry kynges.

    ite ad Stygios, umbrae, portus
    ite, innocuae, quas in primo
    limine vitae scelus oppressit
    patriusque furor;
    ite, iratos visite reges.

Seneca
Hercules Furens, Act iv

703

The whole of the chorus at the end of Act IV of Heywood's HERCULES
FURENS *is very fine, but the last six lines seem to me of singular beauty;
and as the original, too, is a lovely passage, it is both fair and interesting
to quote original and translation. The persons addressed are the dead
children of Hercules, whom he has just slain in his madness. . . . Nothing can be said of such a translation except that it is perfect. It is a last
echo of the earlier tongue, the language of Chaucer, with an overtone
of that Christian piety and pity which disappears with Elizabethan verse.*

T. S. ELIOT
Seneca in Elizabethan Translation (1927)

JOHN MILTON

1 6 0 8 — 1 6 7 4

L'ALLEGRO

Hence loathed Melancholy
   Of *Cerberus*, and blackest midnight born,
In *Stygian* Cave forlorn.
   'Mongst horrid shapes, and shreiks, and sights unholy,
Find out some uncouth cell,
   Where brooding darkness spreads his jealous wings,
And the night-Raven sings;
   There under *Ebon* shades, and low-brow'd Rocks,
As ragged as thy Locks,
   In dark *Cimmerian* desert ever dwell.
But com thou Goddess fair and free,
In Heav'n ycleap'd *Euphrosyne*,
And by men, heart-easing Mirth,
Whom lovely *Venus* at a birth
With two sister Graces more
To Ivy-crowned *Bacchus* bore;
Or whether (as som Sager sing)
The frolick Wind that breathes the Spring,
Zephir with *Aurora* playing,
As he met her once a Maying,
There on Beds of Violets blew,
And fresh-blown Roses washt in dew,
Fill'd her with thee a daughter fair,
So bucksom, blith, and debonair.
Haste thee nymph, and bring with thee

Jest and youthful Jollity,
Quips and Cranks, and wanton Wiles,
Nods, and Becks, and Wreathed Smiles,
Such as hang on *Hebe's* cheek,
And love to live in dimple sleek;
Sport that wrincled Care derides,
And Laughter holding both his sides.
Com, and trip it as you go
On the light fantastick toe,
And in thy right hand lead with thee,
The Mountain Nymph, sweet Liberty;
And if I give thee honour due,
Mirth, admit me of thy crue
To live with her, and live with thee,
In unreproved pleasures free;
To hear the Lark begin his flight,
And singing startle the dull night,
From his watch-towre in the skies,
Till the dappled dawn doth rise;
Then to com in spight of sorrow,
And at my window bid good morrow,
Through the Sweet-Briar, or the Vine,
Or the twisted Eglantine,
While the Cock with lively din,
Scatters the rear of darkness thin,
And to the stack, or the Barn dore,
Stoutly struts his Dames before,
Oft list'ning how the Hounds and Horn
Chearly rouse the slumbring morn,
From the side of som Hoar Hill,
Through the high wood echoing shrill.
Som time walking not unseen
By Hedge-row Elms, on Hillocks green,
Right against the Eastern gate,
Where the great Sun begins his state,
Roab'd in flames, and Amber light,
The clouds in thousand Liveries dight,
While the Plowman neer at hand,
Whistles ore the Furrow'd Land,
And the Milkmaid singeth blithe,
And the Mower whets his sithe,
And every Shepherd tells his tale
Under the Hawthorn in the dale.
Streit mine eye hath caught new pleasures
Whilst the Lantskip round it measures,

Russet Lawns, and Fallows Gray,
Where the nibling flocks do stray,
Mountains on whose barren brest
The labouring clouds do often rest:
Meadows trim with Daisies pide,
Shallow Brooks, and Rivers wide.
Towers, and Battlements it sees
Boosom'd high in tufted Trees,
Wher perhaps som beauty lies,
The Cynosure of neighbouring eyes.
Hard by, a Cottage chimney smokes,
From betwixt two aged Okes,
Where *Corydon* and *Thyrsis* met,
Are at their savory dinner set
Of Hearbs, and other Country Messes,
Which the neat-handed *Phillis* dresses
And then in haste her Bowre she leaves,
With *Thestylis* to bind the Sheaves;
Or if the earlier season lead
To the tann'd Haycock in the Mead,
Some times with secure delight
The up-land Hamlets will invite,
When the merry Bells ring round,
And the jocond rebecks sound
To many a youth, and many a maid,
Dancing in the Chequer'd shade;
And young and old com forth to play
On a Sunshine Holyday,
Till the live-long day-light fail,
Then to the Spicy Nut-brown Ale,
With stories told of many a feat,
How *Faery Mab* the junkets eat,
She was pincht, and pull'd she sed,
And by the Friars Lanthorn led
Tells how the drudging *Goblin* swet,
To ern his Cream-bowle duly set,
When in one night, ere glimps of morn,
His shadowy Flale hath thresh'd the Corn,
That ten day-labourers could not end,
Then lies him down the Lubbar Fend.
And stretch'd out all the Chimney's length,
Basks at the fire his hairy strength;
And Crop-full out of dores he flings,
Ere the first Cock his Mattin rings,

Thus done the Tales, to bed they creep,
By whispering Winds soon lull'd asleep.
Towred Cities please us then,
And the busie humm of men,
Where throngs of Knights and Barons bold,
In weeds of Peace high triumphs hold,
With store of Ladies, whose bright eies
Rain influence, and judge the prise,
Of Wit, or Arms, while both contend
To win her Grace, whom all commend,
There let *Hymen* oft appear
In Saffron robe, with Taper clear,
And pomp, and feast, and revelry,
With mask, and antique Pageantry,
Such sights as youthful Poets dream
On Summer eeves by haunted stream.
Then to the well-trod stage anon,
If *Jonsons* learned Sock be on,
Or sweetest *Shakespear* fancies childe,
Warble his native Wood-notes wilde,
And ever against eating Cares,
Lap me in soft *Lydian* Aires,
Married to immortal verse
Such as the meeting soul may pierce
In notes, with many a winding bout
Of lincked sweetness long drawn out,
With wanton heed, and giddy cunning,
The melting voice through mazes running;
Untwisting all the chains that ty
The hidden soul of harmony.
That *Orpheus* self may heave his head
From golden slumber on a bed
Of heapt *Elysian* flowres, and hear
Such streins as would have won the ear
Of *Pluto*, to have quite set free
His half regain'd *Eurydice*.
These delights, if thou canst give,
Mirth with thee, I mean to live.

(1632)

In none of the works of Milton is his peculiar manner more happily displayed than in the Allegro and the Penseroso. It is impossible to conceive that the mechanism of language can be brought to a more exquisite degree of perfection. These poems differ from others, as attar of roses differs from ordinary rose-water, the close-packed essence from *the thin diluted mixture. They are indeed not so much poems, as collections of hints, from each of which the reader is to make out a poem for himself. Every epithet is a text for a stanza.*

THOMAS BABINGTON MACAULAY
Critical and Historical Essays (1843)

JOHN MILTON

1 6 0 8 — 1 6 7 4

IL PENSEROSO

Hence vain deluding joyes,
    The brood of folly without father bred,
How little you bested,
    Or fill the fixed mind with all your toyes;
Dwell in some idle brain,
    And fancies fond with gaudy shapes possess,
As thick and numberless
    As the gay motes that people the Sun Beams,
Or likest hovering dreams
    The fickle Pensioners of *Morpheus* train.
But hail thou Goddess, sage and holy,
Hail divinest Melancholy,
Whose Saintly visage is too bright
To hit the Sense of human sight;
And therefore to our weaker view,
Ore laid with black staid Wisdoms hue.
Black, but such as in esteem,
Prince *Memnons* sister might beseem,
Or that starr'd *Ethiope* Queen that strove
To set her beauties praise above
The Sea Nymphs, and their powers offended,
Yet thou art higher far descended,
Thee bright-hair'd *Vesta* long of yore,
To solitary *Saturn* bore;
His daughter she (in *Saturns* raign,
Such mixture was not held a stain)
Oft in glimmering Bowres, and glades
He met her, and in secret shades
Of woody *Ida's* inmost grove,
While yet there was no fear of *Jove*.

Com pensive Nun, devout and pure,
Sober, stedfast, and demure,
All in a robe of darkest grain,
Flowing with majestick train,
And sable stole of *Cipres* Lawn,
Over thy decent shoulders drawn.
Com, but keep thy wonted state,
With eev'n step, and musing gate,
And looks commercing with the skies,
Thy rapt soul sitting in thine eyes:
There held in holy passion still,
Forget thy self to Marble, till
With a sad Leaden downward cast,
Thou fix them on the earth as fast.
And joyn with thee calm Peace, and Quiet
Spare Fast, that oft with gods doth diet,
And hears the Muses in a ring,
Ay round about *Joves* Altar sing.
And adde to these retired leasure,
That in trim Gardens takes his pleasure;
But first, and chiefest, with thee bring,
Him that yon soars on golden wing,
Guiding the fiery-wheeled throne,
The Cherub Contemplation,
And the mute Silence hist along,
'Less *Philomel* will deign a Song,
In her sweetest, saddest plight,
Smoothing the rugged brow of night,
While *Cynthia* checks her Dragon yoke,
Gently o're th' accustom'd Oke;
Sweet Bird that shunn'st the noise of folly,
Most musical, most Melancholy!
Thee Chauntress oft the Woods among,
I woo to hear thy Even-Song;
And missing thee, I walk unseen
On the dry smooth-shaven Green,
To behold the wandring Moon,
Riding neer her highest noon,
Like one that had bin led astray
Through the Heav'ns wide pathles way;
And oft, as if her head she bow'd,
Stooping through a fleecy cloud.
Oft on a Plat of rising ground,
I hear the far-off *Curfeu* sound,

Over some wide-water'd shoar,
Swinging slow with sullen roar;
Or if the Ayr will not permit,
Som still removed place will fit,
Where glowing Embers through the room
Teach light to counterfeit a gloom,
Far from all resort of mirth,
Save the Cricket on the hearth,
Or the Belmans drowsie charm,
To bless the dores from nightly harm:
Or let my Lamp at midnight hour,
Be seen in some high lonely Towr,
Where I may oft out-watch the *Bear*,
With thrice great *Hermes*, or unsphear
The spirit of *Plato* to unfold
What Worlds, or what vast Regions hold
The immortal mind that hath forsook
Her mansion in this fleshly nook:
And of those *Dæmons* that are found
In fire, air, flood, or under ground,
Whose power hath a true consent
With Planet, or with Element.
Som time let Gorgeous Tragedy
In Scepter'd Pall com sweeping by,
Presenting *Thebs*, or *Pelops* line,
Or the tale of *Troy* divine.
Or what (though rare) of later age,
Ennobled hath the Buskind stage.
But, O sad Virgin, that thy power
Might raise *Musæus* from his bower,
Or bid the soul of *Orpheus* sing
Such notes as warbled to the string,
Drew Iron tears down *Pluto's* cheek,
And made Hell grant what Love did seek.
Or call up him that left half told
The story of *Cambuscan* bold,
Of *Camball*, and of *Algarsife*,
And who had *Canace* to wife,
That own'd the vertuous Ring and Glass,
And of the wondrous Hors of Brass,
On which the *Tartar* King did ride;
And if ought els, great *Bards* beside,
In sage and solemn tunes have sung,
Of Turneys and of Trophies hung;

Of Forests, and inchantments drear,
Where more is meant then meets the ear.
Thus night oft see me in thy pale career,
Till civil-suited Morn appeer,
Not trickt and frounc't as she was wont,
With the Attick Boy to hunt,
But Cherchef't in a comely Cloud,
While rocking Winds are Piping loud,
Or usher'd with a shower still,
When the gust hath blown his fill,
Ending on the russling Leaves,
With minute drops from off the Eaves.
And when the Sun begins to fling
His flaring beams, me Goddess bring
To arched walks of twilight groves,
And shadows brown that *Sylvan* loves
Of Pine, or monumental Oake,
Where the rude Ax with heaved stroke,
Was never heard the Nymphs to daunt,
Or fright them from their hallow'd haunt.
There in close covert by some Brook,
Where no prophaner eye may look,
Hide me from Day's garish eie,
While the Bee with Honied thie,
That at her flowry work doth sing,
And the Waters murmuring
With such consort as they keep,
Entice the dewy-feather'd Sleep;
And let som strange mysterious dream,
Wave at his Wings in Airy stream,
Of lively portrature display'd,
Softly on my eye-lids laid.
And as I wake, sweet musick breath
Above, about, or underneath,
Sent by som spirit to mortals good,
Or th' unseen Genius of the Wood.
But let my due feet never fail,
To walk the studious Cloysters pale.
And love the high embowed Roof,
With antick Pillars massy proof,
And storied Windows richly dight,
Casting a dimm religious light.
There let the pealing Organ blow,
To the full voic'd Quire below,

In Service high, and Anthems cleer,
As may with sweetness, through mine ear,
Dissolve me into extasies,
And bring all Heav'n before mine eyes.
And may at last my weary age
Find out the peacefull hermitage,
The Hairy Gown and Mossy Cell,
Where I may sit and rightly spell
Of every Star that Heav'n doth shew,
And every Herb that sips the dew;
Till old experience do attain
To something like Prophetic strain.
These pleasures *Melancholy* give,
And I with thee will choose to live.

(1632)

*I have not the least doubt, that the finest poem in the English language,
I mean Milton's Il Penseroso, was composed in the long resounding isle
of a mouldering cloister or ivy'd abbey.*

EDMUND BURKE
Letter to Matthew Smith (1750)

JOHN MILTON

1 6 0 8 — 1 6 7 4

LYCIDAS

*In this Monody the Author bewails a learned Friend, unfortunatly
drown'd in his passage from* CHESTER *on the* IRISH Seas, *1637. And by
occasion foretels the ruine of our corrupted Clergy then in their height.*

Yet once more, O ye Laurels, and once more
Ye Myrtles brown, with Ivy never-sear,
I com to pluck your Berries harsh and crude,
And with forc'd fingers rude,
Shatter your leaves before the mellowing year.
Bitter constraint, and sad occasion dear,
Compels me to disturb your season due:
For *Lycidas* is dead, dead ere his prime
Young *Lycidas*, and hath not left his peer:
Who would not sing for *Lycidas*? he knew
Himself to sing, and build the lofty rhyme.

He must not flote upon his watry bear
Unwept, and welter to the parching wind,
Without the meed of som melodious tear.
    Begin then, Sisters of the sacred well,
That from beneath the seat of *Jove* doth spring,
Begin, and somwhat loudly sweep the string.
Hence with denial vain, and coy excuse,
So may som gentle Muse
With lucky words favour my destin'd Urn,
And as he passes turn,
And bid fair peace be to my sable shrowd.
For we were nurst upon the self-same hill,
Fed the same flocks; by fountain, shade, and rill.
    Together both, ere the high Lawns appear'd
Under the opening eye-lids of the morn,
We drove a field, and both together heard
What time the Gray-fly winds her sultry horn,
Batt'ning our flocks with the fresh dews of night,
Oft till the Star that rose, at Ev'ning, bright
Toward Heav'ns descent had slop'd his westering wheel.
Mean while the Rural ditties were not mute,
Temper'd to th'Oaten Flute,
Rough *Satyrs* danc'd, and *Fauns* with clov'n heel,
From the glad sound would not be absent long,
And old *Damætas* lov'd to hear our song.
    But O the heavy change, now thou art gon,
Now thou art gon, and never must return!
Thee Shepherd, thee the Woods, and desert Caves,
With wilde Thyme and the gadding Vine o'regrown,
And all their echoes mourn.
The Willows, and the Hazle Copses green,
Shall now no more be seen,
Fanning their joyous Leaves to thy soft layes.
As killing as the Canker to the Rose,
Or Taint-worm to the weanling Herds that graze,
Or Frost to Flowers, that their gay wardrop wear,
When first the White thorn blows;
Such, *Lycidas*, thy loss to Shepherds ear.
    Where were ye Nymphs when the remorseless deep
Clos'd o're the head of your lov'd *Lycidas*?
For neither were ye playing on the steep,
Where your old *Bards*, the famous *Druids* ly,
Nor yet on the shaggy top of *Mona* high,
Nor yet where *Deva* spreads her wisard stream:
Ay me, I fondly dream!

Had ye bin there—for what could that have don?
What could the Muse her self that *Orpheus* bore,
The Muse her self, for her inchanting son
Whom Universal nature did lament,
When by the rout that made the hideous roar,
His goary visage down the stream was sent,
Down the swift *Hebrus* to the *Lesbian* shore.

   Alas! what boots it with uncessant care
To tend the homely slighted Shepherds trade,
And strictly meditate the thankles Muse,
Were it not better don as others use,
To sport with *Amaryllis* in the shade,
Or with the tangles of *Neæra's* hair?
Fame is the spur that the clear spirit doth raise
(That last infirmity of Noble mind)
To scorn delights, and live laborious dayes;
But the fair Guerdon when we hope to find,
And think to burst out into sudden blaze,
Comes the blind *Fury* with th'abhorred shears,
And slits the thin-spun life. But not the praise,
Phœbus repli'd, and touch'd my trembling ears;
Fame is no plant that grows on mortal soil,
Nor in the glistering foil
Set off to th'world, nor in broad rumour lies,
But lives and spreds aloft by those pure eyes,
And perfet witnes of all judging *Jove*;
As he pronounces lastly on each deed,
Of so much fame in Heav'n expect thy meed.

   O fountain *Arethuse*, and thou honour'd floud,
Smooth-sliding *Mincius*, crown'd with vocall reeds,
That strain I heard was of a higher mood:
But now my Oate proceeds,
And listens to the Herald of the Sea
That came in *Neptune's* plea,
He ask'd the Waves, and ask'd the Fellon winds,
What hard mishap hath doom'd this gentle swain?
And question'd every gust of rugged wings
That blows from off each beaked Promontory,
They knew not of his story,
And sage *Hippotades* their answer brings,
That not a blast was from his dungeon stray'd,
The Ayr was calm, and on the level brine,
Sleek *Panope* with all her sisters play'd.
It was that fatall and perfidious Bark
Built in th'eclipse, and rigg'd with curses dark,

That sunk so low that sacred head of thine.
   Next *Camus*, reverend Sire, went footing slow,
His Mantle hairy, and his Bonnet sedge,
Inwrought with figures dim, and on the edge
Like to that sanguine flower inscrib'd with woe.
Ah; Who hath reft (quoth he) my dearest pledge?
Last came, and last did go,
The Pilot of the *Galilean* lake,
Two massy Keyes he bore of metals twain,
(The Golden opes, the Iron shuts amain)
He shook his Miter'd locks, and stern bespake,
How well could I have spar'd for thee, young swain,
Anow of such as for their bellies sake,
Creep and intrude, and climb into the fold?
Of other care they little reck'ning make,
Then how to scramble at the shearers feast,
And shove away the worthy bidden guest.
Blind mouthes! that scarce themselves know how to hold
A Sheep-hook, or have learn'd ought els the least
That to the faithfull Herdmans art belongs!
What recks it them? What need they? They are sped;
And when they list, their lean and flashy songs
Grate on their scrannel Pipes of wretched straw,
The hungry Sheep look up, and are not fed,
But swoln with wind, and the rank mist they draw,
Rot inwardly, and foul contagion spread:
Besides what the grim Woolf with privy paw
Daily devours apace, and nothing sed,
But that two-handed engine at the door,
Stands ready to smite once, and smite no more.
   Return *Alpheus*, the dread voice is past,
That shrunk thy streams; Return *Sicilian* Muse,
And call the Vales, and bid them hither cast
Their Bels, and Flourets of a thousand hues.
Ye valleys low where the milde whispers use,
Of shades and wanton winds, and gushing brooks,
On whose fresh lap the swart Star sparely looks,
Throw hither all your quaint enameld eyes,
That on the green terf suck the honied showres,
And purple all the ground with vernal flowres.
Bring the rathe Primrose that forsaken dies.
The tufted Crow-toe, and pale Gessamine,
The white Pink, and the Pansie freakt with jeat,
The glowing Violet.
The Musk-rose, and the well attir'd Woodbine,

715

With Cowslips wan that hang the pensive hed,
And every flower that sad embroidery wears:
Bid *Amaranthus* all his beauty shed,
And Daffadillies fill their cups with tears,
To strew the Laureat Herse where *Lycid* lies.
For so to interpose a little ease,
Let our frail thoughts dally with false surmise.
Ay me! Whilst thee the shores, and sounding Seas
Wash far away, where ere thy bones are hurld,
Whether beyond the stormy *Hebrides,*
Where thou perhaps under the whelming tide
Visit'st the bottom of the monstrous world;
Or whether thou to our moist vows deny'd,
Sleep'st by the fable of *Bellerus* old,
Where the great vision of the guarded Mount
Looks toward *Namancos* and *Bayona's* hold;
Look homeward Angel now, and melt with ruth.
And, O ye *Dolphins*, waft the haples youth.

   Weep no more, woful Shepherds weep no more,
For *Lycidas* your sorrow is not dead,
Sunk though he be beneath the watry floar,
So sinks the day-star in the Ocean bed,
And yet anon repairs his drooping head,
And tricks his beams, and with new spangled Ore,
Flames in the forehead of the morning sky:
So *Lycidas* sunk low, but mounted high,
Through the dear might of him that walk'd the waves
Where other groves, and other streams along,
With *Nectar* pure his oozy Lock's he laves,
And hears the unexpressive nuptiall Song,
In the blest Kingdoms meek of joy and love.
There entertain him all the Saints above,
In solemn troops, and sweet Societies
That sing, and singing in their glory move,
And wipe the tears for ever from his eyes.
Now *Lycidas* the Shepherds weep no more;
Hence forth thou art the Genius of the shore,
In thy large recompense, and shalt be good
To all that wander in that perilous flood.

   Thus sang the uncouth Swain to th'Okes and rills,
While the still morn went out with Sandals gray,
He touch'd the tender stops of various Quills,
With eager thought warbling his *Dorick* lay:
And now the Sun had stretch'd out all the hills,
And now was dropt into the Western bay;

At last he rose, and twitch'd his Mantle blew:
To morrow to fresh Woods, and Pastures new.

(1637)

One of the most staggering performances in any literature.

ALDOUS HUXLEY
Texts & Pretexts (1933)

JOHN MILTON

1 6 0 8 — 1 6 7 4

SATAN GREETS HELL

     Farewel happy Fields
Where Joy for ever dwells: Hail horrours, hail
Infernal world, and thou profoundest Hell
Receive thy new Possessor: One who brings
A mind not to be chang'd by Place or Time.
The mind is its own place, and in it self
Can make a Heav'n of Hell, a Hell of Heav'n.
What matter where, if I be still the same,
And what I should be, all but less then hee
Whom Thunder hath made greater? Here at least
We shall be free; th' Almighty hath not built
Here for his envy, will not drive us hence:
Here we may reign secure, and in my choyce
To reign is worth ambition though in Hell:
Better to reign in Hell, then serve in Heav'n.

Paradise Lost (1667), i

Nothing could be better than that, and nothing is.

MARK VAN DOREN
The Noble Voice (1946)

717

JOHN MILTON

1 6 0 8 — 1 6 7 4

SATAN

He above the rest
In shape and gesture proudly eminent
Stood like a Towr; his form had yet not lost
All her Original brightness, nor appear'd
Less then Arch Angel ruind, and th' excess
Of Glory obscur'd: As when the Sun new ris'n
Looks through the Horizontal misty Air
Shorn of his Beams, or from behind the Moon
In dim Eclips disastrous twilight sheds
On half the Nations, and with fear of change
Perplexes Monarchs.

Paradise Lost (1667), i

We do not anywhere meet a more sublime description than this justly celebrated one of Milton.

EDMUND BURKE
On the Sublime and Beautiful (1756)

JOHN MILTON

1 6 0 8 — 1 6 7 4

DEATH

The other shape,
If shape it might be call'd that shape had none
Distinguishable in member, joynt, or limb,
Or substance might be call'd that shadow seem'd,
For each seem'd either; black it stood as Night,
Fierce as ten Furies, terrible as Hell,
And shook a dreadful Dart; what seem'd his head
The likeness of a Kingly Crown had on.

Paradise Lost (1667), ii

No person seems better to have understood the secret of heightening, or of setting terrible things, if I may use the expression, in their strongest light, by the force of a judicious obscurity, than Milton. His description of Death, in the second book, is admirably studied: it is astonishing with

*what a gloomy pomp, with what a significant and expressive uncertainty
of strokes and coloring, he has finished the portrait of the king of terrors.
... In this description all is dark, uncertain, confused, terrible, and
sublime to the last degree.*

EDMUND BURKE
On the Sublime and Beautiful (1756)

JOHN MILTON

1 6 0 8 — 1 6 7 4

HAIL HOLY LIGHT

Hail holy light, ofspring of Heav'n first-born,
Or of th' Eternal Coeternal beam
May I express thee unblam'd? since God is light,
And never but in unapproached light
Dwelt from Eternitie, dwelt then in thee,
Bright effluence of bright essence increate.
Or hear'st thou rather pure Ethereal stream,
Whose Fountain who shall tell? before the Sun,
Before the Heavens thou wert, and at the voice
Of God, as with a Mantle didst invest
The rising world of water dark and deep,
Won from the void and formless infinite.
Thee I re-visit now with bolder wing,
Escap't the *Stygian* Pool, though long detain'd
In that obscure sojourn, while in my flight
Through utter and through middle darkness borne
With other notes then to th' *Orphean* Lyre
I sung of *Chaos* and *Eternal Night,*
Taught by the heav'nly Muse to venture down
The dark descent, and up to reascend,
Though hard and rare: thee I revisit safe,
And feel thy sovran vital Lamp; but thou
Revisit'st not these eyes, that rowle in vain
To find thy piercing ray, and find no dawn;
So thick a drop serene hath quencht their Orbs,
Or dim suffusion veild. Yet not the more
Cease I to wander where the Muses haunt
Cleer Spring, or shadie Grove, or Sunnie Hill,
Smit with the love of sacred song; but chief
Thee *Sion* and the flowrie Brooks beneath

That wash thy hallowd feet, and warbling flow,
Nightly I visit: nor somtimes forget
Those other two equal'd with me in Fate,
So were I equal'd with them in renown,
Blind *Thamyris* and blind *Mæonides*,
And *Tiresias* and *Phineus* Prophets old.
Then feed on thoughts, that voluntarie move
Harmonious numbers; as the wakeful Bird
Sings darkling, and in shadiest Covert hid
Tunes her nocturnal Note. Thus with the Year
Seasons return, but not to me returns
Day, or the sweet approach of Ev'n or Morn,
Or sight of vernal bloom, or Summers Rose,
Or flocks, or herds, or human face divine;
But cloud in stead, and ever-during dark
Surrounds me, from the chearful wayes of men
Cut off, and for the Book of knowledg fair
Presented with a Universal blanc
Of Natures works to mee expung'd and ras'd,
And wisdome at one entrance quite shut out.
So much the rather thou Celestial light
Shine inward, and the mind through all her powers
Irradiate, there plant eyes, all mist from thence
Purge and disperse, that I may see and tell
Of things invisible to mortal sight.

Paradise Lost (1667), iii

*Not all the poetry of all the world can produce more than a few passages
that equal this in moving power.*

JOHN BAILEY
Milton (1915)

JOHN MILTON

1 6 0 8 — 1 6 7 4

ADAM AND EVE

Now Morn her rosie steps in th' Eastern Clime
Advancing, sow'd the Earth with Orient Pearle,
When *Adam* wak't, so customd, for his sleep
Was Aerie light from pure digestion bred,
And temperat vapors bland, which th' only sound
Of leaves and fuming rills, *Aurora's* fan,

720

Lightly dispers'd, and the shrill Matin Song
Of Birds on every bough; so much the more
His wonder was to find unwak'nd *Eve*
With Tresses discompos'd, and glowing Cheek,
As through unquiet rest: he on his side
Leaning half-rais'd, with looks of cordial Love
Hung over her enamour'd, and beheld
Beautie, which whether waking or asleep,
Shot forth peculiar Graces; then with voice
Milde, as when *Zephyrus* on *Flora* breathes,
Her hand soft touching, whisperd thus. Awake
My fairest, my espous'd, my latest found,
Heav'ns last best gift, my ever new delight,
Awake, the morning shines, and the fresh field
Calls us, we lose the prime, to mark how spring
Our tended Plants, how blows the Citron Grove,
What drops the Myrrhe, and what the balmie Reed,
How Nature paints her colours, how the Bee
Sits on the Bloom extracting liquid sweet.

Paradise Lost (1667), v

The richest melody as well as the sublimest sentiments.

HENRY HOME OF KAMES
Elements of Criticism (1762)

JOHN MILTON

1 6 0 8 — 1 6 7 4

FAR OFF HIS COMING SHONE

Attended with ten thousand thousand Saints,
He onward came, farr off his coming shon.

Paradise Lost (1667), vi

What can be finer in any poet than that beautiful passage in Milton—

. . . *Onward he moved*
And thousands of his saints around.

This is grandeur, but it is grandeur without completeness: but he adds—

Far off their coming shone;

which is the highest sublime. There is TOTAL *completeness.*

S. T. COLERIDGE
Table Talk (1836)

JOHN MILTON

1 6 0 8 — 1 6 7 4

YONDER NETHER WORLD

This most afflicts me, that departing hence,
As from his face I shall be hid, deprivd
His blessed count'nance; here I could frequent,
With worship, place by place where he voutsaf'd
Presence Divine, and to my Sons relate;
On this Mount he appeerd, under this Tree
Stood visible, among these Pines his voice
I heard, here with him at this Fountain talk'd:
So many grateful Altars I would reare
Of grassie Terfe, and pile up every Stone
Of lustre from the brook, in memorie,
Or monument to Ages, and thereon
Offer sweet smelling Gumms and Fruits and Flours:
In yonder nether World where shall I seek
His bright appearances, or footstep trace?
For though I fled him angrie, yet recall'd
To life prolongd and promisd Race, I now
Gladly behold though but his utmost skirts
Of glory, and farr off his steps adore.

Paradise Lost (1667), xi

Nothing can be conceived more sublime and poetical.

JOSEPH ADDISON
The Spectator (April 26, 1712)

JOHN MILTON

1 6 0 8 — 1 6 7 4

CALM AND SINLESS PEACE

And either Tropic now
'Gan thunder, and both ends of Heav'n, the Clouds
From many a horrid rift abortive pour'd
Fierce rain with lightning mixt, water with fire
In ruine reconcil'd: nor slept the winds

Within thir stony caves, but rush'd abroad
From the four hinges of the world, and fell
On the vext Wilderness, whose tallest Pines,
Though rooted deep as high, and sturdiest Oaks
Bow'd their Stiff necks, loaden with stormy blasts,
Or torn up sheer: ill wast thou shrouded then,
O patient Son of God, yet only stoodst
Unshaken; nor yet staid the terror there,
Infernal Ghosts, and Hellish Furies, round
Environ'd thee, some howl'd, some yell'd, some shriek'd,
Some bent at thee their fiery darts, while thou
Sat'st unappall'd in calm and sinless peace.

                            Paradise Regain'd (1671), iv

No such poetry as this has been written since, and little at any time before.

WALTER SAVAGE LANDOR
The Poems of Catullus (1842)

JOHN MILTON

1 6 0 8 — 1 6 7 4

WITH THEM THAT REST

I feel my genial spirits droop,
My hopes all flat, nature within me seems
In all her functions weary of herself;
My race of glory run, and race of shame,
And I shall shortly be with them that rest.

                            Samson Agonistes (1671)

The noblest lines in English poetry. . . . As for ourselves, we will go on wondering whether anything finer than those verses was ever written by Milton or any other mortal man.

WILLIAM PATON KER
The Art of Poetry (1923)

JOHN MILTON

1 6 0 8 — 1 6 7 4

THE ATHENIAN WALLS

To save th' *Athenian* Walls from ruine bare.

Sonnet (1645)

Assonance of long vowels makes [it] .... perhaps the most beautiful line in the language.

HERBERT J. C. GRIERSON and J. C. SMITH
A Critical History of English Poetry (1944)

JOHN MILTON

1 6 0 8 — 1 6 7 4

ON HIS BLINDNESS

When I consider how my light is spent,
  E're half my days, in this dark world and wide,
  And that one Talent which is death to hide,
  Lodg'd with me useless, though my Soul more bent
To serve therewith my Maker, and present
  My true account, least he returning chide,
  Doth God exact day-labour, light deny'd,
  I fondly ask; But patience to prevent
That murmur, soon replies, God doth not need
  Either man's work or his own gifts, who best
  Bear his milde yoak, they serve him best, his State
Is Kingly. Thousands at his bidding speed
  And post o're Land and Ocean without rest:
  They also serve who only stand and waite.

(1673)

Those few supreme words.

ALGERNON CHARLES SWINBURNE
Essays and Studies (1875)

JOHN MILTON

1 6 0 8 — 1 6 7 4

TWO SONNETS

Daughter to that good Earl, once President
  Of *Englands* Counsel, and her Treasury,
  Who liv'd in both, unstain'd with gold or fee,
  And left them both, more in himself content,
Till the sad breaking of that Parlament
  Broke him, as that dishonest victory
  At *Chæronéa*, fatal to liberty
  Kil'd with report that Old man eloquent,
Though later born, then to have known the dayes
  Wherin your Father flourisht, yet by you
  Madam, me thinks I see him living yet;
So well your words his noble vertues praise,
  That all both judge you to relate them true,
  And to possess them, Honour'd *Margaret*.

(1645)

Lawrence of vertuous Father vertuous Son,
  Now that the Fields are dank, and ways are mire,
  Where shall we sometimes meet, and by the fire
  Help wast a sullen day; what may be won
From the hard Season gaining: time will run
  On smoother, till *Favonius* re-inspire
  The frozen earth; and cloth in fresh attire
  The Lillie and Rose, that neither sow'd nor spun.
What neat repast shall feast us, light and choice,
  Of Attick tast, with Wine, whence we may rise
  To hear the Lute well toucht, or artfull voice
Warble immortal Notes and *Tuskan* Ayre?
  He who of those delights can judge, And spare
  To interpose them oft, is not unwise.

(1673)

*In easy majesty and severe beauty, unequalled by any other compositions
of the kind.*

ALEXANDER DYCE
Specimens of English Sonnets (1833)

JOHN MILTON

1 6 0 8 — 1 6 7 4

THE FIFTH ODE OF *HORACE*. LIB. I

Quis multa gracilis te puer in Rosa, *Rendred almost word for word
without Rhyme according to the Latin Measure, as near as the
Language will permit.*

Horatius ex Pyrrhae illecebris tanquam e naufragio enataverat, cujus
amore irretitos affirmat esse miseros.

> What slender Youth bedew'd with liquid odours
> Courts thee on Roses in some pleasant Cave,
> > *Pyrrha* for whom bindst thou
> > In wreaths thy golden Hair,
> Plain in thy neatness; O how oft shall he
> On Faith and changed Gods complain: and Seas
> > Rough with black winds and storms
> > Unwonted shall admire:
> Who now enjoyes thee credulous, all Gold,
> Who alwayes vacant, always amiable
> > Hopes thee; of flattering gales
> > Unmindfull. Hapless they
> To whom thou untry'd seem'st fair. Me in my vow'd
> Picture the sacred wall declares t' have hung
> > My dank and dropping weeds
> > To the stern God of Sea.

> Quis multa gracilis te puer in rosa
> perfusus liquidis urget odoribus
> > grato, Pyrrha, sub antro?
> > cui flavam religas comam,

> simplex munditiis? heu quotiens fidem
> mutatosque deos flebit et aspera
> > nigris aequora ventis
> > emirabitur insolens,

> qui nunc te fruitur credulus aurea,
> qui semper vacuam, semper amabilem
> > sperat, nescius aurae
> > fallacis. miseri, quibus

intemptata nites. me tabula sacer
votiva paries indicat uvida
    suspendisse potenti
      vestimenta maris deo.

Horace
Odes, i, 5

One of the most exquisite lyrics in English.

CYRIL CONNOLLY
The Condemned Playground (1946)

J O H N   M I L T O N

1 6 0 8 — 1 6 7 4

MACBETH

Imaginary Works (n. d.)

*The most fascinating poem—certainly, if play it were, the most fascina-
ting play—ever unwritten.*

ARTHUR QUILLER-COUCH
Poetry (1914)

SIR JOHN SUCKLING

1 6 0 9 — 1 6 4 2

A BALLAD OF A WEDDING

I tell thee, DICK! where I have been,
Where I the rarest things have seen,
   O, things beyond compare!
Such sights again can not be found
In any place on English ground,
   Be it at wake or fair.

At Charing-Cross, hard by the way
Where we, thou know'st, do sell our hay,
   There is a House with stairs;
And there did I see coming down
Such volk as are not in our town,
   Vorty at least, in pairs.

Amongst the rest One pest'lent fine,
His beard no bigger though than thine,
   Walk'd on before the best:
Our Landlord looks like nothing to him;
The King, God bless him! 'twould undo him
   Should he go still so dress'd.

At course-a-park, without all doubt,
He should have first been taken out
   By all the maids i' the town,
Though lusty Roger there had been,
Or little George upon the Green,
   Or Vincent of the Crown.

But wot you what? the Youth was going
To make an end of all his wooing;
   The parson for him stay'd:
Yet by his leave, for all his haste,
He did not so much wish all past,
   Perchance, as did the Maid.

The Maid,—and thereby hangs a tale,
For such a Maid no Widson ale
   Could ever yet produce:
No grape that's kindly ripe could be
So round, so plump, so soft as she,
   Nor half so full of juice.

Her finger was so small the ring
Would not stay on which he did bring,
   It was too wide a peck;
And to say truth, for out it must,
It look'd like the great collar, just,
   About our young colt's neck.

Her feet beneath her petticoat
Like little mice stole in and out,
   As if they fear'd the light;
But, Dick! she dances such a way,
No sun upon an Easter day
   Is half so fine a sight.

He would have kiss'd her once or twice,
But she would not, she was so nice,
   She would not do 't in sight;
And then she look'd as who would say
I will do what I list to-day,
   And you shall do 't at night.

Her cheeks so rare a white was on,
No daisy makes comparison,—
   Who sees them is undone:
For streaks of red were mingled there
Such as are on a Katherine pear,
   The side that's next the sun.

Her lips were red, and one was thin,
Compared to that was next her chin,—
   Some bee had stung it newly:
But, Dick! her eyes so guard her face,
I durst no more upon them gaze
   Than on the sun in Jùly.

Her mouth so small, when she does speak,
Thou 'dst swear her teeth her words did break,
   That they might passage get;
But she so handled still the matter,
They came as good as ours, or better,
   And are not spent a whit.

If wishing should be any sin
The parson himself had guilty been,
   She look'd that day so purely;
And did the Youth so oft the feat
At night as some did in conceit,
   It would have spoil'd him surely.

Passion o' me! how I run on:
There's that that would be thought upon,
  I trow, besides the Bride:
The business of the kitchen's great,
For it is fit that men should eat;
  Nor was it there denied.

Just in the nick the cook knock'd thrice,
And all the waiters in a trice
  His summons did obey;
Each serving-man with dish in hand
March'd boldly up, like our train'd band,
  Presented, and away.

When all the meat was on the table
What man of knife, or teeth, was able
  To stay to be intreated?
And this the very reason was
Before the parson could say grace
  The company was seated.

Now hats fly off, and youths carouse;
Healths first go round, and then the house,—
  The Bride's came thick and thick;
And when 'twas named another's health,
Perhaps he made it her's by stealth:
  And who could help it? Dick!

O' the sudden up they rise and dance;
Then sit again, and sigh, and glance;
  Then dance again and kiss:
Thus several ways the time did pass,
Whilst every woman wish'd her place,
  And every man wish'd his.

By this time all were stolen aside
To counsel and undress the Bride,
  But that he must not know:
But it was thought he guess'd her mind,
And did not mean to stay behind
  Above an hour or so.

When in he came, Dick! there she lay
Like new-fall'n snow melting away,—
  'Twas time, I trow, to part:
Kisses were now the only stay,
Which soon she gave, as who would say
  God b' w' y'! with all my heart.

But just as heavens would have to cross it
In came the bridemaids with the posset;
   The Bridegroom eat in spite:
For had he left the women to 't,
It would have cost two hours to do 't,
   Which were too much that night.

At length the candle 's out, and now
All that they had not done they do:
   What that is who can tell?
But I believe it was no more
Than thou and I have done before
   With Bridget and with Nell.

Twenty-two incomparable verses.

EDMUND GOSSE
in Ward's The English Poets (1880)

THE BIBLE, AUTHORIZED VERSION

1 6 1 1

VISIONS OF THE NIGHT

In thoughts from the visions of the night, when deepe sleepe falleth
on men:
   Feare came vpon me, and trembling, which made all my bones to
shake.
   Then a spirit passed before my face: the haire of my flesh stood vp.
   It stood still, but I could not discerne the forme thereof: an image
was before mine eyes, *there was* silence, and I heard a voyce, *saying,*
   Shall mortall man be more iust then God?

Job, iv, 13–17

Amazingly sublime.

EDMUND BURKE
On the Sublime and Beautiful (1756)

A PSALME OF ASAPH

The mightie God, *euen* the LORD hath spoken, and called the earth from the rising of the sunne, vnto the going downe thereof.

Out of Sion the perfection of beautie, God hath shined.

Our God shall come, and shall not keepe silence: a fire shall deuoure before him, and it shalbe very tempestuous round about him.

He shall call to the heauens from aboue, and to the earth, that hee may iudge his people.

Gather my Saints together vnto mee: those that haue made a couenant with me, by sacrifice.

And the heauens shall declare his righteousnes; for God *is* iudge himselfe. Selah.

Heare, O my people, and I will speake, O Israel, and I will testifie against thee; I *am* God, *euen* thy God.

I will not reproue thee for thy sacrifices, or thy burnt offerings, *to haue bene* continually before me.

I will take no bullocke out of thy house, *nor* hee goates out of thy folds.

For euery beast of the forrest *is* mine, *and* the cattell vpon a thousand hilles.

I know all the foules of the mountaines: and the wild beasts of the field *are* mine.

If I were hungry, I would not tell thee, for the world *is* mine, and the fulnesse thereof.

Will I eate the flesh of bulles, or drinke the blood of goats?

Offer vnto God thankesgiuing, and pay thy vowes vnto the most high.

And call vpon mee in the day of trouble; I will deliuer thee, and thou shalt glorifie me.

But vnto the wicked God saith, What hast thou to doe, to declare my Statutes, or that thou shouldest take my Couenant in thy mouth?

Seeing thou hatest instruction, and casteth my words behinde thee.

When thou sawest a thiefe, then thou consentedst with him, and hast bene partaker with adulterers.

Thou giuest thy mouth to euill, and thy tongue frameth deceit.

Thou sittest *and* speakest against thy brother; thou slanderest thine owne mothers sonne.

These things hast thou done, and I kept silence: thou thoughtest that I was altogether such a one as thy selfe: *but* I will reproue thee, and set *them* in order before thine eyes.

Now consider this, ye that forget God, lest I teare *you* in pieces, and *there be* none to deliuer.

Who so offereth praise, glorifieth me: and to him that ordereth *his* conuersation *aright,* will I shew the saluation of God.

Psalms, l

Comfort ye, comfort ye my people, sayth your God.

Speake ye comfortably to Jerusalem, and cry vnto her, that her warre-fare is accomplished, that her iniquitie is pardoned: for shee hath receiued of the LORDS hand double for all her sinnes.

The voyce of him that cryeth in the wildernesse, Prepare yee the way of the LORD, make straight in the desert a high way for our God.

Euery valley shalbe exalted, and euery mountaine and hill shalbe made low: and the crooked shall be made straight, and the rough places plaine.

And the glory of the LORD shall be reuealed, and all flesh shall see *it* together: for the mouth of the LORD hath spoken *it.*

The voyce sayd; Cry. And hee sayd; What shall I cry? All flesh *is* grasse, and all the goodlinesse thereof *is* as the flowre of the field.

The grass withereth, the flowre fadeth; because the spirit of the LORD bloweth vpon it: surely the people *is* grasse.

The grasse withereth, the flowre fadeth: but the word of our God shall stand for euer.

O Zion, that bringest good tydings, get thee vp into the high moun-taine: O Jerusalem, that bringest good tidings, lift vp thy voyce with strength, lift it vp, be not afraid: say vnto the cities of Judah; Behold your God.

Behold, the Lord GOD will come with strong *hand,* and his arme shall rule for him: behold, his reward *is* with him, and his worke before him.

He shall feede his flocke like a shepheard: he shall gather the lambes with his arme, and carie *them* in his bosome, *and* shall gently lead those that are with yoong.

Who hath measured the waters in the hollow of his hand; and meted out heauen with the spanne, and comprehended the dust of the earth in a measure, and weighed the mountaines in scales, and the hilles in a balance?

Who hath directed the spirit of the LORD, or, being his counseller, hath taught him?

With whom tooke he counsell, and *who* instructed him, and taught him in the path of iudgement; and taught him knowledge, and shewed to him the way of vnderstanding?

Behold, the nations *are* as a drop of a bucket, and are counted as the small dust of the balance: behold, hee taketh vp the yles as a very litle thing.

And Lebanon *is* not sufficient to burne, nor the beasts thereof sufficient for a burnt offring.

All nations before him *are* as nothing, and they are counted to him lesse then nothing, and vanitie.

To whom then will ye liken God? or what likenesse will ye compare vnto him?

The workeman melteth a grauen image, and the goldsmith spreadeth it ouer with golde, and casteth siluer chaines.

He that *is* so impouerished that he hath no oblation, chooseth a tree *that* will not rot; he seeketh vnto him a cunning workeman, to prepare a grauen image *that* shall not be mooued.

Haue yee not knowen? haue yee not heard? hath it not beene tolde you from the beginning? haue yee not vnderstood from the foundations of the earth?

It is he that sitteth vpon the circle of the earth, and the inhabitants thereof *are* as grashoppers; that stretcheth out the heauens as a curtaine, and spreadeth them out as a tent to dwel in:

That bringeth the princes to nothing; hee maketh the Judges of the earth as vanitie.

Yea they shal not be planted, yea they shall not be sowen, yea their stocke shall not take roote in the earth: and he shall also blow vpon them, & they shall wither, and the whirlewinde shall take them away as stubble.

To whom then will ye liken me, or shal I be equall, saith the Holy One?

Lift vp your eyes on high, and behold who hath created these things, that bringeth out their host by number: he calleth them all by names, by the greatnesse of his might, for that hee *is* strong in power, not one faileth.

Why sayest thou, O Jacob, and speakest O Israel, My way is hid from the LORD, and my iudgement is passed ouer from my God?

Hast thou not knowen? hast thou not heard, *that* the euerlasting God, the LORD, the Creatour of the ends of the earth, fainteth not, neither is wearie? there is no searching of his vnderstanding.

He giueth power to the faint, and to them that haue no might, he increaseth strength.

Euen the youths shall faint, and be weary, and the yong men shall vtterly fall.

But they that waite vpon the LORD, shall renew *their* strength: they shall mount vp with wings as Eagles, they shal runne and not be weary, *and* they shall walke, and not faint.

Isaiah, xl

Never was any Greek or Latin ode able to attain the grandeur of the Psalms. For example, that which commences thus "The mighty God, even the Lord hath spoken, and called the earth" surpasses all human

734

imagination. Neither Homer nor any other poet has equalled Isaiah in depicting the majesty of God.

FRANÇOIS DE SALIGNAC FÉNELON
Dialogues sur l'éloquence (1718)

THE BIBLE, AUTHORIZED VERSION

1 6 1 1

DAUID PRAISETH GOD FOR HIS MANIFOLD AND MARUEILOUS BLESSINGS

To the chiefe musicion, *a psalme* of Dauid, the seruant of the LORD, who spake vnto the LORD the words of this song, in the day *that* the LORD deliuered him from the hand of all his enemies, and from the hand of Saul: And he said,

I will loue thee, O LORD, my strength.

The LORD *is* my rocke, and my fortresse, and my deliuerer: my God, my strength in whome I will trust, my buckler, and the horne of my salu-ation, *and* my high tower.

I will call vpon the LORD, who is worthy to be praised: so shall I be saued from mine enemies.

The sorrowes of death compassed me, and the floods of vngodly men made me afraid.

The sorrowes of hell compassed me about: the snares of death preuented me.

In my distresse I called vpon the LORD, and cryed vnto my God: hee heard my voyce out of his temple, and my crie came before him, *euen* into his eares.

Then the earth shooke and trembled; the foundations also of the hilles mooued and were shaken, because hee was wroth.

There went vp a smoke out of his nostrils, and fire out of his mouth deuoured, coales were kindled by it.

He bowed the heauens also, and came downe: and darkenesse *was* vnder his feet.

And he rode vpon a Cherub, and did flie: yea he did flie vpon the wings of the wind.

He made darkenes his secret place: his pauilion round about him, *were* darke waters, *and* thicke cloudes of the skies.

At the brightnes *that was* before him his thicke clouds passed, haile *stones* and coales of fire.

The LORD also thundered in the heauens, and the highest gaue his voyce; haile stones and coales of fire.

Yea, he sent out his arrowes, and scattered them; and he shot out lightnings, and discomfited them.

Then the chanels of waters were seene, and the foundations of the world were discouered: at thy rebuke, O LORD, at the blast of the breath of thy nostrils.

He sent from aboue, he tooke me, he drew me out of many waters.

He deliuered me from my strong enemie, and from them which hated me: for they were too strong for me.

They preuented me in the day of my calamitie: but the LORD was my stay.

He brought me forth also into a large place: he deliuered me, because he delighted in me.

The LORD rewarded me according to my righteousnesse, according to the cleannesse of my hands hath hee recompensed me.

For I haue kept the wayes of the LORD, and haue not wickedly departed from my God.

For all his iudgements *were* before me, and I did not put away his statutes from me.

I was also vpright before him: and I kept my selfe from mine iniquity.

Therefore hath the LORD recompensed me according to my righteousnesse, according to the cleannesse of my hands in his eye-sight.

With the mercifull thou wilt shew thy selfe mercifull, with an vpright man thou wilt shew thy selfe vpright.

With the pure thou wilt shewe thy selfe pure, and with the froward thou wilt shew thy selfe froward.

For thou wilt saue the afflicted people: but wilt bring downe high lookes.

For thou wilt light my candle: the LORD my God will enlighten my darkenesse.

For by thee I haue run through a troupe; and by my God haue I leaped ouer a wall.

As for God, his way is perfect: the word of the LORD is tried: he is a buckler to all those that trust in him.

For who *is* God saue the LORD? or who *is* a rocke saue our God?

It is God that girdeth mee with strength, and maketh my way perfect.

Hee maketh my feete like hindes *feete*, and setteth me vpon my high places.

He teacheth my hands to warre, so that a bow of steele is broken by mine armes.

Thou hast also giuen me the shield of thy saluation: and thy right hand hath holden me vp, and thy gentlenesse hath made me great.

Thou hast enlarged my steppes vnder me; that my feete did not slippe.

I haue pursued mine enemies, and ouertaken them: neither did I turne againe till they were consumed.

I haue wounded them that they were not able to rise: they are fallen vnder my feete.

For thou hast girded mee with strength vnto the battell: thou hast subdued vnder me, those that rose vp against me.

Thou hast also giuen mee the neckes of mine enemies: that I might destroy them that hate me.

They cried, but there was none to saue *them: euen* vnto the LORD, but he answered them not.

Then did I beate them small as the dust before the winde: I did cast them out, as the dirt in the streetes.

Thou hast deliuered me from the striuings of the people, *and* thou hast made mee the head of the heathen: a people *whom* I haue not knowen, shall serue me.

As soone as they heare of mee, they shall obey me: the strangers shall submit themselues vnto me.

The strangers shall fade away, and be afraid out of their close places.

The LORD liueth, and blessed *be* my rocke: and let the God of my saluation be exalted.

It is God that auengeth mee, and subdueth the people vnder me.

He deliuereth me from mine enemies: yea thou liftest mee vp aboue those that rise vp against me; thou hast deliuered me from the violent man.

Therefore will I giue thankes vnto thee, (O LORD) among the heathen: and sing prayses vnto thy name.

Great deliuerance giueth he to his King: and sheweth mercy to his Annointed, to Dauid, and to his seede for euermore.

Psalms, xviii

We must concede that this sublimity is as far above all other sublimity as the spirit of God is above the mind of man. We see here the conception of grandeur in its essence, the rest is only a shadow, as created intelligence is only a feeble emanation of creative intelligence, as fiction, when it is beautiful, is only the shadow of truth, and draws all its merit from a basic resemblance.

JEAN FRANÇOIS DE LA HARPE
Le Psautier français (1797–8)

A VINE OUT OF EGYPT

Thou hast brought a vine out of Egypt: thou hast cast out the heathen, and planted it.

Thou preparedst *roome* before it: and didst cause it to take deepe root, and it filled the land.

The hilles were couered with the shadow of it, and the boughs thereof were like the goodly cedars.

She sent out her boughs vnto the Sea: and her branches vnto the riuer.

Why hast thou *then* broken downe her hedges: so that all they which passe by the way, doe plucke her?

The boare out of the wood doth waste it: and the wild beast of the field doth deuoure it.

Returne, we beseech thee, O God of hosts: looke downe from heauen, and behold, and visit this vine:

And the vineyard which thy right hand hath planted: and the branch *that* thou madest strong for thy selfe.

Psalms, lxxx, 8–15

A finer or more correct allegory is not to be found.

HENRY HOME OF KAMES
Elements of Criticism (1762)

THE BIBLE, AUTHORIZED VERSION

1 6 1 1

LOVE

Set mee as a seale vpon thine heart, as a seale vpon thine arme: for loue *is* strong as death, iealousie *is* cruel as the graue: the coales thereof *are* coales of fire, *which hath* a most vehement flame.

Many waters cannot quench loue, neither can the floods drowne it: if a man would giue all the substance of his house for loue, it would vtterly be contemned.

Song of Solomon, viii, 6–7

Now the requirement of a perfect prose rhythm is that, while it admits of indication by quantity-marks, and even by divisions into feet, the simplicity and equivalence of feet within the clause answering to the line are absent, and the exact correspondence of clause for clause, that is to say, of line for line, is absent also, and still more necessarily absent. Let us take an example. I know no more perfect example of English prose rhythm than the famous verses of the last chapter of the Canticles in the Authorized Version: I am not certain that I know any so perfect. Here they are arranged for the purpose of exhibition in clause-lines, quantified and divided into feet.

Sĕt mĕ | ăs ă seāl | ŭpŏn thĭne heārt | ăs ă seāl | ŭpŏn thĭne ārm |
Fŏr lōve | ĭs strōng | ăs deāth | jeālŏusў | ĭs cruēl | ăs thĕ grāve |
Thĕ coāls thĕreŏf | āre coāls | ŏf fĭrĕ | whĭch hāth | ă mŏst vē | hĕmĕnt
    flāme |
Mănў wătĕrs | cānnŏt quēnch lōve | neīthĕr | căn thĕ floōds | drōwn ĭt |
If ă mān | shoŭld gīve | ăll thĕ sūb | stānce | ŏf hĭs hoūse | fŏr lōve | ĭt
    shŏuld ūt | tĕrlў bĕ cŏntēmned. |

I by no means give the quantification of this, or the distribution into lines and feet as final or impeccable, though I think it is, on the whole— as a good elocutionist would read the passage—accurate enough. But the disposition will, I think, be sufficient to convince anyone who has an ear and a slight acquaintance with RES METRICA, *that here is a system of rhythm irreducible to poetic form. The movement of the whole is perfectly harmonious, exquisitely modulated, finally complete. But it is the harmony of perfectly modulated speech, not of song; harmony, in short, but not melody, divisible into clauses, but not into bars or staves, having parts which continue each other, but do not correspond to each other.*

GEORGE SAINTSBURY
Specimens of English Prose Style (1886)

THE BIBLE, AUTHORIZED VERSION

1 6 1 1

ZION REDEEMED

Arise, shine, for thy light is come, and the glory of the LORD is risen vpon thee.

   For behold, the darknesse shall couer the earth, and grosse darknesse the people: but the LORD shall arise vpon thee, and his glory shall be seene vpon thee. And the Gentiles shall come to thy light, and kings to the brightnesse of thy rising.

Lift vp thine eyes round about, and see: all they gather themselues together, they come to thee: thy sonnes shall come from farre, and thy daughters shalbe nourced at *thy* side.

Then thou shalt see, and flow together, and thine heart shall feare and be inlarged, because the abundance of the Sea shalbe conuerted vnto thee, the forces of the Gentiles shall come vnto thee.

The multitude of camels shall couer thee, the dromedaries of Midian and Ephah: all they from Sheba shall come: they shal bring gold and incense, and they shall shew forth the praises of the LORD.

All the flockes of Kedar shall be gathered together vnto thee, the rams of Nebaioth shall minister vnto thee: they shall come vp with acceptance on mine altar, and I wil glorifie the house of my glory.

Who *are* these that flie as a cloude, and as the doues to their windowes? Surely the yles shall wait for me, and the ships of Tarshish first, to bring thy sonnes from farre, their siluer and their gold with them, vnto the Name of the LORD thy God, and to the Holy One of Israel, because he hath glorified thee.

And the sonnes of strangers shall build vp thy walles, and their kings shal minister vnto thee: for in my wrath I smote thee, but in my fauour haue I had mercie on thee.

Therefore thy gates shal be open continually, they shall not bee shut day nor night, that *men* may bring vnto thee the forces of the Gentiles, and that their kings may be brought.

For the nation and kingdome that will not serue thee, shall perish, yea those nations shall be vtterly wasted.

The glory of Lebanon shal come vnto thee, the Firre tree, the Pine tree, and the Boxe together, to beautifie the place of my Sanctuarie, and I will make the place of my feete glorious.

The sonnes also of them that afflicted thee, shall come bending vnto thee: and all they that despised thee shal bow themselues downe at the soles of thy feet, and they shall call thee the citie of the LORD, the Zion of the Holy One of Israel.

Whereas thou hast bene forsaken and hated, so that no man went thorow *thee*, I will make thee an eternall excellencie, a ioy of many generations.

Thou shalt also sucke the milke of the Gentiles, and shalt sucke the brest of kings, and thou shalt know that I the LORD *am* thy Sauiour and thy Redeemer, the mightie One of Iacob.

For brasse I will bring gold, and for yron I will bring siluer, and for wood brasse, and for stones yron: I will also make thy officers peace, and thine exactours righteousnesse.

Violence shall no more be heard in thy land, wasting nor destruction within thy borders, but thou shalt call thy walles saluation, and thy gates praise.

The Sunne shall be no more thy light by day, neither for brightnesse shall the moone giue light vnto thee: but the LORD shall be vnto thee an euerlasting light, & thy God thy glory.

Thy Sunne shall no more goe downe, neither shall thy moone withdraw it selfe: for the LORD shall bee thine euerlasting light, and the dayes of thy mourning shall be ended.

Thy people also *shall be* all righteous: they shal inherit the land for euer, the branch of my planting, the worke of my hands, that I may be glorified.

A litle one shall become a thousand, and a small one a strong nation: I the LORD will hasten it in his time.

Isaiah, lx

One of the highest points of English prose is probably reached in the Authorised Version of the sixtieth chapter of ISAIAH. *So utterly magnificent is the rendering that even those dolefullest of creatures—the very Ziim and Ochim and Iim of the fauna of our literature—the Revisers of 1870–1885, hardly dared to touch it at all. To compare it with the same passage in other languages is a liberal education in despising and discarding the idle predominance of "the subject." The subject is the same in all, and the magnificence of the imagery can hardly be obscured by any. Of the Hebrew I cannot unfortunately speak, for at the time when I knew a very little Hebrew I knew nothing about literary criticism; and now, when I know perhaps a little about literary criticism, I have entirely lost my Hebrew. But I can read it with some critical competence in Greek and in Latin, in French and in German; and I can form some idea of what its rhetorical value is in Italian and in Spanish. That any one of the modern languages (even Luther's German) can vie with ours I can hardly imagine any one, who can appreciate both the sound and the meaning of English, maintaining for a moment. With the Septuagint and the Vulgate it is different, for the Greek of the one has not quite lost the glory of the most glorious of all languages, and has in places even acquired a certain additional uncanny witchery from its eastern associations; while as for the Vulgate Latin "there is no mistake about* THAT." *But we can meet and beat them both.*

GEORGE SAINTSBURY
A History of English Prose Rhythm (1912)

THE BIBLE, AUTHORIZED VERSION

1 6 1 1

UNTO THE DAY

Sufficient vnto the day is the euill thereof.

Matthew, vi, 34

The most remarkable, the most self-sustained and powerful sentence.

BENJAMIN DISRAELI

Quoted, Austin Dobson, A Bookman's Budget (1917)

RICHARD CRASHAW

1 6 1 3 ? — 1 6 4 9

A HYMN TO THE NAME AND HONOR OF THE ADMIRABLE SAINTE TERESA

Loue, thou art Absolute sole lord
Of Life & Death. To proue the word,
Wee'l now appeal to none of all
Those thy old Souldiers, Great & tall,
Ripe Men of Martyrdom, that could reach down
With strong armes, their triumphant crown;
Such as could with lusty breath
Speak lowd into the face of death
Their Great Lord's glorious name, to none
Of those whose spatious Bosomes spread a throne
For Love at larg to fill: spare blood & sweat;
And see him take a priuate seat,
Making his mansion in the mild
And milky soul of a soft child.
　　Scarse has she learn't to lisp the name
Of Martyr; yet she thinks it shame
Life should so long play with that breath
Which spent can buy so braue a death.
She neuer vndertook to know
What death with loue should haue to doe;
Nor has she e're yet vnderstood
Why to show loue, she should shed blood

Yet though she cannot tell you why,
She can Love, & she can Dy.

Scarse has she Blood enough to make
A guilty sword blush for her sake;
Yet has she'a Heart dares hope to proue
How much lesse strong is Death then Loue.

Be loue but there; let poor six yeares
Be pos'd with the maturest Feares
Man trembles at, you straight shall find
Love knowes no nonage, nor the Mind.
'Tis Love, not Yeares or Limbs that can
Make the Martyr, or the man.

Love touch't her Heart, & lo it beates
High, & burnes with such braue heates;
Such thirsts to dy, as dares drink vp,
A thousand cold deaths in one cup.
Good reason. For she breathes All fire.
Her weake brest heaues with strong desire
Of what she may with fruitles wishes
Seek for amongst her Mother's kisses.

Since 'tis not to be had at home
She'l trauail to a Martyrdom.
No home for hers confesses she
But where she may a Martyr be.

Sh'el to the Moores; And trade with them,
For this vnualued Diadem.
She'l offer them her dearest Breath,
With Christ's Name in't, in change for death.
Sh'el bargain with them; & will giue
Them God; teach them how to liue
In him: or, if they this deny,
For him she'l teach them how to Dy.
So shall she leaue amongst them sown
Her Lord's Blood; or at lest her own.

Farewel then, all the world! Adieu.
Teresa is no more for you.
Farewell, all pleasures, sports, & ioyes,
(Neuer till now esteemed toyes)
Farewell what ever deare may bee,
Mother's armes or Father's knee
Farewell house, & farewell home!
She's for the Moores, & Martyrdom.

Sweet, not so fast! lo thy fair Spouse
Whom thou seekst with so swift vowes,
Calls thee back, & bidds thee come

743

T'embrace a milder MARTYRDOM.

    Blest powres forbid, Thy tender life
Should bleed vpon a barborous knife;
Or some base hand haue power to race
Thy Brest's chast cabinet, & vncase
A soul kept there so sweet, ô no;
Wise heaun will neuer haue it so
THOV art loue's victime; & must dy
A death more mysticall & high.
Into loue's armes thou shalt let fall
A still-suruiuing funerall.
His is the DART must make the DEATH
Whose stroke shall tast thy hallow'd breath;
A Dart thrice dip't in that rich flame
Which writes thy spouse's radiant Name
Vpon the roof of Heau'n; where ay
It shines, & with a soueraign ray
Beates bright vpon the burning faces
Of soules which in that name's sweet graces
Find euerlasting smiles. So rare,
So spirituall, pure, & fair
Must be th'immortall instrument
Vpon whose choice point shall be sent
A life so lou'd; And that there be
Fitt executioners for Thee,
The fair'st & first-born sons of fire
Blest SERAPHIM, shall leaue their quire
And turn loue's souldiers, vpon THEE
To exercise their archerie.
    O how oft shalt thou complain
Of a sweet & subtle PAIN.
Of intolerable IOYES;
Of a DEATH, in which who dyes
Loues his death, and dyes again.
And would for euer so be slain.
And liues, & dyes; and knowes not why
To liue, But that he thus may neuer leaue to DY.
    How kindly will thy gentle HEART
Kisse the sweetly-killing DART!
And close in his embraces keep
Those delicious Wounds, that weep
Balsom to heal themselues with. Thus
When These thy DEATHS, so numerous,
Shall all at last dy into one,
And melt thy Soul's sweet mansion;

Like a soft lump of incense, hasted
By too hott a fire, & wasted
Into perfuming clouds, so fast
Shalt thou exhale to Heaun at last
In a resoluing SIGH, and then
O what? Ask not the Tongues of men.
Angells cannot tell, suffice,
Thy selfe shall feel thine own full ioyes
And hold them fast for euer. There
So soon as thou shalt first appear,
The MOON of maiden starrs, thy white
MISTRESSE, attended by such bright
Soules as thy shining self, shall come
And in her first rankes make thee room;
Where 'mongst her snowy family
Immortall wellcomes wait for thee.

O what delight, when reueal'd LIFE shall stand
And teach thy lipps heau'n with his hand;
On which thou now maist to thy wishes
Heap vp thy consecrated kisses.
What ioyes shall seize thy soul, when she
Bending her blessed eyes on thee
(Those second Smiles of Heau'n) shall dart
Her mild rayes through thy melting heart!

Angels, thy old freinds, there shall greet thee
Glad at their own home now to meet thee.

All thy good WORKES which went before
And waited for thee, at the door,
Shall own thee there; and all in one
Weaue a constellation
Of CROWNS, with which the KING thy spouse
Shall build vp thy triumphant browes.

All thy old woes shall now smile on thee
And thy paines sitt bright vpon thee
All thy sorrows here shall shine,
All thy SVFFRINGS be diuine.
TEARES shall take comfort, & turn gemms
And WRONGS repent to Diademms.
Eu'n thy DEATHS shall liue; & new
Dresse the soul that erst they slew.
Thy wounds shall blush to such bright scarres
As keep account of the LAMB'S warres.

Those rare WORKES where thou shalt leaue writt,
Loue's noble history, with witt

Taught thee by none but him, while here
They feed our soules, shall cloth THINE there.
Each heaunly word by whose hid flame
Our hard Hearts shall strike fire, the same
Shall flourish on thy browes. & be
Both fire to vs & flame to thee;
Whose light shall liue bright in thy FACE
By glory, in our hearts by grace.
   Thou shalt look round about, & see
Thousands of crown'd Soules throng to be
Themselues thy crown. Sons of thy vowes
The virgin-births with which thy soueraign spouse
Made fruitfull thy fair soul, goe now
And with them all about thee bow
To Him, put on (hee'l say) put on
(My rosy loue) That thy rich zone
Sparkling with the sacred flames
Of thousand soules, whose happy names
Heau'n keeps vpon thy score. (Thy bright
Life brought them first to kisse the light
That kindled them to starrs.) and so
Thou with the LAMB, thy lord, shalt goe;
And whereso'ere he setts his white
Stepps, walk with HIM those wayes of light
Which who in death would liue to see,
Must learn in life to dy like thee.

Carmen Deo Nostro (1652)

The most unerring explosion of passionate feeling to be found in English, perhaps in all poetry.

GEORGE SAINTSBURY
A Short History of English Literature (1898)

RICHARD CRASHAW

1 6 1 3 ? — 1 6 4 9

THE FLAMING HEART

Liue in these conquering leaues; liue all the same;
And walk through all tongues one triumphant FLAME
Liue here, great HEART; & loue and dy & kill;
And bleed & wound; and yeild & conquer still.

Let this immortall life wherere it comes
Walk in a crowd of loues & MARTYRDOMES.
Let mystick DEATHS wait on't; & wise soules be
The loue-slain wittnesses of this life of thee.
O sweet incendiary! shew here thy art,
Vpon this carcasse of a hard, cold, hart,
Let all thy scatter'd shafts of light, that play
Among the leaues of thy larg Books of day,
Combin'd against this BREST at once break in
And take away from me my self & sin,
This gratious Robbery shall thy bounty be;
And my best fortunes such fair spoiles of me.
O thou vndanted daughter of desires!
By all thy dowr of LIGHTS & FIRES;
By all the eagle in thee, all the doue;
By all thy liues & deaths of loue;
By thy larg draughts of intellectuall day,
And by thy thirsts of loue more large then they;
By all thy brim-fill'd Bowles of feirce desire
By thy last Morning's draught of liquid fire;
By the full kingdome of that finall kisse
That seiz'd thy parting Soul, & seal'd thee his;
By all the heau'ns thou hast in him
(Fair sister of the SERAPHIM!
By all of HIM we haue in THEE;
Leaue nothing of my SELF in me.
Let me so read thy life, that I
Vnto all life of mine may dy.

Carmen Deo Nostro (1652)

One of the most astonishing things in English or any other literature.

GEORGE SAINTSBURY
A History of Elizabethan Literature (1887)

RICHARD CRASHAW

1613? — 1649

SANCTA MARIA DOLORVM, OR THE MOTHER OF SORROWS

A patheticall descant vpon the deuout
Plainsong of Stabat Mater Dolorosa.

I

In shade of death's sad TREE
    Stood Dolefull SHEE.
Ah SHE! now by none other
Name to be known, alas, but SORROW's MOTHER.
    Before her eyes
Her's, & the whole world's ioyes,
Hanging all torn she sees; and in his woes
And Paines, her Pangs & throes.
Each wound of His, from euery Part,
All, more at home in her owne heart.

II

    What kind of marble than
    Is that cold man
    Who can look on & see,
Nor keep such noble sorrowes company?
    Sure eu'en from you
    (My Flints) some drops are due
To see so many vnkind swords contest
    So fast for one soft Brest.
While with a faithfull, mutuall, floud
Her eyes bleed TEARES, his wounds weep BLOOD.

III

    O costly intercourse
    Of deaths, & worse,
    Diuided loues. While son & mother
Discourse alternate wounds to one another;
    Quick Deaths that grow
    And gather, as they come & goe:

His Nailes write swords in her, which soon her heart
      Payes back, with more then their own smart
Her SWORDS, still growing with his pain,
Turn SPEARES, & straight come home again.

IV

    She sees her son, her GOD,
    Bow with a load
    Of borrowd sins; And swimme
In woes that were not made for Him.
    Ah hard command
    Of loue! Here must she stand
Charg'd to look on, & with a stedfast ey
    See her life dy:
Leauing her only so much Breath
As serues to keep aliue her death.

V

    O Mother turtle-doue!
    Soft sourse of loue
    That these dry lidds might borrow
Somthing from thy full Seas of sorrow!
    O in that brest
    Of thine (the noblest nest
Both of loue's fires & flouds) might I recline
    This hard, cold, Heart of mine!
The chill lump would relent, & proue
Soft subject for the seige of loue.

VI

    O teach those wounds to bleed
    In me; me, so to read
    This book of loues, thus writ
In lines of death, my life may coppy it
    With loyall cares.
    O let me, here, claim shares;
Yeild somthing in thy sad prærogatiue
    (Great Queen of greifes) & giue
Me too my teares; who, though all stone,
Think much that thou shouldst mourn alone.

VII

Yea let my life & me
Fix here with thee,
And at the Humble foot
Of this fair TREE take our eternall root.
That so we may
At least be in loues way;
And in these chast warres while the wing'd wounds flee
So fast 'twixt him & thee,
My brest may catch the kisse of some kind dart,
Though as at second hand, from either heart.

VIII

O you, your own best Darts
Dear, dolefull hearts!
Hail; & strike home & make me see
That wounded bosomes their own weapons be.
Come wounds! come darts!
Nail'd hands! & peirced hearts!
Come your whole selues, sorrow's great son & mother!
Nor grudge a yonger-Brother
Of greifes his portion, who (had all their due)
One single wound should not haue left for you.

IX

Shall I, sett there
So deep a share
(Dear wounds) & onely now
In sorrows draw no Diuidend with you?
O be more wise
If not more soft, mine eyes!
Flow, tardy founts! & into decent showres
Dissolue my Dayes & Howres.
And if thou yet (faint soul!) deferr
To bleed with him, fail not to weep with her.

X

Rich Queen, lend some releife;
At least an almes of greif
To'a heart who by sad right of sin
Could proue the whole summe (too sure) due to him.
By all those stings
Of loue, sweet bitter things,

750

Which these torn hands transcrib'd on thy true heart
    O teach mine too the art
To study him so, till we mix
Wounds; and become one crucifix.

XI

    O let me suck the wine
    So long of this chast vine
    Till drunk of the dear wounds, I be
A lost Thing to the world, as it to me.
    O faithfull freind
    Of me & of my end!
Fold vp my life in loue; and lay't beneath
    My dear lord's vitall death.
Lo, heart, thy hope's whole Plea! Her pretious Breath
Powr'd out in prayrs for thee; thy lord's in death.

Carmen Deo Nostro (1652)

The eleven stanzas are an inspiration, I would almost say, incomparable in hymnology—a combination of woe and triumph, submission and sovereignty, pathos, spiritual sublimity, everything!

WILLIAM STEBBING
Five Centuries of English Verse (1910)

JEREMY TAYLOR

1 6 1 3 — 1 6 6 7

THE WIDOW OF EPHESUS

The *Ephesian Woman* that the souldier told of in *Petronius*, was the talk of all the town, and the rarest example of a dear affection to her husband; she descended with the corps into the vault, and there being attended with her maiden resolved to weep to death, or dye with famine, or a distempered sorrow: from which resolution nor his, nor her friends, nor the reverence of the principal citizens, who used the intreaties of their charity and their power, could perswade her. But a souldier that watched seven dead bodies hanging upon trees just over against this monument, crept in, and a while stared upon the silent and comely dis-orders of the sorrow: and having let the wonder a while breath out at each others eyes, at last he fetched his supper and a bottle of wine with

751

purpose to eat and drink, and still to feed himself with that sad pretti-
nesse; His pity and first draught of wine made him bold and curious to
try if the maid would drink, who having many hours since felt her resolution faint as her wearied body, took his kindnesse, and the light returned
into her eyes and danced like boyes in a festival; and fearing lest the
pertinaciousnesse of her Mistresse sorrows should cause her evil to re-
vert, or her shame to approach, assayed whether she would endure to
hear an argument to perswade her to drink and live. The violent passion
had layed all her spirits in wildness and dissolution and the maid found
them willing to be gathered into order, at the arrest of any new object;
being weary of the first, of which like leeches they had sucked their fill,
till they fell down and burst. The weeping woman took her cordial and
was not angry with her maid, and heard the souldier talk, and he was so
pleased with the change, that he who first lov'd the silence of the sorrow
was more in love with the musick of her returning voice, especially
which himself had strung and put in tune; and the man began to talk
amorously, and the womans weak heart and head was soon possessed
with a little wine, and grew gay, and talked, and fell in love, and that
very night in the morning of her passion, in the grave of her husband,
in the pompes of mourning, and in her funeral garments, married her
new and stranger Guest. For so the wilde forragers of *Lybia* being spent
with heat, and dissolved by the too fond kisses of the sun, do melt with
their common fires, and die with faintnesse, and descend with motions
slow and unable to the little brooks that descend from heaven in the
wildernesse; and when they drink they return into the vigor of a new
life, & contract strange marriages; & the Lioness is courted by a Panther,
and she listens to his love, and conceives a monster that all men call
unnatural, and the daughter of an equivocal passion and of a sudden
refreshment: and so also it was in the Cave at *Ephesus:* for by this time
the souldier began to think it was fit he should return to his watch, and
observe the dead bodies he had in charge; but when he ascended from
his mourning bridal chamber, he found that one of the bodies was stolne
by the friends of the dead, and that he was fallen into an evil condition,
because by the laws of *Ephesus* his body was to be fixed in the place of
it. The poor man returns to his woman, cryes out bitterly, and in her
presence resolves to dye to prevent his death, and *in secret to prevent
his shame;* but now the womans *love was raging* like her former sad-
nesse, and grew witty, and she comforted her souldier, and perswaded
him to live, lest by losing him who had brought her from death and a
more grievous sorrow, she should return to her old solemnities of dying
and lose her honour for a dream, or the reputation of her constancy
without the change and satisfaction of an enjoyed love. The man would
fain have lived if it had been possible, and she found out this way for
him, that he should take the body of her first husband whose funeral she
had so strangely mourned, and put it upon the gallows in the place of

the stolne thief; he did so and escaped the present danger to possesse a love which might change as violently as her grief had done: But so have I seen a croud of disordered people rush violently and in heaps till their utmost border was restrained by a wall, or had spent the fury of the first fluctuation and watry progress, and by & by it returned to the contrary with the same earnestness, only because it was violent & ungoverned; a raging passion is this croud, which when it is not under discipline and the conduct of reason, and the proportions of temperate humanity, runs passionatly the way it happens, and by and by as greedily to another side, being swayed by its own weight, and driven any whither by chance, in all its pursuits having no rule, but to do all it can, and spend it self in haste and expire with some shame and much undecency.

Holy Dying (1651)

Or for another specimen (where so many beauties crowd, the judgment has yet vanity enough to think it can discern the handsomest, till a second judgment and a third AD INFINITUM *start up to disallow their elder brother's pretensions) turn to the Story of the Ephesian Matron in the second section of the 5th chapter of the same* HOLY DYING *(I still refer to the* DYING *part, because it contains better matter than the 'Holy Living,' which deals more in rules than illustrations—I mean in comparison with the other only, else it has more and more beautiful illustrations—than any prose book besides)—read it yourself and show it to Plumstead (with my* LOVE, *and bid him write to me), and ask him if* WILLY *[Shakespeare] himself has ever told a story with more circumstances of* FANCY *and* HUMOUR.

CHARLES LAMB
Letter to Robert Lloyd (April 6, 1801)

FRANÇOIS DUC DE LA ROCHEFOUCAULD

1 6 1 3 — 1 6 8 0

MAXIMS

Nous avons tous assez de force pour supporter les maux d'autrui.

We all have sufficient fortitude to bear the misfortunes of others.

Le refus des louanges est un désir d'être loué deux fois.

Rejection of compliments means that we desire to be complimented further.

Quelque bien qu'on nous dise de nous, on ne nous apprend rien de nouveau.

We are never surprised when we hear how well people speak of us.

On croit quelquefois haïr la flatterie; mais on ne hait que la manière de flatter.

We sometimes think we dislike flattery, but we dislike only the way it is done.

Les passions les plus violentes nous laissent quelquefois du relâche; mais la vanité nous agite toujours.

The most violent passions give us some respite, but vanity moves us always.

The first French writer to understand completely the wonderful capacities for epigrammatic statement which his language possessed; and in the dexterous precision of pointed phrase no succeeding author has ever surpassed him.

LYTTON STRACHEY
Landmarks in French Literature (1923)

CARDINAL DE RETZ

1 6 1 4 — 1 6 7 9

REVOLUTIONS

Les Suisses paraissaient, pour ainsi parler, si étouffés sous la pesanteur de leurs chaînes, qu'ils ne respiraient plus, quand la révolte de trois de leurs paysans forma les Ligues. Les Hollandais se croyaient subjugués par le duc d'Albe quand le prince d'Orange, par le sort réservé aux grands génies, qui voient devant tous les autres le point de la possibilité, conçut et enfanta leur liberté. Voilà des exemples; la raison y est. Ce qui cause l'assoupissement dans les États qui souffrent est la durée du mal, qui saisit l'imagination des hommes, et qui leur fait croire qu'il ne finira jamais. Aussitôt qu'ils trouvent jour à en sortir, ce qui ne manque jamais lorsqu'il est venu jusques à un certain point, ils sont si surpris, si aises et si emportés, qu'ils passent tout d'un coup à l'autre extrémité, et que bien loin de considérer les révolutions comme impossibles, ils les croient faciles; et cette disposition toute seule est quelquefois capable de les faire. Nous avons éprouvé et senti toutes ces vérités dans notre dernière révolution. Qui eût dit, trois mois devant la petite pointe des troubles, qu'il en eût pu naître dans un État où la maison royale était parfaitement unie, où la cour était esclave du Ministre, où les provinces et la capitale lui étaient soumises, où les armées étaient victorieuses, où les compagnies paraissaient de tout point impuissantes: qui l'eût dit eût passé pour insensé, je ne dis pas dans l'esprit du vulgaire, mais je dis entre les Estrées et les Senneterres.

The Swiss seemed as it were crushed under the weight of their chains, when three of their powerful cantons revolted and formed themselves into a league. The Dutch thought of nothing but an entire subjection to the tyrant Duke of Alva, when the Prince of Orange, by the peculiar destiny of great geniuses, who see further into the future than all the world besides, conceived a plan and restored their liberty. The reason of all this is plain: that which causes a supineness in suffering States is the duration of the evil, which inclines the sufferers to believe it will never have an end; as soon as they have hopes of getting out of it, which never fails when the evil has arrived at a certain pitch, they are so surprised, so glad, and so transported, that they run all of a sudden into the other extreme, and are so far from thinking revolutions impossible that they suppose them easy, and such a disposition alone is sometimes able to bring them about; witness the late revolution in France. Who could have imagined three months before the critical period of our disorders that such a revolution could have happened in a kingdom where all the branches of the Royal Family were strictly united, where the Court was a slave to the Prime Minister, where the capital city and all the provinces were in subjection to him, where the armies were victorious, and where the corporations and societies seemed to have no power?—whoever, I say, had said this would have been thought a madman, not only in the judgment of the vulgar, but in the opinion of a D'Estrées or a Senneterre.

Mémoires (1655–65?), ii
Translation anonymous

The vague humours of public discontent are very quick, in hours of crises, to be caught by emulation, letting the example of a neighbour decide them, and taking the particular form of malady that reigns and circulates. Retz understands and makes us understand all that admirably. Do not suppose that he understands seditions and riots only; he comprehends and divines revolutions. He describes as an observer gifted with an exquisite sensitiveness of tact, their period of oncoming, so brusque sometimes, so unforeseen, and yet so long in preparation. I know no finer page of history than that in which he paints the sudden passage from the discouragement and supineness of minds, making them believe that present evils can never end, to the contrary extreme where, far from considering revolutions as impossible, they think them, in a moment, simple and easy.

C.-A. SAINTE-BEUVE
Causeries du lundi (1851)
Translated by K. P. Wormeley

RICHARD LOVELACE

1 6 1 8 — 1 6 5 8

SONG
TO LUCASTA, *GOING TO THE WARRES*

I.

Tell me not (Sweet) I am unkinde,
    That from the Nunnerie
Of thy chaste breast, and quiet minde,
    To Warre and Armes I flie.

II.

True; a new Mistresse now I chase,
    The first Foe in the Field;
And with a stronger Faith imbrace
    A Sword, a Horse, a Shield.

III.

Yet this Inconstancy is such,
    As you too shall adore;
I could not love thee (Deare) so much,
    Lov'd I not Honour more.

Lucasta (1649)

Contains no line or part of a line that could by any possibility be improved.

EDMUND GOSSE
in Ward's The English Poets (1880)

ANDREW MARVELL

1 6 2 1 — 1 6 7 8

THE GARDEN

I

How vainly men themselves amaze
To win the Palm, the Oke, or Bayes;
And their uncessant Labours see
Crown'd from some single Herb or Tree.
Whose short and narrow verged Shade
Does prudently their Toyles upbraid;
While all Flow'rs and all Trees do close
To weave the Garlands of repose.

II

Fair quiet, have I found thee here,
And Innocence thy Sister dear!
Mistaken long, I sought you then
In busie Companies of Men.
Your sacred Plants, if here below,
Only among the Plants will grow.
Society is all but rude,
To this delicious Solitude.

III

No white nor red was ever seen
So am'rous as this lovely green.
Fond Lovers, cruel as their Flame,
Cut in these Trees their Mistress name.
Little, Alas, they know, or heed,
How far these Beauties Hers exceed!
Fair Trees! where s'eer your barkes I wound,
No Name shall but your own be found.

IV

When we have run our Passions heat,
Love hither makes this best retreat.
The *Gods,* that mortal Beauty chase,
Still in a Tree did end their race.

Apollo hunted *Daphne* so,
Only that She might Laurel grow.
And *Pan* did after *Syrinx* speed,
Not as a Nymph, but for a Reed.

V

What wond'rous Life in this I lead!
Ripe Apples drop about my head;
The Luscious Clusters of the Vine
Upon my Mouth do crush their Wine;
The Nectaren, and curious Peach,
Into my hands themselves do reach;
Stumbling on Melons, as I pass,
Insnar'd with Flow'rs, I fall on Grass.

VI

Mean while the Mind, from pleasure less,
Withdraws into its happiness:
The Mind, that Ocean where each kind
Does streight its own resemblance find;
Yet it creates, transcending these,
Far other Worlds, and other Seas;
Annihilating all that's made
To a green Thought in a green Shade.

VII

Here at the Fountains sliding foot,
Or at some Fruit-trees mossy root,
Casting the Bodies Vest aside,
My Soul into the boughs does glide:
There like a Bird it sits, and sings,
Then whets, and combs its silver Wings;
And, till prepar'd for longer flight,
Waves in its Plumes the various Light.

VIII

Such was that happy Garden-state,
While Man there walk'd without a Mate:
After a Place so pure, and sweet,
What other Help could yet be meet!

But 'twas beyond a Mortal's share
To wander solitary there:
Two Paradises 'twere in one
To live in Paradise alone.

IX

How well the skilful Gardner drew
Of flow'rs and herbes this Dial new;
Where from above the milder Sun
Does through a fragrant Zodiack run;
And, as it works, th' industrious Bee
Computes its time as well as we.
How could such sweet and wholsome Hours
Be reckon'd but with herbs and flow'rs!

Miscellaneous Poems (1681)

One of the loveliest short poems in our language. Its green and leafy summer of rich sun and richer shade will live while our language still lives. This is the poem which contains the immortal

"Annihilating all that's made
 To a green thought in a green shade."

The beauty of this poem is largely dependent upon association and imagery. But there are, also, technical points to be noted about the fifth verse, where the several P's in

"Ripe apples drop about my head"

give a feeling of roundness, like that of the apples they are describing; and where the perfectly managed Sh-sounds in

"The luscious clusters of the vine
 Upon my mouth do crush their wine"

give us the richness of the juice of these ripe grapes. In fact, the leafiness and the richness and the greenness of the world he is describing is conveyed in every syllable.

EDITH SITWELL
The Pleasures of Poetry, First Series (1930)

759

ANDREW MARVELL

1621 — 1678

AN HORATIAN *ODE UPON* CROMWELL'S *RETURN FROM* IRELAND

The forward Youth that would appear
Must now forsake his *Muses* dear,
   Nor in the Shadows sing
   His Numbers languishing.
'Tis time to leave the Books in dust,
And oyl th' unused Armours rust:
   Removing from the Wall
   The Corslet of the Hall.
So restless *Cromwel* could not cease
In the inglorious Arts of Peace,
   But through adventrous War
   Urged his active Star.
And, like the three-fork'd Lightning, first
Breaking the Clouds where it was nurst,
   Did thorough his own Side
   His fiery way divide.
For 'tis all one to Courage high
The Emulous or Enemy;
   And with such to inclose
   Is more then to oppose.
Then burning through the Air he went,
And Pallaces and Temples rent:
   And *Cæsars* head at last
   Did through his Laurels blast.
'Tis Madness to resist or blame
The force of angry Heavens flame:
   And, if we would speak true,
   Much to the Man is due.
Who, from his private Gardens, where
He liv'd reserved and austere,
   As if his highest plot
   To plant the Bergamot,
Could by industrious Valour climbe
To ruine the great Work of Time,
   And cast the Kingdome old
   Into another Mold.
Though Justice against Fate complain,
And plead the antient Rights in vain:

But those do hold or break
As Men are strong or weak.
Nature that hateth emptiness,
Allows of penetration less:
    And therefore must make room
    Where greater Spirits come.
What Field of all the Civil Wars
Where his were not the deepest Scars?
    And *Hampton* shows what part
    He had of wiser Art.
Where, twining subtile fears with hope,
He wove a Net of such a scope,
    That *Charles* himself might chase
    To *Caresbrooks* narrow case.
That thence the *Royal Actor* born
The *Tragick Scaffold* might adorn:
    While round the armed Bands
    Did clap their bloody hands.
He nothing common did or mean
Upon that memorable Scene:
    But with his keener Eye
    The Axes edge did try:
Nor call'd the *Gods* with vulgar spight
To vindicate his helpless Right,
    But bow'd his comely Head,
    Down as upon a Bed.
This was that memorable Hour
Which first assur'd the forced Pow'r.
    So when they did design
    The *Capitols* first Line,
A bleeding Head where they begun,
Did fright the Architects to run;
    And yet in that the *State*
    Foresaw it's happy Fate.
And now the *Irish* are asham'd
To see themselves in one Year tam'd:
    So much one Man can do,
    That does both act and know.
They can affirm his Praises best,
And have, though overcome, confest
    How good he is, how just,
    And fit for highest Trust:
Nor yet grown stiffer with Command,
But still in the *Republick's* hand:

How fit he is to sway
That can so well obey.
He to the *Commons Feet* presents
A *Kingdome*, for his first years rents:
And, what he may, forbears
His Fame to make it theirs:
And has his Sword and Spoyls ungirt,
To lay them at the *Publick's* skirt.
So when the Falcon high
Falls heavy from the Sky,
She, having kill'd, no more does search,
But on the next green Bow to pearch;
Where, when he first does lure,
The Falckner has her sure.
What may not then our *Isle* presume
While Victory his Crest does plume!
What may not others fear
If thus he crown each Year!
A *Cæsar* he ere long to *Gaul*,
To *Italy* an *Hannibal*,
And to all States not free
Shall *Clymacterick* be.
The *Pict* no shelter now shall find
Within his party-colour'd Mind;
But from this Valour sad
Shrink underneath the Plad:
Happy if in the tufted brake
The *English Hunter* him mistake;
Nor lay his Hounds in near
The *Caledonian* Deer.
But thou the Wars and Fortunes Son
March indefatigably on;
And for the last effect
Still keep thy Sword erect:
Besides the force it has to fright
The Spirits of the shady Night,
The same *Arts* that did *gain*
A *Pow'r* must it *maintain*.

(1650)

The most truly classic [ode] in our language.

JAMES RUSSELL LOWELL
Among My Books (1870)

JEAN DE LA FONTAINE

1 6 2 1 — 1 6 9 5

ADONIS AND THE WATER NYMPHS

Les nymphes, de qui l'œil voit les choses futures,
L'avoient fait égarer en des routes obscures.
Le son des cors se perd par un charme inconnu.

The nymphs, who hold the future in their gaze,
Led him to wander in uncertain ways.
The horns are muffled by an unknown spell.

Adonis (1657?)
Translated by Malcolm Cowley

The loveliest verses in the world.

PAUL VALÉRY
Variété (1924)

JEAN DE LA FONTAINE

1 6 2 1 — 1 6 9 5

LE LOUP ET LE CHIEN

Un loup n'avait que les os et la peau,
    Tant les chiens faisaient bonne garde:
Ce loup rencontre un dogue aussi puissant que beau,
Gras, poli, qui s'était fourvoyé par mégarde.
    L'attaquer, le mettre en quartiers,
    Sire loup l'eût fait volontiers:
    Mais il fallait livrer bataille;
    Et le mâtin était de taille
    A se défendre hardiment.
    Le loup donc l'aborde humblement,
      Entre en propos, et lui fait compliment
    Sur son embonpoint qu'il admire.
    Il ne tiendra qu'à vous, beau sire,
D'être aussi gras que moi, lui répartit le chien.
    Quittez les bois, vous ferez bien:
    Vos pareils y sont misérables,
    Cancres, hères, et pauvres diables

Dont la condition est de mourir de faim.
Car, quoi! rien d'assuré! point de franche lippée!
    Tout à la pointe de l'épée!
Suivez-moi, vous aurez un bien meilleur destin.
    Le loup reprit: que me faudra-t-il faire?
Presque rien, dit le chien: donner la chasse aux gens
    Portant bâtons, et mendiants;
Flatter ceux du logis, à son maître complaire:
    Moyennant quoi votre salaire
Sera force reliefs de toutes les façons,
    Os de poulets, os de pigeons,
    Sans parler de mainte caresse.
Le loup déja se forge une félicité
    Qui le fait pleurer de tendresse.
Chemin faisant, il vit le cou du chien pelé:
Qu'est-cela? lui dit-il. Rien. Quoi! rien!
    Peu de chose.
Mais encor? Le collier dont je suis attaché
De ce que vous voyez est peut-être la cause.
Attaché! dit le loup: vous ne courez donc pas
    Où vous voulez? Pas toujours: mais qu'importe?
Il importe si bien, que de tous vos repas
    Je ne veux en aucune sorte,
Et ne voudrais pas même à ce prix un trésor.
Cela dit, maître loup s'enfuit, et court encor.

THE WOLF AND THE DOG

A prowling wolf, whose shaggy skin
(So strict the watch of dogs had been)
    Hid little but his bones,
Once met a mastiff dog astray.
A prouder, fatter, sleeker Tray,
    No human mortal owns.
Sir Wolf in famish'd plight,
    Would fain have made a ration
    Upon his fat relation;
But then he first must fight;
    And well the dog seem'd able
    To save from wolfish table
His carcass snug and tight.
    So, then, in civil conversation
    The wolf express'd his admiration
Of Tray's fine case. Said Tray, politely,
Yourself, good sir, may be as sightly,

Quit but the woods, advised by me.
For all your fellows here, I see,
Are shabby wretches, lean and gaunt,
Belike to die of haggard want.
With such a pack, of course it follows,
One fights for every bit he swallows.
Come, then, with me, and share
On equal terms our princely fare.
But what with you
Has one to do?
Inquires the wolf. Light work indeed,
Replies the dog; you only need
To bark a little now and then,
To chase off duns and beggar men,
To fawn on friends that come or go forth,
Your master please, and so forth;
For which you have to eat
All sorts of well-cook'd meat—
Cold pullets, pigeons, savoury messes—
Besides unnumber'd fond caresses.
The wolf, by force of appetite,
Accepts the terms outright,
Tears glistening in his eyes,
But faring on, he spies
A gall'd spot on the mastiff's neck.
What's that? he cries. O, nothing but a speck.
A speck? Ay, ay; 'tis not enough to pain me;
Perhaps the collar's mark by which they chain me.
Chain! chain you! What! run you not, then,
Just where you please, and when?
Not always, sir; but what of that?
Enough for me, to spoil your fat!
It ought to be a precious price
Which could to servile chains entice;
For me, I'll shun them while I've wit.
So ran Sir Wolf, and runneth yet.

Fables, (1668), i, 5
Translated by E. Wright

La Fontaine offers the unheard of spectacle of a man of genius who was able to realize completely and with absolute perfection the work which he had dreamed.

THÉODORE DE BANVILLE
Les Poëtes français (1861)

JEAN DE LA FONTAINE

1 6 2 1 — 1 6 9 5

THE GLUTTON

Ne nous flattons donc point; voyons sans indulgence
    L'état de notre conscience.
Pour moi, satisfaisant mes appétits gloutons,
    J'ai dévoré force moutons.
    Que m'avoient-ils fait? Nulle offense;
Même il m'est arrivé quelquefois de manger
            Le berger.
Je me dévouerai donc, s'il le faut: mais je pense
Qu'il est bon que chacun s'accuse ainsi que moi:
Car on doit souhaiter, selon toute justice,
    Que le plus coupable périsse.

    Himself let no one spare nor flatter,
    But make clean conscience in the matter.
For me, my appetite has play'd the glutton
    Too much and often upon mutton.
    What harm had e'er my victims done?
        I answer, truly, None.
    Perhaps, sometimes, by hunger press'd,
    I've eat the shepherd with the rest.
    I yield myself, if need there be;
    And yet I think, in equity,
Each should confess his sins with me;
    For laws of right and justice cry,
    The guiltiest alone should die.

Fables (1668), vii, 1
Translated by E. Wright

The fables of La Fontaine are perfection itself, and the ultimate expression of genius. . . . REGARDEZ, MAIS N'Y TOUCHEZ PAS!

THÉODORE DE BANVILLE
Petit Traité de poésie française (1870)

HENRY VAUGHAN

1 6 2 2 — 1 6 9 5

FROM THE NIGHT

There is in God (some say)
A deep, but dazling darkness.

Silex Scintillans (1650)

That is not only sublime—it is sublimity.

FRANCIS THOMPSON
Milton (1913)

MOLIÈRE (JEAN BAPTISTE POQUELIN)

1 6 2 2 — 1 6 7 3

THE HYPOCRITE

Madame Pernelle and Flipote, her servant, Elmire, Mariane, Dorine, Damis, Cléante.

MADAME PERNELLE

Come along, Flipote, come along; let me get away from them.

ELMIRE

You walk so fast that I can scarcely keep up with you.

MADAME PERNELLE

You need not come any further, child. I can dispense with such ceremony.

ELMIRE

We only give what is due to you. But, mother, why are you in such a hurry to leave us?

MADAME PERNELLE

Because I cannot bear to see such goings on and no one takes any pains to meet my wishes. Yes, I leave your house not very well pleased: you ignore all my advice, you do not show any respect for anything, everyone says what he likes, and it is just like the Court of King Pétaud.

DORINE

If . . .

MADAME PERNELLE

You are far too free with your tongue for your position, my lass, and too saucy. You offer your advice about everything.

DAMIS

But . . .

MADAME PERNELLE

You are a fool thrice over, my boy, though it is your own grandmother who says it. I have told your father a hundred times that you will become a ne'er-do-weel, and will cause him nothing but trouble.

MARIANE

I think . . .

MADAME PERNELLE

As for you, his sister, you put on such a demure air that it is difficult to catch you tripping. But, as the saying is, still waters are the most dangerous, and I hate your underhand ways.

ELMIRE

But, mother . . .

MADAME PERNELLE

Let me tell you, daughter, that your whole conduct is entirely wrong. You ought to set them a good example: their late mother did much better. You are extravagant: I am shocked to see you decked out like a princess. If a woman wishes to please her husband only, she has no need for so much finery, my child.

CLÉANTE

But, madam, after all . . .

MADAME PERNELLE

As for you, sir, who are her brother, I think very highly of you, and I both love and respect you, but, at the same time, if I were my son, her husband, I should request you not to enter our house. You are always laying down rules of conduct which respectable people should not follow. I speak rather frankly to you, but that is my nature: I do not mince matters when I have anything on my mind.

DAMIS

Your Mr. Tartuffe is, no doubt, an excellent person . . .

MADAME PERNELLE

He is a very worthy man, one who should be listened to; and it makes me very angry to hear him sneered at by a fool like you.

DAMIS

What! Am I to permit a censorious bigot to exercise a tyrannical influence in the family; and are we not to be allowed any pleasures unless this good gentleman condescends to give his consent?

DORINE

Were we to listen to him and to put faith in his maxims, we should look upon all our acts as criminal, for the zealous critic finds fault with everything.

768

MADAME PERNELLE

And whatever he finds fault with deserves censure. He wants to lead you to Heaven, and it is my son's duty to teach you to value him.

DAMIS

No; look here, grandmother, neither my father nor anyone else shall ever induce me to think well of him: I should be false to myself were I to speak otherwise. His ways irritate me constantly. I can see what the consequence will be: that underbred fellow and I will soon quarrel.

DORINE

Surely it is a scandalous thing to see a stranger exercise such authority in this house: to see a beggar, who, when he came, had not shoes on his feet, and whose whole clothing may have been worth twopence, so far forget himself as to interfere with everything, and play the master.

MADAME PERNELLE

Ah! mercy on me! it would be much better if everything were done in accordance with his good rules.

DORINE

He is a saint in your opinion, but, in mine, he is a hypocrite.

MADAME PERNELLE

What language!

DORINE

I should not like to trust myself either with him or with his man Laurent, without good security.

MADAME PERNELLE

I do not know what the servant may be at heart, but I will swear the master is a worthy man. You all hate and flout him because he tells you unpleasant truths. His anger is directed against sin, and his only desire is to further the cause of Heaven.

DORINE

Yes; but why, especially for some time past, can he not bear any one to come to the house? Why is a polite call so offensive to Heaven that he needs make noise enough about it to split our heads? Between ourselves I will tell you what I think. Upon my word, I believe that he is jealous of Madame.

MADAME PERNELLE

Hold your tongue, and take care what you say. He is not the only person who blames these visits. The whole neighbourhood is annoyed by the bustle of the people you receive, their carriages always waiting before the door, and the noisy crowd of servants. I am willing to believe that there is no actual harm done, but people will talk, and it is better not to give them cause.

CLÉANTE

Ah! madam, how can you stop people talking? It would be a sorry thing if in this world we had to give up our best friends, because of idle chatter aimed at us. And even if we could bring ourselves to do so, do you think it would stop people's tongues? There is not any protection against slander. Do not let us pay any attention to foolish gossip, but endeavour to live honestly and leave the scandal-mongers to say what they will.

DORINE

Probably our neighbour Daphné, and her little husband, are at the bottom of all this slander. Those who are the most ridiculous in their own conduct are always the first to libel others. They are quick to get hold of the slightest rumour of a love-affair, to spread it abroad with high glee, giving the story just what twist they like. They paint the actions of others in their own colours, thinking thereby to justify their own conduct to the world; and in the vain hope of a resemblance they try to give their intrigues some show of innocence, or else to shift to other shoulders a part of that blame with which they themselves are overburdened.

MADAME PERNELLE

All these arguments have nothing to do with the matter. Everybody knows that Orante leads an exemplary life, and that all her thoughts are towards heaven. Well, I have been told that she strongly disapproves of the company who visit here.

DORINE

The example is admirable, and the lady is beyond reproach! It is true that she lives an austere life, but age is responsible for her fervent zeal, and people know that she is a prude because she cannot help it. She made the most of all her advantages while she had the power of attracting attention. But now that her eyes have lost their lustre she renounces the world which renounces her, and hides under the pompous cloak of prudence the decay of her worn-out charms. Such is the last shift of a modern coquette. Mortified to see their lovers fall away from them, their gloomy despair sees nothing for it, when thus forsaken, but the rôle of prudery; and in their strictness these good women censure everything and pardon nothing. They loudly condemn the actions of others, not from principles of charity, but out of envy, since they cannot bear to see another taste those pleasures for which age has taken away their appetite.

MADAME PERNELLE

These are idle tales told to please you. I have to be silent in your house, my child, for madam keeps the ball rolling all day long. Still, I mean to have my say in my turn. I tell you that my son never did a wiser act than when he received this good man into his family; Heaven mercifully sent him into your house to convert your erring thoughts. You ought to hear him for your soul's sake, since he censures nothing but that which deserves censure. All these visits, these balls, these tales, are inventions of the evil one. Not one good word is heard at them, nothing but idle gossip, songs and chatter. Often enough the neighbour comes in for his share, and there is scandal right and left. Indeed the heads of sensible people are quite turned by the distraction of these gatherings. A thousand ill-natured stories are spread abroad in no time; and, as a certain doctor very truly said the other day, it is a perfect tower of Babylon, for every one babbles as long as he likes. And to tell the story which brought this up . . . Here is this gentleman giggling already! Go and find the fools who make you laugh, and without . . . Good-bye, my child. I'll say no more. My regard for your house has fallen by one-half, and it will be a very long time before I set foot in it again. *(Slapping Flipote's face.)* Come along, you, don't stand there dreaming and gaping. Good Lord! I'll warm your ears for you, come on, hussy, come on.

Tartuffe (1664), Act i, Scene i
Translated by A. R. Waller

I asked how a piece must be constructed so as to be fit for the theatre.
"It must be symbolical," replied Goethe; "that is to say, each incident must be significant in itself, and lead to another still more important. The TARTUFFE *of Molière is, in this respect, a great example. Only think what an introduction is the first scene! From the very beginning everything is highly significant, and leads us to expect something still more important. The beginning of Lessing's* MINNA VON BARNHELM *is also admirable; but that of the* TARTUFFE *comes only once into the world: it is the greatest and best thing that exists of the kind."*

JOHANN WOLFGANG VON GOETHE
J. P. ECKERMANN Gespräche mit Goethe (1837–48)
Translated by John Oxenford

BLAISE PASCAL

1 6 2 3 — 1 6 6 2

CHARITY IS SUPERNATURAL

La distance infinie des corps aux esprits figure la distance infiniment plus infinie des esprits à la charité, car elle est surnaturelle.

Tout l'éclat des grandeurs n'a point de lustre pour les gens qui sont dans les recherches de l'esprit.

La grandeur des gens d'esprit est invisible aux rois, aux riches, aux capitaines, à tous ces grands de chair.

La grandeur de la sagesse, qui n'est nulle sinon de Dieu, est invisible aux charnels et aux gens d'esprit. Ce sont trois ordres différents de genre.

Les grands génies ont leur empire, leur éclat, leur grandeur, leur victoire, leur lustre et n'ont nul besoin des grandeurs charnelles, où elles n'ont pas de rapport. Ils sont vus non des yeux, mais des esprits, c'est assez.

Les saints ont leur empire, leur éclat, leur victoire, leur lustre, et n'ont nul besoin des grandeurs charnelles ou spirituelles, où elles n'ont nul rapport, car elles n'y ajoutent ni ôtent. Ils sont vus de Dieu et des anges, et non des corps ni des esprits curieux: Dieu leur suffit.

Archimède, sans éclat, serait en même vénération. Il n'a pas donné des batailles pour les yeux, mais il a fourni à tous les esprits ses inventions. Oh! qu'il a éclaté aux esprits!

Jésus-Christ, sans biens et sans aucune production au dehors de science, est dans son ordre de sainteté. Il n'a point donné d'invention, il n'a point régné; mais il a été humble, patient, saint, saint, saint à Dieu, terrible aux démons, sans aucun péché. Oh! qu'il est venu en grande pompe et en une prodigieuse magnificence, aux yeux du cœur et qui voient la sagesse!

Il eût été inutile à Archimède de faire le prince dans ses livres de géométrie, quoiqu'il le fût.

Il eût été inutile à Notre Seigneur Jésus-Christ, pour éclater dans son règne de sainteté, de venir en roi; mais il y est bien venu avec l'éclat de son ordre!

Il est bien ridicule de se scandaliser de la bassesse de Jésus-Christ, comme si cette bassesse était du même ordre, duquel est la grandeur qu'il venait faire paraître. Qu'on considère cette grandeur-là dans sa vie, dans sa passion, dans son obscurité, dans sa mort, dans l'élection des siens, dans leur abandon, dans sa secrète résurrection, et dans le reste: on la verra si grande qu'on n'aura pas sujet de se scandaliser d'une bassesse qui n'y est pas.

Mais il y en a qui ne peuvent admirer que les grandeurs charnelles, comme s'il n'y en avait pas de spirituelles; et d'autres qui n'admirent que les spirituelles, comme s'il n'y en avait pas d'infiniment plus hautes dans la sagesse.

Tous les corps, le firmament, les étoiles, la terre et ses royaumes, ne valent pas le moindre des esprits; car il connaît tout cela, et soi; et les corps, rien.

Tous les corps ensemble, et tous les esprits ensemble, et toutes leurs productions, ne valent pas le moindre mouvement de charité. Cela est d'un ordre infiniment plus élevé.

De tous les corps ensemble, on ne saurait en faire réussir une petite pensée: cela est impossible, et d'un autre ordre. De tous les corps et esprits, on n'en saurait tirer un mouvement de vraie charité, cela est impossible, et d'un autre ordre, surnaturel.

The infinite distance between body and mind is a type of the infinitely more infinite distance between mind and charity, for charity is supernatural.

All the splendour of greatness lacks lustre for those who seek understanding.

The greatness of men of understanding is invisible to kings, the rich, leaders, to all who are great according to the flesh.

The greatness of wisdom which has no existence save in God, is invisible to the carnal-minded and the men of understanding. These are three orders, differing in kind.

Men of exalted genius have their empire, their splendour, their greatness, their victory, their lustre, and do not need material greatness, with which they have nothing to do. They are seen, not by the outward eye, but by the mind, and that is enough for them.

The saints have their empire, their splendour, their victory, their lustre, and need no worldly or intellectual greatness, with which they have nothing to do, for these add nothing to them, nor do they take anything away from them. They are seen by God and the angels, and not by the bodily eye, nor by the enquiring mind; God suffices them.

Archimedes, without splendour, would have had the same reverence. He fought no battles for the eyes to gaze upon, but he left his discoveries for all minds. And how splendid he was to the mind!

Jesus Christ, without wealth or any outward scientific equipment, is in His own order of holiness. He furnished no scientific discovery, and He never reigned; but He was humble, patient, holy, holy, holy, in God's sight, terrible to devils, and sinless. Oh, in what great pomp, and with what transcendent magnificence did He come, to the eyes of the heart that can discern wisdom!

There would have been no need for Archimedes, though of princely birth, to play the prince in his books on geometry.

There would have been no need for our Lord Jesus Christ, for the purpose of shining in His kingdom of holiness, to come as a king; but He did come in the glory proper to His order.

It is most unreasonable to be offended by the lowliness of Jesus Christ, as if this lowliness were in the same order as the greatness He came to set forth. Let us consider this greatness in His life, His Passion, His obscurity and His death; in the selection of His disciples, in their desertion of Him, in His secret resurrection, and the rest; and it will seem so vast that there will be no room for offence at a lowliness which is of another order.

But there are those who can only admire worldly greatness, as if there were no intellectual greatness; and others who only admire intellectual greatness, as if there were not infinitely greater heights in wisdom.

All bodies, the firmament, the stars, the earth and its kingdoms, are not to be compared with the lowest mind, for mind knows all these, and itself; the bodies know nothing.

All bodies together, and all minds together, and all they can effect, are not to be compared with the least motion of charity, for that is of an order infinitely more exalted.

All bodies together cannot furnish one spark of thought; it is an impossibility, for thought is of another order. All bodies and minds cannot produce a single motion of true charity; it is an impossibility, for charity is of another, a supernatural order.

Pensées (1670)
Translated by Lilian A. Clare

*A page that illuminates all Pascal's work, and which has been called,
not without reason, the most beautiful in the French language.*

JACQUES CHEVALIER
Pascal (1922)

BLAISE PASCAL

1 6 2 3 — 1 6 6 2

HEAR GOD

Quelle chimère est-ce donc que l'homme? quelle nouveauté, quel monstre, quel chaos, quel sujet de contradiction, quel prodige! Juge de toutes choses, imbécile ver de terre, dépositaire du vrai, cloaque d'incertitude et d'erreur, gloire et rebut de l'univers.

What a chimera then is man! What a novelty! What a monster, what a chaos, what a contradiction, what a prodigy! Judge of all things, imbecile worm of the earth; depository of truth, a sink of uncertainty and error; the pride and refuse of the universe!

Nous sommes plaisans de nous reposer dans la société de nos semblables. Misérables comme nous, impuissans comme nous, ils ne nous aideront pas; on mourra seul.

We are fools to depend upon the society of our fellow-men. Wretched as we are, powerless as we are, they will not aid us; we shall die alone.

Le dernier acte est sanglant, quelque belle que soit la comédie en tout le reste. On jette enfin de la terre sur la tête, et en voilà pour jamais.

The last act is tragic, however happy all the rest of the play is; at the last a little earth is thrown upon our head, and that is the end for ever.

Connoissez donc, superbe, quel paradoxe vous êtes à vous-même. Humiliez-vous, raison impuissante; taisez-vous, nature imbécile: apprenez que l'homme passe infiniment l'homme, et entendez de votre maître votre condition véritable que vous ignorez. Écoutez Dieu.

Know then, proud man, what a paradox you are to yourself. Humble yourself, weak reason; be silent, foolish nature; learn that man infinitely transcends man, and learn from your Master your true condition, of which you are ignorant. Hear God.

Pensées (1670)
Translated by William Finlayson Trotter

In the LETTRES PROVINCIALES *Pascal created French prose—the French prose that we know to-day, the French prose which ranks by virtue of its vigour, elegance, and precision as a unique thing in the literature of the world. . . .*

In sheer genius Pascal ranks among the very greatest writers who have lived upon this earth. And his genius was not simply artistic; it displayed itself no less in his character and in the quality of his thought. These are the sides of him which are revealed with extraordinary splendour in his PENSÉES—*a collection of notes intended to form the basis for an elaborate treatise in defence of Christianity which Pascal did not live to complete. The style of many of these passages surpasses in brilliance and force even that of the* LETTRES PROVINCIALES. *In addition, one hears the intimate voice of Pascal, speaking upon the profoundest problems of existence—the most momentous topics which can agitate the mind of men. Two great themes compose his argument: the miserable insignificance of all that is human—human reason, human knowledge, human ambition; and the transcendent glory of God. Never was the wretchedness of mankind painted with a more passionate power.*

LYTTON STRACHEY
Landmarks in French Literature (1923)

THE CLIMAX OF IMPIETY

—O mon père! lui dis-je, il n'y a point de patience que vous ne mettiez à bout, et on ne peut ouïr sans horreur les choses que je viens d'entendre. —Ce n'est pas de moi-même, dit-il. —Je le sais bien, mon père, mais vous n'en avez point d'aversion; et, bien loin de détester les auteurs de ces maximes, vous avez de l'estime pour eux. Ne craignez-vous pas que votre consentement ne vous rende participant de leur crime? Et pouvez-vous ignorer que saint Paul juge "dignes de mort, non-seulement les auteurs des maux, mais aussi ceux qui y consentent?" Ne suffisoit-il pas d'avoir permis aux hommes tant de choses défendues par les palliations que vous y avez apportées? falloit-il encore leur donner l'occasion de commettre les crimes mêmes que vous n'avez pu excuser par la facilité et l'assurance de l'absolution que vous leur en offrez, en détruisant à ce dessein la puissance des prêtres, et les obligeant d'absoudre, plutôt en esclaves qu'en juges, les pécheurs les plus envieillis, sans changement de vie, sans aucun signe de regret, que des promesses cent fois violées; sans pénitence, *s'ils n'en veulent point accepter;* et sans quitter les occasions des vices, *s'ils en reçoivent de l'incommodité?*

"Mais on passe encore au delà, et la licence qu'on a prise d'ébranler les règles les plus saintes de la conduite chrétienne se porte jusqu'au renversement entier de la loi de Dieu. On viole *le grand commandement, qui comprend la loi et les prophètes;* on attaque la piété dans le cœur; on en ôte l'esprit qui donne la vie; on dit que l'amour de Dieu n'est pas nécessaire au salut; et on va même jusqu'à prétendre que *cette dispense d'aimer Dieu est l'avantage que Jésus-Christ a apporté au monde.* C'est le comble de l'impiété. Le prix du sang de Jésus-Christ sera de nous obtenir la dispense de l'aimer! Avant l'incarnation, on étoit obligé d'aimer Dieu; mais depuis que *Dieu a tant aimé le monde, qu'il lui a donné son Fils unique,* le monde, racheté par lui, sera déchargé de l'aimer! Etrange théologie de nos jours! On ose lever *l'anathème* que saint Paul prononce *contre ceux qui n'aiment pas le Seigneur Jésus!* On ruine ce que dit saint Jean, que *qui n'aime point demeure en la mort;* et ce que dit Jésus-Christ même, que *qui ne l'aime point ne garde point ses préceptes!* Ainsi on rend dignes de jouir de Dieu dans l'éternité ceux qui n'ont jamais aimé Dieu en toute leur vie! Voilà le mystère d'iniquité accompli. Ouvrez enfin les yeux, mon père; et si vous n'avez point été touché par les autres égaremens de vos casuistes, que ces derniers vous en retirent par leurs excès. Je le souhaite de tout mon cœur pour vous et pour tous vos pères; et je prie Dieu qu'il daigne leur faire connoître combien est fausse la lumière qui les a conduits jusqu'à de tels précipices, et qu'il remplisse de son amour ceux qui en osent dispenser les hommes."

Après quelques discours de cette sorte, je quittai le père, et je ne vois guère d'apparence d'y retourner. Mais n'y ayez pas de regret; car s'il étoit nécessaire de vous entretenir encore de leurs maximes, j'ai assez lu leurs livres pour pouvoir vous en dire à peu près autant de leur morale, et peut-être plus de leur politique, qu'il n'eût fait lui-même. Je suis, etc.

"O father!" cried I; "no patience can stand this any longer. It is impossible to listen without horror to the sentiments I have just heard."

"They are not my sentiments," said the monk.

"I grant it, sir," said I; "but you feel no aversion to them; and, so far from detesting the authors of these maxims, you hold them in esteem. Are you not afraid that your consent may involve you in a participation of their guilt? and are you not aware that St. Paul judges worthy of death, not only the authors of evil things, but also 'those who have pleasure in them that do them?' Was it not enough to have permitted men to indulge in so many forbidden things, under the covert of your palliations? Was it necessary to go still further, and hold out a bribe to them to commit even those crimes which you found it impossible to excuse, by offering them an easy and certain absolution; and for this purpose nullifying the power of the priests, and obliging them, more as slaves than as judges, to absolve the most inveterate sinners—without any amendment of life—without any sign of contrition except promises a hundred times broken—without penance 'unless they choose to accept of it'—and without abandoning the occasions of their vices, 'if they should thereby be put to any inconvenience?'

"But your doctors have gone even beyond this; and the license which they have assumed to tamper with the most holy rules of Christian conduct amounts to a total subversion of the law of God. They violate 'the great commandment on which hang all the law and the prophets'; they strike at the very heart of piety; they rob it of the spirit that giveth life; they hold that to love God is not necessary to salvation; and go so far as to maintain that 'this dispensation from loving God is the privilege which Jesus Christ has introduced into the world!' This, sir, is the very climax of impiety. The price of the blood of Jesus Christ paid to obtain us a dispensation from loving him! Before the incarnation, it seems men were obliged to love God; but since 'God has so loved the world as to give his only-begotten Son,' the world, redeemed by him, is released from loving him! Strange divinity of our days—to dare to take off the 'anathema' which St. Paul denounces on those 'that love not the Lord Jesus!' To cancel the sentence of St. John: 'He that loveth not, abideth in death!' and that of Jesus Christ himself: 'He that loveth me not keepeth not my precepts!' and thus to render those worthy of enjoying God through eternity who never loved God all their life! Behold the Mystery of Iniquity fulfilled! Open your eyes at length, my dear father, and if the other aberrations of your casuists have made no impression on you, let these last, by their very extravagance, compel you to abandon them. This is what I desire from the bottom of my heart, for your own sake and for the sake of your doctors; and my prayer to God is, that he would vouchsafe to convince them how false the light must be that has guided them to such precipices; and that he would fill their hearts with that love of himself from which they have dared to give man a dispensation!"

After some remarks of this nature, I took my leave of the monk, and I see no great likelihood of my repeating my visits to him. This, however, need not occasion you any regret; for, should it be necessary to continue these communications on their maxims, I have studied their books sufficiently to tell you as much of their morality, and more, perhaps, of their policy, than he could have done himself.—I am, &c.

Lettres Provinciales (1656), x
Translated by Thomas M'Crie

All the gifts of the writer are combined in Pascal to the point of perfection which no one excels. His style is, perhaps, of all the great styles of the seventeenth and eighteenth centuries, the most lofty.

DÉSIRÉ NISARD
Histoire de la littérature française (1844)

MADAME DE SÉVIGNÉ

1 6 2 6 — 1 6 9 6

THE MARRIAGE OF MADEMOISELLE

Je m'en vais vous mander la chose la plus étonnante, la plus surprenante, la plus merveilleuse, la plus miraculeuse, la plus triomphante, la plus étourdissante, la plus inouïe, la plus singulière, la plus extraordinaire, la plus incroyable, la plus imprévue, la plus grande, la plus petite, la plus rare, la plus commune, la plus éclatante, la plus secrète jusqu'à aujourd'hui, la plus brillante, la plus digne d'envie; enfin une chose dont on ne trouve qu'un exemple dans les siècles passés, encore cet exemple n'est-il pas juste, une chose que nous ne saurions croire à Paris, comment la pourrait-on croire à Lyon? une chose qui fait crier miséricorde à tout le monde; une chose qui comble de joie madame de Rohan et madame d'Hauterive; une chose, enfin, qui se fera dimanche, où ceux qui la verront croiront avoir la *berlue;* une chose qui se fera dimanche, et qui ne sera peut-être pas faite lundi. Je ne puis me résoudre à la dire, devinez-la; je vous le donne en trois; *jetez-vous votre langue aux chiens?* Hé bien! il faut donc vous la dire: M. de Lauzun épouse dimanche au Louvre, devinez qui? Je vous le donne en quatre, je vous le donne en dix, je vous le donne en cent. Madame de Coulanges dit: Voilà qui est bien difficile à deviner: c'est madame de la Vallière. Point du tout, Madame; c'est donc mademoiselle de Retz? Point du tout; vous êtes bien provinciale. Ah, vraiment, nous sommes bien bêtes! dites-vous; c'est mademoiselle Colbert. Encore moins. C'est assurément mademoiselle de Créqui? Vous n'y êtes pas. Il faut donc à la fin vous le dire: il épouse, dimanche au Louvre, avec la permission du roi, mademoiselle, mademoiselle de . . . . mademoiselle: devinez le nom; il épouse Mademoiselle, ma foi! par ma foi! ma foi jurée! MADEMOISELLE, la grande Mademoiselle, Mademoiselle, fille de feu MONSIEUR, Mademoiselle, petite-fille de HENRI IV, mademoiselle d'Eu, mademoiselle de Dombes, mademoiselle de Montpensier, mademoiselle d'Orléans, Mademoiselle, cousine germaine du roi; Mademoiselle, destinée au trône; Mademoiselle, le seul parti de France qui fût digne de MONSIEUR. Voilà un beau sujet de discourir. Si vous criez, si vous êtes hors de vous-même, si vous dites que nous avons menti, que cela est faux, qu'on se moque de vous, que voilà une belle raillerie, que cela est bien fade à imaginer; si enfin vous nous dites des injures, nous trouverons que vous avez raison; nous en avons fait autant que vous. Adieu; les lettres qui seront portées par cet ordinaire vous feront voir si nous disons vrai ou non.

I am going to tell you a thing the most astonishing, the most surprising, the most marvellous, the most miraculous, the most magnificent, the most confounding, the most unheard of, the most singular, the most extraordinary, the most incredible, the most unforeseen, the greatest, the least, the rarest, the most common, the most public, the most private till to-day, the most brilliant, the most enviable; in short, a thing of which there is but one example in past ages, and that not an exact one neither; a thing that we cannot believe at Paris; how then will it gain credit at Lyons? a thing which makes everybody cry, "Lord, have mercy upon us!" a thing which causes the greatest joy to Madame de Rohan and Madame de Hauterive; a thing, in fine, which is to happen on Sunday next, when those who are present will doubt the evidence of their senses; a thing which, though it is to be done on Sunday, yet perhaps will not be finished on Monday. I cannot bring myself to tell it you: guess what it is. I give you three times to do it in. What, not a word to throw at a dog? Well then, I find I must tell you. Monsieur de Lauzun is to be married next Sunday at the Louvre, to ———, pray guess to whom! I give you four times to do it in, I give you six, I give you a hundred. Says Madame de Coulanges, "It is really very hard to guess: perhaps it is Madame de la Vallière." Indeed, Madam, it is not. "It is Mademoiselle de Retz, then." No, nor she neither; you are extremely provincial. "Lord, bless me," say you, "what stupid wretches we are! it is Mademoiselle de Colbert all the while." Nay, now you are still farther from the mark. "Why then it must certainly be Mademoiselle de Crequi." You have it not yet. Well, I find I must tell you at last. He is to be married next Sunday, at the Louvre, with the King's leave, to Mademoiselle, Mademoiselle de—Mademoiselle—guess, pray guess her name: he is to be married to Mademoiselle, the great Mademoiselle; Mademoiselle, daughter to the late Monsieur; Mademoiselle, granddaughter of Henry the Fourth; Mademoiselle d'Eu, Mademoiselle de Dombes, Mademoiselle de Montpensier, Mademoiselle d'Orléans, Mademoiselle, the King's cousin-german, Mademoiselle, destined to the Throne, Mademoiselle, the only match in France that was worthy of Monsieur. What glorious matter for talk! If you should burst forth like a bedlamite, say we have told you a lie, that it is false, that we are making a jest of you, and that a pretty jest it is without wit or invention; in short, if you abuse us, we shall think you quite in the right; for we have done just the same things ourselves. Farewell, you will find by the letters you receive this post, whether we tell you truth or not.

Letter to M. de Coulanges (December 15, 1670)
Translation Anonymous

Perhaps the most famous and remarkable of all letter-writers in literature.

GEORGE SAINTSBURY
A Short History of French Literature (1882)

JACQUES BÉNIGNE BOSSUET

1627 — 1704

SAINT PAUL

Il ira, cet ignorant dans l'art de bien dire, avec cette locution rude, avec cette phrase qui sent l'étranger, il ira en cette Grèce polie, la mère des philosophes et des orateurs; et malgré la résistance du monde, il y établira plus d'Eglises, que Platon n'y a gagné de disciples par cette éloquence qu'on a crue divine. Il prêchera Jésus dans Athènes, et le plus savant de ses sénateurs passera de l'Aréopage en l'école de ce barbare. Il poussera encore plus loin ses conquêtes; il abattra aux pieds du Sauveur la majesté des faisceaux romains en la personne d'un pro-consul, et il fera trembler dans leurs tribunaux les juges devant lesquels on le cite. Rome même entendra sa voix; et un jour cette ville maîtresse se tiendra bien plus honorée d'une lettre du style de Paul, adressée à ses citoyens, que de tant de fameuses harangues qu'elle a entendues de son Cicéron.

Et d'où vient cela, chrétiens? C'est que Paul a des moyens pour per-suader que la Grèce n'enseigne pas, et que Rome n'a pas appris. Une puissance surnaturelle, qui se plaît de relever ce que les superbes méprisent, s'est répandue et mêlée dans l'auguste simplicité de ses paroles. De là vient que nous admirons dans ses admirables Epîtres une certaine vertu plus qu'humaine, qui persuade contre les règles, ou plutôt qui ne persuade pas tant, qu'elle captive les entendements; qui ne flatte pas les oreilles, mais qui porte ses coups droit au cœur. De même qu'on voit un grand fleuve qui retient encore, coulant dans la plaine, cette force violente et impétueuse, qu'il avoit acquise aux montagnes d'où il tire son origine; ainsi cette vertu céleste, qui est contenue dans les Ecrits de saint Paul, même dans cette simplicité de style conserve toute la vigueur qu'elle apporte du ciel, d'où elle descend.

Yes, this man, so ignorant of the art of the polished speaker, will go, with his rugged speech and his foreign phrase and accent, into Greece, the mother of philosophers and orators, and in spite of the world's re-sistance, will establish there more churches than Plato gained disciples by that eloquence which was thought divine. St. Paul will preach Jesus Christ in Athens, and the most learned of her senators will pass from the Areopagus into the school of this barbarian. He will pursue his triumph; he will lay prostrate at the feet of Jesus the majesty of the Roman fasces, in the person of a proconsul, and he will cause the very judges, before whom he is arraigned, to quake on their tribunals. Rome herself shall hear his voice, and the day will come when this city, this mistress of the world, will esteem herself more honoured by a letter addressed by him to her citizens, than by all the harangues which she has heard from her Cicero.

And how, Christians, how happens all this? It is that Paul has means of persuasion which Greece does not teach and which Rome has not learned. A supernatural power, which exalts that which the haughty despise, mingles with the august simplicity of his language, and breathes in every word he utters. Hence it is that in his amazing Epistles we feel some subtle charm, a certain superhuman force, which does not flatter the taste and tickle the ear, but which grips and stirs the soul, leading captive the understanding and going straight to the heart. Just as a mighty river retains, when flowing through the plain, all that violent and impetuous force which it had acquired in the mountains whence it derived its source, so does this Divine virtue that resides in St. Paul's Epistles preserve undiminished, even in the plainness of his style, all the vigour and power which it brings from the Heaven whence it has descended.

Panégyrique de l'Apôtre Saint Paul (1657)
Translated by D. O'Mahony

The limit of beauty.

C.-A. SAINTE-BEUVE
Causeries du lundi (1854)

JACQUES BÉNIGNE BOSSUET

1627 — 1704

MADAME IS DEAD

O nuit désastreuse! ô nuit effroyable! où retentit tout à coup, comme un éclat de tonnerre, cette étonnante nouvelle: MADAME se meurt! MADAME est morte!

O disastrous night! O dreadful night! that resounded suddenly like a clap of thunder with the shocking news: Madame is dying, Madame is dead!

Oraison Funèbre de Henriette-Anne d'Angleterre (1670)

The splendid words flow out like a stream of lava, molten and glowing, and then fix themselves for ever in adamantine beauty.

LYTTON STRACHEY
Landmarks in French Literature (1923)

JOHN BUNYAN

1628 — 1688

THE WILDERNESS OF THIS WORLD

As I walked through the wilderness of this world, I lighted on a certain place where was a Den, and I laid me down in that place to sleep: and, as I slept, I dreamed a dream. I dreamed, and behold, I saw a man clothed with rags, standing in a certain place, with his face from his own house, a book in his hand, and a great burden upon his back.

*   *   *   *

Now I saw in my dream that these two men went in at the gate: and lo, as they entered, they were transfigured, and they had raiment put on that shone like gold. There was also that met them with harps and crowns, and gave them to them—the harps to praise withal, and the crowns in token of honour. Then I heard in my dream that all the bells in the city rang again for joy.

Now, just as the gates were opened to let in the men, I looked in after them, and, behold, the City shone like the sun; the streets also were paved with gold, and in them walked many men, with crowns on their heads, palms in their hands, and golden harps to sing praises withal.

There were also of them that had wings, and they answered one another without intermission, saying, *Holy, holy, holy, is the Lord.* And after that they shut up the gates; which, when I had seen, I wished myself among them.

The Pilgrim's Progress (1678)

The first half-dozen lines of THE PILGRIM'S PROGRESS *give an example of a perfect beginning. . . . In these few words, as in a few strokes by some master of etching, the atmosphere is made, the movement is launched, the effect is got for the whole narrative. But even more remarkable is the skill with which he brings it to an end. . . . Notice the beautiful cadence of these last words. They give the quiet ending which was insisted upon by Greek art, and which is so conspicuous in Milton at the close both of the* PARADISE LOST *and of the* SAMSON.

J. W. MACKAIL
Studies in Humanism (1938)

SIR WILLIAM TEMPLE

1 6 2 8 — 1 6 9 9

HUMAN LIFE

When all is done, Humane Life is at the greatest and the best, but like a froward Child, that must be Play'd with, and Humour'd a little, to keep it quiet, till it falls asleep, and then the Care is over.

Miscellanea (1690)

The most beautiful to me is Temple's sentence on Life. . . . There is
a cadence there to thrill along the nerves as in no other sentence I can
recall.

HAVELOCK ELLIS
Impressions and Comments, Second Series (1923)

JOHN DRYDEN

1 6 3 1 — 1 7 0 0

ABSALOM AND ACHITOPHEL

In pious times, e'r Priest-craft did begin,
Before *Polygamy* was made a Sin;
When Man on many multipli'd his kind,
E'r one to one was cursedly confin'd,
When Nature prompted and no Law deni'd
Promiscuous Use of Concubine and Bride;
Then *Israel's* Monarch, after Heavens own heart,
His vigorous warmth did, variously, impart
To Wives and Slaves: And, wide as his Command,
Scatter'd his Maker's Image through the Land.
Michal, of Royal Blood, the Crown did wear,
A soil ungrateful to the Tiller's care:
Not so the rest; for several Mothers bore
To God-like *David* several sons before.
But since like Slaves his Bed they did ascend,
No True Succession could their Seed attend.
Of all this Numerous Progeny was none
So Beautiful so Brave as *Absalon:*
Whether, inspir'd by some diviner Lust,
His father got him with a greater Gust,
Or that his Conscious Destiny made way
By manly Beauty to Imperial Sway.
Early in Foreign Fields he won Renown
With Kings and States allied to *Israel's* Crown:
In Peace the thoughts of War he coud remove
And seem'd as he were onely born for Love.
What e'r he did was done with so much ease,
In him alone, 'twas Natural to please;
His motions all accompanied with grace;
And *Paradise* was open'd in his face.

With secret joy, indulgent *David* view'd
His Youthful Image in his Son renew'd;
To all his wishes Nothing he deni'd
And made the Charming *Annabel* his Bride.
What faults he had (for who from faults is free?)
His father coud not or he woud not see.
Some warm excesses, which the Law forbore,
Were constru'd Youth that purg'd by boiling o'r:
And *Amnon's* Murther, by a specious Name,
Was call'd a Just Revenge for injur'd Fame.
Thus Prais'd and Lov'd, the Noble Youth remain'd,
While *David*, undisturb'd, in *Sion* reign'd.
But Life can never be sincerely blest:
Heav'n punishes the bad, and proves the best.
The *Jews*, a Headstrong, Moody, Murm'ring race
As ever tri'd th' extent and stretch of grace;
God's pamper'd People, whom, debauch'd with ease,
No King could govern nor no God could please;
(Gods they had tri'd of every shape and size
That God-smiths could produce or Priests devise:)
These *Adam*-wits, too fortunately free,
Began to dream they wanted liberty;
And when no rule, no president was found
Of men, by Laws less circumscrib'd and bound;
They led their wild desires to Woods and Caves;
And thought that all but Savages were Slaves.
They who, when *Saul* was dead, without a blow
Made foolish *Ishbosheth* the Crown forgo;
Who banisht *David* did from *Hebron* bring,
And, with a General shout, proclaim'd him King:
Those very *Jews* who at their very best
Their Humour more than Loyalty exprest,
Now wondred why so long they had obey'd
An Idol-Monarch which their hands had made;
Thought they might ruine him they could create
Or melt him to that Golden Calf, a State.
But these were random Bolts: No form'd Design
Nor Interest made the Factious Croud to join:
The sober part of *Israel*, free from stain,
Well knew the value of a peaceful reign;
And, looking backward with a wise afright,
Saw Seams of wounds, dishonest to the sight:
In contemplation of whose ugly Scars,
They curst the memory of Civil Wars.

The moderate sort of Men, thus qualifi'd,
Inclin'd the Ballance to the better side;
And *David's* mildness manag'd it so well,
The bad found no occasion to Rebel.
But, when to Sin our byast Nature leans,
The careful Devil is still at hand with means;
And providently Pimps for ill desires:
The Good Old Cause, reviv'd, a Plot requires,
Plots, true or false, are necessary things,
To raise up Common-wealths and ruin Kings.

Th' inhabitants of old *Jerusalem*,
Were *Jebusites;* the Town so call'd from them;
And their's the Native right—
But when the chosen People grew more strong,
The rightful cause at length became the wrong;
And every loss the men of *Jebus* bore,
They still were thought God's enemies the more.
Thus, worn and weaken'd, well or ill content,
Submit they must to *David's* Government:
Impoverish't and depriv'd of all Command,
Their Taxes doubled as they lost their Land;
And, what was harder yet to flesh and blood,
Their Gods disgrac'd, and burnt like common Wood.
This set the Heathen Priesthood in a flame,
For Priests of all Religions are the same:
Of whatsoe'er descent their Godhead be,
Stock, Stone, or other homely Pedigree,
In his defence his Servants are as bold,
As if he had been born of beaten Gold.
The *Jewish Rabbins,* though their Enemies,
In this conclude them honest men and wise:
For 'twas their duty, all the Learned think,
T' espouse his Cause by whom they eat and drink.
From hence began that Plot, the Nations Curse,
Bad in itself, but represented worse,
Rais'd in extremes, and in extremes decri'd,
With Oaths affirm'd, with dying Vows deni'd,
Not weigh'd or winnow'd by the Multitude,
But swallow'd in the Mass, unchewed and crude.
Some Truth there was, but dashed and brew'd with Lies;
To please the Fools, and puzzle all the Wise.
Succeeding Times did equal Folly call
Believing nothing or believing all.

The *Egyptian* Rites the *Jebusites* embrac'd,
Where Gods were recommended by their taste.
Such sav'ry Deities must needs be good
As serv'd at once for Worship and for Food.
By force they could not Introduce these Gods,
For Ten to One in former days was odds.
So Fraud was us'd, (the Sacrificers Trade,)
Fools are more hard to Conquer than Persuade.
Their busie Teachers mingled with the *Jews*
And rak'd for Converts even the Court and Stews:
Which *Hebrew* Priests the more unkindly took,
Because the Fleece accompanies the Flock.
Some thought they God's Anointed meant to slay
By Guns, invented since full many a day:
Our Author swears it not; but who can know
How far the Devil and *Jebusites* may go?
This Plot, which fail'd for want of common Sense,
Had yet a deep and dangerous Consequence;
For as, when raging Fevers boil the Blood
The standing Lake soon floats into a Floud;
And ev'ry hostile Humour which before
Slept quiet in its Channels bubbles o're:
So, several Factions from this first Ferment
Work up to Foam, and threat the Government.
Some by their Friends, more by themselves thought wise,
Oppos'd the Pow'r to which they could not rise.
Some had in Courts been Great and, thrown from thence,
Like Fiends were hardened in Impenitence.
Some, by their Monarch's fatal mercy grown,
From Pardon'd Rebels, Kinsmen to the Throne
Were raised in Pow'r and Publick Office high;
Strong Bands, if Bands ungrateful men coud tie.
Of these the false *Achitophel* was first,
A Name to all succeeding Ages curst.
For close Designs and crooked Counsels fit,
Sagacious, Bold, and Turbulent of wit,
Restless, unfixt in Principles and Place,
In Pow'r unpleased, impatient of Disgrace;
A fiery Soul, which working out its way,
Fretted the Pigmy Body to decay:
And o'r informed the Tenement of Clay.
A daring Pilot in extremity;
Pleas'd with the Danger, when the Waves went high
He sought the Storms; but, for a Calm unfit,
Would Steer too nigh the Sands to boast his Wit.

Great Wits are sure to Madness near alli'd
And thin Partitions do their Bounds divide;
Else, why should he, with Wealth and Honour blest,
Refuse his Age the needful hours of Rest?
Punish a Body which he coud not please,
Bankrupt of Life, yet Prodigal of Ease?
And all to leave what with his Toil he won
To that unfeather'd two-legg'd thing, a Son:
Got, while his Soul did huddled Notions trie;
And born a shapeless Lump, like Anarchy.
In Friendship false, implacable in Hate,
Resolv'd to Ruine or to Rule the State;
To Compass this the Triple Bond he broke;
The Pillars of the Publick Safety shook,
And fitted *Israel* for a Foreign Yoke;
Then, seiz'd with Fear, yet still affecting Fame,
Usurp'd a Patriot's All-attoning Name.
So easie still it proves in Factious Times
With publick Zeal to cancel private Crimes:
How safe is Treason and how sacred ill,
Where none can sin against the Peoples Will,
Where Crouds can wink; and no offence be known,
Since in anothers guilt they find their own.
Yet, Fame deserv'd, no Enemy can grudge;
The Statesman we abhor, but praise the Judge.
In *Israels* courts ne'er sat an *Abbethdin*
With more discerning Eyes or Hands more clean,
Unbrib'd, unsought, the Wretched to redress;
Swift of Dispatch and easie of Access.
Oh, had he been content to serve the Crown
With Vertues onely proper to the Gown,
Or had the rankness of the Soil been freed
From Cockle that opprest the Noble Seed,
David for him his tuneful Harp had strung,
And Heav'n had wanted one Immortal Song.
But wild Ambition loves to slide, not stand,
And Fortunes Ice prefers to Vertues Land.
Achitophel, grown weary to possess
A lawful Fame, and lazie Happiness,
Disdain'd the Golden Fruit to gather free
And lent the Crowd his Arm to shake the Tree.
Now, manifest of Crimes, contriv'd long since,
He stood at bold Defiance with his Prince:
Held up the Buckler of the Peoples Cause
Against the Crown; and sculk'd behind the Laws.

The wish'd occasion of the Plot he takes;
Some Circumstances finds, but more he makes.
By buzzing Emissaries, fills the ears
Of listening Crouds, with Jealousies and Fears
Of Arbitrary Counsels brought to light,
And proves the King himself a *Jebusite*.
Weak Arguments! which yet he knew full well,
Were strong with People easie to Rebel.
For, govern'd by the *Moon*, the giddy *Jews*
Tread the same Track when she the Prime renews:
And once in twenty Years, their Scribes record,
By natural Instinct they change their Lord.
Achitophel still wants a Chief, and none
Was found so fit as Warlike *Absalon*:
Not, that he wish'd his Greatness to create,
(For Polititians neither love nor hate:)
But, for he knew his Title not allow'd,
Would keep him still depending on the Croud,
That Kingly pow'r, thus ebbing out, might be
Drawn to the Dregs of a Democracie.
Him he attempts with studied Arts to please
And sheds his Venome in such words as these.

    Auspicious Prince! at whose Nativity
Some Royal Planet rul'd the Southern Sky;
Thy longing Countries Darling and Desire,
Their cloudy Pillar, and their guardian Fire,
Their second *Moses*, whose extended Wand
Divides the Seas and shows the promis'd Land,
Whose dawning Day, in every distant Age,
Has exercised the Sacred Prophets rage,
The Peoples Pray'r, the glad Diviners Theam,
The Young mens Vision and the Old mens Dream!
Thee, *Saviour*, Thee the Nations Vows confess;
And, never satisfi'd with seeing, bless:
Swift, unbespoken Pomps, thy steps proclaim,
And stammering Babes are taught to lisp thy Name.
How long wilt thou the general Joy detain;
Starve, and defraud the People of thy Reign?
Content ingloriously to pass thy days,
Like one of Vertues Fools that Feeds on Praise;
Till thy fresh Glories, which now shine so bright,
Grow Stale and Tarnish with our dayly sight.
Believe me, Royal Youth, thy Fruit must be
Or gather'd Ripe, or rot upon the Tree.

Heav'n has to all allotted, soon or late,
Some lucky Revolution of their Fate:
Whose Motions, if we watch and guide with Skill,
(For humane Good depends on humane Will,)
Our Fortune rolls as from a smooth Descent
And, from the first impression, takes the Bent;
But, if unseiz'd, she glides away like wind;
And leaves repenting Folly far behind.
Now, now she meets you with a glorious prize
And spreads her Locks before her as she flies.
Had thus Old *David*, from whose Loins you spring,
Not dar'd, when Fortune call'd him, to be King,
At *Gath* an Exile he might still remain,
And Heavens Anointing Oil had been in vain.
Let his successful Youth your hopes engage,
But shun th' example of Declining Age.
Behold him setting in his Western Skies,
The Shadows lengthening as the Vapours rise.
He is not now, as when, on *Jordan's* Sand,
The Joyful People throng'd to see him Land,
Cov'ring the *Beach* and blackning all the *Strand:*
But like the Prince of Angels, from his height,
Comes tumbling downward with diminish'd light:
Betray'd by one poor Plot to publick Scorn,
(Our onely blessing since his curst Return,)
Those heaps of People which one Sheaf did bind,
Blown off and scatter'd by a puff of Wind.
What strength can he to your Designs oppose,
Naked of Friends, and round beset with Foes?
If *Pharaoh's* doubtful succour he should use,
A Foreign Aid would more incense the *Jews:*
Proud *Egypt* woud dissembled Friendship bring;
Foment the War, but not support the King:
Nor woud the Royal Party e'r unite
With *Pharaoh's* arms t' assist the *Jebusite;*
Or if they shoud, their Interest soon would break,
And, with such odious Aid, make *David* weak.
All sorts of men, by my successful Arts
Abhorring Kings, estrange their altered Hearts
From *David's* Rule: And 'tis the general Cry,
Religion, Common-wealth, and Liberty.
If you, as Champion of the Publique Good,
Add to their Arms a Chief of Royal Blood;
What may not *Israel* hope, and what Applause
Might such a General gain by such a Cause?

Not barren Praise alone, that Gaudy Flow'r,
Fair onely to the sight, but solid Pow'r:
And Nobler is a limited Command,
Giv'n by the Love of all your Native Land,
Than a Successive Title, Long, and Dark,
Drawn from the Mouldy Rolls of *Noah's* ark.

    What cannot Praise effect in Mighty Minds,
When Flattery Sooths and when Ambition Blinds!
Desire of Pow'r, on Earth a Vitious Weed,
Yet, sprung from High is of Cœlestial Seed;
In God 'tis Glory: And when Men Aspire,
'Tis but a Spark too much of Heavenly Fire.
Th' Ambitious Youth, too Covetous of Fame,
Too Full of Angels Metal in his Frame,
Unwarily was led from Vertues ways,
Made Drunk with Honour, and debauch'd with Praise.
Half loath and half consenting to the Ill,
(For Loyal Blood within him strugled still,)
He thus repli'd—And what Pretence have I
To take up Arms for Publick Liberty?
My Father Governs with unquestion'd Right;
The Faiths Defender and Mankinds Delight,
Good, Gracious, Just, observant of the Laws;
And Heav'n by Wonders has espous'd his Cause.
Whom has he Wrong'd in all his Peaceful Reign?
Who sues for Justice to his Throne in Vain?
What Millions has he pardoned of his Foes
Whom Just Revenge did to his Wrath expose?
Mild, Easie, Humble, Studious of our Good,
Enclin'd to Mercy, and averse from Blood.
If Mildness Ill with Stubborn *Israel* Suit,
His Crime is God's beloved Attribute.
What could he gain, his People to Betray
Or change his Right, for Arbitrary Sway?
Let Haughty *Pharaoh* Curse with such a Reign
His Fruitful *Nile*, and Yoak a Servile Train.
If *David's* Rule *Jerusalem* Displease,
The *Dog-star* heats their Brains to this Disease.
Why then should I, Encouraging the Bad,
Turn Rebel and run Popularly Mad?
Were he a Tyrant who, by Lawless Might,
Opprest the *Jews* and rais'd the *Jebusite*,
Well might I Mourn; but Nature's holy Bands
Would Curb my Spirits, and Restrain my Hands;

The People might assert their Liberty;
But what was Right in them, were Crime in me.
His Favour leaves me nothing to require;
Prevents my Wishes and out-runs Desire
What more can I expect while *David* lives?
All but his Kingly Diadem he gives:
And that: But there he paus'd; then Sighing, said,
Is Justly destin'd for a Worthier head.
For when my Father from his Toyls shall Rest
And late Augment the Number of the Blest:
His Lawful Issue shall the Throne ascend,
Or the *Collat'ral* Line, where that shall end.
His Brother, though Opprest with Vulgar Spight,
Yet Dauntless and Secure of Native Right,
Of every Royal Vertue stands possest;
Still Dear to all the Bravest and the Best.
His Courage Foes, his Friends his Truth Proclaim;
His Loyalty the King, the World his Fame.
His Mercy ev'n th' Offending Croud will find,
For sure he comes of a Forgiving Kind.
Why shoud I then Repine at Heavens Decree
Which gives me no Pretence to Royalty?
Yet oh that Fate, Propitiously Inclin'd,
Had rais'd my Birth, or had debas'd my Mind;
To my large Soul, not all her Treasure lent,
And then betrai'd it to a mean Descent.
I find, I find my mounting Spirits Bold,
And *David's* part disdains my Mothers Mold.
Why am I scanted by a Niggard Birth?
My soul Disclaims the Kindred of her Earth:
And, made for Empire, Whispers me within;
Desire of Greatness is a God-like Sin.

Him Staggering so when Hells dire Agent found,
While fainting Vertue scarce maintain'd her Ground,
He pours fresh Forces in, and thus Replies:
Th' eternal God, Supreamly Good and Wise,
Imparts not these Prodigious Gifts in vain;
What Wonders are Reserv'd to bless your Reign?
Against your will your Arguments have shown,
Such Vertue's only giv'n to guide a Throne.
Not that your Father's Mildness I contemn,
But manly Force becomes the Diadem.
'Tis true he grants the People all they crave;
And more perhaps than Subject ought to have:

For Lavish Grants suppose a Monarch tame
And more his Goodness than his Wit proclaim.
But when should People strive their Bonds to break,
If not when Kings are Negligent or Weak?
Let him give on till he can give no more,
The thrifty Sanhedrin shall keep him poor:
And every Sheckle which he can receive
Shall cost a Limb of his Prerogative.
To ply him with new Plots shall be my care;
Or plunge him deep in some Expensive War;
Which, when his Treasure can no more supply,
He must, with the Remains of Kingship, buy.
His faithful Friends our Jealousies and Fears
Call *Jebusites;* and *Pharaoh's* Pensioners,
Whom, when our Fury from his Aid has torn,
He shall be naked left to publick Scorn.
The next Successor, whom I fear and hate,
My Arts have made obnoxious to the State;
Turn'd all his Vertues to his Overthrow,
And gain'd our Elders to pronounce a Foe.
His Right, for Sums of necessary Gold,
Shall first be Pawn'd, and afterwards be Sold;
Till time shall Ever-wanting *David* draw,
To pass your doubtful Title into Law.
If not; the People have a Right Supreme
To make their Kings; for Kings are made for them.
All Empire is no more than Pow'r in Trust,
Which, when resum'd, can be no longer Just.
Succession, for the general Good design'd,
In its own wrong a Nation cannot bind:
If altering that, the People can relieve,
Better one suffer, than a Nation grieve.
The *Jews* well know their pow'r: e'r *Saul* they chose
God was their King, and God they durst Depose.
Urge now your Piety, your Filial Name,
A Father's Right and Fear of future Fame;
The Publick Good, that Universal Call,
To which even Heav'n submitted, answers all.
Nor let his Love enchant your generous Mind;
'Tis Natures trick to propagate her Kind.
Our fond Begetters, who would never die,
Love but themselves in their Posterity.
Or let his kindness by th' Effects be tried
Or let him lay his vain Pretence aside.

God said he loved your Father; coud he bring
A better Proof than to anoint him King?
It surely shew'd, He lov'd the Shepherd well
Who gave so fair a Flock as *Israel.*
Would *David* have you thought his Darling Son?
What means he then, to Alienate the Crown?
The name of Godly he may blush to bear:
'Tis after Gods own heart to Cheat his Heir.
He to his Brother gives Supreme Command;
To you a Legacie of Barren Land:
Perhaps th' old Harp on which he thrums his Lays:
Or some dull *Hebrew* Ballad in your Praise.
Then the next Heir, a Prince, Severe and Wise,
Already looks on you with Jealous Eyes,
Sees through the thin Disguises of your Arts,
And marks your Progress in the Peoples Hearts.
Though now his mighty Soul its Grief contains;
He meditates Revenge who least Complains.
And like a Lion, Slumb'ring in the way,
Or Sleep dissembling, while he waits his Prey,
His fearless Foes within his Distance draws,
Constrains his Roaring, and Contracts his Paws:
Till at the last, his time for Fury found,
He shoots with sudden Vengeance from the Ground:
The Prostrate Vulgar, passes o'r and Spares;
But with a Lordly Rage, his Hunters tears;
Your Case no tame Expedients will afford;
Resolve on Death, or Conquest by the Sword,
Which for no less a Stake than Life, you Draw,
And Self-defence is Natures Eldest Law.
Leave the warm People no Considering time;
For then Rebellion may be thought a Crime.
Prevail your self of what Occasion gives,
But trie your Title while your Father lives;
And, that your Arms may have a fair Pretence,
Proclaim, you take them in the King's Defence;
Whose Sacred Life each minute woud Expose,
To Plots, from seeming Friends and secret Foes,
And who can sound the depth of *David's* Soul?
Perhaps his fear, his kindness may Controul.
He fears his Brother, though he loves his Son,
For plighted Vows too late to be undone.
If so, by Force he wishes to be gain'd,
Like Womens Leachery to seem Constrain'd:

Doubt not; but, when he most affects the Frown,
Commit a pleasing Rape upon the Crown.
Secure his Person to secure your Cause;
They who possess the Prince, possess the Laws.

    He said, And this Advice above the rest
With *Absalom's* Mild Nature suited best;
Unblamed of Life (Ambition set aside,)
Not stain'd with Cruelty, nor puft with pride.
How happy had he been, if Destiny
Had higher placed his Birth, or not so high!
His Kingly Vertues might have claim'd a Throne
And blest all other Countries but his own:
But charming Greatness, since so few refuse;
'Tis Juster to Lament him, than Accuse.
Strong were his hopes a Rival to remove,
With Blandishments to gain the publick Love,
To Head the Faction while their Zeal was hot,
And Popularly Prosecute the Plot.
To farther this, *Achitophel* Unites
The Malecontents of all the Israelites:
Whose differing Parties he could wisely Join
For several Ends, to serve the same Design.
The Best, and of the Princes some were such,
Who thought the pow'r of Monarchy too much:
Mistaken Men, and Patriots in their Hearts;
Not Wicked, but seduc'd by Impious Arts.
By these the Springs of Property were bent,
And wound so high, they Crack'd the Government.
The next for Interest sought t' embroil the State,
To sell their Duty at a dearer rate;
And make their *Jewish* Markets of the Throne;
Pretending Publick Good, to serve their own.
Others thought Kings an useless heavy Load,
Who Cost too much, and did too little Good.
These were for laying Honest *David* by
On Principles of pure good Husbandry.
With them join'd all th' Haranguers of the Throng
That thought to get Preferment by the Tongue.
Who follow next, a double danger bring,
Not onely hating *David*, but the King;
The *Solymæan* Rout; well Vers'd of old
In Godly Faction, and in Treason bold;
Cowring and Quaking at a Conqu'ror's Sword,
But Lofty to a Lawful Prince Restored;

Saw with Disdain an *Ethnick* Plot begun
And Scorned by *Jebusites* to be Out-done.
Hot *Levites* Headed these; who pul'd before
From th' *Ark*, which in the Judges days they bore,
Resum'd their Cant, and with a Zealous Crie
Pursu'd their old belov'd Theocracie.
Where Sanhedrin and Priest enslav'd the Nation
And justifi'd their Spoils by Inspiration:
For who so fit for Reign as *Aaron's* Race,
If once Dominion they could found in Grace?
These led the Pack; though not of surest scent,
Yet deepest mouth'd against the Government.
A numerous Host of dreaming Saints succeed;
Of the true old Enthusiastick Breed:
'Gainst Form and Order they their Pow'r imploy,
Nothing to Build, and all things to Destroy.
But far more numerous was the Herd of such,
Who think too little, and who talk too much.
These, out of meer instinct, they knew not why,
Adored their Fathers' God, and Property:
And, by the same blind Benefit of Fate,
The Devil and the *Jebusite* did hate:
Born to be sav'd, even in their own despight;
Because they could not help believing right.
Such were the Tools; but a whole Hydra more
Remains, of sprouting heads too long to score.
Some of their Chiefs were Princes of the Land;
In the first Rank of these did *Zimri* stand:
A man so various, that he seem'd to be
Not one, but all Mankind's Epitome.
Stiff in Opinions, always in the wrong;
Was Every thing by starts, and Nothing long:
But, in the course of one revolving Moon,
Was Chymist, Fidler, States-man, and Buffoon;
Then all for Women, Painting, Rhiming, Drinking,
Besides ten thousand Freaks that died in thinking.
Blest Madman, who coud every hour employ,
With something New to wish, or to enjoy!
Railing and praising were his usual Theams;
And both (to shew his Judgment) in Extreams:
So over Violent, or over Civil,
That every Man, with him, was God or Devil.
In squandring Wealth was his peculiar Art:
Nothing went unrewarded, but Desert.

Begger'd by fools, whom still he found too late:
He had his Jest, and they had his Estate.
He laugh'd himself from Court; then sought Relief
By forming Parties, but could ne'r be Chief:
For, spight of him, the weight of Business fell
On *Absalom* and wise *Achitophel:*
Thus wicked but in Will, of Means bereft,
He left not Faction, but of that was left.

   Titles and Names 'twere tedious to Reherse
Of Lords, below the Dignity of Verse.
Wits, Warriors, Commonwealths-men were the best:
Kind Husbands and meer Nobles all the rest.
And, therefore in the name of Dulness, be
The well-hung *Balaam* and cold *Caleb* free;
And Canting *Nadab* let Oblivion damn,
Who made new Porridge for the Paschal Lamb.
Let Friendships holy Band some Names assure,
Some their own Worth, and some let Scorn secure.
Nor shall the Rascal Rabble here have Place,
Whom Kings no Titles gave, and God no Grace:
Not Bull-fac'd *Jonas*, who coud Statutes draw
To mean Rebellion, and make Treason Law.
But he, though bad, is follow'd by a worse,
The Wretch, who Heav'ns Anointed dar'd to Curse.
Shimei, whose Youth did early Promise bring
Of Zeal to God, and Hatred to his King;
Did wisely from Expensive Sins refrain,
And never broke the Sabbath, but for Gain:
Nor ever was he known an Oath to vent,
Or curse, unless against the Government.
Thus, heaping Wealth, by the most ready way
Among the *Jews,* which was to Cheat and Pray;
The City, to reward his pious Hate
Against his Master, chose him Magistrate:
His Hand a Vare of Justice did uphold;
His Neck was loaded with a Chain of Gold.
During his Office, Treason was no Crime.
The Sons of *Belial* had a Glorious Time:
For *Shimei,* though not prodigal of pelf,
Yet lov'd his wicked Neighbour as himself:
When two or three were gather'd to declaim
Against the Monarch of *Jerusalem,*
Shimei was always in the midst of them.
And, if they Curst the King when he was by,
Would rather Curse, than break good Company.

If any durst his Factious Friends accuse,
He pact a jury of dissenting *Jews:*
Whose fellow-feeling, in the godly Cause
Would free the suff'ring Saint from Humane Laws.
For Laws are onely made to Punish those
Who serve the King, and to protect his Foes.
If any leisure time he had from Pow'r,
(Because 'tis Sin to misimploy an hour;)
His bus'ness was by Writing to persuade
That Kings were Useless, and a Clog to Trade:
And that his noble Stile he might refine,
No *Rechabite* more shund the fumes of Wine.
Chaste were his Cellars; and his Shrieval Board
The Grossness of a City Feast abhor'd:
His Cooks, with long disuse, their Trade forgot;
Cool was his Kitchin, though his Brains were hot.
Such frugal Vertue Malice may accuse;
But sure 'twas necessary to the *Jews:*
For Towns once burnt, such Magistrates require
As dare not tempt Gods Providence by Fire.
With Spiritual Food he fed his Servants well,
But free from Flesh that made the *Jews* rebel:
And *Moses's* Laws he held in more account,
For forty days of Fasting in the Mount.
To speak the rest, who better are forgot,
Would tire a well-breath'd Witness of the Plot:
Yet, *Corah,* thou shalt from Oblivion pass;
Erect thy self thou Monumental Brass:
High as the Serpent of thy Metal made,
While Nations stand secure beneath thy shade.
What though his Birth were base, yet Comets rise
From Earthy Vapours, e'r they shine in Skies.
Prodigious Actions may as well be done
By Weaver's issue as by Prince's son.
This Arch-Attestor for the Publick Good
By that one Deed enobles all his Bloud.
Who ever ask'd the Witnesses high race
Whose Oath with Martyrdom did *Stephen* grace?
Ours was a *Levite,* and as times went then,
His tribe were God-almighties Gentlemen.
Sunk were his Eyes, his Voice was harsh and loud,
Sure signs he neither Cholerick was, nor Proud:
His long Chin prov'd his Wit; his Saint-like Grace
A Church Vermilion, and a *Moses's* Face.

His Memory, miraculously great,
Coud Plots, exceeding mans belief, repeat;
Which, therefore cannot be accounted Lies,
For humane Wit coud never such devise.
Some future Truths are mingled in his Book;
But where the Witness fail'd, the Prophet spoke:
Some things like Visionary flights appear;
The Spirit caught him up, the Lord knows where:
And gave him his *Rabinical* degree,
Unknown to Foreign University.
His Judgment yet his Mem'ry did excel,
Which piec'd his wondrous Evidence so well:
And suited to the temper of the Times;
Then groaning under *Jebusitick* Crimes.
Let *Israels* foes suspect his Heav'nly call,
And rashly judge his Writ Apocryphal;
Our Laws for such affronts have Forfeits made:
He takes his Life, who takes away his Trade.
Were I myself in Witness *Corah's* place,
The Wretch who did me such a dire disgrace
Should whet my memory, though once forgot,
To make him an Appendix of my Plot.
His Zeal to Heav'n, made him his Prince despise,
And load his Person with indignities:
But Zeal peculiar priviledge affords,
Indulging latitude to deeds and words:
And *Corah* might for *Agag's* murther call,
In terms as course as *Samuel* us'd to *Saul.*
What others in his Evidence did join,
(The best that coud be had for love or coin,)
In *Corah's* own predicament will fall
For *Witness* is a Common Name to all.

Surrounded thus with Friends of every sort,
Deluded *Absalom* forsakes the Court:
Impatient of high hopes, urg'd with renown,
And Fir'd with near possession of a Crown.
The admiring Croud are dazled with surprize
And on his goodly person feed their eyes:
His joy conceal'd, he sets himself to show;
On each side bowing popularly low:
His looks, his gestures, and his words he frames
And with familiar ease repeats their Names.
Thus, form'd by Nature, furnished out with Arts,
He glides unfelt into their secret hearts:

Then with a kind compassionating look,
And sighs, bespeaking pity e'r he spoke.
Few words he said, but easie those and fit,
More slow than Hybla drops, and far more sweet.

  I mourn, my Country-men, your lost Estate,
Though far unable to prevent your Fate:
Behold a Banish'd man, for your dear cause
Expos'd a prey to Arbitrary Laws!
Yet oh! that I alone coud be undone,
Cut off from Empire, and no more a Son!
Now all your Liberties a spoil are made;
Egypt and *Tyrus* intercept your Trade,
And *Jebusites* your Sacred Rites invade.
My Father, whom with reverence yet I name,
Charm'd into Ease, is careless of his Fame:
And, brib'd with petty sums of Foreign Gold,
Is grown in *Bathsheba's* Embraces old:
Exalts his Enemies, his Friends destroys,
And all his pow'r against himself imploys.
He gives, and let him give my right away;
But why should he his own and yours betray?
He onely, he can make the Nation bleed,
And he alone from my revenge is freed.
Take then my tears (with that he wiped his Eyes)
'Tis all the Aid my present pow'r supplies:
No Court-Informer can these Arms accuse;
These Arms may Sons against their Fathers use;
And, 'tis my wish, the next Successor's reign
May make no other *Israelite* complain.

  Youth, Beauty, Graceful Action seldom fail:
But Common Interest always will prevail:
And pity never Ceases to be shown
To him, who makes the Peoples wrongs his own.
The Croud, (that still believe their Kings oppress,)
With lifted hands their young *Messiah* bless:
Who now begins his Progress to ordain
With Chariots, Horsemen, and a num'rous train;
From East to West his Glories he displays:
And, like the Sun, the Promis'd Land surveys.
Fame runs before him as the Morning-Star,
And shouts of Joy salute him from afar:
Each house receives him as a Guardian God;
And Consecrates the Place of his abode:

But hospitable Treats did most commend
Wise *Issachar*, his wealthy Western Friend.
This moving Court that caught the Peoples Eyes,
And seem'd but Pomp, did other Ends disguise:
Achitophel had form'd it, with intent
To sound the depths, and fathom where it went,
The Peoples hearts distinguish Friends from Foes;
And trie their strength before they came to Blows.
Yet all was colour'd with a smooth pretence
Of specious love, and duty to their Prince.
Religion, and Redress of Grievances,
Two names, that always cheat and always please,
Are often urg'd; and good King *David's* life
Endanger'd by a Brother and a Wife.
Thus, in a Pageant Shew, a Plot is made;
And Peace it self is War in Masquerade.
Oh foolish *Israel!* never warn'd by Ill:
Still the same Bait, and circumvented still!
Did ever men forsake their present ease,
In midst of health imagine a Disease;
Take pains Contingent mischiefs to foresee,
Make Heirs for Monarchs, and for God decree?
What shall we think! Can People give away
Both for themselves and Sons their Native sway?
Then they are left Defenceless, to the Sword
Of each unbounded, Arbitrary Lord:
And Laws are vain, by which we Right enjoy,
If Kings unquestion'd can those Laws destroy.
Yet if the Croud be Judge of Fit and Just,
And Kings are onely Officers in Trust,
Then this resuming Cov'nant was declar'd
When Kings were made, or is for ever bar'd:
If those who gave the Scepter, coud not tie
By their own Deed their own Posterity,
How then coud *Adam* bind his future Race?
How coud his Forfeit on Mankind take place?
Or how coud heavenly Justice damn us all
Who ne'r consented to our Fathers Fall?
Then Kings are Slaves to those whom they command,
And Tenants to their Peoples pleasure stand.
Add that the Pow'r, for Property allow'd,
Is mischievously seated in the Croud;
For who can be secure of private Right,
If Sovereign Sway may be dissolv'd by Might?

Nor is the Peoples Judgment always true:
The Most may err as grosly as the Few.
And faultless Kings run down, by Common Cry,
For Vice, Oppression, and for Tyranny.
What Standard is there in a fickle rout,
Which, flowing to the Mark, runs faster out?
Nor onely crouds, but Sanhedrins may be
Infected with this publick Lunacy:
And Share the madness of Rebellious Times,
To Murther Monarchs for Imagin'd crimes.
If they may Give and Take when e'r they please,
Not Kings alone, (the Godheads Images,)
But Government it self at length must fall
To Natures state, where all have Right to all.
Yet, grant our Lords the People, Kings can make,
What prudent men a setled Throne woud shake?
For whatsoe'r their Sufferings were before,
That Change they Covet makes them suffer more.
All other Errors but disturb a State;
But Innovation is the Blow of Fate.
If ancient Fabricks nod, and threat to fall,
To Patch the Flaws, and Buttress up the Wall,
Thus far 'tis Duty; but here fix the Mark:
For all beyond it is to touch our Ark.
To change Foundations, cast the Frame anew,
Is work for Rebels who base Ends pursue:
At once Divine and Humane Laws controul,
And mend the Parts by ruine of the Whole.
The tamp'ring World is subject to this Curse,
To Physick their Disease into a Worse.

Now what Relief can Righteous *David* bring?
How Fatal 'tis to be too good a King!
Friends he has few, so high the madness grows;
Who dare be such, must be the People's Foes:
Yet some there were ev'n in the worst of days;
Some let me name, and Naming is to praise.

In this short File *Barzillai* first appears;
Barzillai crown'd with Honour and with Years:
Long since, the rising Rebels he withstood
In Regions Waste, beyond the *Jordans* Flood:
Unfortunately Brave to buoy the State;
But sinking underneath his Master's Fate:

In Exile with his God-like Prince he Mourn'd,
For him he Suffer'd, and with him Return'd.
The Court he practis'd, not the Courtier's Art:
Large was his Wealth, but larger was his Heart:
Which, well the Noblest Objects knew to chuse,
The Fighting Warriour, and Recording Muse.
His Bed coud once a Fruitful Issue boast:
Now more than half a Father's Name is lost.
His Eldest Hope, with every Grace adorn'd,
By me (so Heav'n will have it) always Mourn'd
And always honour'd, snatch'd in manhoods prime
B' unequal Fates and Providences crime:
Yet not before the Goal of Honour won,
All Parts fulfill'd of Subject and of Son;
Swift was the Race, but short the Time to run.
Oh Narrow Circle, but of Pow'r Divine,
Scanted in Space, but perfect in thy Line!
By Sea, by Land, the Matchless Worth was known;
Arms thy Delight, and War was all thy Own:
Thy force, Infus'd, the fainting *Tyrians* prop'd;
And haughty *Pharaoh* found his Fortune stop'd.
Oh Ancient Honour, Oh unconquered Hand,
Whom Foes unpunish'd never coud withstand!
But *Israel* was unworthy of thy Name:
Short is the date of all Immoderate Fame.
It looks as Heav'n our Ruine had design'd,
And durst not trust thy Fortune and thy Mind.
Now, free from Earth, thy disencumbred Soul
Mounts up, and leaves behind the Clouds and Starry Pole:
From thence thy kindred Legions maist thou bring,
To aid the Guardian Angel of thy King.
Here stop my Muse, here cease thy painful flight;
No pinions can pursue Immortal height:
Tell good *Barzillai* thou canst sing no more,
And tell thy Soul she should have fled before;
Or fled she with his life, and left this Verse
To hang on her departed Patron's Herse?
Now take thy steepy flight from Heav'n, and see
If thou canst find on Earth another *He;*
Another he would be too hard to find;
See then whom thou canst see not far behind.
Zadock the priest, whom, shunning Pow'r and Place,
His lowly mind advanc'd to *David's* Grace:
With him the *Sagan* of *Jerusalem,*
Of hospitable Soul and noble Stem;

Him of the Western dome, whose weighty sense
Flows in fit words and heavenly eloquence.
The Prophets Sons, by such Example led,
To Learning and to Loyalty were bred:
For *Colleges* on bounteous Kings depend,
And never Rebel was to Arts a Friend.
To these succeed the Pillars of the Laws,
Who best coud plead, and best can judge a Cause.
Next them a train of Loyal Peers ascend:
Sharp judging *Adriel,* the Muses Friend,
Himself a Muse:—In Sanhedrins debate
True to his Prince, but not a Slave of State.
Whom *David's* love with Honours did adorn,
That from his disobedient Son were torn.
Jotham of piercing Wit and pregnant Thought,
Endew'd by nature and by learning taught
To move Assemblies, who but onely tri'd
The worse a while, then chose the better side;
Nor chose alone, but turned the Balance too;
So much the weight of one brave man can do.
Hushai the friend of *David* in distress,
In publick storms of manly stedfastness;
By Foreign Treaties he inform'd his Youth;
And join'd Experience to his Native Truth.
His frugal care suppli'd the wanting Throne;
Frugal for that, but bounteous of his own:
'Tis easie Conduct when Exchequers flow;
But hard the task to manage well the low:
For Sovereign Power is too deprest or high,
When Kings are forced to sell, or Crouds to buy.
Indulge one labour more, my weary Muse,
For *Amiel;* who can *Amiel's* praise refuse?
Of ancient race by birth, but nobler yet
In his own worth, and without Title great:
The Sanhedrin long time as Chief he rul'd,
Their Reason guided, and their Passion cool'd:
So dextrous was he in the Crown's defence,
So form'd to speak a Loyal Nations Sense,
That, as their Band was *Israels* Tribes in small,
So fit was he to represent them all.
Now rasher Charioteers the Seat ascend,
Whose loose Carriers his steady Skill commend:
They, like th' unequal Ruler of the Day,
Misguide the Seasons, and mistake the Way;

While he withdrawn at their mad Labour smiles
And safe enjoys the Sabbath of his Toils.

   These were the chief; a small but faithful Band
Of Worthies in the Breach who dar'd to stand
And tempt th' united Fury of the Land.
With grief they view'd such powerful Engines bent
To batter down the lawful Government.
A numerous Faction with pretended frights,
In Sanhedrins to plume the Regal Rights.
The true Successor from the Court removed:
The plot, by hireling Witnesses improv'd.
These Ills they saw, and, as their Duty bound,
They shew'd the King the danger of the Wound:
That no Concessions from the Throne woud please;
But Lenitives fomented the Disease;
That *Absalom*, ambitious of the Crown,
Was made the Lure to draw the People down:
That false *Achitophel's* pernitious Hate
Had turn'd the Plot to ruine Church and State;
The Council violent, the Rabble worse:
That *Shimei* taught *Jerusalem* to Curse.

   With all these loads of Injuries opprest,
And long revolving in his careful Brest
Th' event of things; at last his patience tir'd,
Thus from his Royal Throne, by Heav'n inspir'd,
The God-like *David* spoke; with awful fear
His Train their Maker in their Master hear.

   Thus long have I by Native Mercy sway'd,
My Wrongs dissembl'd, my Revenge delay'd;
So willing to forgive th' Offending Age;
So much the Father did the King asswage.
But now so far my Clemency they slight,
Th' Offenders question my Forgiving Right.
That one was made for many, they contend;
But 'tis to Rule, for that's a Monarch's End.
They call my tenderness of Blood, my Fear,
Though Manly tempers can the longest bear.
Yet since they will divert my Native course,
'Tis time to show I am not Good by Force.
Those heap'd Affronts that haughty Subjects bring,
Are burdens for a Camel, not a King:

Kings are the publick Pillars of the State,
Born to sustain and prop the Nations weight:
If my young *Sampson* will pretend a Call
To shake the Column, let him share the Fall:
But oh that yet he woud repent and live!
How easie 'tis for Parents to forgive!
With how few Tears a Pardon might be won
From Nature, pleading for a Darling Son!
Poor pitied youth, by my Paternal care,
Rais'd up to all the Height his Frame coud bear:
Had God ordain'd his Fate for Empire born,
He woud have giv'n his Soul another turn:
Gull'd with a Patriot's name, whose Modern sense
Is one that woud by Law supplant his Prince:
The Peoples Brave, the Politicians Tool;
Never was Patriot yet, but was a Fool.
Whence comes it that Religion and the Laws
Should more be *Absalom's* than *David's* Cause?
His old Instructor, e'r he lost his Place,
Was never thought indu'd with so much Grace.
Good heav'ns, how Faction can a Patriot Paint!
My Rebel ever proves my Peoples Saint:
Woud *They* impose an Heir upon the Throne?
Let Sanhedrins be taught to give their Own.
A king's at least a part of Government;
And mine as requisite as their Consent:
Without my leave a future King to choose,
Infers a Right the present to Depose:
True, they petition me t' approve their Choice:
But *Esau's* Hands suit ill with *Jacob's* Voice.
My Pious Subjects for my Safety pray,
Which to Secure, they take my Pow'r away.
From Plots and Treasons Heav'n preserve my Years,
But save me most from my Petitioners.
Unsatiate as the barren Womb or Grave;
God cannot Grant so much as they can Crave.
What then is left but with a Jealous Eye
To guard the Small remains of Royalty?
The Law shall still direct my peaceful Sway,
And the same Law teach Rebels to obey:
Votes shall no more Established Pow'r controul,
Such Votes as make a Part exceed the Whole:
No groundless Clamours shall my Friends remove
Nor Crouds have pow'r to Punish e'r they Prove;

For Gods and God-like kings their Care express,
Still to defend their Servants in distress.
Oh that my Pow'r to Saving were confin'd:
Why am I forc'd, like Heav'n, against my mind,
To make Examples of another Kind?
Must I at length the Sword of Justice draw?
Oh curst Effects of necessary Law!
How ill my Fear they by my Mercy scan,
Beware the Fury of a Patient Man.
Law they require, let Law then shew her Face;
They could not be content to look on Grace,
Her hinder parts, but with a daring Eye
To tempt the terror of her Front, and Die.
By their own Arts 'tis Righteously decreed,
Those dire Artificers of Death shall bleed.
Against themselves their Witnesses will Swear,
Till, Viper-like, their Mother Plot they tear,
And suck for Nutriment that bloudy gore
Which was their Principle of Life before.
Their *Belial* with their *Belzebub* will fight;
Thus on my Foes, my Foes shall do me Right.
Nor doubt th' event; for Factious crouds engage
In their first Onset, all their Brutal Rage;
Then let 'em take an unresisted Course;
Retire and Traverse, and Delude their Force:
But when they stand all Breathless, urge the fight,
And rise upon 'em with redoubled might:
For Lawful Pow'r is still Superiour found,
When long driv'n back, at length it stands the ground.

    He said. Th' Almighty, nodding, gave consent;
And peals of Thunder shook the Firmament.
Henceforth a Series of new time began,
The mighty Years in long Procession ran:
Once more the God-like *David* was Restor'd,
And willing Nations knew their Lawful Lord.

(1681)

In 1822 Byron wrote . . . . THE VISION OF JUDGEMENT * . . . . *with*
ABSALOM AND ACHITOPHEL, *the greatest political satire in our language.*
HERBERT J. C. GRIERSON and J. C. SMITH
A Critical History of English Poetry (1944)

---

* For an extract from *The Vision of Judgment,* see page 1089.

JOHN DRYDEN

1631 — 1700

RELIGIO LAICI

Dim, as the borrow'd beams of Moon and Stars
To *lonely, weary, wandring* Travellers
Is *Reason* to the *Soul:* And as on high
Those rowling Fires *discover* but the Sky
Not light us *here;* So *Reason's* glimmering Ray
Was lent, not to *assure* our *doubtfull* way,
But *guide* us upward to a *better Day.*
And as those nightly Tapers disappear
When Day's bright Lord ascends our Hemisphere;
So pale grows *Reason* at *Religions* sight;
So *dyes,* and so *dissolves* in *Supernatural Light.*
Some few, whose Lamp shone brighter, have been led
From Cause to Cause to *Natures* secret head;
And found that *one first principle* must be;
But *what,* or *who,* that UNIVERSAL HE;
Whether some *Soul* incompassing this Ball,
Unmade, unmov'd; yet *making, moving All;*
Or various *Atom's,* interfering Dance
Leapt into *Form* (the Noble work of *Chance,*)
Or this great *All* was from *Eternity;*
Not ev'n the *Stagirite* himself could see;
And *Epicurus Guess'd* as well as He.
As *blindly grop'd* they for a *future State,*
As *rashly Judg'd* of *Providence* and *Fate:*
But least of all could their Endeavours find
What most concern'd the good of Humane kind:
For *Happiness* was never to be found;
But vanish'd from 'em, like Enchanted ground.
One thought *Content* the Good to be enjoyed:
This, every little *Accident* destroyed:
The *wiser Madmen* did for *Vertue* toyl,
A Thorny, or at best a barren Soil:
In *Pleasure* some their glutton Souls would steep,
But found their Line too short, the Well too deep,
And leaky Vessels which no *Bliss* cou'd keep.
Thus, *anxious Thoughts* in *endless Circles* roul,
Without a *Centre* where to fix the *Soul:*
In this wilde Maze their vain Endeavours end:
How can the *less* the *Greater* comprehend?

Or *finite Reason* reach *Infinity?*
For what cou'd *Fathom* GOD were *more* than *He.*

    The *Deist* thinks he stands on firmer ground,
Cries εὕρεχα: the mighty Secret's found:
God is that *Spring* of *Good; Supreme* and *Best,*
We, made to *serve,* and in that Service *blest;*
If so, some *Rules* of Worship must be given,
Distributed alike to all by Heaven:
Else *God* were *partial,* and to *some* deny'd
The Means His Justice shou'd for *all* provide.
This *general Worship* is to PRAISE, and PRAY:
One part to *borrow* Blessings, one to *pay:*
And when frail Nature slides into *Offence,*
The *Sacrifice* for *Crimes* is *Penitence.*
Yet, since th' Effects of Providence, we find
Are variously dispensed to Humane kind;
That *Vice Triumphs* and *Virtue suffers* here,
(A Brand that Sovereign justice cannot bear;)
Our Reason prompts us to a *future* State,
The *last Appeal* from *Fortune,* and from *Fate,*
Where God's all-righteous ways will be declar'd,
The *Bad* meet *Punishment,* the *Good, Reward.*

    Thus Man by his own strength to Heaven wou'd soar:
And wou'd not be Obliged to God for more.
Vain, wretched Creature, how art thou misled
To think thy Wit these God-like notions bred!
These Truths are not the product of thy Mind,
But dropt from Heaven, and of a Nobler kind.
Reveal'd Religion first inform'd thy sight,
And *Reason* saw not till *Faith* sprung the Light.
Hence all thy *Natural Worship* takes the *Source:*
'Tis *Revelation* what thou thinkst *Discourse.*
Else how com'st *Thou* to see these truths so clear,
Which so obscure to *Heathens* did appear?
Not *Plato* these, nor *Aristotle* found.
Nor He whose wisedom *Oracles* renown'd.
Hast thou a Wit so deep, or so sublime,
Or canst thou lower dive, or higher climb?
Canst *Thou,* by *Reason,* more of *God-head* know
Than *Plutarch, Seneca,* or *Cicero?*
Those Gyant Wits, in happyer Ages born,
(When *Arms,* and *Arts* did *Greece* and *Rome* adorn,)

Knew no such *Systeme:* no such Piles cou'd raise
Of *Natural Worship,* built on *Pray'r* and *Praise,*
To One sole GOD:
Nor did Remorse, to Expiate Sin, prescribe:
But slew their fellow Creatures for a Bribe:
The guiltless *Victim* groan'd for their Offence;
And *Cruelty* and *Blood,* was *Penitence.*
If *Sheep* and *Oxen* cou'd Attone for Men
Ah! at how cheap a rate the *Rich* might Sin!
And great Oppressours might Heavens Wrath beguile
By offering his own Creatures for a Spoil!

Dar'st thou, poor Worm, offend *Infinity?*
And must the Terms of Peace be given by *Thee?*
Then *Thou* art *Justice* in the *last Appeal;*
Thy easie God instructs Thee to *rebell:*
And, like a King remote, and weak, must take
What Satisfaction *Thou* art pleased to make.

But if there be a *Pow'r* too *Just,* and *strong*
To wink at *Crimes* and bear unpunish'd *Wrong;*
Look humbly upward, see his Will disclose
The *Forfeit* first, and then the *Fine* impose
A *Mulct thy* poverty cou'd never pay
Had not *Eternal Wisedom* found the way
And with Cœlestial Wealth supply'd thy Store;
His Justice makes the *Fine, his Mercy* quits the *Score.*
See God descending in thy Humane Frame;
Th' *offended,* suffering in th' *Offenders* name:
All thy Misdeeds to Him imputed see,
And all his Righteousness devolv'd on thee.

For granting we have Sin'd, and that th' offence
Of *Man,* is made against *Omnipotence,*
Some Price, that bears *proportion,* must be paid
And *Infinite* with *Infinite* be weigh'd.
See then the *Deist lost: Remorse* for *Vice*
Not paid, or *paid, inadequate* in price:
What farther means can *Reason* now direct,
Or what Relief from *humane Wit* expect?
That shews us *sick;* and sadly are we sure
Still to be *Sick,* till *Heav'n* reveal the *Cure:*
If then *Heaven's Will* must needs be understood,
(Which must, if we want *Cure,* and *Heaven* be *Good,*)

810

Let all Records of *Will reveal'd* be shown;
With *Scripture*, all in equal ballance thrown,
And *our one Sacred Book* will be *That one.*

    Proof needs not here; for whether we compare
That Impious, Idle, Superstitious Ware
Of *Rites, Lustrations, Offerings,* (which before,
In various Ages, various Countries bore,)
With *Christian Faith and Vertues,* we shall find
None answ'ring the great ends of humane kind,
But *This one rule of Life;* That shews us best
How *God* may be *appeas'd,* and *mortals blest.*
Whether from length of *Time* its worth we draw,
The *World* is scarce more *Ancient* than the *Law:*
Heav'ns early Care prescrib'd for every Age;
First, in the *Soul,* and after, in the *Page.*
Or, whether more abstractedly we look,
Or on the *Writers,* or the *written* Book,
Whence, but from *Heav'n* cou'd men, unskilled in Arts,
In several Ages born, in several parts,
Weave such *agreeing Truths?* or *how* or *why*
Shou'd *all* conspire to cheat us with a *Lye?*
Unask'd their *Pains, ungratefull* their *Advice,*
Starving their *Gain* and *Martyrdom* their *Price.*

    If on the Book itself we cast our view,
Concurrent Heathens prove the Story *True:*
The *Doctrine, Miracles;* which must convince,
For *Heav'n* in *Them* appeals to *humane Sense;*
And though they *prove* not, they *Confirm* the Cause,
When what is *Taught* agrees with *Natures Laws.*

    Then for the *Style, Majestick* and *Divine,*
It speaks no less than God in every Line;
Commanding words; whose *Force* is still the same
As the first *Fiat* that produc'd our Frame.
All Faiths *beside,* or did by *Arms* ascend;
Or *Sense* indulg'd has made *Mankind* their *Friend;*
This *onely* Doctrine does our *Lusts* oppose:
Unfed by Natures Soil, in which it grows;
Cross to our *Interests,* curbing Sense and Sin;
Oppress'd without, and undermin'd within,
It thrives through pain; its own Tormentours tires;
And with a stubborn patience still aspires.

811

To what can *Reason* such Effects assign,
Transcending *Nature*, but to *Laws Divine?*
Which in that Sacred Volume are contain'd;
Sufficient, clear, and for that use ordained.

But stay: the *Deist* here will urge anew,
No *Supernatural Worship* can be *True:*
Because a *general Law* is that alone
Which must to *all* and every *where* be known:
A Style so large as not *this* Book can claim,
Nor aught that bears *reveal'd* Religions *Name.*
'Tis said the sound of a *Messiah's Birth*
Is gone through all the habitable Earth:
But still that Text must be confin'd alone
To what was *Then* inhabited, and known:
And what Provision could from *thence* accrue
To *Indian* Souls, and Worlds discovered *New?*
In other parts it helps, that Ages past,
The Scriptures there were *known,* and were *imbrac'd,*
Till Sin spread once again the Shades of Night:
What's that to these who never *saw* the Light?

Of all Objections this indeed is chief
To startle Reason, stagger frail Belief:
We grant, 'tis true, that Heav'n from humane Sense
Has hid the secret paths of *Providence;*
But *boundless Wisedom, boundless Mercy,* may
Find ev'n for those *be-wildred* Souls, a *way:*
If from his *Nature Foes* may Pity claim,
Much more may *Strangers* who ne'er heard his *Name.*
And though *no Name* be for *Salvation* known,
But that of His *Eternal Sons* alone;
Who knows how far transcending Goodness can
Extend the *Merits* of *that Son* to *Man?*
Who knows what *Reasons* may his *Mercy* lead;
Or *Ignorance invincible* may plead?
Not onely *Charity* bids hope the *best,*
But *more* the great Apostle has exprest:
That, if the Gentiles, (whom no Law inspir'd,)
By Nature did what was by *Law required,*
They, who the written Rule had never known,
Were to themselves both Rule and Law alone:
To Natures plain indictment they shall plead;
And, by their Conscience, be condemn'd or freed.

Most Righteous Doom! because a *Rule reveal'd*
Is *none* to *Those*, from whom it was *conceal'd.*
Then those who follow'd *Reasons* Dictates right;
Liv'd up, and lifted high their *Natural Light;*
With *Socrates* may see their Maker's Face,
While Thousand *Rubrick-Martyrs* want a place.

　　Nor does it baulk my Charity to find
Th' *Egyptian* Bishop of another mind:
For, though his *Creed Eternal Truth* contains,
'Tis hard for *Man* to doom to *endless pains*
All who believ'd not all, his Zeal requir'd;
Unless he first cou'd prove he was inspir'd.
Then let us either think he meant to say
This Faith, where *publish'd,* was the onely way;
Or else conclude that, *Arius* to confute,
The good old Man, too eager in dispute,
Flew high; and, as his *Christian* Fury rose,
Damn'd all for *Hereticks* who durst *oppose.*

　　Thus far my Charity this path has try'd,
(A much unskilfull, but well meaning guide:)
Yet what they are, even these crude thoughts were bred
By reading that, which better thou hast read,
Thy Matchless Author's work: which thou, my Friend,
By well translating better dost commend:
Those youthfull hours, which of thy Equals most
In *Toys* have *squander'd,* or in Vice have *lost,*
Those hours hast thou to Nobler use employ'd;
And the severe Delights of Truth enjoy'd.
Witness this weighty Book, in which appears
The crabbed Toil of many thoughtfull years,
Spent by thy Authour in the Sifting Care
Of *Rabbins'* old Sophisticated Ware
From Gold Divine, which he who well can sort
May afterwards make *Algebra* a Sport.
A Treasure which, if *Country-Curates* buy,
They *Junius,* and *Tremellius* may defy:
Save pains in various readings, and Translations,
And without *Hebrew* make most learn'd quotations.
A Work so full with various Learning fraught,
So nicely pondred, yet so strongly wrought,
As Natures height and Arts last hand requir'd:
As much as Man cou'd compass, uninspir'd.

Where we may see what *Errours* have been made
Both in the *Copiers* and *Translaters Trade:*
How *Jewish, Popish,* Interests have prevail'd,
And where *Infallibility* has *fail'd.*

For some, who have his secret meaning ghes'd,
Have found our Authour not too *much* a *Priest;*
For *Fashion-sake* he seems to have recourse
To *Pope,* and *Councils,* and *Traditions* force:
But he that *old* Traditions cou'd subdue,
Cou'd not but find the weakness of the *New:*
If *Scripture,* though deriv'd from *heav'nly birth,*
Has been but carelessly preserved on *Earth;*
If *God's own People,* who of *God* before
Knew what we know, and had been promis'd more,
In fuller Terms of Heaven's assisting Care,
And who did neither *Time,* nor *Study* spare
To keep this Book *untainted, unperplext;*
Let in gross *Errours* to corrupt the *Text,*
Omitted *paragraphs,* embroyl'd the *Sense,*
With vain *Traditions* stopt the gaping Fence,
Which every common hand pull'd up with ease:
What Safety from such *brushwood-helps* as these?
If *written words* from time are not secur'd,
How can we think have *oral Sounds* endur'd?
Which *thus* transmitted, if *one* Mouth has fail'd,
Immortal Lyes on *Ages* are intail'd;
And that some such have been, is prov'd too plain;
If we consider *Interest, Church,* and *Gain.*

Oh but, says one, *Tradition* set aside,
Where can we hope for an *unerring Guid?*
For since th' *original* Scripture has been lost,
All Copies *disagreeing, maim'd* the *most,*
Or *Christian Faith* can have no *certain* ground
Or *Truth* in *Church Tradition* must be found.

Such an *Omniscient* Church we wish indeed;
'Twere worth *Both Testaments,* and cast in the *Creed:*
But if *this Mother* be a *Guid* so sure
As can all *doubts resolve,* all *truth secure,*
Then her *Infallibility,* as well
Where Copies are *corrupt,* or *lame,* can tell;
Restore *lost Canon* with as little pains,
As *truly explicate* what still *remains:*

Which yet no *Council* dare *pretend* to doe;
Unless like *Esdras*, they could *write* it new:
Strange Confidence, still to *interpret* true,
Yet not be sure that all they have explain'd,
Is in the blest *Original* contain'd.
More Safe, and much more modest 'tis to say
God wou'd not leave Mankind without a way:
And that the *Scriptures*, though not *every where*
Free from Corruption, or intire, or clear,
Are uncorrupt, sufficient, clear, intire,
In all things which our needfull *Faith* require.
If *others* in the *same Glass better* see,
'Tis for *Themselves* they look, but not for *me:*
For MY Salvation must its Doom receive
Not from what OTHERS, but what I believe.

Must *all tradition* then be set aside?
This to affirm were Ignorance or Pride.
Are there not many points, some needfull sure
To saving Faith, that Scripture leaves obscure?
Which every Sect will wrest a several way
(For what *one* Sect interprets, *all* Sects *may:*)
We hold, and say we prove from Scripture plain,
That *Christ* is GOD; the bold *Socinian*
From the *same* Scripture urges he's but MAN.
Now what Appeal can end th' important Suit;
Both parts *talk* loudly, but the *Rule* is *mute.*

Shall I speak plain, and in a Nation free
Assume an honest *Layman's Liberty?*
I think (according to my little Skill,)
To my own Mother-Church submitting still)
That many have been sav'd, and many may,
Who never heard this Question brought in play.
Th' *unletter'd* Christian, who believes in *gross,*
Plods on to *Heaven* and ne'er is at a loss:
For the *Streight-gate* would be made *streighter* yet,
Were *none* admitted there but men of *Wit.*
The few, by Nature form'd, with Learning fraught,
Born to instruct, as others to be taught,
Must Study well the Sacred Page; and see
Which Doctrine, this, or that, does best agree
With the whole *Tenour* of the Work Divine:
And plainlyest points to Heaven's reveal'd Design:

Which Exposition flows from *genuine Sense;*
And which is *forc'd* by *Wit* and *Eloquence.*
Not that Traditions parts are useless here:
When general, old, disinteress'd and clear:
That Ancient Fathers thus expound the Page
Gives *Truth* the reverend Majesty of *Age,*
Confirms its force by biding every *Test;*
For best *Authority's,* next *Rules,* are best.
And still the nearer to the Spring we go
More limpid, more unsoyl'd, the Waters flow.
Thus, *first Traditions* were a proof alone;
Cou'd we be *certain* such they *were,* so *known:*
But since some Flaws in long descent may be,
They make not *Truth* but *Probability.*
Even *Arius* and *Pelagius* durst provoke
To what the *Centuries preceding* spoke.
Such difference is there in an oft-told Tale:
But Truth by its own Sinews will prevail.
Tradition written therefore more commends
Authority, than what from *Voice* descends:
And this, as perfect as its kind can be,
Rouls down to us the Sacred History:
Which, from the *Universal Church* receiv'd,
Is *try'd,* and *after* for its *self* believed.

The partial *Papists* wou'd infer from hence,
Their Church, in last resort, shou'd Judge the *Sense.*
But first they would assume, with wondrous Art,
Themselves to be the *whole,* who are but *part*
Of that vast Frame, the Church; yet grant they were
The handers down, can they from thence infer
A right t' interpret? or wou'd they alone
Who brought the Present claim it for their own?
The *Book's* a *Common Largess* to *Mankind;*
Not more for *them* than *every* Man design'd;
The *welcome News* is in the *Letter* found;
The *Carrier's* not Commission'd to *expound.*
It *speaks* it *Self,* and what it does contain,
In all things *needfull* to be *known,* is *plain.*

In times o'ergrown with Rust and Ignorance,
A gainfull Trade their Clergy did advance:
When want of Learning kept the *Laymen* low,
And none but *Priests* were *Authoriz'd* to *know;*

When what small Knowledge was, in them did dwell;
And he a *God* who cou'd but *Reade* or *Spell;*
Then *Mother Church* did mightily prevail:
She parcel'd out the Bible by *retail:*
But still *expounded* what She *sold* or *gave;*
To keep it in *her Power* to *Damn* and *Save:*
Scripture was *scarce,* and as the Market went,
Poor *Laymen* took *Salvation* on *Content;*
As needy men take Money, good or bad:
God's Word they had not, but the *Priests* they had.
Yet, whate'er *false Conveyances* they made,
The *Lawyer* still was *certain* to be paid.
In those dark times they learn'd their knack so well,
That by long use they grew *Infallible:*
At last, a knowing Age began t' enquire
If *they* the *Book,* or *That* did *them* inspire:
And, making narrower search they found, thô' late,
That what they thought the *Priest's* was *Their Estate,*
Taught by the *Will produc'd,* (the written Word,)
How long they had been *cheated* on *Record.*
Then, every man who saw the title fair,
Claim'd a Child's part, and put in for a Share:
Consulted Soberly his private good;
And sav'd himself as cheap as e'er he cou'd.

'Tis true, my Friend, (and far be Flattery hence)
This good had full as bad a Consequence:
The Book thus put in every vulgar hand,
Which each presum'd he best cou'd understand,
The *Common Rule* was made the *common Prey;*
And at the mercy of the *Rabble* lay.
The tender Page with horney Fists was gaul'd;
And he was gifted most that loudest baul'd;
The *Spirit* gave the *Doctoral Degree,*
And every member of a *Company*
Was of *his Trade* and of the *Bible free.*
Plain *Truths* enough for needfull *use* they found;
But men wou'd still be itching to *expound;*
Each was ambitious of th' obscurest place,
No measure ta'n from *Knowledge,* all from GRACE.
Study and *Pains* were now no more their Care;
Texts were explain'd by *Fasting* and by *Prayer:*
This was the Fruit the *private Spirit* brought;
Occasion'd by *great Zeal* and *little Thought.*

While Crouds unlearn'd, with rude Devotion warm,
About the Sacred Viands buz and swarm,
The *Fly-blown Text* creates a *crawling Brood;*
And turns to *Maggots* what was meant for *Food.*
A *Thousand daily Sects rise up, and dye;*
A *Thousand more the perish'd Race supply:*
So all we make of Heavens discover'd Will
Is, not to have it, or to use it ill.
The Danger's much the same; on several Shelves
If *others* wreck *us* or *we* wreck our *selves.*

What then remains, but, waving each Extreme,
The Tides of Ignorance, and Pride to stem?
Neither so rich a Treasure to forgo;
Nor proudly seek beyond our pow'r to know:
Faith is not built on disquisitions vain;
The things we *must* believe, are *few* and *plain:*
But since men *will* believe more than they *need;*
And very man will make *himself* a Creed,
In doubtful questions 'tis the safest way
To learn what unsuspected Ancients say:
For 'tis not likely *we* should higher Soar
In search of Heav'n than *all the Church before:*
Nor can we be deceiv'd, unless we see
The *Scripture* and the *Fathers disagree.*
If after all, they stand suspected still,
(For no man's Faith depends upon his Will;)
'Tis some Relief, that points not clearly known,
Without much hazard may be let alone:
And after hearing what our Church can say,
If still our Reason runs another way,
That private Reason 'tis more Just to curb,
Than by Disputes the publick Peace disturb.
For points obscure are of small use to learn:
But *Common quiet* is *Mankind's concern.*

Thus have I made my own Opinions clear:
Yet neither Praise expect, not Censure fear:
And this unpolish'd, rugged Verse I chose;
As fittest for Discourse, and nearest prose;
For while from *Sacred Truth* I do not swerve,
Tom Sternhold's or *Tom Sha—ll's Rhimes* will serve.

(1682)

818

The RELIGIO LAICI *is one of the most admirable poems in the language. The argumentative part is conducted with singular skill, upon those topics which occasioned the principal animosity between the religious sects; and the deductions are drawn in favour of the church of England with so much apparent impartiality, that those who could not assent, had at least no title to be angry. The opinions of the various classes of free-thinkers are combated by an appeal to those feelings of the human mind, which always acknowledge an offended Deity, and to the various modes in which all ages and nations have shewn their sense of the necessity of an atonement by sacrifice and penance. . . .*

The doctrine of the RELIGIO LAICI *is admirably adapted to the subject; though treating of the most abstruse doctrines of Christianity, it is as clear and perspicuous as the most humble prose, while it has all the elegance and effect which argument is capable of receiving from poetry. Johnson, usually sufficiently niggard of praise, has allowed, that this "is a composition of great excellence in its kind, in which the familiar is very properly diversified with the solemn, and the grave with the humorous; in which metre has neither weakened the force, nor clouded the perspicuity of argument; nor will it be easy to find another example, equally happy, of this middle kind of writing, which, though prosaic in some parts, rises to high poetry in others, and neither towers to the skies, nor creeps along the ground."*

SIR WALTER SCOTT
The Works of John Dryden (1821)

JOHN DRYDEN

1 6 3 1 — 1 7 0 0

TO THE MEMORY OF MR. OLDHAM

Farewell, too little and too lately known,
Whom I began to think and call my own:
For sure our Souls were near alli'd, and thine
Cast in the same poetick mold with mine.
One common Note on either Lyre did strike,
And Knaves and Fools we both abhorr'd alike.
To the same Goal did both our Studies drive:
The last set out the soonest did arrive.
Thus *Nisus* fell upon the slippery place,
Whilst his young Friend perform'd and won the Race.

O early ripe! to thy abundant Store
What could advancing Age have added more?
It might (what Nature never gives the Young)
Have taught the Numbers of thy Native Tongue.
But Satire needs not those, and Wit will shine
Through the harsh Cadence of a rugged Line.
A noble Error, and but seldom made,
When Poets are by too much force betray'd.
Thy gen'rous Fruits, though gather'd ere their prime,
Still shew'd a Quickness; and maturing Time
But mellows what we write to the dull Sweets of Rhyme.
Once more, hail, and farewell! farewell, thou young,
But ah! too short, *Marcellus* of our Tongue!
Thy Brows with Ivy and with Laurels bound;
But Fate and gloomy Night encompass thee around.

(1684)

He was partial to literary history and literary parallels as subjects for
poems, and no one in English has done better criticism in metre.

MARK VAN DOREN
The Poetry of John Dryden (1920)

JOHN DRYDEN

1 6 3 1 — 1 7 0 0

TO THE PIOUS MEMORY OF THE ACCOMPLISHT YOUNG LADY MRS. ANNE KILLIGREW,

EXCELLENT IN THE TWO SISTER-ARTS OF POESIE AND PAINTING. *AN ODE.*

1

Thou youngest Virgin-Daughter of the Skies,
Made in the last Promotion of the *Blest;*
Whose Palms, new pluckt from Paradise,
In spreading *Branches* more sublimely rise,
Rich with Immortal Green above the rest:
Whether, adopted to some Neighbouring Star,
Thou rol'st above us in thy wand'ring Race,
Or, in Procession fixt and regular,

Mov'd with the Heavens Majestick pace;
   Or, call'd to more Superiour *Bliss,*
Thou tread'st, with Seraphims, the vast *Abyss:*
Whatever happy region is thy place,
Cease thy Celestial Song a little space;
(Thou wilt have time enough for Hymns Divine,
Since Heav'ns Eternal Year is thine.)
Hear then a Mortal Muse thy praise rehearse
     In no ignoble Verse;
But such as thy own voice did practise here,
When thy first Fruits of Poesie were given,
To make thyself a welcome Inmate there;
    While yet a young Probationer,
     And Candidate of Heav'n.

2

If by Traduction came thy Mind,
   Our Wonder is the less to find
A Soul so charming from a Stock so good;
Thy Father was transfus'd into thy *Blood:*
So wert thou born into the tuneful strain,
(An early, rich, and inexhausted Vein.)
   But if thy Præ-existing Soul
Was form'd, at first, with Myriads more,
   It did through all the Mighty Poets roul
Who *Greek* or *Latine* Laurels wore,
And was that *Sappho* last, which once it was before.
   If so, then cease thy flight, *O Heav'n-born Mind!*
Thou hast no *Dross* to purge from thy Rich Ore:
   Nor can thy Soul a fairer Mansion find
   Than was the *Beauteous* Frame she left behind:
Return, to fill or mend the Quire of thy Celestial kind.

3

May we presume to say, that at thy *Birth,*
New joy was sprung in HEAV'N as well as here on *Earth?*
For sure the Milder Planets did combine
On thy *Auspicious* Horoscope to shine,
And ev'n the most Malicious were in Trine.
Thy *Brother-Angels* at thy *Birth*
   Strung each his Lyre, and tun'd it high,
    That all the People of the Skie

Might know a Poetess was born on Earth.
  And then if ever, Mortal Ears
  Had heard the Musick of the Spheres!
  And if no clust'ring Swarm of *Bees*
On thy sweet Mouth distill'd their golden Dew,
  'Twas that, such vulgar Miracles
  Heav'n had not Leasure to renew:
For all the *Blest* Fraternity of Love
Solemniz'd there thy *Birth,* and kept thy Holyday above.

4

  O Gracious God! How far have we
  Prophan'd thy Heav'nly Gift of Poesy!
  Made prostitute and profligate the Muse,
  Debas'd to each obscene and impious use,
  Whose Harmony was first ordain'd *Above,*
  For Tongues of *Angels* and for *Hymns* of *Love!*
Oh wretched We! why were we hurry'd down
  This lubrique and adult'rate age,
  (Nay, added fat Pollutions of our own)
  T' increase the steaming Ordures of the Stage?
What can we say t' excuse our *Second Fall?*
Let this thy *Vestal,* Heav'n, atone for all:
  Her *Arethusian* Stream remains unsoil'd,
  Unmixt with Forreign Filth and undefil'd,
Her Wit was more than Man, her Innocence a Child.

5

Art she had none, yet wanted none,
  For Nature did that Want supply:
So rich in Treasures of her Own,
  She might our boasted Stores defy:
Such Noble Vigour did her Verse adorn,
That it seem'd borrow'd, where 'twas only born.
Her Morals too were in her *Bosom* bred
  By great Examples daily fed,
What in the best of *Books,* her Father's Life, she read.
  And to be read her self she need not fear;
  Each Test, and ev'ry Light, her Muse will bear,
  Though *Epictetus* with his Lamp were there.
  Ev'n Love (for Love sometimes her Muse exprest),
Was but a Lambent-flame which play'd about her *Breast:*

Light as the Vapours of a Morning Dream,
So cold herself, whilst she such Warmth exprest,
'Twas *Cupid* bathing in *Diana's* Stream.

6

Born to the Spacious Empire of the Nine,
One wou'd have thought, she should have been content
To manage well that Mighty Government;
But what can young ambitious Souls confine?
  To the next Realm she stretcht her Sway,
  For *Painture* near adjoyning lay,
A plenteous Province, and alluring Prey.
A *Chamber of Dependences* was fram'd,
(As Conquerors will never want Pretence,
  When arm'd, to justifie th' Offence),
And the whole Fief, in right of Poetry she claim'd.
  The Country open lay without Defence;
For Poets frequent In-rodes there had made,
  And perfectly cou'd represent
  The Shape, the Face, with ev'ry Lineament;
And all the large Demains which the Dumb-sister sway'd;
  All bow'd beneath her Government,
  Receiv'd in Triumph wheresoe're she went.
Her Pencil drew whate're her Soul design'd
And oft the *happy Draught* surpass'd the *Image* in her *Mind.*
  The *Sylvan* Scenes of Herds and Flocks
  And fruitful Plains and barren Rocks,
  Of shallow *Brooks* that flow'd so clear,
  The bottom did the top appear;
  Of deeper too and ampler Floods
  Which as in Mirrors, shew'd the Woods;
  Of lofty Trees, with Sacred Shades
  And Perspectives of pleasant Glades,
  Where Nymphs of brightest Form appear,
  And shaggy Satyrs standing near,
  Which them at once admire and fear.
  The Ruines too of some Majestick Piece,
  Boasting the Pow'r of ancient *Rome* or *Greece,*
  Whose Statues, Freezes, Columns, broken lie,
  And, tho' defac'd, the Wonder of the Eye;
  What *Nature, Art,* bold *Fiction,* e're durst frame,
  Her forming Hand gave Feature to the Name.
  So strange a Concourse ne're was seen before,
But when the peopl'd *Ark* the whole Creation bore.

7

The Scene then chang'd; with bold Erected Look
Our Martial King the sight with Reverence strook:
For, not content t' express his Outward Part,
Her hand call'd out the Image of his Heart,
His Warlike Mind, his Soul devoid of Fear,
His High-designing *Thoughts* were figurd' there,
As when, by Magick, Ghosts are made appear.
    Our Phenix queen was portrai'd too so bright,
Beauty alone cou'd *Beauty* take so right:
Her Dress, her Shape, her matchless Grace,
Were all observ'd, as well as heav'nly Face.
With such a Peerless Majesty she stands,
As in that Day she took the Crown from Sacred hands:
Before a Train of Heroins was seen,
In *Beauty* foremost, as in Rank, the Queen!
    Thus nothing to her Genius was deny'd,
But like a *Ball* of Fire, the farther thrown,
Still with a greater *Blaze* she shone,
    And her bright Soul broke out on ev'ry side.
What next she had design'd, Heaven only knows:
To such Immod'rate Growth her Conquest rose
That Fate alone its Progress cou'd oppose.

Now all those Charms, that blooming Grace,
The well-proportion'd Shape and beauteous Face,
Shall never more be seen by Mortal Eyes;
In Earth the much-lamented Virgin lies!
    Not Wit nor Piety cou'd Fate prevent;
    Nor was the cruel *Destiny* content
      To finish all the Murder at a blow,
      To sweep at once her *Life* and *Beauty* too;
But, like a hardn'd Fellon, took a pride
      To work more Mischievously slow,
And plunder'd first, and then destroy'd.
O double Sacriledge on things Divine,
To rob the Relique, and deface the Shrine!
    But thus *Orinda* dy'd:
Heav'n, by the same Disease, did both translate,
As equal were their Souls, so equal was their fate.

Mean time, her *Warlike Brother* on the Seas
His waving Streamers to the Winds displays,
And vows for his Return, with vain Devotion, pays.
  Ah, Generous Youth! that Wish forbear,
  The Winds too soon will waft thee here!
  Slack all thy Sails, and fear to come,
Alas, thou know'st not, thou art wreck'd at home!
No more shalt thou behold thy Sister's Face,
Thou hast already had her last Embrace.
But look aloft, and if thou ken'st from far,
Among the *Pleiad's*, a New-kindl'd star,
If any sparkles, than the rest, more bright,
'Tis she that shines in that propitious Light.

10

When in mid-Air the Golden Trump shall sound,
  To raise the Nations under ground;
  When in the Valley of *Jehosaphat*
The Judging God shall close the book of Fate;
  And there the last *Assizes* keep
  For those who Wake and those who Sleep;
  When ratling *Bones* together fly
  From the four Corners of the Skie,
When Sinews o're the Skeletons are spread,
Those cloath'd with Flesh, and Life inspires the Dead;
The Sacred Poets first shall hear the Sound,
And formost from the Tomb shall bound:
For they are cover'd with the lightest ground;
And streight, with in-born Vigour, on the Wing,
Like mounting Larks, to the New Morning sing.
There *Thou*, sweet Saint, before the Quire shalt go,
As Harbinger of Heav'n, the Way to show,
The Way which thou so well hast learn'd below.

(1693)

Undoubtedly the noblest ode that our language has ever produced. The first part flows with a torrent of enthusiasm. FERVET IMMENSUSQUE RUIT.

SAMUEL JOHNSON
The Lives of the Poets (1779–81)

JOHN DRYDEN

1 6 3 1 — 1 7 0 0

LINES PRINTED UNDER THE
ENGRAVED PORTRAIT OF MILTON

Three Poets, in three distant Ages born,
Greece, Italy, and *England* did adorn.
The first in Loftiness of Thought surpass'd,
The next in Majesty, in both the last:
The Force of Nature could no farther go;
To make a third she join'd the former two.

> In Tonson's Folio Edition
> of the 'Paradise Lost' (1688)

It is a remarkable fact, that the very finest epigram in the English language happens also to be the worst. EPIGRAM *I call it in the austere Greek sense; which thus far resembled our modern idea of an epigram, that something pointed and allied to wit was demanded in the management of the leading thought at its close, but otherwise nothing tending towards the comic or the ludicrous. The epigram I speak of is the well-known one of Dryden dedicated to the glorification of Milton. It is irreproachable as regards its severe brevity. Not one word is there that could be spared; nor could the wit of man have cast the movement of the thought into a better mould. There are three couplets. In the first couplet we are reminded of the fact that this earth had, in three different stages of its development, given birth to a trinity of transcendent poets; meaning narrative poets, or, even more narrowly, epic poets. The duty thrown upon the second couplet is to characterize these three poets, and to value them against each other, but in such terms as that, whilst nothing less than the very highest praise should be assigned to the two elder poets in this trinity—the Greek and the Roman—nevertheless, by some dexterous artifice, a higher praise than the highest should suddenly unmask itself, and drop, as it were, like a diadem from the clouds upon the brows of their English competitor. In the kind of expectation raised, and in the extreme difficulty of adequately meeting this expectation, there was pretty much the same challenge offered to Dryden as was offered, somewhere about the same time, to a British ambassador when dining with his political antagonists. One of these—the ambassador of France—had proposed to drink his master, Louis XIV., under the character of the sun, who dispensed life and light to the whole political system. To this there was no objection; and immediately, by way of intercepting any further draughts upon the rest of the solar system, the Dutch ambassador rose, and proposed the health of their high mightinesses the Seven*

United States, as the moon and six planets, who gave light in the absence of the sun. The two foreign ambassadors, Monsieur and Mynheer, secretly enjoyed the mortification of their English brother, who seemed to be thus left in a state of bankruptcy, 'no funds' being available for retaliation, or so they fancied. But suddenly our British representative toasted HIS master as Joshua, the son of Nun, that made the sun and moon stand still. All had seemed lost for England, when in an instant of time both her antagonists were checkmated. Dryden assumed something of the same position. He gave away the supreme jewels in his exchequer; apparently nothing remained behind; all was exhausted. To Homer he gave A; to Virgil he gave B; and, behold! after these were given away, there remained nothing at all that would not have been a secondary praise. But, in a moment of time, by giving A AND B to Milton, at one sling of his victorious arm he raised him above Homer by the whole extent of B, and above Virgil by the whole extent of A. This felicitous evasion of the embarrassment is accomplished in the second couplet; and, finally, the third couplet winds up with graceful effect, by making a RESUMÉ, or recapitulation of the logic concerned in the distribution of prizes just announced. Nature, he says, had it not in her power to provide a third prize separate from the first and second; her resource was, to join the first and second in combination: 'To make a third, she joined the former two.'

Such is the abstract of this famous epigram; and, judged simply by the outline and tendency of the thought, it merits all the vast popularity which it has earned. But in the meantime, it is radically vicious as regards the filling in of this outline; for the particular quality in which Homer is accredited with the pre-eminence, viz., LOFTINESS OF THOUGHT, happens to be a mere variety of expression for that quality, viz. MAJESTY, in which the pre-eminence is awarded to Virgil. Homer excels Virgil in the very point in which lies Virgil's superiority to Homer; and that synthesis, by means of which a great triumph is reserved to Milton, becomes obviously impossible, when it is perceived that the supposed analytic elements of this synthesis are blank reiterations of each other.

Exceedingly striking it is, that a thought should have prospered for one hundred and seventy years, which, on the slightest steadiness of examination, turns out to be no thought at all, but mere blank vacuity. There is, however, this justification of the case, that the mould, the set of channels, into which the metal of the thought is meant to run, really HAS the felicity which it appears to have: the form is perfect; and it is merely in the MATTER, in the accidental filling up of the mould, that a fault has been committed. Had the Virgilian point of excellence been LOVELINESS instead of MAJESTY, or any word whatever suggesting the common antithesis of sublimity and beauty; or had it been power on the one side, matched against grace on the other, the true lurking tendency

of the thought would have been developed, and the sub-conscious pur-
pose of the epigram would have fulfilled itself to the letter.

N.B.—*It is not meant that* LOFTINESS OF THOUGHT *and* MAJESTY *are*
expressions so entirely interchangeable, as that no shades of difference
could be suggested; it is enough that these 'shades' are not substantial
enough, or broad enough, to support the weight of opposition which
the epigram assigns to them. GRACE *and* ELEGANCE, *for instance, are*
far from being in all relations synonymous; but they are so to the full
extent of any purposes concerned in this epigram.

Nevertheless, it is probable enough that Dryden had moving in his
thoughts a relation of the word MAJESTY, *which, if developed, would*
have done justice to his meaning. It was, perhaps, the decorum and sus-
tained dignity of the COMPOSITION—*the workmanship apart from the*
native grandeur of the materials—the majestic style of the artistic treat-
ment as distinguished from the original creative power—which Dryden,
the translator of the Roman poet, familiar therefore with his weakness
and with his strength, meant in this place to predicate as character-
istically observable in Virgil.

THOMAS DE QUINCEY
The Note Book of An English Opium-Eater (1855)

JOHN DRYDEN

1 6 3 1 — 1 7 0 0

ALEXANDER'S FEAST;
OR, THE POWER OF MUSIQUE.

AN ODE IN HONOUR OF ST. CECILIA'S DAY: 1697.

I

'Twas at the Royal Feast, for *Persia* won,
  By *Philip's* Warlike Son:
  Aloft in awful State
  The God-like Heroe sate
  On his Imperial Throne;
His valiant Peers were plac'd around;
Their Brows with Roses and with Myrtles bound.
 (So should Desert in Arms be Crown'd:)
 The lovely *Thais* by his side,
 Sate like a blooming *Eastern* Bride

In Flow'r of Youth and Beauty's Pride.
          Happy, happy, happy Pair!
              None but the Brave,
              None but the Brave,
      None but the Brave deserves the Fair.

          Happy, happy, happy Pair!
              None but the Brave,
              None but the Brave,
      None but the Brave deserves the Fair.

II

          Timotheus plac'd on high
              Amid the tuneful Quire,
      With the flying Fingers touch'd the Lyre:
          The trembling Notes ascend the Sky,
              And Heav'nly Joys inspire.
      The Song began from *Jove;*
      Who left his blissful Seats above,
      (Such is the Pow'r of mighty Love.)
      A Dragon's fiery Form bely'd the God:
      Sublime on Radiant Spires He rode,
      When He to fair *Olympia* press'd:
      And while He sought her snowy Breast:
      Then, round her slender Waist he curl'd,
And stamp'd an Image of himself, a Sov'raign of the World.
      The list'ning crowd admire the lofty Sound,
      A present Deity, they shout around:
      A present Deity, the vaulted Roofs rebound.
              With ravish'd Ears,
              The Monarch hears,
              Assumes the God,
              Affects to nod,
      And seems to shake the Spheres.

              With ravish'd Ears
              The Monarch hears,
              Assumes the God,
              Affects to nod,
      And seems to shake the Spheres.

III

The Praise of *Bacchus* then the sweet Musician sung,
  Of *Bacchus* ever Fair, and ever Young:
    The jolly God in Triumph comes;
    Sound the Trumpets; beat the Drums;
      Flush'd with a purple Grace
      He shows his honest Face:
Now give the Hautboys breath; He comes, He comes.
      Bacchus ever Fair and Young
      Drinking Joys did first ordain;
    Bacchus Blessings are a Treasure;
    Drinking is the Soldiers Pleasure;
        Rich the Treasure;
        Sweet the Pleasure;
      Sweet is Pleasure after Pain.

CHORUS

    Bacchus *Blessings are a Treasure,*
    Drinking is the Soldier's Pleasure;
        Rich the Treasure,
        Sweet the Pleasure,
      Sweet is Pleasure after Pain.

IV

  Sooth'd with the Sound the King grew vain;
    Fought all his Battails o'er again;
And thrice He routed all his Foes, and thrice he slew the slain.
    The Master saw the Madness rise,
    His glowing Cheeks, his ardent Eyes;
    And while He Heav'n and Earth defy'd,
  Chang'd his Hand, and check'd his Pride.
      He chose a Mournful Muse,
      Soft Pity to infuse;
    He sung *Darius* Great and Good,
      By too severe a Fate,
    Fallen, fallen, fallen, fallen,
      Fallen from his high Estate,
    And weltring in his Blood:
    Deserted at his utmost Need
    By those his former Bounty fed;
    On the bare Earth expos'd He lies,
    With not a Friend to close his Eyes.

With down-cast Looks the joyless Victor sate,
　　Revolving in his alter'd Soul
　　　The various Turns of Chance below;
　　And, now and then, a Sigh he stole,
　　　And Tears began to flow.

CHORUS

Revolving in his alter'd Soul
　　The various Turns of Chance below;
And, now and then, a Sigh he stole,
　　And Tears began to flow.

V

The Mighty Master smil'd to see
That Love was in the next Degree;
'Twas but a Kindred-Sound to move,
For Pity melts the Mind to Love.
　　Softly sweet, in *Lydian* Measures,
　　Soon he sooth'd his Soul to Pleasures.
War, he sung, is Toil and Trouble;
Honour but an empty Bubble.
　　Never ending, still beginning,
Fighting still, and still destroying,
　　If the World be worth thy Winning,
Think, O think, it worth Enjoying.
　　Lovely *Thais* sits beside thee,
　　Take the Good the Gods provide thee.
The Many rend the Skies, with loud applause;
So Love was Crown'd, but Musique won the Cause.
　　The Prince, unable to conceal his Pain,
　　　　Gaz'd on the Fair
　　　　Who caus'd his Care,
　　And sigh'd and look'd, sigh'd and look'd,
　　Sigh'd and look'd, and sigh'd again:
At length, with Love and Wine at once oppress'd,
The vanquish'd Victor sunk upon her Breast.

CHORUS

The Prince, unable to conceal his Pain,
　　　Gaz'd on the fair
　　　Who caus'd his Care,
　　And sigh'd and look'd, sigh'd and look'd,
　　Sigh'd and look'd, and sigh'd again;
At length, with Love and Wine at once oppress'd,
The vanquish'd Victor sunk upon her Breast.

VI

Now strike the Golden Lyre again;
A lowder yet, and yet a lowder Strain.
Break his Bands of Sleep asunder,
And rouze him, like a rattling Peal of Thunder.
    Hark, hark, the horrid Sound
      Has rais'd up his Head;
      As awak'd from the Dead,
    And amaz'd, he stares around.
Revenge, revenge, *Timotheus* cries
    See the Furies arise!
    See the Snakes that they rear,
    How they hiss in their Hair,
And the Sparkles that flash from their Eyes!
    Behold a ghastly Band,
    Each a Torch in his Hand!
Those are *Grecian* Ghosts, that in Battail were slain,
    And unbury'd remain
    Inglorious on the Plain:
    Give the Vengeance due
    To the Valiant Crew.
Behold how they toss their Torches on high,
    How they point to the *Persian* Abodes,
And glitt'ring Temples of their Hostile Gods.
The Princes applaud with a furious Joy;
And the King seized a Flambeau with Zeal to destroy;
    Thais led the Way,
    To light him to his Prey,
And, like another *Hellen*, fir'd another *Troy*.

CHORUS

And the King seiz'd a Flambeau with Zeal to destroy;
    Thais *led the Way,*
    To light him to his Prey,
And, like another Hellen, *fir'd another Troy.*

VII

    Thus long ago,
'Ere heaving Bellows learn'd to blow,
    While Organs yet were mute,
    Timotheus, to his breathing Flute
    And sounding Lyre,
Cou'd swell the Soul to rage, or kindle soft Desire.

At last Divine *Cecilia* came,
Inventress of the Vocal Frame;
The Sweet Enthusiast, from her Sacred Store,
Enlarg'd the former narrow Bounds,
And added Length to solemn Sounds,
With Nature's Mother-Wit, and Arts unknown before.
Let old *Timotheus* yield the Prize,
Or both divide the Crown:
He rais'd a Mortal to the Skies;
She drew an Angel down.

GRAND CHORUS

At last Divine Cecilia *came,*
Inventress of the Vocal Frame;
The sweet Enthusiast, from her Sacred Store,
Enlarg'd the former narrow Bounds,
And added Length to solemn Sounds,
With Nature's Mother-Wit, and Arts unknown before.
Let old Timotheus *yield the Prize,*
Or both divide the Crown:
He rais'd a Mortal to the Skies;
She drew an Angel down.

(1700)

We have had in our language no other odes of the sublime kind, than
that of Dryden on St. Cecilia's day.

THOMAS GRAY
The Progress of Poesy (1754)

JOHN DRYDEN

1 6 3 1 — 1 7 0 0

CYMON AND IPHIGENIA

The deep Recesses of the Grove he gain'd;
Where, in a Plain, defended by the Wood,
Crept through the matted Grass a Chrystal Flood,
By which an Alabaster Fountain stood:
And on the Margin of the Fount was laid
(Attended by her Slaves) a sleeping Maid

Like *Dian* and her Nymphs, when, tir'd with Sport,
To rest by cool *Eurotas* they resort:
The Dame herself the Goddess well express'd,
Not more distinguish'd by her Purple Vest,
Than by the charming Features of her Face,
And ev'n in Slumber a superiour Grace:
Her comely Limbs compos'd with decent Care,
Her Body shaded with a slight Cymarr;
Her Bosom to the view was only bare:
Where two beginning Paps were scarcely spy'd
For yet their Places were but signify'd:
The fanning Wind upon her Bosom blows,
To meet the fanning Wind the Bosom rose;
The fanning Wind, and purling Streams continue her repose.
   The Fool of Nature, stood with stupid Eyes
And gaping Mouth, that testify'd Surprize,
Fix'd on her Face, nor cou'd remove his Sight,
New as he was to Love, and Novice in Delight:
Long mute he stood, and leaning on his Staff,
His Wonder witness'd with an Ideot laugh;
Then would have spoke, but by his glimmering Sense
First found his want of Words, and fear'd Offence:
Doubted for what he was he should be known,
By his Clown-Accent and his Country-Tone.
   Through the rude Chaos thus the running Light
Shot the first Ray that pierc'd the Native Night:
Then Day and Darkness in the Mass were mix'd,
Till gather'd in a Globe, the Beams were fix'd:
Last shon the Sun who, radiant in his Sphere
Illumin'd Heav'n, and Earth, and rowl'd around the Year.
So Reason in this Brutal Soul began:
Love made him first suspect he was a Man;
Love made him doubt his broad barbarian Sound;
By Love his want of Words and Wit he found;
That sense of want prepar'd the future way
To Knowledge, and disclos'd the promise of a Day.
   What not his Father's Care, nor Tutor's Art
Cou'd plant with Pains in his unpolish'd Heart,
The best Instructor Love at once inspir'd,
As barren Grounds to Fruitfulness are fir'd;
Love taught him Shame, and Shame with Love at Strife
Soon taught the sweet Civilities of Life;
His gross material Soul at once could find
Somewhat in her excelling all her Kind:

Exciting a Desire till then unknown,
Somewhat unfound, or found in her alone.
This made the first Impression in his Mind,
Above, but just above, the Brutal Kind.
For Beasts can like, but not distinguish too,
Nor their own liking by reflection know;
Nor why they like or this, or t'other Face,
Or judge of this or that peculiar Grace;
But love in gross, and stupidly admire;
As Flies allur'd by Light, approach the Fire.
Thus our Man-Beast advancing by degrees
First likes the whole, then sep'rates what he sees;
On sev'ral Parts, a sev'ral Praise bestows,
The ruby Lips, the well-proportion'd Nose,
The snowy Skin, in Raven-glossy Hair,
The dimpled Cheek, the Forehead rising fair,
And ev'n in Sleep it self a smiling Air.
From thence his Eyes descending view'd the rest,
Her plump round Arms, white Hands, and heaving Breast.
Long on the last he dwelt, though ev'ry part
A pointed Arrow sped to pierce his Heart.
    Thus in a trice a Judge of Beauty grown,
(A Judge erected from a Country-Clown)
He long'd to see her Eyes in Slumber hid,
And wish'd his own cou'd pierce within the Lid:
He wou'd have wak'd her, but restrain'd his Thought,
And Love new-born the first good Manners taught.
An awful Fear his ardent Wish withstood,
Nor durst disturb the Goddess of the Wood;
For such she seem'd by her celestial Face,
Excelling all the rest of human Race:
And Things divine, by common Sense he knew,
Must be devoutly seen at distant view:
So checking his Desire, with trembling Heart
Gazing he stood, nor would, nor could depart;
Fix'd as a Pilgrim wilder'd in his way,
Who dares not stir by Night for fear to stray;
But stands with awful Eyes to watch the dawn of Day.

Fables Antient and Modern (1700)

There is not in our language a strain of more beautiful and melodious poetry.

SIR WALTER SCOTT
The Works of John Dryden (1808)

JOHN DRYDEN

1 6 3 1 — 1 7 0 0

THE TWENTY-NINTH ODE OF THE THIRD BOOK OF HORACE

PARAPHRASED IN PINDARICK VERSE, AND INSCRIBED TO THE
RIGHT HON. LAURENCE EARL OF ROCHESTER.

I

Descended of an ancient Line,
   That long the *Tuscan* Scepter sway'd,
Make haste to meet the generous Wine,
   Whose piercing is for thee delay'd:
The rosie wreath is ready made;
   And artful hands prepare
The fragrant *Syrian* Oyl, that shall perfume thy hair.

II

When the Wine sparkles from a far,
   And the well-natur'd Friend cries, come away;
Make haste, and leave thy business and thy care:
   No mortal int'rest can be worth thy stay.

III

Leave for a while thy costly Country Seat;
   And, to be Great indeed, forget
The nauseous pleasures of the Great:
   Make haste and come:
Come, and forsake thy cloying store;
   Thy Turret that surveys, from high,
The smoke, and wealth, and noise of *Rome;*
   And all the busie pageantry
That wise men scorn, and fools adore:
Come, give thy Soul a loose, and taste the pleasures of the poor.

IV

Sometimes 'tis grateful to the Rich, to try
A short vicissitude, and fit of Poverty:
   A savoury Dish, a homely Treat,
   Where all is plain, where all is neat,

Without the stately spacious Room,
The *Persian* Carpet, or the *Tyrian* Loom,
Clear up the cloudy foreheads of the Great.

V

The Sun is in the Lion mounted high;
    The *Syrian* Star
    Barks from afar,
And with his sultry breath infects the Sky;
The ground below is parch'd, the heav'ns above us fry.
    The Shepheard drives his fainting Flock
    Beneath the covert of a Rock,
    And seeks refreshing Rivulets nigh
    The *Sylvans* to their shades retire,
Those very shades and streams new shades and streams require,
And want a cooling breeze of wind to fan the raging fire.

VI

Thou, what befits the new Lord May'r,
And what the City Faction dare,
And what the *Gallique* arms will do,
And what the Quiverbearing foe,
Art anxiously inquisitive to know:
But God has, wisely, hid from humane sight
    The dark decrees of future fate;
    And sown their seeds in depth of night;
He laughs at all the giddy turns of State;
When Mortals search too soon, and fear too late.

VII

Enjoy the present smiling hour;
    And put it out of Fortunes pow'r:
The tide of bus'ness, like the running stream,
    Is sometimes high, and sometimes low,
A quiet ebb, or a tempestuous flow,
        And alwayes in extream.
    Now with a noiseless gentle course
    It keeps within the middle Bed;
    Anon it lifts aloft the head,
And bears down all before it with impetuous force:
    And trunks of Trees come rowling down,
    Sheep and their Folds together drown:

Both House and Homested into Seas are borne;
And Rocks are from their old foundations torn,
And woods, made thin with winds, their scatter'd honours mourn.

VIII

Happy the Man, and happy he alone,
    He, who can call to day his own:
    He who, secure within, can say,
To morrow do thy worst, for I have liv'd to-day.
    Be fair, or foul, or rain, or shine,
The joys I have possest, in spight of fate, are mine.
Not Heav'n it self upon the past has pow'r;
But what has been, has been, and I have had my hour.

IX

Fortune, that with malicious joy
    Does Man her slave oppress,
Proud of her Office to destroy,
    Is seldome pleas'd to bless:
Still various, and unconstant still,
But with an inclination to be ill.
Promotes, degrades, delights in strife,
    And makes a Lottery of life.
I can enjoy her while she's kind;
But when she dances in the wind,
    And shakes the wings, and will not stay.
    I puff the Prostitute away:
The little or the much she gave, is quietly resign'd:
Content with poverty, my Soul I arm;
And Vertue, tho' in rags, will keep me warm.

X

What is't to me,
Who never sail in her unfaithful Sea,
    If Storms arise, and Clouds grow black;
    If the Mast split, and threaten wreck?
Then let the greedy Merchant fear
    For his ill gotten gain;
And pray to Gods that will not hear,
While the debating winds and billows bear
    His Wealth into the Main
For me, secure from Fortunes blows
(Secure of what I cannot lose,)

In my small Pinnace I can sail,
Contemning all the blustring roar;
    And running with a merry gale,
With friendly Stars my safety seek
Within some little winding Creek;
    And see the storm a shore.

Horace
Odes, iii, 29

One of the great poems in English.

CYRIL CONNOLLY
The Condemned Playground (1946)

JOHN LOCKE

1 6 3 2 — 1 7 0 4

WIT AND JUDGMENT

And hence, perhaps, may be given some Reason of that common Observation, That Men who have a great deal of Wit, and prompt Memories, have not always the clearest Judgment, or deepest Reason. For *Wit* lying most in the assemblage of *Ideas,* and putting those together with quickness and variety, wherein can be found any resemblance or congruity, thereby to make up pleasant Pictures, and agreeable Visions in the Fancy: *Judgment,* on the contrary, lies quite on the other side, in separating carefully *Ideas* one from another, wherein can be found the least difference, thereby to avoid being misled by Similitude, and by affinity to take one thing for another. This is a way of proceeding quite contrary to Metaphor and Allusion, wherein, for the most part, lies that entertainment and pleasantry of Wit, which strikes so lively on the Fancy; and therefore so acceptable to all People.

An Essay Concerning Humane Understanding (1690)

This is, I think, the best and most philosophical account that I have ever met with of wit.

JOSEPH ADDISON
The Spectator (May 11, 1711)

NICOLAS BOILEAU-DESPRÉAUX

1636 — 1711

ANTITHESIS

Et, pour le rendre libre, il le faut enchaîner.

To set him free, he must be enchained.

This verse alone was worth a pension from Louis. It is indeed the most violent antithesis that ever was constructed.

WALTER SAVAGE LANDOR
Imaginary Conversations, Abbé Delille and Landor (1824–9)

NICOLAS BOILEAU-DESPRÉAUX

1636 — 1711

MALHERBE

Dans mes vers recousus mettre en pièces Malherbe.

In my patched-up verses to tear Malherbe to pieces.
Satires, ii (1664)

I would give the most beautiful of my verses to have written this one.

JEAN DE LA FONTAINE
Quoted, Désiré Nisard, Histoire de la littérature française (1844)

JEAN RACINE

1639 — 1699

THE OPENING LINES OF *BAJAZET*

ACOMAT
Viens, suis-moi. La Sultane en ce lieu se doit rendre.
Je pourrai cependant te parler et t'entendre.
OSMIN
Et depuis quand, Seigneur, entre-t-on dans ces lieux

Dont l'accès était même interdit à nos yeux?
Jadis une mort prompte eût suivi cette audace.

ACOMAT

Quand tu seras instruit de tout ce qui se passe,
Mon entrée en ces lieux ne te surprendra plus.
Mais laissons, cher Osmin, les discours superflus.
Que ton retour tardait à mon impatience!
Et que d'un œil content je te vois dans Byzance!
Instruis-moi des secrets que peut t'avoir appris
Un voyage si long pour moi seul entrepris.
De ce qu'ont vu tes yeux parle en témoin sincère:
Songe que du récit, Osmin, que tu vas faire
Dépendent les destins de l'empire ottoman.
Qu'as-tu vu dans l'armée, et que fait le Sultan?

OSMIN

Babylone, Seigneur, à son prince fidèle,
Voyait sans s'étonner notre armée autour d'elle;
Les Persans rassemblés marchaient à son secours,
Et du camp d'Amurat s'approchaient tous les jours.
Lui-même, fatigué d'un long siège inutile,
Semblait vouloir laisser Babylone tranquille,
Et sans renouveler ses assauts impuissants,
Résolu de combattre, attendait les Persans.
Mais, comme vous savez, malgré ma diligence,
Un long chemin sépare et le camp et Byzance;
Mille obstacles divers m'ont même traversé,
Et je puis ignorer tout ce qui s'est passé.

ACOMAT

Que faisaient cependant nos braves janissaires?
Rendent-ils au Sultan des hommages sincères?
Dans le secret des cœurs, Osmin, n'as-tu rien lu?
Amurat jouit-il d'un pouvoir absolu?

OSMIN

Amurat est content, si nous le voulons croire,
Et semblait se promettre une heureuse victoire.
Mais en vain par ce calme il croit nous éblouir:
Il affecte un repos dont il ne peut jouir.
C'est en vain que forçant ses soupçons ordinaires,
Il se rend accessible à tous les janissaires:
Il se souvient toujours que son inimitié,
Voulut de ce grand corps retrancher la moitié,
Lorsque, pour affermir sa puissance nouvelle,
Il voulait, disait-il, sortir de leur tutelle.
Moi-même, j'ai souvent entendu leurs discours;
Comme il les craint sans cesse, ils le craignent toujours.

Ses caresses n'ont point effacé cette injure.
Votre absence est pour eux un sujet de murmure.
Ils regrettent le temps, à leur grand cœur si doux,
Lorsqu' assurés de vaincre ils combattaient sous vous.

ACOMAT

Quoi? tu crois, cher Osmin, que ma gloire passée
Flatte encor leur valeur et vit dans leur pensée?
Crois-tu qu'ils me suivraient encore avec plaisir,
Et qu'ils reconnaîtraient la voix de leur vizir?

ACOMAT

Here, *Osmyn*, we may reason unobserv'd.
The Sultaness, from yonder high-rais'd Terras,
Views the wide *Euxine*, and enjoys the Breeze.

OSMYN

Where am I, Vizier! Whither do you lead me?
'Tis Death to breathe within these Walls; this Place
Our earthly Gods hold Sacred: The *Seraglio*
Is fenc'd by *Mahomet's* severest Laws:
'Tis Sacrilege, 'tis Height of Prophanation,
For vulgar Feet to tread where the dread Race
Of *Ottoman* is form'd.—But tell me, General,
How durst those tongueless Slaves, who guard this Palace
In dreadful Silence, open to your Signal?
I dare no farther press.

ACOMAT

Yet check a while
Thy curious Fears: I am thy Guide. Say, *Osmyn*,
Why didst thou suffer *Acomat* thus long
To wait thy needful Presence in *Bysantium*?
What Seas, what Sands, what Dangers hast thou cross'd
To serve thy Friend? What Tidings of Importance?
What Secret dost thou bring? What of our Army?
What of our Sultan knowest thou? Open all.
Speak, *Osmyn:* Ease my impatient Heart: Thy *own*,
Thy Vizier's *Fate*, the *Fate* of a whole Empire
Lyes in thy Breast, and hangs upon thy Words.

OSMYN

Still *Babylon* stands faithful to her Prince:
Unshaken yet, she sees our turban'd Hosts
Surround her Walls. Mean Time, the *Persians* arm:
From every Side their num'rous Bands advancing,
Move to her Aid; and each succeeding Morn,
Gain on the Sight, and thicken to the View.

The *Sultan*, weary'd with a fruitless Siege,
No more renews his vain Assaults; resolv'd
To wait their Arms before those lofty Bulwarks;
In one decisive Hour to try his Fate,
And fix at once the Empire of the East.

ACOMAT

Go on, my Soldier: I am all Attention.

OSMYN

Since that, I little know. Long tedious Leagues
Divide this City from the Camp; each Day
New Obstacles have cross'd my speedy Course,
And intercepted all my Diligence.

ACOMAT

How do our Gallant Janizaries bear
Their great Imperial Master's jealous Eye?
Or is the Homage which they pay, Sincere?

OSMYN

Proud *Amurat* puts on a pleasing Look,
And seems secure of Conquest; but in vain
He smooths his troubl'd Brow; the thin Disguise
Serves but to render him yet more suspected,
In vain he courts his hardy Janizaries:
Their Hearts are inaccessible: They think,
And think with secret Malice, on the Attempt
The *Sultan* made to break their Gallant Troops.
They fear him, Sir; and whom they fear, they hate.
I know they murmur at their *Vizier's* Absence;
And oftentimes regret those Days of Glory,
When you conducted them to certain Conquest.

ACOMAT

Dost thou then think, dear *Osmyn*, those bless'd Days
Still swell their Hearts, and make them full of me?
Think'st thou they still will follow where I lead,
And recognize once more their *Vizier's* Voice?

Bajazet (1672)
Act i, Scene i
The Charles Johnson Version (1717)

*What would be, for example, the best model for the opening passage of
a tragedy? It would be that of* BAJAZET. . . . *This passage is conceded
to be a masterpiece of the human mind.*

F. M. AROUET DE VOLTAIRE
Lettre à l'Académie Française (1776)

JEAN RACINE

1 6 3 9 — 1 6 9 9

MONIME ANSWERS HER LOVER'S FATHER

Et, quand il n'en perdroit que l'amour de son père,
Il en mourra, Seigneur.

If he loses naught but his father's love he will die of it, my lord.

Mithridate (1673)
Act iv, Scene iv

Sublime words, in that domain of delicate thoughts and verities of the heart, where Racine is without an equal as without a model.

DÉSIRÉ NISARD
Histoire de la littérature française (1844)

JEAN RACINE

1 6 3 9 — 1 6 9 9

DEATH

Mais la mort fuit encor sa grande âme trompée.

But Death still shuns his great defrauded soul.

Mithridate (1673)
Act v, Scene iv
Translated by Maurice Baring

One of the most poignant lines in poetry.

MAURICE BARING
Have You Anything to Declare? (1936)

844

JEAN RACINE

1 6 3 9 — 1 6 9 9

PHÆDRA

La fille de Minos et de Pasiphaé.

Daughter of Minos and Pasiphaë.

Phèdre (1677)
Act i, Scene i

The most beautiful line in all French literature, a phrase of eternal and sublime beauty.

GUSTAVE FLAUBERT
Quoted, J. G. Palache, Gautier and the Romantics (1926)

JEAN RACINE

1 6 3 9 — 1 6 9 9

PHÆDRA DECLARES HER LOVE
FOR HER STEPSON

PHÈDRE, HIPPOLYTE, OENONE.

PHÈDRE, à OENONE

Le voici. Vers mon cœur tout mon sang se retire.
J'oublie, en le voyant, ce que je viens lui dire.

OENONE

Souvenez-vous d'un fils qui n'espère qu'en vous.

PHÈDRE

On dit qu'un prompt départ vous éloigne de nous,
Seigneur. A vos douleurs je viens joindre mes larmes.
Je vous viens pour un fils expliquer mes alarmes.
Mon fils n'a plus de père; et le jour n'est pas loin
Qui de ma mort encor doit le rendre témoin.
Déjà mille ennemis attaquent son enfance.
Vous seul pouvez contre eux embrasser sa défense.

Mais un secret remords agite mes esprits.
Je crains d'avoir fermé votre oreille à ses cris.
Je tremble que sur lui votre juste colère
Ne poursuive bientôt une odieuse mère.

HIPPOLYTE

Madame, je n'ai point des sentiments si bas.

PHÈDRE

Quand vous me haïriez, je ne m'en plaindrois pas,
Seigneur. Vous m'avez vue attachée à vous nuire;
Dans le fond de mon cœur vous ne pouviez pas lire.
A votre inimitié j'ai pris soin de m'offrir.
Aux bords que j'habitois je n'ai pu vous souffrir.
En public, en secret, contre vous déclarée,
J'ai voulu par des mers en être séparée;
J'ai même défendu, par une expresse loi,
Qu'on osât prononcer votre nom devant moi.
Si pourtant à l'offense on mesure la peine,
Si la haine peut seule attirer votre haine,
Jamais femme ne fut plus digne de pitié,
Et moins digne, Seigneur, de votre inimitié.

HIPPOLYTE

Des droits de ses enfants une mère jalouse
Pardonne rarement au fils d'une autre épouse.
Madame, je le sais. Les soupçons importuns
Sont d'un second hymen les fruits les plus communs.
Toute autre auroit pour moi pris les mêmes ombrages,
Et j'en aurois peut-être essuyé plus d'outrages.

PHÈDRE

Ah! Seigneur, que le ciel, j'ose ici l'attester,
De cette loi commune a voulu m'excepter!
Qu'un soin bien différent me trouble et me dévore!

HIPPOLYTE

Madame, il n'est pas temps de vous troubler encore.
Peut-être votre époux voit encore le jour;
Le ciel peut à nos pleurs accorder son retour.
Neptune le protége, et ce dieu tutélaire
Ne sera pas en vain imploré par mon père.

PHÈDRE

On ne voit point deux fois le rivage des morts,
Seigneur. Puisque Thésée a vu les sombres bords,
En vain vous espérez qu'un dieu vous le renvoie;
Et l'avare Achéron ne lâche point sa proie.
Que dis-je? Il n'est point mort, puisqu'il respire en vous.
Toujours devant mes yeux je crois voir mon époux.

Je le vois, je lui parle; et mon cœur. . . . Je m'égare,
Seigneur, ma folle ardeur malgré moi se déclare.

HIPPOLYTE

Je vois de votre amour l'effet prodigieux.
Tout mort qu'il est, Thésée est présent à vos yeux;
Toujours de son amour votre âme est embrasée.

PHÈDRE

Oui, Prince, je languis, je brûle pour Thésée.
Je l'aime, non point tel que l'ont vu les enfers,
Volage adorateur de mille objets divers,
Qui va du dieu des morts déshonorer la couche;
Mais fidèle, mais fier, et même un peu farouche,
Charmant, jeune, traînant tous les cœurs après soi,
Tel qu'on dépeint nos dieux, ou tel que je vous **voi.**
Il avoit votre port, vos yeux, votre langage,
Cette noble pudeur coloroit son visage
Lorsque de notre Crète il traversa les flots,
Digne sujet des vœux des filles de Minos.
Que faisiez-vous alors? Pourquoi, sans Hippolyte,
Des héros de la Grèce assembla-t-il l'élite?
Pourquoi, trop jeune encor, ne pûtes-vous alors
Entrer dans le vaisseau qui le mit sur nos bords?
Par vous auroit péri le monstre de la Crète,
Malgré tous les détours de sa vaste retraite.
Pour en développer l'embarras incertain,
Ma sœur du fil fatal eût armé votre main.
Mais non, dans ce dessein je l'aurois devancée
L'amour m'en eût d'abord inspiré la pensée.
C'est moi, Prince, c'est moi dont l'utile secours
Vous eût du Labyrinthe enseigné les détours.
Que de soins m'eût coûtés cette tête charmante!
Un fil n'eût point assez rassuré votre amante.
Compagne du péril qu'il vous falloit chercher,
Moi-même devant vous j'aurois voulu marcher;
Et Phèdre au Labyrinthe avec vous descendue
Se seroit avec vous retrouvée, ou perdue.

HIPPOLYTE

Dieux! qu'est-ce que j'entends? Madame, oubliez-**vous**
Que Thésée est mon père, et qu'il est votre époux?

PHÈDRE

Et sur quoi jugez-vous que j'en perds la mémoire,
Prince? Aurois-je perdu tout le soin de ma gloire?

HIPPOLYTE

Madame, pardonnez. J'avoue, en rougissant,
Que j'accusois à tort un discours innocent.

847

Ma honte ne peut plus soutenir votre vue;
Et je vais. . . .

                    Ah! cruel, tu m'as trop entendue.
Je t'en ai dit assez pour te tirer d'erreur.
Hé bien! connois donc Phèdre et toute sa fureur.
J'aime. Ne pense pas qu'au moment que je t'aime,
Innocente à mes yeux, je m'approuve moi-même;
Ni que du fol amour qui trouble ma raison
Ma lâche complaisance ait nourri le poison.
Objet infortuné des vengeances célestes,
Je m'abhorre encor plus que tu ne me détestes.
Les Dieux m'en sont témoins, ces Dieux qui dans mon flanc
Ont allumé le feu fatal à tout mon sang;
Ces Dieux qui se sont fait une gloire cruelle
De séduire le cœur d'une foible mortelle.
Toi-même en ton esprit rappelle le passé.
C'est peu de t'avoir fui, cruel, je t'ai chassé;
J'ai voulu te paroître odieuse, inhumaine;
Pour mieux te résister, j'ai recherché ta haine.
De quoi m'ont profité mes inutiles soins?
Tu me haïssois plus, je ne t'aimois pas moins.
Tes malheurs te prêtoient encor de nouveaux charmes.
J'ai langui, j'ai séché, dans les feux, dans les larmes.
Il suffit de tes yeux pour t'en persuader,
Si tes yeux un moment pouvoient me regarder.
Que dis-je? Cet aveu que je te viens de faire,
Cet aveu si honteux, le crois-tu volontaire?
Tremblante pour un fils que je n'osois trahir,
Je te venois prier de ne le point haïr.
Foibles projets d'un cœur trop plein de ce qu'il aime!
Hélas! je ne t'ai pu parler que de toi-même.
Venge-toi, punis-moi d'un odieux amour.
Digne fils du héros qui t'a donné le jour,
Délivre l'univers d'un monstre qui t'irrite.
La veuve de Thésée ose aimer Hippolyte!
Crois-moi, ce monstre affreux ne doit point t'échapper.
Voilà mon cœur. C'est là que ta main doit frapper.
Impatient déjà d'expier son offense,
Au-devant de ton bras je le sens qui s'avance.
Frappe. Ou si tu le crois indigne de tes coups,
Si ta haine m'envie un supplice si doux,
Ou si d'un sang trop vil ta main seroit trempée,

Au défaut de ton bras prête-moi ton épée.
Donne.

OENONE

Que faites-vous, Madame? Justes Dieux!
Mais on vient. Évitez des témoins odieux;
Venez, rentrez, fuyez une honte certaine.

PHÆDRA (*to* OENONE).

Look, I see him!
My blood forgets to flow,—tongue will not speak
What I have come to say!

OENONE

Think of your son.
And think that all his hopes depend on you.

PHÆDRA

They tell me that you leave us, hastily.
I come to add my own tears to your sorrow,
And I would plead my fears for my young son.
He has no father, now; 'twill not be long
Until the day that he will see my death,
And even now, his youth is much imperiled
By a thousand foes. You only can defend him.
And in my inmost heart, remorse is stirring,—
Yes, and fear, too, lest I have shut your ears
Against his cries; I fear that your just anger
May, before long, visit on him that hatred
His mother earned.

HIPPOLYTUS

Madam, you need not fear.
Such malice is not mine.

PHÆDRA

I should not blame you
If you should hate me; I have injured you.
So much you know;—you could not read my heart.
Yes, I have tried to be your enemy,
For the same land could never hold us both.
In private and abroad I have declared it;—
I was your enemy! I found no peace
Till seas had parted us; and I forbade
Even your name to be pronounced to me.
And yet, if punishment be meted out
Justly, by the offense;—if only hatred
Deserves a hate, then never was there woman
Deserved more pity, and less enmity.

849

HIPPOLYTUS

A mother who is jealous for her children
Will seldom love the children of a mother
Who came before her. Torments of suspicion
Will often follow on a second marriage.
Another would have felt that jealousy
No less than you; perhaps more violently.

PHÆDRA

Ah, prince, but Heaven made me quite exempt
From what is usual, and I can call
That Heaven as my witness! 'Tis not this—
No, quite another ill devours my heart!

HIPPOLYTUS

This is no time for self-reproaching, madam.
Perhaps your husband still beholds the light,
Perhaps he may be granted safe return
In answer to our prayers; his guarding god
Is Neptune, whom he never called in vain.

PHÆDRA

He who has seen the mansions of the dead
Returns not thence. Since Theseus has gone
Once to those gloomy shores, we need not hope,
For Heaven will not send him back again.
Prince, there is no release from Acheron;—
It is a greedy maw,—and yet I think
He lives and breathes in you,—and still I see him
Before me here; I seem to speak to him—
My heart—! Oh, I am mad! Do what I will,
I cannot hide my passion.

HIPPOLYTUS

Yes, I see
What strange things love will do, for Theseus, dead,
Seems present to your eyes, and in your soul
A constant flame is burning.

PHÆDRA

Ah, for Theseus
I languish and I long, but not, indeed,
As the Shades have seen him, as the fickle lover
Of a thousand forms, the one who fain would ravish
The bride of Pluto;—but one faithful, proud,
Even to slight disdain,—the charm of youth
That draws all hearts, even as the gods are painted,—
Or as yourself. He had your eyes, your manner,—
He spoke like you, and he could blush like you,
And when he came across the waves to Crete,

My childhood home, worthy to win the love
Of Minos' daughters,—what were you doing then?
Why did my father gather all these men,
The flower of Greece, and leave Hippolytus?
Oh, why were you too young to have embarked
On board the ship that brought your father there?
The monster would have perished at your hands,
Despite the windings of his vast retreat.
My sister would have armed you with the clue
To guide your steps, doubtful within the maze.—
But no—for Phædra would have come before her,
And love would first have given me the thought,
And I it would have been, whose timely aid
Had taught you all the labyrinthine ways!
The care that such a dear life would have cost me!
No thread could satisfy my lover's fears.
I would have wished to lead the way myself,
And share the peril you were sure to face.
Yes, Phædra would have walked the maze with you,—
With you come out in safety, or have perished!

HIPPOLYTUS

Gods! What is this I hear? Have you forgotten
That Theseus is my father and your husband?

PHÆDRA

Why should you fancy I have lost remembrance
And that I am regardless of my honor?

HIPPOLYTUS

Forgive me, madam! With a blush I own
That I mistook your words, quite innocent.
For very shame I cannot see you longer—
Now I will go—

PHÆDRA

Ah, prince, you understood me,—
Too well, indeed! For I had said enough.
You could not well mistake. But do not think
That in those moments when I love you most
I do not feel my guilt. No easy yielding
Has helped the poison that infects my mind.
The sorry object of divine revenge,
I am not half so hateful to your sight
As to myself. The gods will bear me witness,—
They who have lit this fire within my veins,—
The gods who take their barbarous delight
In leading some poor mortal heart astray!
Nay, do you not remember, in the past,

How I was not content to fly?—I drove you
Out of the land, so that I might appear
Most odious—and to resist you better
I tried to make you hate me—and in vain!
You hated more, and I loved not the less,
While your misfortunes lent you newer charms.
I have been drowned in tears and scorched by fire!
Your own eyes might convince you of the truth
If you could look at me, but for a moment!
What do I say? You think this vile confession
That I have made, is what I meant to say?
I did not dare betray my son. For him
I feared,—and came to beg you not to hate him.
This was the purpose of a heart too full
Of love for you to speak of aught besides.
Take your revenge, and punish me my passion!
Prove yourself worthy of your valiant father,
And rid the world of an offensive monster!
Does Theseus' widow dare to love his son?
Monster indeed! Nay, let her not escape you!
Here is my heart! Here is the place to strike!
It is most eager to absolve itself!
It leaps impatiently to meet your blow!—
Strike deep! Or if, indeed, you find it shameful
To drench your hand in such polluted blood,—
If that be punishment too mild for you,—
Too easy for your hate,—if not your arm,
Then lend your sword to me.—Come! Give it now!—

ŒNONE

What would you do, my lady? Oh, just gods!
But someone comes;—go quickly. Run from shame.
You cannot fly, if they should find you thus.

Phèdre (1677)
Act ii, Scene v
Translated by Robert Henderson

As for the tremendous "scene of the declaration" it is a crime of LÈSE-
LITTÉRATURE *to mutilate it in the slightest degree. It is fairly safe to
say that such a variety of emotion—fear, loss of conscious control, voluptuous abandonment, indignation, pride, shame, anger, remorse—has
not elsewhere been compressed within a little over one hundred lines.*

A. F. B. CLARK
Jean Racine (1939)

PHÆDRA JEALOUS

PHÈDRE

Ils s'aimeront toujours.
Au moment que je parle, ah! mortelle pensée!
Ils bravent la fureur d'une amante insensée.
Malgré ce même exil qui va les écarter,
Ils font mille serments de ne se point quitter.
   Non, je ne puis souffrir un bonheur qui m'outrage,
Œnone, prends pitié de ma jalouse rage:
Il faut perdre Aricie. Il faut de mon époux
Contre un sang odieux réveiller le courroux.
Qu'il ne se borne pas à des peines légères:
Le crime de la sœur passe celui des frères.
Dans mes jaloux transports je le veux implorer.
   Que fais-je? Où ma raison se va-t-elle égarer?
Moi jalouse! et Thésée est celui que j'implore!
Mon époux est vivant, et moi je brûle encore!
Pour qui? Quel est le cœur où prétendent mes vœux?
Chaque mot sur mon front fait dresser mes cheveux.
Mes crimes désormais ont comblé la mesure.
Je respire à la fois l'inceste et l'imposture.
Mes homicides mains, promptes à me venger,
Dans le sang innocent brûlent de se plonger.
Misérable! et je vis? et je soutiens la vue
De ce sacré soleil dont je suis descendue?
J'ai pour aïeul le père et le maître des Dieux:
Le ciel, tout l'univers est plein de mes aïeux.
Où me cacher? Fuyons dans la nuit infernale.
Mais que dis-je? mon père y tient l'urne fatale;
Le sort, dit-on, l'a mise en ses sévères mains:
Minos juge aux enfers tous les pâles humains.
Ah! combien frémira son ombre épouvantée,
Lorsqu'il verra sa fille à ses yeux présentée,
Contrainte d'avouer tant de forfaits divers,
Et des crimes peut-être inconnus aux enfers!
Que diras-tu, mon père, à ce spectacle horrible?
Je crois voir de ta main tomber l'urne terrible;
Je crois te voir, cherchant un supplice nouveau,
Toi-même de ton sang devenir le bourreau.

Pardonne. Un Dieu cruel a perdu ta famille;
Reconnais sa vengeance aux fureurs de ta fille.
Hélas! du crime affreux dont la honte me suit
Jamais mon triste cœur n'a recueilli le fruit.
Jusqu'au dernier soupir de malheurs poursuivie,
Je rends dans les tourments une pénible vie.

PHÆDRA
Love will stay,
And it will stay forever. While I speak—
O dreadful thought—they laugh and scorn my madness
And my distracted heart. In spite of exile,
In spite of that which soon must come to part them,
They make a thousand oaths to bind their union.
Œnone, can I bear this happiness
Which so insults me? I would have your pity.
Yes, she must be destroyed. My husband's fury
Against her hated race shall be renewed.
The punishment must be a heavy one.
Her guilt outruns the guilt of all her brothers.
I'll plead with Theseus, in my jealousy,—
What do I say? Oh, have I lost my senses?
Is Phædra jealous? will she, then, go begging
For Theseus' help? He lives,—and yet I burn.
For whom? Whose heart is this I claim as mine?
My hair stands up with horror at my words,
And from this time, my guilt has passed all bounds!
Hypocrisy and incest breathe at once
Through all I do. My hands are ripe for murder,
To spill the guiltless blood of innocence.
Do I still live, a wretch, and dare to face
The holy Sun, from whom I have my being?
My father's father was the king of gods;
My race is spread through all the universe.—
Where can I hide? In the dark realms of Pluto?
But there my father holds the fatal urn.
His hands award the doom irrevocable.—
Minos is judge of all the ghosts in hell.
And how his awful shade will start and shudder
When he shall see his daughter brought before him,
And made confess such many-colored sins,
Such crimes, perhaps, as hell itself knows not!
O father, what will be thy words at seeing
So dire a sight? I see thee drop the urn,

Turning to seek some punishment unheard of,--
To be, thyself, mine executioner!
O spare me! For a cruel deity
Destroys thy race. O look upon my madness,
And in it see her wrath. This aching heart
Gathers no fruit of pleasure from its crime.
It is a shame which hounds me to the grave,
And ends a life of misery in torment.

Phèdre (1677)
Act iv, Scene vi
Translated by Robert Henderson

The play contains one of the most finished and beautiful, and at the same time one of the most overwhelming studies of passion in the literature of the world. The tremendous rôle of Phèdre—which, as the final touchstone of great acting, holds the same place on the French stage as that of Hamlet on the English—dominates the piece, rising in intensity as act follows act, and "horror on horror's head accumulates." Here, too, Racine has poured out all the wealth of his poetic powers. He has performed the last miracle, and infused into the ordered ease of the Alexandrine a strange sense of brooding mystery and indefinable terror and the awful approaches of fate. The splendour of the verse reaches its height in the fourth act, when the ruined queen, at the culmination of her passion, her remorse, and her despair, sees in a vision Hell opening to receive her, and the appalling shade of her father Minos dispensing his unutterable doom. The creator of this magnificent passage, in which the imaginative grandeur of the loftiest poetry and the supreme force of dramatic emotion are mingled in a perfect whole, has a right to walk beside Sophocles in the high places of eternity.

LYTTON STRACHEY
Landmarks in French Literature (1923)

JEAN DE LA BRUYÈRE

1 6 4 5 — 1 6 9 6

THE LOVER OF FLOWERS

Vous le voyez planté, et qui a pris racine au milieu de ses tulipes et devant la *Solitaire:* il ouvre de grands yeux, il frotte ses mains, il se baisse, il la voit de plus près, il ne l'a jamais vue si belle, il a le cœur épanoui de joie; il la quitte pour l'*Orientale;* de là il va à la *Veuve;* il passe au *Drap d'or,* de celle-ci à l'*Agathe,* d'où il revient enfin à la *Solitaire,* où il se fixe, où il se lasse, où il s'assit, où il oublie de dîner: aussi est-elle nuancée, bordée, huilée, à pièces emportées; elle a un beau vase ou un beau calice: il la contemple, il l'admire. Dieu et la nature sont en tout cela ce qu'il n'admire point; il ne va pas plus loin que l'oignon de sa tulipe, qu'il ne livrerait pas pour mille écus, et qu'il donnera pour rien quand les tulipes seront négligées et que les œillets auront prévalu. Cet homme raisonnable, qui a une âme, qui a un culte et une religion, revient chez soi fatigué, affamé, mais fort content de sa journée: il a vu des tulipes.

You see him standing there, and would think he had taken root in the midst of his tulips before his "Solitaire;" he opens his eyes wide, rubs his hands, stoops down and looks closer at it; it never before seemed to him so handsome; he is in an ecstasy of joy, and leaves it to go to the "Orient," then to the "Veuve," from thence to the "Cloth of Gold," on to the "Agatha," and at last returns to the "Solitaire," where he remains, is tired out, sits down, and forgets his dinner; he looks at the tulip and admires its shade, shape, colour, sheen, and edges, its beautiful form and calix; but God and nature are not in his thoughts, for they do not go beyond the bulb of his tulip, which he would not sell for a thousand crowns, though he will give it to you for nothing when tulips are no longer in fashion, and carnations are all the rage. This rational being, who has a soul and professes some religion, comes home tired and half-starved, but very pleased with his day's work; he has seen some tulips.

Les Caractères (1688)
Translated by Henri van Laun

The rhythm is absolutely perfect, and, with its suspensions, its elaborations, its gradual crescendos, its unerring conclusions, seems to carry the sheer beauty of expressiveness to the farthest conceivable point.

LYTTON STRACHEY
Landmarks in French Literature (1923)

BOOK OF COMMON PRAYER

1 6 6 2

NO MAN MAY DELIVER

But no man may deliver his brother: nor make agreement unto God for him.

Psalms, xlix, 7

That is to me poetry so moving that I can hardly keep my voice steady in reading it.

A. E. HOUSMAN
The Name and Nature of Poetry (1933)

MATTHEW PRIOR

1 6 6 4 — 1 7 2 1

EPIGRAM

To John I ow'd great Obligation;
  But John, unhappily, thought fit
To publish it to all the Nation:
  Sure John and I are more than Quit.

ANOTHER

Yes, every Poet is a Fool:
  By Demonstration Ned can show it:
Happy, cou'd Ned's inverted Rule
  Prove every Fool to be a Poet.

FOR MY OWN TOMB-STONE

To Me 'twas giv'n to die: to Thee 'tis giv'n
  To live: Alas! one Moment sets us ev'n.
Mark! how impartial is the Will of Heav'n?

Poems on Several Occasions (1718)

As an epigrammatist he is unrivalled in English.

AUSTIN DOBSON
in Ward's The English Poets (1880)

MATTHEW PRIOR

1 6 6 4 — 1 7 2 1

TO CLOE JEALOUS, A BETTER ANSWER

I court others in Verse; but I love Thee in Prose:
    And They have my Whimsies; but Thou hast my Heart.
                        Poems on Several Occasions (1718)

*Prior is probably the greatest of all who dally with the light lyre which
thrills to the wings of fleeting Loves—the greatest English writer of*
VERS DE SOCIÉTÉ.

ANDREW LANG
Letters on Literature (1889)

MATTHEW PRIOR

1 6 6 4 — 1 7 2 1

AN ODE

I

The Merchant, to secure his Treasure,
    Conveys it in a borrow'd Name:
Euphelia serves to grace my Measure;
    But Cloe is my real Flame.

II

My softest Verse, my darling Lyre
    Upon Euphelia's Toylet lay;
When Cloe noted her Desire,
    That I should sing, that I should play.

III

My Lyre I tune, my Voice I raise;
    But with my Numbers mix my Sighs:
And whilst I sing Euphelia's Praise,
    I fix my Soul on Cloe's Eyes.

IV

Fair Cloe blush'd: Euphelia frown'd:
  I sung and gaz'd: I play'd and trembl'd:
And Venus to the Loves around
  Remark'd, how ill We all dissembl'd.

Poems on Several Occasions (1718)

TO A CHILD OF QUALITY,

FIVE YEARS OLD, THE AUTHOR FORTY

I

Lords, knights, and squires, the num'rous band,
  That wear the fair miss Mary's fetters,
Were summon'd by her high command,
  To show their passions by their letters.

II

My pen amongst the rest I took,
  Lest those bright eyes that cannot read
Shou'd dart their kindling fires, and look,
  The power they have to be obey'd.

III

Nor quality, nor reputation,
  Forbid me yet my flame to tell,
Dear five years old befriends my passion,
  And I may write till she can spell.

IV

For while she makes her silk-worms beds,
  With all the tender things I swear,
Whilst all the house my passion reads,
  In papers round her baby's hair.

V

She may receive and own my flame,
  For tho' the strictest prudes shou'd know it,
She'll pass for a most virtuous dame,
  And I for an unhappy poet.

VI

Then too alas! when she shall tear
   The lines some younger rival sends,
She'll give me leave to write I fear,
   And we shall still continue friends.

VII

For as our diff'rent ages move,
   'Tis so ordain'd, wou'd fate but mend it,
That I shall be past making love
   When she begins to comprehend it.

(1704)

The perfection of VERS DE SOCIÉTÉ.

WALTER HEADLAM
A Book of Greek Verse (1907)

JONATHAN SWIFT

1 6 6 7 — 1 7 4 5

TO THEIR EXCELLENCIES THE LORDS JUSTICES OF IRELAND

THE HUMBLE PETITION OF FRANCES HARRIS,

Who must Starve, and Die a Maid if it miscarries.

Anno 1700

Humbly Sheweth.

That I went to warm my self in Lady *Betty's* Chamber, because I was
   cold,
And I had in a Purse, seven Pound, four Shillings and six Pence, besides
   Farthings, in Money, and Gold;
So because I had been buying things for my *Lady* last Night,
I was resolved to tell my Money, to see if it was right:
Now you must know, because my Trunk has a very bad Lock,
Therefore all the Money, I have, which, *God* knows, is a very small
   Stock,
I keep in my Pocket ty'd about my Middle, next my Smock.

So when I went to put up my Purse, as *God* would have it, my Smock
    was unript,
And, instead of putting it into my Pocket, down it slipt:
Then the Bell rung, and I went down to put my *Lady* to Bed,
And, *God* knows, I thought my Money was as safe as my Maidenhead.
So when I came up again, I found my Pocket feel very light,
But when I search'd, and miss'd my Purse, *Lord!* I thought I should
    have sunk outright:
Lord! Madam, says *Mary*, how d'ye do? Indeed, says I, never worse;
But pray, *Mary*, can you tell what I have done with my Purse!
Lord help me, said *Mary*, I never stirr'd out of this Place!
Nay, said I, I had it in Lady *Betty's* Chamber, that's a plain Case.
So *Mary* got me to bed, and cover'd me up warm;
However, she stole away my Garters, that I might do my self no Harm:
So I tumbl'd and toss'd all Night, as you may very well think,
But hardly ever set my Eyes together, or slept a Wink.
So I was a-dream'd, methought, that we went and search'd the Folks
    round,
And in a Corner of Mrs. *Dukes's* Box, ty'd in a Rag, the Money was
    found.
So next Morning we told *Whittle*, and he fell a Swearing;
Then my Dame *Wadgar* came, and she, you know, is thick of Hearing;
Dame, said I, as loud as I could bawl, Do you know what a Loss I have
    had?
Nay, said she, my Lord *Collway's* Folks are all very sad,
For my Lord *Dromedary* comes a *Tuesday* without fail;
Pugh! said I, but that's not the Business that I ail.
Says *Cary*, says he, I have been a Servant this Five and Twenty Years,
    come Spring,
And in all the Places I Liv'd, I never heard of such a Thing.
Yes, says the *Steward*, I remember when I was at my Lady *Shrewsbury's*,
Such a Thing as this happen'd, just about the time of *Goosberries*.
So I went to the Party suspected, and I found her full of Grief;
(Now you must know, of all Things in the World, I hate a Thief.)
However I was resolv'd to bring the Discourse slily about,
Mrs. *Dukes*, said I, here's an ugly Accident has happen'd out;
'Tis not that I value the Money three Skips of a Louse;
But the Thing I stand upon, is the Credit of the House;
'Tis true, seven Pounds, four Shillings and six Pence, makes a great Hole
    in my Wages,
Besides, as they say, Service is no Inheritance in these Ages.
Now, Mrs. *Dukes*, you know, and every Body understands,
That tho' 'tis hard to judge, yet Money can't go without Hands.
The *Devil* take me, said she, (blessing her self,) is ever I saw't!
So she roar'd like a *Bedlam*, as tho' I had call'd her all to naught;

So you know, what could I say to her any more,
I e'en left her, and came away as wise as I was before.
Well: But then they would have had me gone to the Cunning Man;
No, said I, 'tis the same Thing, the *Chaplain* will be here anon.
So the *Chaplain* came in; now the Servants say, he is my Sweet-heart,
Because he's always in my Chamber, and I always take his Part;
So, as the *Devil* would have it, before I was aware, out I blunder'd,
Parson, said I, can you cast a *Nativity*, when a Body's plunder'd?
(Now you must know, he hates to be call'd *Parson*, like the *Devil*.)
Truly, says he, Mrs. *Nab*, it might become you to be more civil:
If your Money be gone, as a Learned *Divine* says, d'ye see,
You are no *Text* for my Handling, so take that from me:
I was never taken for a *Conjurer* before, I'd have you to know.
Lord, said I, don't be angry, I'm sure I never thought you so;
You know, I honour the Cloth, I design to be a *Parson's* Wife,
I never took one in *Your Coat* for a *Conjurer* in all my Life.
With that, he twisted his Girdle at me like a Rope, as who should say,
Now you may go hang your self for me, and so went away.
Well; I thought I should have swoon'd; *Lord*, said I, what shall I do?
I have lost my *Money*, and shall lose my *True-Love* too.
Then my *Lord* call'd me; *Harry*, said my *Lord*, don't cry,
I'll give something towards thy Loss; and says my *Lady*, so will I.
Oh! but, said I, what if after all my Chaplain won't *come to*?
For that, he said, (an't please your *Excellencies*) I must petition You.
The Premises tenderly consider'd, I desire your *Excellencies* Protection,
And that I may have a Share in next *Sunday's* Collection:
And over and above, that I may have your *Excellencies* Letter,
With an Order for the *Chaplain* aforesaid: or instead of Him, a Better:
And then your poor *Petitioner*, both Night and Day,
Or the *Chaplain*, (for 'tis his *Trade*) as in Duty bound, shall ever *Pray*.

Perhaps this is the most humorous piece of verse in the English language.
FREDERICK LOCKER-LAMPSON
Lyra Elegantiarum (1867)

JONATHAN SWIFT

1 6 6 7 — 1 7 4 5

THE EPISTLE DEDICATORY,
TO HIS ROYAL HIGHNESS PRINCE POSTERITY

SIR,

I here present *Your Highness* with the Fruits of a very few leisure Hours, stollen from the short Intervals of a World of Business, and of an Employment quite alien from such Amusements as this: The poor Production of that Refuse of Time which has lain heavy upon my Hands, during a long Prorogation of Parliament, a great Dearth of Forein News, and a tedious Fit of rainy Weather: For which, and other Reasons, it cannot chuse extreamly to deserve such a Patronage as that of *Your Highness*, whose numberless Virtues in so few Years, make the World look upon You as the future Example to all Princes: For altho' *Your Highness* is hardly got clear of Infancy, yet has the universal learned World already resolv'd upon appealing to Your future Dictates with the lowest and most resigned Submission: Fate having decreed You sole Arbiter of the Productions of human Wit, in this polite and most accomplish'd Age. Methinks, the Number of Appellants were enough to shock and startle any Judge of a Genius less unlimited than Yours: But in order to prevent such glorious Tryals, the *Person* (it seems) to whose Care the Education of *Your Highness* is committed, has resolved (as I am told) to keep you in almost an universal Ignorance of our Studies, which it is Your inherent Birth-right to inspect.

IT is amazing to me, that this *Person* should have Assurance in the face of the Sun, to go about persuading *Your Highness*, that our Age is almost wholly illiterate, and has hardly produc'd one Writer upon any Subject. I know very well, that when *Your Highness* shall come to riper Years, and have gone through the Learning of Antiquity, you will be too curious to neglect inquiring into the Authors of the very age before You: And to think that this *Insolent*, in the Account he is preparing for Your View, designs to reduce them to a Number so insignificant as I am asham'd to mention; it moves my Zeal and my Spleen for the Honor and Interest of our vast flourishing Body, as well as of my self, for whom I know by long Experience, he has profess'd, and still continues a peculiar Malice.

'TIS not unlikely, that when *Your Highness* will one day peruse what I am now writing, You may be ready to expostulate with Your *Governour* upon the Credit of what I here affirm, and command Him to shew You some of our Productions. To which he will answer, (for I am well informed of his Designs) by asking *Your Highness*, where they are? and what is become of them? and pretend it a Demonstration that there never were any, because they are not then to be found: Not to be found! Who has mislaid them? Are they sunk in the Abyss of Things? 'Tis certain, that in their own Nature they were *light* enough to swim upon the Surface for all Eternity. Therefore the Fault is in Him, who tied Weights so heavy to their Heels, as to depress them to the Center. Is their very Essence destroyed? Who has annihilated them? Were they drowned by *Purges* or martyred by *Pipes?* Who administred them to the Posteriors of ———? But that it may no longer be a Doubt with *Your Highness,* who is to be the Author of this universal Ruin; I beseech You to observe that large and terrible *Scythe* which your *Governour* affects to bear continually about him. Be pleased to remark the Length and Strength, the Sharpness and Hardness of his *Nails* and *Teeth:* Consider his baneful abominable *Breath,* Enemy to Life and Matter, infectious and corrupting: And then reflect whether it be possible for any mortal Ink and Paper of this Generation to make a suitable Resistance. Oh, that *Your Highness* would one day resolve to disarm this Usurping *Maitre du Palais,* of his furious Engins, and bring Your Empire *hors de Page.*

IT were endless to recount the several Methods of Tyranny and Destruction, which Your *Governour* is pleased to practise upon this Occasion. His inveterate Malice is such to the Writings of our Age, that of several Thousands produced yearly from this renowned City, before the next Revolution of the Sun, there is not one to be heard of: Unhappy Infants, many of them barbarously destroyed, before they have so much as learnt their *Mother-Tongue* to beg for Pity. Some he stifles in their Cradles, others he frights into Convulsions, whereof they suddenly die; Some he flays alive, others he tears Limb from Limb. Great Numbers are offered to *Moloch,* and the rest tainted by his Breath, die of a languishing Consumption.

BUT the Concern I have most at Heart, is for our Corporation of *Poets,* from whom I am preparing a Petition to *Your Highness,* to be subscribed with the Names of one hundred thirty six of the first Rate, but whose immortal Productions are never likely to reach your Eyes, tho' each of them is now an humble and an earnest Appellant for the Laurel, and has large comely Volumes ready to shew for a Support to his Pretensions. The *never-dying* Works of these illustrious Persons, Your *Governour,* Sir, has devoted to unavoidable Death, and *Your Highness* is to be made believe, that our Age has never arrived at the Honor to produce one single Poet.

WE confess *Immortality* to be a great and powerful Goddess, but in vain we offer up to her our Devotions and our Sacrifices, if *Your Highness's Governour,* who has usurped the *Priesthood,* must by an unparallel'd Ambition and Avarice, wholly intercept and devour them.

TO affirm that our Age is altogether Unlearned, and devoid of

Writers in any kind, seems to be an Assertion so bold and so false, that I have been sometime thinking, the contrary may almost be proved by uncontroulable Demonstration. 'Tis true indeed, that altho' their Numbers be vast, and their Productions numerous in proportion, yet are they hurryed so hastily off the Scene, that they escape our Memory, and delude our Sight. When I first thought of this Address, I had prepared a copious List of *Titles* to present *Your Highness* as an undisputed Argument for what I affirm. The Originals were posted fresh upon all Gates and Corners of Streets; but returning in a very few Hours to take a Review, they were all torn down, and fresh ones in their Places: I enquired after them among Readers and Booksellers, but I enquired in vain, the *Memorial of them was lost among Men, their Place was no more to be found:* and I was laughed to scorn, for a *Clown* and a *Pedant*, without all Taste and Refinement, little versed in the Course of *present* Affairs, and that knew nothing of what had pass'd in the best Companies of Court and Town. So that I can only avow in general to *Your Highness*, that we do abound in Learning and Wit; but to fix upon Particulars, is a Task too slippery for my slender Abilities. If I should venture in a windy Day, to affirm to *Your Highness*, that there is a large Cloud near the *Horizon* in the Form of a *Bear*, another in the *Zenith* with the Head of an *Ass*, a third to the Westward with Claws like a *Dragon;* and *Your Highness* should in a few Minutes think fit to examine the Truth, 'tis certain, they would all be changed in Figure and Position, new ones would arise, and all we could agree upon would be, that Clouds there were, but that I was grossly mistaken in the *Zoography* and *Topography* of them.

BUT Your *Governour*, perhaps, may still insist, and put the Question: What is then become of those immense Bales of Paper, which must needs have been employ'd in such Numbers of Books? Can these also be wholly annihilate, and so of a sudden as I pretend? What shall I say in return of so invidious an Objection? It ill befits the Distance between *Your Highness* and Me, to send You for ocular Conviction to a *Jakes*, or an *Oven;* to the Windows of a *Bawdy-house*, or to a sordid *Lanthorn*. Books, like Men their Authors, have no more than one Way of coming into the World, but there are ten Thousand to go out of it, and return no more.

I profess to *Your Highness*, in the Integrity of my Heart, that what I am going to say is literally true this Minute I am writing: What Revolutions may happen before it shall be ready for your Perusal, I can by no means warrant: However I beg You to accept it as a Specimen of our Learning, our Politeness and our Wit. I do therefore affirm upon the Word of a sincere Man, that there is now actually in being, a certain Poet called *John Dryden*, whose Translation of *Virgil* was lately printed in a large Folio, well bound, and if diligent search were made, for ought I know, is yet to be seen. There is another call'd *Nahum Tate*, who is ready to make Oath that he has caused many Rheams of Verse to be published, whereof both himself and his Bookseller (if lawfully required) can still produce authentick Copies, and therefore wonders why the World is pleased to make such a Secret of it. There is a Third, known by the Name of *Tom Durfey,* a Poet of a vast Comprehension, an universal Genius, and most profound Learning. There are also one Mr. *Rymer,* and one Mr. *Dennis,* most profound Criticks. There is a Person styl'd Dr. *B--tl-y,* who has written near a thousand Pages of immense Erudition, *giving a full and true Account* of a certain *Squable* of wonderful Importance between himself and a Bookseller: He is a Writer of infinite Wit and Humour; no Man raillyes with a better Grace, and in more sprightly Turns. Farther, I avow to *Your Highness,* that with these Eyes I have beheld the Person of *William W--tt--n,* B.D. who has written a good sizeable volume against a *Friend of Your Governor,* (from whom, alas! he must therefore look for little Favour) in a most gentlemanly Style, adorned with utmost Politeness and Civility; replete with Discoveries equally valuable for their Novelty and Use: and embellish'd with *Traits* of Wit so poignant and so apposite, that he is a worthy Yokemate to his foremention'd *Friend.*

WHY should I go upon farther Particulars, which might fill a Volume with the just Elogies of my cotemporary Brethren? I shall bequeath this Piece of Justice to a larger Work: wherein I intend to write a Character of the present Set of *Wits* in our Nation: Their Persons I shall describe particularly, and at Length, their Genius and Understandings in *Mignature.*

IN the mean time, I do here make bold to present *Your Highness* with a faithful Abstract drawn from the Universal Body of all Arts and Sciences, intended wholly for your Service and Instruction: Nor do I doubt in the least, but *Your Highness* will peruse it as carefully, and make as considerable Improvements, as *other* young *Princes* have already done by the many Volumes of late Years written for a Help to their Studies.

THAT *Your Highness* may advance in Wisdom and Virtue, as well as Years, and at last out-shine all Your Royal Ancestors, shall be the daily Prayer of,

SIR,

Decemb.
1697.

Your Highness's
Most devoted, &c.

A Tale of a Tub (1704)

Of all English prose Swift's has the most of flexibility, the most of nervous and of sinewy force; it is the most perfect as an instrument, and the most deadly in its unerring accuracy of aim. It often disdains grammatical correctness, and violates not infrequently the rules of con-

struction and arrangement. But it is significant that Swift attained the perfection of his art, not by deliberately setting aside the proprieties of diction, but by setting before himself consistently the first and highest ideal of simplicity, by disdaining eccentricity and paradox and the caprice of fashion, and that although he wrote "his own English," as no other did before or since, he was inspired from first to last by a deep reverence for the language, and an ardent desire to maintain its dignity and its purity unchanged and unimpaired.

HENRY CRAIK
English Prose (1906)

JONATHAN SWIFT

1 6 6 7 — 1 7 4 5

A MODEST PROPOSAL

*for preventing the Children of Poor People from being a Burthen to
to their Parents, or the Country, and for making them
Beneficial to the Publick.*

It is a melancholly Object to those, who walk through this great Town, or travel in the Country, when they see the *Streets,* the *Roads,* and *Cabbin-Doors,* crowded with *Beggars* of the female Sex, followed by three, four, or six Children, *all in Rags,* and importuning every Passenger for an Alms. . . .

I think it is agreed by all Parties, that this prodigious number of Children. . . . is *in the present deplorable state of the Kingdom,* a very great additional grievance; and therefore whoever could find out a fair, cheap and easy method of making these Children sound and useful Members of the common-wealth would deserve so well of the publick, as to have his Statue set up for a preserver of the Nation. . . .

I shall now therefore humbly propose my own thoughts, which I hope will not be lyable to the least Objection.

I have been assured by a very knowing *American* of my acquaintance in *London,* that a young healthy Child well Nursed is at a year Old a most delicious, nourishing, and wholesome Food, whether *Stewed, Roasted, Baked,* or *Boyled,* and I make no doubt that it will equally serve in a *Fricasie,* or a *Ragoust.*

I do therefore humbly offer it to *publick consideration,* that of the hundred and twenty thousand Children, already computed, twenty thousand may be reserved for Breed, whereof only one fourth part to be Males. . . . That the remaining hundred thousand may at a year

867

Old be offered in Sale to the *persons of Quality,* and *Fortune,* through the Kingdom, always advising the Mother to let them Suck plentifully in the last Month, so as to render them Plump, and Fat for a good Table. A Child will make two Dishes at an Entertainment for Friends, and when the Family dines alone, the fore or hind Quarter will make a reasonable Dish, and seasoned with a little Pepper or Salt will be very good Boiled on the fourth Day, especially in Winter.

I have reckoned upon a Medium, that a Child just born will weigh 12 pounds, and in a solar Year if tollerably nursed encreaseth to 28 Pound. . . .

I have already computed the Charge of nursing a Beggars Child (in which list I reckon all *Cottagers, Labourers,* and four fifths of the *Farmers*) to be about two Shillings *per Annum,* Rags included, and I believe no Gentleman would repine to give Ten Shillings for the *Carcass of a good fat Child,* which, as I have said will make four Dishes of excellent Nutritive Meat. . . .

Those who are more thrifty (*as I must confess the Times require*) may flay the Carcass; the Skin of which, Artificially dressed, will make admirable *Gloves for Ladies,* and *Summer Boots for fine Gentlemen.*

As to our City of *Dublin,* Shambles may be appointed for this purpose, in the most convenient parts of it, and Butchers we may be assured will not be wanting, although I rather recommend buying the Children alive, and dressing them hot from the Knife, as we do *roasting Pigs.* . . .

Some Persons of a desponding Spirit are in great concern about that vast Number of poor People, who are aged, diseased, or maimed, and I have been desired to imploy my thoughts what Course may be taken, to ease the Nation of so grievous an Incumbrance. But I am not in the least pain about the matter, because it is very well known, that they are every Day *dying,* and *rotting,* by *cold,* and *famine,* and *filth,* and *vermin,* as fast as can be reasonably expected. And as to the younger Labourers they are now in almost as hopeful a Condition. They cannot get Work, and consequently pine away for want of Nourishment, to a degree, that if at any time they are accidentally hired to common Labour, they have not strength to perform it, and thus the Country and themselves are happily delivered from the Evils to come. . . .

I think the advantages by the Proposal which I have made are obvious and many as well as of the highest importance.

For first, as I have already observed, it would greatly lessen *the Number of Papists,* with whom we are Yearly over-run, being the principal Breeders of the Nation, as well as our most dangerous Enemies. . . .

Thirdly, Whereas the Maintenance of an hundred thousand Children, from two Years old, and upwards, cannot be computed at less than Ten Shillings a piece *per Annum,* the Nation's Stock will be thereby encreased fifty thousand pounds *per Annum,* besides the profit of a new Dish, introduced to the Tables of all *Gentlemen of Fortune* in the

Kingdom, who have any refinement in Taste, and the Money will circulate among our selves, the Goods being entirely of our own Growth and Manufacture. . . .

Sixthly, This would be a great Inducement to Marriage, which all wise Nations have either encouraged by Rewards, or enforced by Laws and Penalties. It would encrease the care and tenderness of Mothers towards their Children, when they were sure of a Settlement for Life, to the poor Babes, provided in some sort by the Publick to their Annual profit instead of Expence. . . .

Many other advantages might be enumerated: For Instance, the addition of some thousand Carcases in our exportation of Barreled Beef. The Propagation of *Swines Flesh,* and Improvement in the Art of making good *Bacon.* . . . But this, and many others I omit, being studious of Brevity. . . .

I Profess in the sincerity of my Heart that I have not the least personal Interest in endeavouring to promote this necessary Work having no other Motive than the *publick Good of my Country, by advancing our Trade, providing for Infants, relieving the Poor, and giving some Pleasure to the Rich.* I have no Children, by which I can propose to get a single Penny; the youngest being nine Years old, and my Wife past Childbearing.

(1729)

I give it almost entire; it merits it. I know nothing its equal in any literature.

HIPPOLYTE TAINE
Histoire de la littérature anglaise (1863)

JONATHAN SWIFT

1 6 6 7 — 1 7 4 5

INSCRIPTION ACCOMPANYING A LOCK OF STELLA'S HAIR

Only a woman's hair.

The riddle of the painful earth in one of its forms expressed more poignantly and finally than it has been expressed by any uninspired human being excepting Shakespeare.

GEORGE SAINTSBURY
The Peace of the Augustans (1916)

JEAN-BAPTISTE ROUSSEAU

1 6 6 9 — 1 7 4 1

EPIGRAM

Le traducteur qui rima l'Iliade,
De douze chants prétendit l'abréger:
Mais par son style, aussi triste que fade,
De douze en sus il a su l'allonger.
Or, le lecteur, qui se sent affliger,
Le donne au diable, et dit, perdant haleine:
Hé! finissez, rimeur à la douzaine!
Vos abrégés sont longs au dernier point.
Ami lecteur, vous voilà bien en peine;
Rendons-les courts en ne les lisant point.

The translator who rhymed the Iliad claimed to have shortened it twelve cantos; but through his tasteless and sorry style, he lengthened it twelve cantos more. Now, the aggrieved reader consigns it to hell, and says, out of breath: Hey! be done, you cheap rhymster! Your abbreviations are excessively lengthy. Dear Reader, you are in a sorry fix; let us save time by not reading them at all.

Rousseau without doubt has reached the supreme height in this minor genre in which perfection is rare, as it is everywhere.

PIERRE MALITOURNE
Les Poëtes français (1861)

WILLIAM CONGREVE

1 6 7 0 — 1 7 2 9

VALENTINE AND HIS FATHER
DISCUSS PATERNAL RESPONSIBILITY

JEREMY
He is here, Sir.
VALENTINE
Your Blessing, Sir.

SIR SAMPSON

You've had it already, Sir, I think I sent it you to Day in a Bill of Four thousand Pound: A great deal of Mony, Brother *Foresight.*

FORESIGHT

Ay indeed, Sir *Sampson,* a great deal of Mony for a young Man, I wonder what he can do with it!

SIR SAMPSON

Body o'me, so do I.—Hark ye, *Valentine,* if there be too much, refund the Superfluity; Do'st hear Boy?

VALENTINE

Superfluity, Sir, it will scarce pay my Debts,—I hope you will have more Indulgence, than to oblige me to those hard Conditions, which my Necessity sign'd to.

SIR SAMPSON

Sir, how, I beseech you, what were you pleas'd to intimate, concerning Indulgence?

VALENTINE

Why, Sir, that you wou'd not go to the extremity of the Conditions, but release me at least from some Part.—

SIR SAMPSON

Oh Sir, I understand you—that's all, ha?

VALENTINE

Yes, Sir, all that I presume to ask.—But what you, out of Fatherly Fondness, will be pleas'd to add, shall be doubly welcome.

SIR SAMPSON

No doubt of it, sweet Sir, but your filial Piety, and my fatherly Fondness wou'd fit like two Tallies.—Here's a Rogue, Brother *Foresight,* makes a Bargain under Hand and Seal in the Morning, and would be releas'd from it in the Afternoon; here's a Rogue, Dog, here's Conscience and Honesty; this is your Wit now, this is the Morality of your Wits! You are a Wit, and have been a Beau, and may be a— Why Sirrah, is it not here under Hand and Seal—Can you deny it?

VALENTINE

Sir, I don't deny it.—

SIR SAMPSON

Sirrah, you'll be hang'd; I shall live to see you go up *Holborn-Hill* —Has he not a Rogue's Face?—Speak, Brother, you understand Physiognomy, a hanging Look to me—of all my Boys the most unlike me; he has a damn'd *Tyburn*-Face, without the Benefit o'the Clergy.

FORESIGHT

Hum—truly I don't care to discourage a young Man,—he has a violent Death in his Face; but I hope no Danger of Hanging.

VALENTINE

Sir, is this Usage for your Son?—for that old Weather-headed Fool, I know how to laugh at him; but you, Sir—

SIR SAMPSON

You, Sir; and you, Sir:—Why, who are you, Sir?

VALENTINE

Your Son, Sir.

SIR SAMPSON

That's more than I know, Sir, and I believe not.

VALENTINE

Faith, I hope not.

SIR SAMPSON

What, wou'd you have your Mother a Whore! Did you ever hear the like! Did you ever hear the like! Body o'me—

VALENTINE

I would have an Excuse for your Barbarity and unnatural Usage.

SIR SAMPSON

Excuse! Impudence! Why, Sirrah, mayn't I do what I please? Are not you my Slave? Did not I beget you? And might not I have chosen whether I would have begot you or no? 'Oons who are you? Whence came you? What brought you into the World? How came you here, Sir? Here, to stand here, upon those two Legs, and look erect with that audacious Face, hah? Answer me that? Did you come a Volunteer into the World? Or did I, with the lawful Authority of a Parent, press you to the Service?

VALENTINE

I know no more why I came, than you do why you call'd me. But here I am, and if you don't mean to provide for me, I desire you would leave me as you found me.

SIR SAMPSON

With all my Heart: Come, uncase, strip, and go naked out of the World, as you came into't.

VALENTINE

My Cloaths are soon put off:—But you must also divest me of Reason, Thought, Passions, Inclinations, Affections, Appetites, Senses, and the huge Train of Attendants that you begot along with me.

SIR SAMPSON

Body o'me, what a many-headed Monster have I propagated!

VALENTINE

I am of my self, a plain easie simple Creature; and to be kept at small Expence; but the Retinue that you gave me are craving and invincible; they are so many Devils that you have rais'd, and will have Employment.

SIR SAMPSON

'Oons, what had I to do to get Children,—can't a private Man be born without all these Followers?—Why nothing under an Emperor should be born with Appetites,—Why at this rate a Fellow that has but a Groat in his Pocket, may have a Stomach capable of a Ten Shilling Ordinary.

JEREMY

Nay that's as clear as the Sun; I'll make Oath of it before any Justice in *Middlesex*.

SIR SAMPSON

Here's a Cormorant too,—'S'heart this Fellow was not born with you?—I did not beget him, did I?—

JEREMY

By the Provision that's made for me, you might have begot me too: —Nay, and to tell your Worship another Truth, I believe you did, for I find I was born with those same Whoreson Appetites too, that my Master speaks of.

SIR SAMPSON

Why look you there now,—I'll maintain it, that by the Rule of right Reason, this Fellow ought to have been born without a Palate. 'S'heart, what shou'd he do with a distinguishing Taste?—I warrant now he'd rather eat a Pheasant, than a Piece of poor *John;* and smell, now, why I warrant he can smell, and loves Perfumes above a Stink.—Why there's it; and Musick, don't you love Musick, Scoundrel?

JEREMY

Yes, I have a reasonable good Ear, Sir, as to Jiggs and Country Dances; and the like; I don't much matter your *Solo's* or *Sonata's,* they give me the Spleen.

SIR SAMPSON

The Spleen, ha, ha, ha, a Pox confound you—*Solo's* or *Sonata's?* 'Oons whose Son are you? How were you engendred, Muckworm?

JEREMY

I am by my Father, the Son of a Chairman; my Mother sold Oisters in Winter, and Cucumbers in Summer; and I came up Stairs into the World; for I was born in a Cellar.

FORESIGHT

By your Looks, you shou'd go up Stairs out of the World too, Friend.

SIR SAMPSON

And if this Rogue were Anatomiz'd now, and dissected, he has his Vessels of Digestion and Concoction, and so forth, large enough for the inside of a Cardinal, this Son of a Cucumber.—These things are unaccountable and unreasonable,—Body o'me, why was not I a Bear? that my Cubs might have liv'd upon sucking their Paws; Nature has been provident only to Bears and Spiders; the one has its Nutriment in his own Hands; and t'other spins his Habitation out of his own Entrails.

VALENTINE

Fortune was provident enough to supply all the Necessities of my Nature; if I had my right of Inheritance.

SIR SAMPSON

Again! 'Oons han't you four thousand Pound—if I had it again, I wou'd not give thee a Groat,—What, would'st thou have me turn Pelican, and feed thee out of my own Vitals?—'S'heart, live by your Wits,—You were always fond of the Wits,—Now let's see, if you have Wit enough to keep your self—Your Brother will be in Town to Night, or to Morrow Morning, and then look you perform Covenants, and so your Friend and Servant.—Come Brother *Foresight*.

Love for Love (1695)

Act ii, Scene vii

One of the most admirable scenes in all comedy.

EDMUND GOSSE

Life of William Congreve (1924)

WILLIAM CONGREVE

1 6 7 0 — 1 7 2 9

THE TEMPLE

ALMERIA

It was a fancy'd Noise, for all is hush'd.

LEONORA

It bore the Accent of a Human Voice.

ALMERIA

It was thy Fear, or else some transient Wind
Whistling thro' Hollows of this vaulted Isle.
We'll listen—

LEONORA

Hark!

ALMERIA

No, all is hush'd, and still as Death—'Tis dreadful!
How reverend is the Face of this tall Pile,
Whose ancient Pillars rear their Marble Heads,
To bear aloft its arch'd and pond'rous Roof,
By its own Weight made stedfast and immoveable,
Looking Tranquility. It striks an Awe
And Terror on my aking Sight; the Tombs

And Monumental Caves of Death look cold,
And shoot a Chilness to my trembling Heart.
Give me thy Hand, and let me hear thy Voice;
Nay, quickly speak to me, and let me hear
Thy Voice—my own affrights me with its Echo's.

The Mourning Bride (1697)
Act ii, Scene iii

If I were required to select from the whole mass of English poetry the most poetical paragraph, I know not what I could prefer to an exclamation in THE MOURNING BRIDE. . . . *He who reads those lines enjoys for a moment the powers of a poet; he feels what he remembers to have felt before, but he feels it with great increase of sensibility; he recognizes a familiar image, but meets it again amplified and expanded, embellished with beauty, and enlarged with majesty.*

SAMUEL JOHNSON
The Lives of the Poets (1779–81)

Johnson said, that the description of the temple, in the MOURNING BRIDE, *was the finest poetical passage he had ever read: he recollected none in Shakspeare equal to it. 'But, (said Garrick, all alarmed for the 'God of his idolatry,') we know not the extent and variety of his powers. We are to suppose there are such passages in his works. Shakspeare must not suffer from the badness of our memories.' Johnson, diverted by this enthusiastick jealousy, went on with greater ardour: 'No, Sir; Congreve has* NATURE;' *(smiling on the tragick eagerness of Garrick;) but composing himself, he added, 'Sir, this is not comparing Congreve on the whole, with Shakspeare on the whole; but only maintaining that Congreve has one finer passage than any that can be found in Shakspeare. Sir, a man may have no more than ten guineas in the world, but he may have those ten guineas in one piece; and so may have a finer piece than a man who has ten thousand pounds: but then he has only one ten-guinea piece. What I mean is, that you can shew me no passage where there is simply a description of material objects, without any intermixture of moral notions, which produces such an effect.'*

JAMES BOSWELL
The Life of Samuel Johnson L.L.D. (1799)

WILLIAM CONGREVE

1 6 7 0 — 1 7 2 9

MRS. MILLAMANT IS SEEN
COMING THROUGH THE CROWD
IN ST. JAMES'S PARK

Here she comes I'faith full Sail, with her Fan spread and Streamers
out, and a Shoal of Fools for Tenders— Ha, no, I cry her Mercy.

The Way of the World (1700)

Act ii, Scene i

SHE DENIES THAT BEING LOVED
MAKES WOMEN BEAUTIFUL

Beauty the Lover's Gift— Lord, what is a Lover, that it can give?
Why one makes Lovers as fast as one pleases, and they live as long as
one pleases, and they die as soon as one pleases: And then if one
pleases one makes more.

The Way of the World (1700)

Act ii, Scene i

THE WAY OF THE WORLD *is throughout authentic Congreve, and is of
incomparable beauty in its kind. Here, whatever he may have learned
from his predecessors, he made something peculiarly his own, impossible to imitate. For sinewy flexibility and point, combined with seduc-
tive gentleness; for the full gamut of vowel sounds and the varied
spacing of stresses, English literature had to wait for Landor until it
once more heard a voice that had something of the especial quality
of Congreve. . . .*

*The beauty of that [sentence that ushers in Mrs. Millamant for the
first time] needs no insistence; the delicate play of the vowels, the dancing rhythm, with the sharp uptake at the end attended with the entirely new sound of 'cry', sweep us away with their effect of spontaneity.
And see, too, a little later in the same scene, [when Mrs. Millamant
denies that being loved is what makes women beautiful] how skilfully he
can now play on one note, recurring to the same word. . . . 'How it
chimes, and cries tink in the close, divinely!' The reiteration never
gives the ear the smallest bother, because, said as they must be to gain
the full meaning, the phrases only gather their weight upon 'pleases'
in the last instance, the stresses otherwise playing all around it. At*

last the voice fatefully pounces upon the word, as a hawk, after several feints, lands upon a predestined prey.

Those extracts are from that miraculous second act, which shows a more consummate mastery than any other passage in the dramatic literature of the period.

BONAMY DOBRÉE
Variety of Ways (1932)

JOSEPH ADDISON

1 6 7 2 — 1 7 1 9

A LADY'S LIBRARY

Some months ago, my friend Sir Roger, being in the country, enclosed a letter to me, directed to a certain lady whom I shall here call by the name of Leonora, and as it contained matters of consequence, desired me to deliver it to her with my own hand. Accordingly I waited upon her ladyship pretty early in the morning, and was desired by her woman to walk into her lady's library, till such time as she was in readiness to receive me. The very sound of a lady's library gave me a great curiosity to see in it; and as it was some time before the lady came to me, I had an opportunity of turning over a great many of her books, which were ranged together in a very beautiful order. At the end of the folios (which were finely bound and gilt) were great jars of China placed one above another in a very noble piece of architecture. The quartos were separated from the octavos by a pile of smaller vessels, which rose in a delightful pyramid. The octavos were bounded by tea-dishes of all shapes, colours, and sizes, which were so disposed on a wooden frame, that they looked like one continued pillar indented with the finest strokes of sculpture, and stained with the greatest variety of dyes. That part of the library which was designed for the reception of plays and pamphlets, and other loose papers, was enclosed in a kind of square, consisting of one of the prettiest grotesque works that ever I saw, and made up of scaramouches, lions, monkeys, mandarines, trees, shells, and a thousand other odd figures in China ware. In the midst of the room was a little Japan table, with a quire of gilt paper upon it, and on the paper a silver snuff-box made in the shape of a little book. I found there were several other counterfeit books upon the upper shelves, which were carved in wood, and served only to fill up the numbers, like fagots in the muster of a regiment. I was wonderfully pleased with such a mixt kind of furniture, as seemed very suitable to both the lady and the scholar, and did not know at first whether I should fancy myself in a grotto, or in a library.

The Spectator (April 12, 1711)

That is a little jewel of Addisonian prose. There is a slightly periodic character about the first sentence. Otherwise, the order of words in each sentence is simple and idiomatic. Nor is there apparently any attempt to give an emphatic close to each sentence. In the first, "with my own hand" ends the sentence well because it gives the reason of his visit. But "till such time as she was in readiness to receive me," "which were ranged together in a very beautiful order," "in a very noble piece of architecture," "which rose in a delightful pyramid," etc.—none of these SEEM *very weighty statements, but they are, in fact, fine strokes of Addisonian irony. The end of each sentence* IS *emphatic; and the emphasis thus thrown on trifling and apparently irrelevant details contributes delicately and penetratingly to what is intended to be the pervading innuendo of the whole paragraph and essay—that Leonora is more interested in the elegant accessories of her books than in their contents.*

HERBERT J. C. GRIERSON
Rhetoric and English Composition (1945)

LOUIS DE SAINT-SIMON

1 6 7 5 — 1 7 5 5

THE DEATH OF MONSEIGNEUR

While Meudon was filled with horror, all was tranquil at Versailles, without the least suspicion. We had supped. The company some time after had retired, and I was talking with Madame de Saint-Simon, who had nearly finished undressing herself to go to bed, when a servant of Madame la Duchesse de Berry, who had formerly belonged to us, entered, all terrified. He said that there must be some bad news from Meudon, since Monseigneur le Duc de Bourgogne had just whispered in the ear of M. le Duc de Berry, whose eyes had at once become red, that he left the table, and that all the company shortly after him rose with precipitation. So sudden a change rendered my surprise extreme. I ran in hot haste to Madame la Duchesse de Berry's. Nobody was there. Everybody had gone to Madame la Duchesse de Bourgogne. I followed on with all speed.

I found all Versailles assembled on arriving, all the ladies hastily dressed—the majority having been on the point of going to bed—all the doors open, and all in trouble. I learnt that Monseigneur had received the extreme unction, that he was without consciousness and beyond hope, and that the King had sent word to Madame de Bourgogne that he was going to Marly, and that she was to meet him as he passed through the avenue between the two stables.

The spectacle before me attracted all the attention I could bestow. The two Princes and the two Princesses were in the little cabinet behind the bed. The bed toilette was as usual in the chamber of the Duchesse de Bourgogne, which was filled with all the Court in confusion. She came and went from the cabinet to the chamber, waiting for the moment when she was to meet the King; and her demeanour, always distinguished by the same graces, was one of trouble and compassion, which the trouble and compassion of others induced them to take for grief. Now and then, in passing, she said a few rare words. All present were in truth expressive personages. Whoever had eyes, without any knowledge of the Court, could see the interests of all interested painted on their faces, and the indifference of the indifferent; these tranquil, the former penetrated with grief, or gravely attentive to themselves to hide their emancipation and their joy.

For my part, my first care was to inform myself thoroughly of the state of affairs, fearing lest there might be too much alarm for too trifling a cause; then, recovering myself, I reflected upon the misery common to all men, and that I myself should find myself some day at the gates of death. Joy, nevertheless, found its way through the momentary reflections of religion and of humanity, by which I tried to master myself. My own private deliverance seemed so great and so unhoped for, that it appeared to me that the State must gain everything by such a loss. And with these thoughts I felt, in spite of myself, a lingering fear lest the sick man should recover, and was extremely ashamed of it.

Wrapped up thus in myself, I did not fail, nevertheless, to cast clandestine looks upon each face, to see what was passing there. I saw Madame la Duchesse d'Orléans arrive, but her countenance, majestic and constrained, said nothing. She went into the little cabinet, whence she presently issued with the Duc d'Orléans, whose activity and turbulent air marked his emotion at the spectacle more than any other sentiment. They went away, and I noticed this expressly, on account of what happened afterwards in my presence.

Soon afterwards I caught a distant glimpse of the Duc de Bourgogne, who seemed much moved and troubled; but the glance with which I probed him rapidly, revealed nothing tender, and told merely of a mind profoundly occupied with the bearings of what had taken place.

Valets and chamber-women were already indiscreetly crying out; and *their* grief showed well that they were about to lose something!

Towards half-past twelve we had news of the King, and immediately after Madame de Bourgogne came out of the little cabinet with the

Duke, who seemed more touched than when I first saw him. The Princess took her carf and her coifs from the toilette, standing with a deliberate air, her eyes scarcely wet—a fact betrayed by inquisitive glances cast rapidly to the right and left—and, followed only by her ladies, went to her coach by the great staircase.

I took the opportunity to go to the Duchesse d'Orléans, where I found many people. Their presence made me very impatient; the Duchess, who was equally impatient, took a light and went in. I whispered in the ear of the Duchesse de Villeroy, who thought as I thought of this event. She nudged me, and said in a very low voice that I must contain myself. I was smothered with silence, amidst the complaints and the narrative surprises of these ladies; but at last M. le Duc d'Orléans appeared at the door of his cabinet, and beckoned me to come to him.

I followed him into the cabinet, where we were alone. What was my surprise, remembering the terms on which he was with Monseigneur, to see the tears streaming from his eyes.

"Sir!" exclaimed I, rising. He understood me at once; and answered in a broken voice, really crying: "You are right to be surprised—I am surprised myself; but such a spectacle touches. He was a man with whom I passed much of my life, and who treated me well when he was uninfluenced. I feel very well that my grief won't last long; in a few days I shall discover motives of joy; at present, blood, relationship, humanity,—all work; and my entrails are moved." I praised his sentiments, but repeated my surprise. He rose, thrust his head into a corner, and with his nose there, wept bitterly and sobbed, which if I had not seen I could not have believed.

After a little silence, however, I exhorted him to calm himself. I represented to him that, everybody knowing on what terms he had been with Monseigneur, he would be laughed at, as playing a part, if his eyes showed that he had been weeping. He did what he could to remove the marks of his tears, and we then went back into the other room.

The interview of the Duchesse de Bourgogne with the King had not been long. She met him in the avenue between the two stables, got down, and went to the door of the carriage. Madame de Maintenon cried out, "Where are you going? We bear the plague about with us." I do not know what the King said or did. The Princess returned to her carriage, and came back to Versailles, bringing in reality the first news of the actual death of Monseigneur.

Acting upon the advice of M. de Beauvilliers, all the company had gone into the salon. The two Princes, Monseigneur de Bourgogne and M. de Berry, were there, seated on one sofa, their Princesses at their sides; all the rest of the company were scattered about in confusion, seated or standing, some of the ladies being on the floor, near the sofa. There could be no doubt of what had happened. It was plainly written on every face in the chamber and throughout the apartment. Monseigneur was no more: it was known: it was spoken of: constraint with respect to him no longer existed. Amidst the surprise, the confusion, and the movements that prevailed, the sentiments of all were painted to the life in looks and gestures.

In the outside rooms were heard the constrained groans and sighs of the valets—grieving for the master they had lost as well as for the master that had succeeded. Farther on began the crowd of courtiers of all kinds. The greater number—that is to say the fools—pumped up sighs as well as they could, and with wandering but dry eyes, sung the praises of Monseigneur—insisting especially on his goodness. They pitied the King for the loss of so good a son. The keener began already to be uneasy about the health of the King; and admired themselves for preserving so much judgment amidst so much trouble, which could be perceived by the frequency of their repetitions. Others, really afflicted—the discomfited cabal—wept bitterly, and kept themselves under with an effort as easy to notice as sobs. The most strong-minded or the wisest, with eyes fixed on the ground, in corners, meditated on the consequences of such an event—and especially on their own interests. Few words passed in conversation—here and there an exclamation wrung from grief was answered by some neighbouring grief—a word every quarter of an hour—sombre and haggard eyes—movements quite involuntary of the hands—immobility of all other parts of the body. Those who already looked upon the event as favourable in vain exaggerated their gravity so as to make it resemble chagrin and severity; the veil over their faces was transparent and hid not a single feature. They remained as motionless as those who grieved most, fearing opinion, curiosity, their own satisfaction, their every movement; but their eyes made up for their immobility. Indeed they could not refrain from repeatedly changing their attitude like people ill at ease, sitting or standing, from avoiding each other too carefully, even from allowing their eyes to meet—nor repress a manifest air of liberty—nor conceal their increased liveliness— nor put out a sort of brilliancy which distinguished them in spite of themselves.

The two Princes, and the two Princesses who sat by their sides, were more exposed to view than any other. The Duc de Bourgogne wept with tenderness, sincerity, and gentleness, the tears of nature, of religion, and patience. M. le Duc de Berry also sincerely shed abundance of tears, but bloody tears, so to speak, so great appeared their bitterness; and he uttered not only sobs, but cries, nay, even yells. He was silent sometimes, but from suffocation, and then would burst out again with such a noise, such a trumpet sound of despair, that the majority present burst out also at these dolorous repetitions, either impelled by affliction or decorum. He became so bad, in fact, that his people were forced to undress him then and there, put him to bed, and call in the doctor. Madame la Duchesse de Berry was beside herself, and we shall soon see why. The most bitter despair was painted with horror on her face. There was seen written, as it were, a sort of furious grief, based on interest, not affection; now and then came dry lulls deep and sullen, then a torrent of tears and involuntary gestures, yet restrained, which showed extreme bitterness of mind, fruit of the profound meditation that had preceded. Often aroused by the cries of her husband, prompt to assist him, to support him, to embrace him, to give her smelling-bottle, her care for him was evident; but soon came another profound reverie —then a gush of tears assisted to suppress her cries. As for Madame la Duchesse de Bourgogne she consoled her husband with less trouble than she had to appear herself in want of consolation. Without attempting to play a part, it was evident that she did her best to acquit herself of a pressing duty of decorum. But she found extreme difficulty in keeping up appearances. When the Prince her brother-in-law howled, she blew her nose. She had brought some tears along with her and kept them up with care; and these combined with the art of the handkerchief, enabled her to redden her eyes, and make them swell, and smudge her face; but her glances often wandered on the sly to the countenances of all present.

Madame arrived, in full dress she knew not why, and howling she knew not why, inundated everybody with her tears in embracing them, making the château echo with renewed cries, and furnished the odd spectacle of a Princess putting on her robes of ceremony in the dead of night to come and cry among a crowd of women with but little on except their night-dresses,—almost as masqueraders.

In the gallery several ladies, Madame la Duchesse d'Orléans, Madame de Castries, and Madame de Saint-Simon among the rest, finding no one close by, drew near each other by the side of a tent-bedstead, and began to open their hearts to each other, which they did with the more freedom, inasmuch as they had but one sentiment in common upon what had occurred. In this gallery, and in the salon, there were always during the night several beds, in which, for security's sake, certain Swiss guards and servants slept. These beds had been put in their usual place this evening before the bad news came from Meudon. In the midst of the conversation of the ladies, Madame de Castries touched the bed, felt something move, and was much terrified. A moment after they saw a sturdy arm, nearly naked, raise on a sudden the curtains, and thus show them a great brawny Swiss under the sheets, half awake, and wholly amazed. The fellow was a long time in making out his position, fixing his eyes upon every face one after the other; but at last, not judging it advisable to get up in the midst of such a grand company, he reburied himself in his bed, and closed the curtains. Apparently the good man had gone to bed before anything had transpired, and had slept so soundly ever since that he had not been aroused until then. The saddest sights have often the most ridiculous contrasts. This caused some of the ladies to laugh, and Madame d'Orléans fear lest the conversation should have been overheard. But after reflection, the sleep and the stupidity of the sleeper reassured her.

I had some doubts yet as to the event that had taken place; for I did not like to abandon myself to belief, until the word was pronounced by some one in whom I could have faith. By chance I met D'O, and I asked him. He answered me clearly that Monseigneur was no more. Thus answered, I tried not to be glad. I know not if I succeeded well, but at least it is certain, that neither joy nor sorrow blunted my curiosity, and that while taking due care to preserve all decorum, I did not consider myself in any way forced to play the doleful. I no longer feared any fresh attack from the citadel of Meudon, nor any cruel charges from its implacable garrison. I felt, therefore, under no constraint, and followed every face with my glances, and tried to scrutinise them unobserved. It must be admitted, that for him who is well acquainted with the privacies of a Court, the first sight of rare events of this nature, so interesting in so many different respects, is extremely satisfactory. Every countenance recalls the cares, the intrigues, the labours employed in the advancement of fortunes—in the overthrow of rivals: the relations, the coldness, the hatreds, the evil offices done, the baseness of all; hope, despair, rage, satisfaction, express themselves in the features. See how all eyes wander to and fro examining what passes around—how some are astonished to find others more mean, or less mean than was expected! Thus this spectacle produced a pleasure, which, hollow as it may be, is one of the greatest a Court can bestow.

The turmoil in this vast apartment lasted about an hour, at the end of which M. de Beauvilliers thought it was high time to deliver the Princes of their company. The rooms were cleared. M. le Duc de Berry went away to his rooms, partly supported by his wife. All through the night he asked, amid tears and cries, for news from Meudon; he would not understand the cause of the King's departure to Marly. When at length the mournful curtain was drawn from before his eyes, the state he fell into cannot be described. The night of Monseigneur and Madame de Bourgogne was more tranquil. Some one having said to the Princess, that having no real cause to be affected, it would be terrible to play a part, she replied, quite naturally, that without feigning, pity touched her and decorum controlled her; and indeed she kept herself within these bounds with truth and decency. Their chamber, in which they invited several ladies to pass the night in arm-chairs, became immediately a palace of Morpheus. All quietly fell asleep. The curtains were left open, so that the Prince and Princess could be seen sleeping profoundly. They woke up once or twice for a moment. In the morning the Duke and Duchess rose early, their tears quite dried up. They shed

no more for this cause, except on special and rare occasions. The
ladies who had watched and slept in their chamber, told their friends
how tranquil the night had been. But nobody was surprised, and as
there was no longer a Monseigneur, nobody was scandalised. Madame
de Saint-Simon and I remained up two hours before going to bed, and
then went there without feeling any want of rest. In fact, I slept so
little that at seven in the morning I was up; but it must be admitted
that such restlessness is sweet, and such re-awakenings are savoury.

Mémoires (1829–30)
Translated by Bayle St. John

*A scene that surpasses anything imaginable for sagacity of observation
and genius of expression in human matters.*

C.-A. SAINTE-BEUVE
Causeries du lundi (1851)

ALEXANDER POPE

1 6 8 8 — 1 7 4 4

THE HEIGHTS OF ARTS

Fir'd at first sight with what the Muse imparts,
In fearless youth we tempt the heights of Arts,
While from the bounded level of our mind,
Short views we take, nor see the lengths behind;
But more advanc'd, behold with strange surprize
New distant scenes of endless science rise!
So pleas'd at first the tow'ring Alps we try,
Mount o'er the vales, and seem to tread the sky,
Th' eternal snows appear already past,
And the first clouds and mountains seem the last:
But, those attain'd, we tremble to survey
The growing labours of the lengthen'd way,
Th' increasing prospect tires our wand'ring eyes,
Hills peep o'er hills, and Alps on Alps arise!

Essay on Criticism (1711)

*I cannot forbear to observe, that the comparison of a student's progress
in the sciences with the journey of a traveller in the Alps, is perhaps the
best that English poetry can show. A simile, to be perfect, must both*

illustrate and ennoble the subject; must show it to the understanding in a clearer view, and display it to the fancy with greater dignity; but either of these qualities may be sufficient to recommend it. In didactic poetry, of which the great purpose is instruction, a simile may be praised which illustrates, though it does not ennoble; in heroics, that may be admitted which ennobles, though it does not illustrate. That it may be complete, it is required to exhibit, independently of its references, a pleasing image; for a simile is said to be a short episode. To this antiquity was so attentive, that circumstances were sometimes added, which, having no parallels, served only to fill the imagination, and produced what Perrault ludicrously called "comparisons with a long tail." In their similes the greatest writers have sometimes failed; the ship-race, compared with the chariot-race, is neither illustrated or aggrandised; land and water make all the difference: when Apollo, running after Daphne, is likened to a greyhound chasing a hare, there is nothing gained; the ideas of pursuit and flight are too plain to be made plainer; and a god and the daughter of a god, are not represented much to their advantage by a hare and dog. The simile of the Alps has no useless parts, yet affords a striking picture by itself; it makes the foregoing position better understood, and enables it to take faster hold on the attention; it assists the apprehension, and elevates the fancy.

SAMUEL JOHNSON
The Lives of the Poets (1779–81)

ALEXANDER POPE

1 6 8 8 — 1 7 4 4

THE SOUND AND THE SENSE

'Tis not enough no harshness gives offence,
The sound must seem an Echo to the sense:
Soft is the strain when Zephyr gently blows,
And the smooth stream in smoother numbers flows;
But when loud surges lash the sounding shoar,
The hoarse, rough verse should like the torrent roar:
When Ajax strives some rock's vast weight to throw,
The line too labours, and the words move slow;
Not so, when swift Camilla scours the plain,
Flies o'er th' unbending corn, and skims along the main.

Essay on Criticism (1711)

A celebrated passage and the most perfect of its kind, perhaps, that exists in modern writing.

C.-A. SAINTE-BEUVE
Nouveaux lundis (1864)

ALEXANDER POPE

1 6 8 8 — 1 7 4 4

THE RAPE OF THE LOCK

Canto I

What dire offence from am'rous causes springs,
What mighty contests rise from trivial things,
I sing—This verse to *Caryll*, Muse! is due:
This, ev'n Belinda may vouchsafe to view:
Slight is the subject, but not so the praise,
If she inspire, and he approve my lays.
   Say what strange motive, Goddess! could compel
A well-bred Lord t' assault a gentle Belle?
O say what stranger cause, yet unexplor'd,
Could make a gentle Belle reject a Lord?
In tasks so bold, can little men engage,
And in soft bosoms dwells such mighty Rage?
   Sol thro' white curtains shot a tim'rous ray,
And oped those eyes that must eclipse the day:
Now lapdogs give themselves the rousing shake,
And sleepless lovers, just at twelve, awake:
Thrice rung the bell, the slipper knock'd the ground,
And the press'd watch return'd a silver sound.
Belinda still her downy pillow prest,
Her guardian Sylph prolong'd the balmy rest:
'Twas He had summon'd to her silent bed
The morning-dream that hover'd o'er her head;
A Youth more glitt'ring than a Birth-night Beau,
(That ev'n in slumber caus'd her cheek to glow)
Seem'd to her ear his winning lips to lay,
And thus in whispers said, or seem'd to say.
   Fairest of mortals, thou distinguish'd **care**
Of thousand bright Inhabitants of Air!
If e'er one vision touch'd thy infant thought,
Of all the Nurse and all the Priest have taught;

Of airy Elves by moonlight shadows seen,
The silver token, and the circled green,
Or virgins visited by Angel-pow'rs,
With golden crowns and wreaths of heav'nly flow'rs;
Hear and believe! thy own importance know,
Nor bound thy narrow views to things below.
Some secret truths, from learned pride conceal'd,
To Maids alone and Children are reveal'd:
What tho' no credit doubting Wits may give?
The Fair and Innocent shall still believe.
Know, then, unnumber'd Spirits round thee fly,
The light Militia of the lower sky:
These, tho' unseen, are ever on the wing,
Hang o'er the Box, and hover round the Ring.
Think what an equipage thou hast in Air,
And view with scorn two Pages and a Chair.
As now your own, our beings were of old,
And once inclos'd in Woman's beauteous mould;
Thence, by a soft transition, we repair
From earthly Vehicles to these of air.
Think not, when Woman's transient breath is fled,
That all her vanities at once are dead;
Succeeding vanities she still regards,
And tho' she plays no more, o'erlooks the cards.
Her joy in gilded Chariots, when alive,
And love of Ombre, after death survive.
For when the Fair in all their pride expire,
To their first Elements their Souls retire:
The Sprites of fiery Termagants in Flame
Mount up, and take a Salamander's name.
Soft yielding minds to Water glide away,
And sip, with Nymphs, their elemental Tea.
The graver Prude sinks downward to a Gnome,
In search of mischief still on Earth to roam.
The light Coquettes in Sylphs aloft repair,
And sport and flutter in the fields of Air.
    Know further yet; whoever fair and chaste
Rejects mankind, is by some Sylph embrac'd:
For Spirits, freed from mortal laws, with ease
Assume what sexes and what shapes they please.
What guards the purity of melting Maids,
In courtly balls, and midnight masquerades,
Safe from the treach'rous friend, the daring spark,
The glance by day, the whisper in the dark,
When kind occasion prompts their warm desires,

When music softens, and when dancing fires?
'Tis but their Sylph, the wise Celestials know,
Tho' Honour is the word with Men below.
　　Some nymphs there are, too conscious of their face,
For life predestin'd to the Gnomes' embrace.
These swell their prospects and exalt their pride,
When offers are disdain'd, and love deny'd:
Then gay Ideas crowd the vacant brain,
While Peers, and Dukes, and all their sweeping train,
And Garters, Stars, and Coronets appear,
And in soft sounds, Your Grace salutes their ear.
'Tis these that early taint the female soul,
Instruct the eyes of young Coquettes to roll,
Teach infant-cheeks a bidden blush to know,
And little hearts to flutter at a Beau.
　　Oft, when the world imagine women stray,
The Sylphs thro' mystic mazes guide their way,
Thro' all the giddy circle they pursue,
And old impertinence expel by new.
What tender maid but must a victim fall
To one man's treat, but for another's ball?
When Florio speaks what virgin could withstand,
If gentle Damon did not squeeze her hand?
With varying vanities, from ev'ry part,
They shift the moving Toyshop of their heart;
Where wigs with wigs, with sword-knots sword-knots strive,
Beaux banish beaux, and coaches coaches drive.
This erring mortals Levity may call;
Oh blind to truth! the Sylphs contrive it all.
　　Of these am I, who thy protection claim,
A watchful sprite, and Ariel is my name.
Late, as I rang'd the crystal wilds of air,
In the clear Mirror of thy ruling Star
I saw, alas! some dread event impend,
Ere to the main this morning sun descend,
But heav'n reveals not what, or how, or where:
Warn'd by the Sylph, oh pious maid, beware!
This to disclose is all thy guardian can:
Beware of all, but most beware of Man!
　　He said; when Shock, who thought she slept too long,
Leap'd up, and wak'd his mistress with his tongue.
'Twas then, Belinda, if report say true,
Thy eyes first open'd on a Billet-doux;
Wounds, Charms and Ardours were no sooner read,
But all the Vision vanish'd from thy head.

And now, unveil'd, the Toilet stands display'd,
Each silver Vase in mystic order laid.
First, rob'd in white, the Nymph intent adores,
With head uncover'd, the Cosmetic pow'rs.
A heav'nly image in the glass appears,
To that she bends, to that her eyes she rears;
Th' inferior Priestess, at her altar's side,
Trembling begins the sacred rites of Pride.
Unnumber'd treasures ope at once, and here
The various off'rings of the world appear;
From each she nicely culls with curious toil,
And decks the Goddess with the glitt'ring spoil.
This casket India's glowing gems unlocks,
And all Arabia breathes from yonder box.
The Tortoise here and Elephant unite,
Transform'd to combs, the speckled, and the white.
Here files of pins extend their shining rows,
Puffs, Powders, Patches, Bibles, Billet-doux.
Now awful Beauty puts on all its arms;
The fair each moment rises in her charms,
Repairs her smiles, awakens ev'ry grace,
And calls forth all the wonders of her face;
Sees by degrees a purer blush arise,
And keener lightnings quicken in her eyes.
The busy Sylphs surround their darling care,
These set the head, and those divide the hair,
Some fold the sleeve, whilst others plait the gown;
And Betty's prais'd for labours not her own.

Canto II

Not with more glories, in th' etherial plain,
The Sun first rises o'er the purpled main,
Than, issuing forth, the rival of his beams
Launch'd on the bosom of the silver Thames.
Fair Nymphs, and well-drest Youths around her shone,
But ev'ry eye was fix'd on her alone.
On her white breast a sparkling Cross she wore,
Which Jews might kiss, and Infidels adore.
Her lively looks a sprightly mind disclose,
Quick as her eyes, and as unfix'd as those:
Favours to none, to all she smiles extends;
Oft she rejects, but never once offends.
Bright as the sun, her eyes the gazers strike,
And, like the sun, they shine on all alike.

Yet graceful ease, and sweetness void of pride,
Might hide her faults, if Belles had faults to hide:
If to her share some female errors fall,
Look on her face, and you'll forget 'em all.

This Nymph, to the destruction of mankind,
Nourish'd two Locks, which graceful hung behind
In equal curls, and well conspir'd to deck
With shining ringlets the smooth iv'ry neck.
Love in these labyrinths his slaves detains,
And mighty hearts are held in slender chains.
With hairy springes we the birds betray,
Slight lines of hair surprise the finny prey,
Fair tresses man's imperial race ensnare
And beauty draws us with a single hair.

Th' advent'rous Baron the bright locks admir'd;
He saw, he wish'd, and to the prize aspir'd.
Resolv'd to win, he meditates the way,
By force to ravish, or by fraud betray;
For when success a Lover's toil attends,
Few ask, if fraud or force attain'd his ends.

For this, ere Phœbus rose, he had implor'd
Propitious heav'n, and ev'ry pow'r ador'd,
But chiefly Love—to Love an Altar built,
Of twelve vast French Romances, neatly gilt.
There lay three garters, half a pair of gloves;
And all the trophies of his former loves;
With tender Billet-doux he lights the pyre,
And breathes three am'rous sighs to raise the fire.
Then prostrate falls, and begs with ardent eyes
Soon to obtain, and long possess the prize:
The pow'rs gave ear, and granted half his pray'r,
The rest, the winds dispers'd in empty air.

But now secure the painted vessel glides,
The sun-beams trembling on the floating tides:
While melting music steals upon the sky,
And soften'd sounds along the waters die;
Smooth flow the waves, the Zephyrs gently play,
Belinda smil'd, and all the world was gay.
All but the Sylph—with careful thoughts opprest,
Th' impending woe sat heavy on his breast.
He summons strait his Denizens of air;
The lucid squadrons round the sails repair:
Soft o'er the shrouds aërial whispers breathe,
That seem'd but Zephyrs to the train beneath.

Some to the sun their insect-wings unfold,
Waft on the breeze, or sink in clouds of gold;
Transparent forms, too fine for mortal sight,
Their fluid bodies half dissolv'd in light,
Loose to the wind their airy garments flew,
Thin glitt'ring textures of the filmy dew,
Dipt in the richest tincture of the skies,
Where light disports in ever-mingling dyes,
While ev'ry beam new transient colours flings,
Colours that change whene'er they wave their wings.
Amid the circle, on the gilded mast,
 uperior by the head, was Ariel plac'd;
His purple pinions op'ning to the sun,
He rais'd his azure wands, and thus begun.

Ye Sylphs and Sylphids, to your chief give ear.
Fays, Fairies, Genii, Elves, and Dæmons, hear!
Ye know the spheres and various tasks assign'd
By laws eternal to th' aërial kind.
Some in the fields of purest Æther play,
And bask and whiten in the blaze of day.
Some guide the course of wand'ring orbs on high,
Or roll the planets thro' the boundless sky.
Some less refin'd, beneath the moon's pale light
Pursue the stars that shoot athwart the night,
Or suck the mists in grosser air below,
Or dip their pinions in the painted bow,
Or brew fierce tempests on the wintry main,
Or o'er the glebe distil the kindly rain.
Others on earth o'er human race preside,
Watch all their ways, and all their actions guide:
Of these the chief the care of Nations own,
And guard with Arms divine the British Throne.

Our humbler province is to tend the Fair,
Not a less pleasing, tho' less glorious care;
To save the powder from too rude a gale,
Nor let th' imprison'd essences exhale;
To draw fresh colours from the vernal flow'rs;
To steal from rainbows e'er they drop in show'rs
A brighter wash; to curl their waving hairs,
Assist their blushes, and inspire their airs;
Nay oft, in dreams, invention we bestow,
To change a Flounce, or add a Furbelow.

This day, black Omens threat the brightest **Fair,**
That e'er deserv'd a watchful spirit's care;

Some dire disaster, or by force, or slight;
But what, or where, the fates have wrapt in night.
Whether the nymph shall break Diana's law,
Or some frail China jar receive a flaw;
Or stain her honour or her new brocade;
Forget her pray'rs, or miss a masquerade;
Or lose her heart, or necklace, at a ball;
Or whether Heav'n has doom'd that Shock must fall.
Haste, then, ye spirits! to your charge repair:
The flutt'ring fan be Zephyretta's care;
The drops to thee, Brillante, we consign;
And, Momentilla, let the watch be thine;
Do thou, Crispissa, tend her fav'rite Lock;
Ariel himself shall be the guard of Shock.

   To fifty chosen Sylphs, of special note,
We trust th' important charge, the Petticoat:
Oft have we known that seven-fold fence to fail,
Tho' stiff with hoops, and arm'd with ribs of whale;
Form a strong line about the silver bound,
And guard the wide circumference around.

   Whatever spirit, careless of his charge,
His post neglects, or leaves the fair at large,
Shall feel sharp vengeance soon o'ertake his sins,
Be stopp'd in vials, or transfix'd with pins;
Or plung'd in lakes of bitter washes lie,
Or wedg'd whole ages in a bodkin's eye:
Gums and Pomatums shall his flight restrain,
While clogg'd he beats his silken wings in vain;
Or Alum styptics with contracting pow'r
Shrink his thin essence like a rivel'd flow'r:
Or, as Ixion fix'd, the wretch shall feel
The giddy motion of the whirling Mill,
In fumes of burning Chocolate shall glow,
And tremble at the sea that froths below!

   He spoke; the spirits from the sails descend;
Some, orb in orb, around the nymph extend;
Some thrid the mazy ringlets of her hair;
Some hang upon the pendants of her ear:
With beating hearts the dire event they wait,
Anxious, and trembling for the birth of Fate.

Canto III

Close by those meads, for ever crown'd with flow'rs,
Where Thames with pride surveys his rising tow'rs,

There stands a structure of majestic frame,
Which from the neighb'ring Hampton takes its name.
Here Britain's statesmen oft the fall foredoom
Or foreign Tyrants and of Nymphs at home;
Here thou, great ANNA! whom three realms obey,
Dost sometimes counsel take—and sometimes Tea.

Hither the heroes and the nymphs resort,
To taste awhile the pleasures of a Court;
In various talk th' instructive hours they past,
Who gave the ball, or paid the visit last;
One speaks the glory of the British Queen,
And one describes a charming Indian screen;
A third interprets motions, looks, and eyes;
At ev'ry word a reputation dies.
Snuff, or the fan, supply each pause of chat,
With singing, laughing, ogling, *and all that.*

Mean while, declining from the noon of day,
The sun obliquely shoots his burning ray;
The hungry Judges soon the sentence sign,
And wretches hang that jury-men may dine;
The merchant from th' Exchange returns in peace,
And the long labours of the Toilet cease.
Belinda now, whom thirst of fame invites,
Burns to encounter two advent'rous Knights,
At Ombre singly to decide their doom;
And swells her breast with conquests yet to come.
Straight the three bands prepare in arms to join,
Each band the number of the sacred nine.
Soon as she spreads her hand, th' aërial guard
Descend, and sit on each important card:
First Ariel perch'd upon a Matadore,
Then each, according to the rank they bore;
For Sylphs, yet mindful of their ancient race,
Are, as when women, wondrous fond of place.

Behold four Kings in majesty revered,
With hoary whiskers and a forky beard;
And four fair Queens whose hands sustain a flow'r,
Th' expressive emblem of their softer pow'r;
Four Knaves in garbs succinct, a trusty band,
Caps on their heads, and halberts in their hand;
And particolour'd troops, a shining train,
Draw forth to combat on the velvet plain.

The skilful Nymph reviews her force with care:
Let Spades be trumps! she said, and trumps they were.

Now move to war her sable Matadores,
In show like leaders of the swarthy Moors.
Spadillio first, unconquerable Lord!
Led off two captive trumps, and swept the board.
As many more Manillio forc'd to yield,
And march'd a victor from the verdant field.
Him Basto follow'd, but his fate more hard
Gain'd but one trump and one Plebeian card.
With his broad sabre next, a chief in years,
The hoary Majesty of Spades appears,
Puts forth one manly leg, to sight reveal'd,
The rest, his many-colour'd robe conceal'd.
The rebel Knave, who dares his prince engage,
Proves the just victim of his royal rage.
Ev'n mighty Pam, that Kings and Queens o'erthrew
And mow'd down armies in the fights of Lu,
Sad chance of war! now destitute of aid,
Falls undistinguish'd by the victor spade!

   Thus far both armies to Belinda yield;
Now to the Baron fate inclines the field.
His warlike Amazon her host invades,
Th' imperial consort of the crown of Spades.
The Club's black Tyrant first her victim dy'd,
Spite of his haughty mien, and barb'rous pride:
What boots the regal circle on his head,
His giant limbs, in state unwieldy spread;
That long behind he trails his pompous robe,
And, of all monarch's, only grasps the globe?

   The Baron now his Diamonds pours apace;
Th' embroider'd King who shows but half his face,
And his refulgent Queen, with pow'rs combin'd
Of broken troops an easy conquest find.
Clubs, Diamonds, Hearts, in wild disorder seen,
With throngs promiscuous strow the level green.
Thus when dispers'd a routed army runs,
Of Asia's troops, and Afric's sable sons,
With like confusion different nations fly,
Of various habit, and of various dye,
The pierced battalions disunited fall,
In heaps on heaps; one fate o'erwhelms them all.

   The Knave of Diamonds tries his wily arts,
And wins (oh shameful chance!) the Queen of Hearts.
At this, the blood the virgin's cheek forsook,
A livid paleness spreads o'er all her look;

She sees, and trembles at th' approaching ill,
Just in the jaws of ruin, and Codille.
And now (as oft in some distemper'd State)
On one nice Trick depends the gen'ral fate.
An Ace of Hearts steps forth: The King unseen
Lurk'd in her hand, and mourn'd his captive Queen:
He springs to Vengeance with an eager pace,
And falls like thunder on the prostrate Ace.
The nymph exulting fills with shouts the sky;
The walls, the woods, and long canals reply.

Oh thoughtless mortals! ever blind to fate,
Too soon dejected, and too soon elate.
Sudden, these honours shall be snatch'd away,
And curs'd for ever this victorious day.

For lo! the board with cups and spoons is crown'd,
The berries crackle, and the mill turns round;
On shining altars of Japan they raise
The silver lamp; the fiery spirits blaze:
From silver spouts the grateful liquors glide,
While China's earth receives the smoking tide:
At once they gratify their scent and taste,
And frequent cups prolong the rich repast.
Straight hover round the Fair her airy band;
Some, as she sipp'd, the fuming liquor fann'd,
Some o'er her lap their careful plumes display'd,
Trembling, and conscious of the rich brocade.
Coffee, (which makes the politician wise,
And see thro' all things with his half-shut eyes)
Sent up in vapours to the Baron's brain
New Stratagems, the radiant Lock to gain.
Ah cease, rash youth! desist ere 'tis too late,
Fear the just Gods, and think of Scylla's Fate!
Chang'd to a bird, and sent to flit in air,
She dearly pays for Nisus' injur'd hair!

But when to mischief mortals bend their will,
How soon they find fit instruments of ill!
Just then, Clarissa drew with tempting grace
A two-edg'd weapon from her shining case:
So Ladies in Romance assist their Knight,
Present the spear, and arm him for the fight.
He takes the gift with rev'rence, and extends
The little engine on his fingers' ends;
This just behind Belinda's neck he spread,
As o'er the fragrant steams she bends her head.

Swift to the Lock a thousand Sprites repair,
A thousand wings, by turns, blow back the hair;
And thrice they twitch'd the diamond in her ear;
Thrice she look'd back, and thrice the foe drew near.
Just in that instant, anxious Ariel sought
The close recesses of the Virgin's thought;
As on the nosegay in her breast reclin'd,
He watch'd th' Ideas rising in her mind,
Sudden he view'd, in spite of all her art,
An earthly Lover lurking at her heart.
Amaz'd, confus'd, he found his pow'r expir'd,
Resign'd to fate, and with a sigh retir'd.

    The Peer now spreads the glitt'ring Forfex wide,
T' inclose the Lock; now joins it, to divide.
Ev'n then, before the fatal engine clos'd,
A wretched Sylph too fondly interpos'd;
Fate urg'd the shears, and cut the Sylph in twain,
(But airy substance soon unites again)
The meeting points the sacred hair dissever
From the fair head, for ever, and for ever!

    Then flash'd the living lightning from her eyes,
And screams of horror rend th' affrighted skies.
Not louder shrieks to pitying heav'n are cast,
When husbands, or when lapdogs breathe their last;
Or when rich China vessels fall'n from high,
In glitt'ring dust and painted fragments lie!

    Let wreaths of triumph now my temples twine,
(The victor cry'd) the glorious Prize is mine!
While fish in streams, or birds delight in air,
Or in a coach and six the British Fair,
As long as Atalantis shall be read,
Or the small pillow grace a Lady's bed,
While visits shall be paid on solemn days,
When num'rous wax-lights in bright order blaze,
While nymphs take treats, or assignations give,
So long my honour, name, and praise shall live!
What Time would spare, from Steel receives its date,
And monuments, like men, submit to fate!
Steel could the labour of the Gods destroy,
And strike to dust th' imperial tow'rs of Troy;
Steel could the works of mortal pride confound,
And hew triumphal arches to the ground.
What wonder then, fair nymph! thy hairs should feel,
The conqu'ring force of unresisted steel?

But anxious care the pensive nymph oppress'd,
And secret passions labour'd in her breast.
Not youthful kings in battle seiz'd alive,
Not scornful virgins who their charms survive,
Not ardent lovers robb'd of all their bliss,
Not ancient ladies when refus'd a kiss,
Not tyrants fierce that unrepenting die,
Not Cynthia when her manteau's pinn'd awry,
E'er felt such rage, resentment, and despair,
As thou, sad Virgin! for thy ravish'd Hair.

 For, that sad moment, when the Sylphs withdrew
And Ariel weeping from Belinda flew,
Umbriel, a dusky, melancholy sprite,
As ever sully'd the fair face of light,
Down to the central earth, his proper scene,
Repair'd to search the gloomy Cave of Spleen.

 Swift on his sooty pinions flits the Gnome,
And in a vapour reach'd the dismal dome.
No cheerful breeze this sullen region knows,
The dreaded East is all the wind that blows.
Here in a grotto, shelter'd close from air,
And screen'd in shades from day's detested glare,
She sighs for ever on her pensive bed,
Pain at her side, and Megrim at her head.

 Two handmaids wait the throne: alike in place,
But diff'ring far in figure and in face.
Here stood Ill-nature like an ancient maid,
Her wrinkled form in black and white array'd;
With store of pray'rs, for mornings, nights, and noons,
Her hand is fill'd; her bosom with lampoons.

 There Affectation, with a sickly mien,
Shows in her cheek the roses of eighteen,
Practis'd to lisp, and hang the head aside,
Faints into airs, and languishes with pride,
On the rich quilt sinks with becoming woe,
Wrapt in a gown, for sickness, and for show.
The fair ones feel such maladies as these,
When each new night-dress gives a new disease.

 A constant Vapour o'er the palace flies;
Strange phantoms rising as the mists arise;
Dreadful, as hermit's dreams in haunted shades,
Or bright, as visions of expiring maids.

Now glaring fiends, and snakes on rolling spires,
Pale spectres, gaping tombs, and purple fires:
Now lakes of liquid gold, Elysian scenes,
And crystal domes, and angels in machines.
　　Unnumber'd throngs on every side are seen,
Of bodies char.g'd to various forms by Spleen.
Here living Tea-pots stand, one arm held out,
One bent; the handle this, and that the spout:
A Pipkin there, like Homer's Tripod walks;
Here sighs a Jar, and there a Goose-pie talks;
Men prove with child, as pow'rful fancy works,
And maids turn'd bottles, call aloud for corks.
　　Safe past the Gnome thro' this fantastic band,
A branch of healing Spleenwort in his hand.
Then thus address'd the pow'r: "Hail, wayward Queen!
Who rule the sex to fifty from fifteen:
Parent of vapours and of female wit,
Who give th' hysteric, or poetic fit,
On various tempers act by various ways,
Make some take physic, other scribble plays;
Who cause the proud their visits to delay,
And send the godly in a pet to pray.
A nymph there is, that all thy pow'r disdains,
And thousands more in equal mirth maintains.
But oh! if e'er thy Gnome could spoil a grace,
Or raise a pimple on a beauteous face,
Like Citron-waters matrons' cheeks inflame,
Or change complexions at a losing game;
If e'er with airy horns I planted heads,
Or rumpled petticoats, or tumbled beds,
Or caus'd suspicion when no soul was rude,
Or discompos'd the head-dress of a Prude,
Or e'er to costive lap-dog gave disease,
Which not the tears of brightest eyes could ease:
Hear me, and touch Belinda with chagrin,
That single act gives half the world the spleen."
　　The Goddess with a discontented air
Seems to reject him, tho' she grants his pray'r.
A wond'rous Bag with both her hands she binds,
Like that where once Ulysses held the winds;
There she collects the force of female lungs,
Sighs, sobs, and passions, and the war of tongues.
A Vial next she fills with fainting fears,
Soft sorrows, melting griefs, and flowing tears.

The Gnome rejoicing bears her gifts away,
Spreads his black wings, and slowly mounts to day.
    Sunk in Thalestris' arms the nymph he found,
Her eyes dejected and her hair unbound.
Full o'er their heads the swelling bag he rent,
And all the Furies issu'd at the vent.
Belinda burns with more than mortal ire,
And fierce Thalestris fans the rising fire.
"O wretched maid!" she spread her hands, and cry'd,
(While Hampton's echoes, "Wretched maid!" reply'd)
"Was it for this you took such constant care
The bodkin, comb, and essence to prepare?
For this your locks in paper durance bound,
For this with tort'ring irons wreath'd around?
For this with fillets strain'd your tender head,
And bravely bore the double loads of lead?
Gods! shall the ravisher display your hair,
While the Fops envy, and the Ladies stare!
Honour forbid! at whose unrivall'd shrine
Ease, pleasure, virtue, all our sex resign.
Methinks already I your tears survey,
Already hear the horrid things they say,
Already see you a degraded toast,
And all your honour in a whisper lost!
How shall I, then, your hapless fame defend?
'Twill then be infamy to seem your friend!
And shall this prize, th' inestimable prize,
Expos'd thro' crystal to the gazing eyes,
And heighten'd by the diamond's circling rays,
On that rapacious hand for ever blaze?
Sooner shall grass in Hyde-park Circus grow,
And wits take lodgings in the sound of Bow;
Sooner let earth, air, sea, to Chaos fall,
Men, monkeys, lap-dogs, parrots, perish all!"
    She said; then raging to Sir Plume repairs,
And bids her Beau demand the precious hairs:
(Sir Plume of amber snuff-box justly vain,
And the nice conduct of a clouded cane)
With earnest eyes, and round unthinking face,
He first the snuff-box open'd, then the case,
And thus broke out—"My Lord, why, what the devil?
"Z—ds! damn the lock! 'fore Gad, you must be civil!
"Plague on't! 'tis past a jest—nay prithee, pox!
"Give her the hair"—he spoke, and rapp'd his box.

"It grieves me much" (reply'd the Peer again)
"Who speaks so well should ever speak in vain.
But by this Lock, this sacred Lock I swear,
(Which never more shall join its parted hair;
Which never more its honours shall renew,
Clipp'd from the lovely head where late it grew)
That while my nostrils draw the vital air,
This hand, which won it, shall for ever wear."
He spoke, and speaking, in proud triumph spread
The long-contended honours of her head.

But Umbriel, hateful Gnome! forbears not so;
He breaks the Vial whence the sorrows flow.
Then see! the nymph in beauteous grief appears,
Her eyes half-languishing, half-drown'd in tears;
On her heav'd bosom hung her drooping head,
Which, with a sigh, she rais'd; and thus she said.

"For ever curs'd be this detested day,
Which snatch'd my best, my fav'rite curl away!
Happy! ah ten times happy had I been,
If Hampton-Court these eyes had never seen!
Yet am not I the first mistaken maid,
By love of Courts to num'rous ills betray'd.
Oh had I rather un-admir'd remain'd
In some lone isle, or distant Northern land;
Where the gilt Chariot never marks the way,
Where none learn Ombre, none e'er taste Bohea!
There kept my charms conceal'd from mortal eye,
Like roses, that in deserts bloom and die.
What mov'd my mind with youthful Lords to roam?
Oh had I stay'd, and said my pray'rs at home!
'Twas this, the morning omens seem'd to tell,
Thrice from my trembling hand the patch-box fell;
The tott'ring China shook without a wind,
Nay, Poll sat mute, and Shock was most unkind!
A Sylph too warn'd me of the threats of fate,
In mystic visions, now believ'd too late!
See the poor remnants of these slighted hairs!
My hands shall rend what ev'n thy rapine spares:
These in two sable ringlets taught to break,
Once gave new beauties to the snowy neck;
The sister-lock now sits uncouth, alone,
And in its fellow's fate foresees its own;
Uncurl'd it hangs, the fatal shears demands,
And tempts once more, thy sacrilegious hands.

Oh hadst thou, cruel! been content to seize
Hairs less in sight, or any hairs but these!"

Canto V

She said: the pitying audience melt in tears,
But Fate and Jove had stopp'd the Baron's ears.
In vain Thalestris with reproach assails,
For who can move when fair Belinda fails?
Not half so fix'd the Trojan could remain,
While Anna begg'd and Dido rag'd in vain.
Then grave Clarissa graceful wav'd her fan;
Silence ensu'd, and thus the nymph began.
  "Say why are Beauties prais'd and honour'd most,
The wise man's passion, and the vain man's toast?
Why deck'd with all that land and sea afford,
Why Angels call'd, and Angel-like ador'd?
Why round our coaches croud the white-glov'd Beaux,
Why bows the side-box from its inmost rows;
How vain are all these glories, all our pains,
Unless good sense preserve what beauty gains:
That men may say, when we the front-box grace:
'Behold the first in virtue as in face!'
Oh! if to dance all night, and dress all day,
Charm'd the small-pox, or chas'd old-age away;
Who would not scorn what housewife's cares produce,
Or who would learn one earthly thing of use?
To patch, nay ogle, might become a Saint,
Nor could it sure be such a sin to paint.
But since, alas! frail beauty must decay,
Curl'd or uncurl'd, since Locks will turn to grey;
Since painted, or not painted, all shall fade,
And she who scorns a man, must die a maid;
What then remains but well our pow'r to use,
And keep good-humour still whate'er we lose?
And trust me, dear! good-humour can prevail,
When airs, and flights, and screams, and scolding fail.
Beauties in vain their pretty eyes may roll;
Charms strike the sight, but merit wins the soul."
  So spoke the Dame, but no applause ensu'd;
Belinda frown'd, Thalestris call'd her Prude.
"To arms, to arms!" the fierce Virago cries,
And swift as lightning to the combat flies.
All side in parties, and begin th' attack;
Fans clap, silks rustle, and tough whalebones crack;

Heroes' and Heroines' shouts confus'dly rise,
And bass, and treble voices strike the skies.
No common weapons in their hands are found,
Like Gods they fight, nor dread a mortal wound.
    So when bold Homer makes the Gods engage,
And heav'nly breasts with human passions rage;
'Gainst Pallas, Mars; Latona, Hermes arms;
And all Olympus rings with loud alarms:
Jove's thunder roars, heav'n trembles all around,
Blue Neptune storms, the bellowing deeps resound:
Earth shakes her nodding tow'rs, the ground gives way,
And the pale ghosts start at the flash of day!
    Triumphant Umbriel on a sconce's height
Clapp'd his glad wings, and sate to view the fight:
Propp'd on their bodkin spears, the Sprites survey
The growing combat, or assist the fray.
    While thro' the press enrag'd Thalestris flies,
And scatters death around from both her eyes,
A Beau and Witling perish'd in the throng,
One died in metaphor, and one in song.
"O cruel nymph! a living death I bear,"
Cry'd Dapperwit, and sunk beside his chair.
A mournful glance Sir Fopling upwards cast,
"Those eyes are made so killing"—was his last.
Thus on Mæander's flow'ry margin lies
Th' expiring Swan, and as he sings he dies.
    When bold Sir Plume had drawn Clarissa down,
Chloe stepp'd in, and kill'd him with a frown;
She smil'd to see the doughty hero slain,
But, at her smile, the Beau reviv'd again.
    Now Jove suspends his golden scales in air,
Weighs the Men's wits against the Lady's hair;
The doubtful beam long nods from side to side;
At length the wits mount up, the hairs subside.
    See, fierce Belinda on the Baron flies,
With more than usual lightning in her eyes:
Nor fear'd the Chief th' unequal fight to try,
Who sought no more than on his foe to die.
But this bold Lord with manly strength endu'd,
She with one finger and a thumb subdu'd:
Just where the breath of life his nostrils drew,
A charge of Snuff the wily virgin threw;
The Gnomes direct, to ev'ry atom just,
The pungent grains of titillating dust.

Sudden, with starting tears each eye o'erflows,
And the high dome re-echoes to his nose.
  Now meet thy fate, incens'd Belinda cry'd,
And drew a deadly bodkin from her side.
(The same, his ancient personage to deck,
Her great great grandsire wore about his neck,
In three seal-rings; which after, melted down,
Form'd a vast buckle for his widow's gown:
Her infant grandame's whistle next it grew,
The bells she jingled, and the whistle blew;
Then in a bodkin grac'd her mother's hairs,
Which long she wore, and now Belinda wears.)
  "Boast not my fall" (he cry'd) "insulting foe!
Thou by some other shalt be laid as low,
Nor think, to die dejects my lofty mind:
All that I dread is leaving you behind!
Rather than so, ah let me still survive,
And burn in Cupid's flames—but burn alive."
  "Restore the Lock!" she cries; and all around
"Restore the Lock!" the vaulted roofs rebound.
Not fierce Othello in so loud a strain
Roar'd for the handkerchief that caus'd his pain.
But see how oft ambitious aims are cross'd,
And chiefs contend 'till all the prize is lost!
The Lock, obtain'd with guilt, and kept with pain,
In ev'ry place is sought, but sought in vain:
With such a prize no mortal must be blest,
So heav'n decrees! with heav'n who can contest?
  Some thought it mounted to the Lunar sphere,
Since all things lost on earth are treasur'd there.
There Hero's wits are kept in pond'rous vases,
And beau's in snuff-boxes and tweezer-cases.
There broken vows and death-bed alms are found,
And lovers' hearts with ends of riband bound,
The courtier's promises, and sick man's pray'rs,
The smiles of harlots, and the tears of heirs,
Cages for gnats, and chains to yoke a flea,
Dry'd butterflies, and tomes of casuistry.
  But trust the Muse—she saw it upward rise,
Tho' mark'd by none but quick, poetic eyes:
(So Rome's great founder to the heav'ns withdrew,
To Proculus alone confess'd in view)
A sudden Star, it shot thro' liquid air,
And drew behind a radiant trail of hair.

Not Berenice's Locks first rose so bright,
The heav'ns bespangling with dishevell'd light.
The Sylphs behold it kindling as it flies,
And pleas'd pursue its progress thro' the skies.
   This the Beau monde shall from the Mall survey,
And hail with music its propitious ray.
This the blest Lover shall for Venus take,
And send up vows from Rosamonda's lake.
This Partridge soon shall view in cloudless skies,
When next he looks thro' Galileo's eyes;
And hence th' egregious wizard shall foredoom
The fate of Louis, and the fall of Rome.
   Then cease, bright Nymph! to mourn thy ravish'd hair,
Which adds new glory to the shining sphere!
Not all the tresses that fair head can boast,
Shall draw such envy as the Lock you lost.
For, after all the murders of your eye,
When, after millions slain, yourself shall die:
When those fair suns shall set, as set they must,
And all those tresses shall be laid in dust,
This Lock, the Muse shall consecrate to fame,
And 'midst the stars inscribe Belinda's name.

(1712)

It is one of the few things wholly without a flaw.

WILLIAM PATON KER
The Art of Poetry (1923)

ALEXANDER POPE

1 6 8 8 — 1 7 4 4

LORD MAYOR'S SHOW

Now Night descending, the proud scene was o'er,
But liv'd, in Settle's numbers, one day more.°

The Dunciad (1728), i

The finest piece of wit I know of.

WILLIAM HAZLITT
Lectures on the English Comic Writers (1818)

° Settle was poet to the city of London and composed yearly panegyrics upon the Lord Mayors.

ALEXANDER POPE

1 6 8 8 — 1 7 4 4

A GOLDEN RULE

Never elated while one man's oppress'd;
Never dejected while another's bless'd.

An Essay on Man (1734), iv

The most complete, concise, and lofty expression of moral temper exist-
ing in English words.

JOHN RUSKIN
Lectures on Art (1887)

ALEXANDER POPE

1 6 8 8 — 1 7 4 4

COMPLIMENTS

Despise low joys, low gains;
Disdain whatever Cornbury disdains;
Be virtuous, and be happy for your pains.

The Sixth Epistle of the First Book of Horace (1738)

Conspicuous scene! another yet is nigh
(More silent far), where Kings and Poets lie;
Where Murray (long enough his country's pride)
Shall be no more than Tully or than Hyde!

The Sixth Epistle of the First Book of Horace (1738)

Why rail they then if but a wreath of mine,
O all-accomplish'd St. John! deck thy shrine?

Epilogue to the Satires (1738)

A. But why then publish? P. Granville the polite,
And knowing Walsh, would tell me I could write;
Well-natured Garth inflamed with early praise,
And Congreve lov'd, and Swift endured my lays;
The courtly Talbot, Somers, Sheffield, read;
Ev'n mitred Rochester would nod the head,

And St. John's self (great Dryden's friends before)
With open arms receiv'd one poet more.
Happy my studies, when by these approv'd!
Happier their author, when by these belov'd!
From these the world will judge of men and books,
Not from the Burnets, Oldmixons, and Cookes.

Epistle to Dr. Arbuthnot (1735)

"Compliments! I did not know he ever made any."—"The finest," said Lamb, "that were ever paid by the wit of man. Each of them is worth an estate for life—nay, is an immortality."

CHARLES LAMB
Quoted, William Hazlitt, Of Persons One Would Wish
to Have Seen (1826)

JACQUES RANCHIN

C . 1 6 9 0

THE KING OF TRIOLETS

Le premier jour du mois de mai
Fut le plus heureux de ma vie:
Le beau dessein que je formais,
Le premier jour du mois de mai!
Je vous vis et je vous aimais.
Si ce dessein vous plut, Sylvie,
Le premier jour du mois de mai
Fut le plus heureux de ma vie.

The first day in the month of May
Counts for the happiest in my life.
How fair a plan I formed that day,
The first day in the month of May!
I saw you and I loved straightway;
And if my plan pleased you, my wife,
The first day in the month of May
Counts for the happiest in my life.

Translated by J. G. Legge

The King of Triolets.

GILLES MÉNAGE
Menagiana (1715)

F. M. AROUET DE VOLTAIRE

1694 — 1778

NO TIME FOR JESTING

Ce n'est plus le temps de plaisanter; les bons mots ne conviennent point aux massacres. Quoi! des Busiris en robe font périr dans les plus horribles supplices des enfans de seize ans! et cela malgré l'avis de dix juges intègres et humains! et la nation le souffre! A peine en parle-t-on un moment, on court ensuite à l'Opéra-Comique; et la barbarie, devenue plus insolente par notre silence, égorgera demain qui elle voudra juridiquement; et vous surtout, qui aurez élevé la voix contre elle deux ou trois minutes. Ici Calas roué, là Sirven pendu, plus loin un bâillon dans la bouche d'un lieutenant-général; quinze jours après, cinq jeunes gens condamnés aux flammes pour des folies qui méritaient Saint-Lazare. Qu'importe l'avant-propos du roi de Prusse? Apporte-t-il le moindre remède à ces maux exécrables? est-ce là le pays de la philosophie et des agrémens? c'est celui de la Saint-Barthélemi. L'inquisition n'aurait pas osé faire ce que des juges jansénistes viennent d'exécuter. . . . Vous voulez prendre le parti de rire, mon cher Platon! il faudrait prendre celui de se venger, ou du moins quitter un pays où se commettent tous les jours tant d'horreurs. . . .

Non, encore une fois, je ne puis souffrir que vous finissiez votre lettre en disant: *Je rirai.* Ah! mon cher ami, est-ce là le temps de rire? riait-on en voyant chauffer le taureau de Phalaris?

This is no longer a time for jesting: witty things do not go well with massacres. What? These Busirises in wigs destroy in the midst of horrible tortures children of sixteen! And that in face of the verdict of ten upright and humane judges! And the victim suffers it! People talk about it for a moment, and the next they are hastening to the comic opera; and barbarity, become the more insolent for our silence, will to-morrow cut throats juridically at pleasure. Here Calas broken on the wheel, there Sirven condemned to be hung, further off a gag thrust into the mouth of a lieutenant-general, a fortnight after that five youths condemned to the flames for extravagances that deserved nothing worse than Saint Lazare. Is this the country of philosophy and pleasure? It is the country rather of the Saint Bartholomew massacre. Why, the Inquisition would not have ventured to do what these Jansenist judges have done. . . . What, you would be content to laugh? We ought rather to resolve to seek vengeance, or at any rate to leave a country where day after day such horrors are committed. . . . No, once more, I cannot bear that you should finish your letter by saying, I mean to laugh. Ah, my friend, is it a time for laughing? Did men laugh when they saw Phalaris's bull being made red-hot?

Letters to D'Alembert (July 18–23, 1766)
Translated by John Morley

These atrocities kindled in Voltaire a blaze of anger and pity, that remains among the things of which humanity has most reason to be proud. Everybody who has read much of the French writing of the middle of the eighteenth century, is conscious from time to time of a sound of mocking and sardonic laughter in it. This laugh of the eighteenth century has been too often misunderstood as the expression of a cynical hardness of heart, proving the hollowness of the humanitarian pretensions in the midst of which it is heard. It was in truth something very different; it was the form in which men sought a little relief from the monotony of the abominations which oppressed them, and from whose taint they had such difficulty to escape. This refrain, that after all a man can do nothing better than laugh, apparently so shallow and inhuman, in reality so penetrated with melancholy, we may count most certainly on finding at the close of the narration of some more than usually iniquitous or imbecile exploit of those in authority. It was when the thought of the political and social and intellectual degradation of their country became too vivid to be endured, that men like Voltaire and D'Alembert would abruptly turn away from it, and in the bitterness of their impotence cry that there was nothing for it but to take the world and all that befalls therein in merriment. It was the grimacing of a man who jests when he is perishing of hunger, or is shrinking under knife or cautery.

JOHN MORLEY
Voltaire (1903)

F. M. AROUET DE VOLTAIRE

1694 — 1778

CANDIDE

"Je sçai aussi, dit Candide, qu'il faut cultiver nôtre jardin. — Vous avez raison, dit Pangloss; car quand l'homme fut mis dans le jardin d'Eden, il y fut mis, *ut operaretur eum,* pour qu'il travaillat; ce qui prouve que l'homme n'est pas né pour le repos. — Travaillons sans raisonner, dit **Martin**, c'est le seul moyen de rendre la vie suportable."

Toute la petite societé entra dans ce louable dessein; chacun se mit à exercer ses talents. La petite terre raporta beaucoup. Cunégonde était à la vérité bien laide; mais elle devint une excellente patissiére; Paquette broda; la Vieille eut soin du linge. Il n'y eut pas jusqu'à Frère Giroflée qui ne rendit service; il fut un très bon menuisier, & même devint honnête homme: & Pangloss disait quelquefois à Candide: "Tous les événements sont enchainés dans le meilleur des Mondes possibles; car enfin, si vous n'aviez pas été chassé d'un beau Château à grands coups de pied dans le derrière, pour l'amour de Mademoiselle Cunégonde, si vous n'aviez pas été mis à l'Inquisition, si vous n'aviez pas couru l'Amérique à pied si vous n'aviez pas donné un bon coup d'épée au Baron, si vous n'aviez pas perdu tous vos moutons du bon pays d'Eldorado, vous ne mangeriez pas ici des cédras confits & des pistaches.— Cela est bien dit, répondit Candide, mais il faut cultiver nôtre jardin."

"Yes," said Candide, "and I know too that we must attend to our garden."

"You are right," said Pangloss; "for when man was put into the Garden of Eden, he was placed there 'ut operaretur eum,'—to dress it and to keep it, which proves that man is not born for idleness and repose."

"Let us work without arguing," said Martin; "that is the only way of rendering life tolerable."

All the little company entered into this praiseworthy resolution, and each began busily to exert his or her peculiar talents. The small orchard brought forth abundant crops. Cunegund, it could not be denied, was very ugly, but she became an excellent hand at making pastry; Paquette embroidered; the old woman took care of the linen. There was no one who did not make himself useful, not even friar Giroflée; he was a first-rate carpenter, and actually turned out an honest fellow.

Pangloss used sometimes to say to Candide: "All events are inextricably linked together in this best of all possible worlds; for, look you, if you had not been driven out of a magnificent castle by hearty kicks upon your hinder parts for presuming to make love to Miss Cunegund, if you had not been put into the Inquisition, if you had not roamed over America on foot, if you had never run your sword through the Baron, or lost all your sheep from the fine country of El Dorado, you would not be here now eating candied citrons and pistachio-nuts."

"Well said!" answered Candide; "but we must attend to our garden."

Candide, ou l'optimisme (1758)
Translated by R. Bruce Boswell

The book is a catalogue of all the woes, all the misfortunes, all the degradations, and all the horrors that can afflict humanity; and through-

out it Voltaire's grin is never for a moment relaxed. As catastrophe follows catastrophe, and disaster succeeds disaster, not only does he laugh himself consumedly, but he makes his reader laugh no less; and it is only when the book is finished that the true meaning of it is borne in upon the mind. Then it is that the scintillating pages begin to exercise their grim unforgettable effect; and the pettiness and misery of man seem to borrow a new intensity from the relentless laughter of Voltaire.

But perhaps the most wonderful thing about CANDIDE is that it contains, after all, something more than mere pessimism—it contains a positive doctrine as well. Voltaire's common sense withers the Ideal; but it remains common sense. "Il faut cultiver notre jardin" is his final word—one of the very few pieces of practical wisdom ever uttered by a philosopher.

Voltaire's style reaches the summit of its perfection in CANDIDE; but it is perfect in all that he wrote. His prose is the final embodiment of the most characteristic qualities of the French genius. If all that that great nation had ever done or thought were abolished from the world, except a single sentence of Voltaire's, the essence of their achievement would have survived.

LYTTON STRACHEY
Landmarks in French Literature (1923)

F. M. AROUET DE VOLTAIRE

1694 — 1778

SUR UN CHRIST HABILLÉ EN JÉSUITE

Admirez l'artifice extrême
De ces moines industrieux;
Ils vous ont habillé comme eux,
Mon Dieu, de peur qu'on ne vous aime.

ON A CHRIST IN JESUIT ROBES

Consider, pray, the artfulness
Industrious monks like these can show.
My God, they've clothed Thee in their dress,
Lest men should love Thee here below!

SUR SON PORTRAIT ENTRE CEUX DE LA BEAUMELLE ET DE FRÉRON

Le Jay vient de mettre Voltaire
Entre La Beaumelle et Fréron;
Ce serait vraiment un Calvaire,
S'il s'y trouvait un bon larron.

ON HIS PORTRAIT BETWEEN TWO OTHERS

'Twixt Fréron and La Beaumelle me!
What can Le Jay by this have meant?
It were indeed a Calvary,
Had either thief been penitent.

Translated by J. G. Legge

Here are two of his bitterest epigrams, and they are probably not to be equalled for keen, incisive, cruel wit in all literature. The first is an example of the attacks he indulged in against the Church and its ministers. The second indicates his intolerant contempt for authors he fell foul of; Le Jay, a publisher, had produced a title-page with his portrait between those of two of his pet aversions, Fréron, a leading critic and an estimable man, and La Beaumelle, an old teacher of Voltaire.

J. G. LEGGE
Chanticleer (1935)

ANONYMOUS

SEVENTEENTH CENTURY

CHANSON DE RENAUD

I

Quand Jean Renaud de guerre r'vint,
Tenait ses tripes dans ses mains.
Sa mère à la fenêtre en haut:
"Voici venir mon fils Renaud."

911

II

"Bonjour, Renaud, bonjour, mon fils,
Ta femme est accouché' d'un fils.
—Ni de ma femm', ni de mon fils
Je ne saurais me réjouir.

III

"Que l'on me fass' vite un lit blanc
Pour que je m'y couche dedans."
Et quand ce vint sur le minuit,
Le beau Renaud rendit l'esprit.

IV

"Dites-moi, ma mère, ma mie,
Qu'est-c' que j'entends pleurer ici?
—C'est un p'tit pag' qu'on a fouetté
Pour un plat d'or qu'est égaré.

V

—Dites-moi, ma mère, ma mie,
Qu'est-c' que j'entends coigner ici?
—Ma fille, ce sont les maçons
Qui raccommodent la maison.

VI

—Dites-moi, ma mère, ma mie,
Qu'est-c' que j'entends sonner ici?
—C'est le p'tit Dauphin nouveau-né
Dont le baptême est retardé.

VII

—Dites-moi, ma mère, ma mie,
Qu'est-c' que j'entends chanter ici?
—Ma fille, c' sont les processions
Qui font le tour de la maison.

VIII

—Dites-moi, ma mère, ma mie,
Quell' robe mettrai-je aujourd'hui?
—Mettez le blanc, mettez le gris,
Mettez le noir pour mieux choisi.

912

—Dites-moi, ma mère, ma mie,
Qu'est-c' que ce noir-là signifie?
—Tout' femme qui relèv' d'un fils
Du drap de saint Maur doit se vêti.

X

—Dites-moi, ma mère, ma mie,
Irai-je à la messe aujourd'hui?
—Ma fille, attendez à demain,
Et vous irez pour le certain."

XI

Quand ell' fut dans les champs allée,
Trois p'tits garçons s' sont écriés:
"Voilà la femm' de ce seigneur
Qu'on enterra hier à trois heures."

XII

Quand ell' fut dans l'église entrée,
D' l'eau bénite on y a présenté;
Et puis, levant les yeux en haut,
Elle aperçut le grand tombeau.

XIII

"Dites-moi, ma mère, ma mie,
Qu'est-c' que c' tombeau-là signifie?
—Ma fille, je n' puis vous l' cacher,
C'est vot' mari qu'est trépassé.

XIV

"Renaud, Renaud, mon réconfort,
Te voilà donc au rang des morts!
Divin Renaud, mon réconfort,
Te voilà donc au rang des morts!"

XV

Elle se fit dire trois messes,
A la première, ell' se confesse,
A la seconde, ell' communia,
A la troisième, elle expira.

SONG OF RENAUD

I

When Jean Renaud returned from war, he held his bowels in his hands. His mother said at the window above: "Here comes my son, Renaud."

II

"Good day, Renaud, good day, my son, your wife has had a son." "—Neither in my wife, nor in my son can I rejoice."

III

"Let them quickly make a white bed for me to lie in." And when midnight arrived, fair Renaud gave up the ghost.

IV

"Tell me, mother my dear, what is the weeping that I hear?" "—It's a little page who has been whipped for a golden plate that is lost."

V

"Tell me, mother my dear, what is the knocking that I hear?" "—My child, it is the masons repairing the house."

VI

"Tell me, mother my dear, what is the ringing that I hear?" "—It is the little new-born Dauphin, whose baptism is delayed."

VII

"Tell me, mother my dear, what is the singing that I hear?" "—My child, it is the processions that wind about the house."

VIII

"Tell me, mother my dear, what dress shall I wear today?" "—Wear the white, wear the gray, wear the black as a better choice."

IX

"Tell me, mother my dear, what does the black mean?" "—All women who give birth to a son should dress in the drapery of Saint Maur."

X

"Tell me, mother my dear, shall I go to Mass today?" "—My child, wait till tomorrow, and you will surely go."

XI

When she went into the fields, three little boys cried out: "There's the wife of the nobleman who was buried yesterday at three o'clock."

XII

When she entered the church, she was given some holy water; and then, raising her eyes on high, she noticed the great tomb.

XIII

"Tell me, mother my dear, what does that tomb mean?" "—My child, I cannot hide it from you, it is your husband that has passed away."

XIV

"Renaud, Renaud, soul of my soul, you are then among the dead! Divine Renaud, soul of my soul, you are then among the dead!"

XV

She had three Masses said; at the first, she confessed; at the second, she took communion; at the third, she died.

One of the most beautiful inspirations of untutored genius.

ANATOLE FRANCE
La Vie littéraire (1888–92)

HENRY FIELDING

1 7 0 7 — 1 7 5 4

GREATNESS

1. Never to do more mischief to another than was necessary to the effecting his purpose; for that mischief was too precious a thing to be thrown away.

2. To know no distinction of men from affection; but to sacrifice all with equal readiness to his interest.

3. Never to communicate more of an affair than was necessary to the person who was to execute it.

4. Not to trust him who hath deceived you, nor who knows he hath been deceived by you.

5. To forgive no enemy; but to be cautious and often dilatory in revenge.

6. To shun poverty and distress, and to ally himself as close as possible to power and riches.

7. To maintain a constant gravity in his countenance and behaviour, and to affect wisdom on all occasions.

8. To foment eternal jealousies in his gang, one of another.

9. Never to reward any one equal to his merit; but always to insinuate that the reward was above it.

10. That all men were knaves or fools, and much the greater number a composition of both.

11. That a good name, like money, must be parted with, or at least greatly risked, in order to bring the owner any advantage.

12. That virtues, like precious stones, were easily counterfeited; that the counterfeits in both cases adorned the wearer equally, and that very few had knowledge or discernment sufficient to distinguish the counterfeit jewel from the real.

13. That many men were undone by not going deep enough in roguery; as in gaming any man may be a loser who doth not play the whole game.

14. That men proclaim their own virtues, as shopkeepers expose their goods, in order to profit by them.

15. That the heart was the proper seat of hatred, and the countenance of affection and friendship.

> The History of The Life of the Late
> Mr. Jonathan Wild the Great (1743)

Jonathan Wild is a personage of undeviating criminality; the beautiful consistency of his life is marred by scarce a single generous deed or decent impulse. From the time of his youthful captaincy over a gang of orchard robbers, when he was invariably "treasurer of the booty, some little part of which he would now and then, with wonderful generosity, bestow on those who took it," until his consummation on the scaffold or "tree of glory," when he found breath to deliver "a hearty curse" upon the assembled crowd, he showed himself to be "not restrained by any of those weaknesses which disappoint the views of mean and vulgar souls, and which are comprehended in one general term of honesty, which is a corruption of HONOSTY, *a word derived from what the Greeks call an ass." From the title-page to the closing sentence there is an incessant harping on the word "greatness," used in this scheme of irony to mean material success without moral goodness. And when, near the end, Fielding reduces the career of his infamous protagonist to a list of elementary principles of "greatness," behold! that list exactly defines and delineates the practices by which Fielding saw eminence achieved in the most respected careers of his own 18th century world. His purpose is to show how a boot-licking society worshipped prestige no matter how gained; his method is to draw a grotesque parallel between the successful man of the great world and the successful criminal of the underworld, and to signify that the one is as little worthy of admiration as the other. This catalogue of principles, as applicable to a Robert Walpole as to a Jonathan Wild, seems to me to be among the most ingenious and pointed uses of savage irony in English.*

WILSON FOLLETT
The Modern Novel (1918)

SAMUEL JOHNSON

1 7 0 9 — 1 7 8 4

THE METAPHYSICAL POETS

Cowley, like other poets who have written with narrow views, and, instead of tracing intellectual pleasure to its natural sources in the mind of man, paid their court to temporary prejudices, has been at one time too much praised, and too much neglected at another.

Wit, like all other things subject by their nature to the choice of man, has its changes and fashions, and at different times takes different forms. About the beginning of the seventeenth century appeared a race of writers that may be termed the metaphysical poets; of whom, in a criticism on the works of Cowley, it is not improper to give some account.

The metaphysical poets were men of learning, and to show their learning was their whole endeavour; but, unluckily resolving to shew it in rhyme, instead of writing poetry, they only wrote verses, and very often such verses as stood the trial of the finger better than of the ear; for

917

the modulation was so imperfect, that they were only found to be verses by counting the syllables.

If the father of criticism has rightly denominated poetry τέχνη μιμητική, *an imitative art,* these writers will, without great wrong, lose their right to the name of poets; for they cannot be said to have imitated any thing; they neither copied nature nor life; neither painted the forms of matter, nor represented the operations of intellect.

Those, however, who deny them to be poets, allow them to be wits. Dryden confesses of himself and his contemporaries, that they fall below Donne in wit, but maintains that they surpass him in poetry.

If Wit be well described by Pope, as being 'that which has been often thought, but was never before so well expressed,' they certainly never attained, nor ever sought it; for they endeavoured to be singular in their thoughts, and were careless of their diction. But Pope's account of wit is undoubtedly erroneous: he depresses it below its natural dignity, and reduces it from strength of thought to happiness of language.

If by a more noble and more adequate conception that be considered as Wit, which is at once natural and new, that which, though not obvious, is, upon its first production, acknowledged to be just; if it be that, which he that never found it, wonders how he missed; to wit of this kind the metaphysical poets have seldom risen. Their thoughts are often new, but seldom natural; they are not obvious, but neither are they just; and the reader, far from wondering that he missed them, wonders more frequently by what perverseness of industry they were ever found.

But Wit, abstracted from its effects upon the hearer, may be more rigorously and philosophically considered as a kind of *discordia concors;* a combination of dissimilar images, or discovery of occult resemblances in things apparently unlike. Of wit, thus defined, they have more than enough. The most heterogeneous ideas are yoked by violence together; nature and art are ransacked for illustrations, comparisons, and allusions; their learning instructs, and their subtilty surprises; but the reader commonly thinks his improvement dearly bought, and, though he sometimes admires, is seldom pleased.

From this account of their composition it will be readily inferred, that they were not successful in representing or moving the affections. As they were wholly employed on something unexpected and surprising, they had no regard to that uniformity of sentiment which enables us to conceive and to excite the pains and the pleasure of other minds: they never enquired what, on any occasion, they should have said or done; but wrote rather as beholders than partakers of human nature; as Beings looking upon good and evil, impassive and at leisure; as Epicurean deities making remarks on the actions of men, and the vicissitudes of life, without interest and without emotion. Their courtship was void of fondness, and their lamentation of sorrow. Their wish was only to say what they hoped had been never said before.

Nor was the sublime more within their reach than the pathetick; for they never attempted that comprehension and expanse of thought which at once fills the whole mind, and of which the first effect is sudden astonishment, and the second rational admiration. Sublimity is produced by aggregation, and littleness by dispersion. Great thoughts are always general, and consist in positions not limited by exceptions, and in descriptions not descending to minuteness. It is with great propriety that Subtlety, which in its original import means exility of particles, is taken in its metaphorical meaning for nicety of distinction. Those writers who lay on the watch for novelty could have little hope of greatness; for great things cannot have escaped former observation. Their attempts were always analytick; they broke every image into fragments: and could no more represent, by their slender conceits and laboured particularities, the prospects of nature, or the scenes of life, than he, who dissects a sunbeam with a prism, can exhibit the wide effulgence of a summer noon.

What they wanted however of the sublime, they endeavoured to supply by hyperbole; their amplification had no limits; they left not only reason but fancy behind them; and produced combinations of confused magnificence, that not only could not be credited, but could not be imagined.

Yet great labour, directed by great abilities, is never wholly lost: if they frequently threw away their wit upon false conceits, they likewise sometimes struck out unexpected truth: if their conceits were far-fetched, they were often worth the carriage. To write on their plan, it was at least necessary to read and think. No man could be born a metaphysical poet, nor assume the dignity of a writer, by descriptions copied from descriptions, by imitations borrowed from imitations, by traditional imagery, and hereditary similes, by readiness of rhyme, and volubility of syllables.

In perusing the works of this race of authors, the mind is exercised either by recollection or inquiry; either something already learned is to be retrieved, or something new is to be examined. If their greatness seldom elevates, their acuteness often surprises; if the imagination is not always gratified, at least the powers of reflection and comparison are employed; and in the mass of materials which ingenious absurdity has thrown together, genuine wit and useful knowledge may be sometimes found, buried perhaps in grossness of expression, but useful to those who know their value; and such as, when they are expanded to perspicuity, and polished to elegance, may give lustre to works which have more propriety though less copiousness of sentiment.

The Lives of the Poets (1779–81)

Johnson's style is not seen in its richness and perfection, nor in its consummate ease, until we come to his last and greatest work—the LIVES OF THE POETS. *That was not begun until he was nearly seventy years of age. His time for careful and methodic labour was now past. His opinions were fixed, and he was not likely to examine or modify them. He was undisputed literary dictator, and indisposed to bend to others' views. But all these circumstances contributed to the consummate literary qualities of the book. This is not the place either to impugn or defend the justice of his literary criticisms. But for vigour and ease and variety of style, for elasticity of confidence, for keenness of sarcasm, for brightness of humour, the* LIVES *hold the first place, absolutely free from competition, amongst all works of English criticism of similar range. We may carp at Johnson's judgments, and rail against the prejudice and injustice of his decrees. We may be disposed to accord to more modern critics, all the advantages of balanced judgment and sympathetic insight which they may claim; but they must yield to Johnson the palm for boldness, for wit, for extent of range, and for brilliancy of style.*

HENRY CRAIK
English Prose (1895)

SAMUEL JOHNSON

1 7 0 9 — 1 7 8 4

THE PYRAMIDS

"We have now," said Imlac, "gratified our minds with an exact view of the greatest work of man, except the wall of China.

"Of the wall it is very easy to assign the motive. It secured a wealthy and timorous nation from the incursions of barbarians, whose unskilfulness in arts made it easier for them to supply their wants by rapine than by industry, and who from time to time poured in upon the habitations of peaceful commerce as vultures descend upon domestic fowl. Their celerity and fierceness made the wall necessary, and their ignorance made it efficacious.

"But for the Pyramids no reason has ever been given, adequate to the cost and labor of the work. The narrowness of the chamber proves that it could afford no retreat from enemies, and treasures might have been reposited at far less expense with equal security. It seems to have been erected only in compliance with that hunger of imagination which preys incessantly upon life, and must be always appeased by some employment. Those who have already all that they can enjoy must enlarge their desires. He that has built for use, till use is supplied, must begin to build for vanity, and extend his plan to the utmost power of human performance, that he may not be soon reduced to form another wish.

"I consider this mighty structure as a monument of the insufficiency of human enjoyments. A king, whose power is unlimited, and whose treasures surmount all real and imaginary wants, is compelled to solace, by the erection of a pyramid, the satiety of dominion and tastelessness of pleasures, and to amuse the tediousness of declining life, by seeing thousands laboring without end, and one stone for no purpose laid upon another. Whoever thou art, that, not content with a moderate condition, imaginest happiness in royal magnificence, and dreamest that command or riches can feed the appetite of novelty with perpetual gratifications, survey the Pyramids and confess thy folly!"

Rasselas, Prince of Abyssinia (1759)

Perhaps, in all literature, the most magnificent tribute ever paid to the power of Boredom.

JOSEPH WOOD KRUTCH
Samuel Johnson (1944)

OLIVER EDWARDS

1 7 1 1 — 1 7 9 1

PHILOSOPHY

'You are a philosopher, Dr. Johnson. I have tried too in my time to be a philosopher; but, I don't know how, cheerfulness was always breaking in.'

Boswell's Life of Johnson (April 17, 1778)

On the Good Friday following the series of dinner-parties Johnson, accompanied by Boswell, followed his usual practice of attending divine service at St. Clement Danes. They had, as usual, talked too long after breakfast and arrived at church late—at the second lesson in fact. But on the return from this service there occurred an encounter that was unusual. It was with Oliver Edwards, who had been an undergraduate with Johnson at Pembroke College, Oxford. It was when they had reached Johnson's house that Mr. Edwards delivered himself of his immortal apologia.

S. C. ROBERTS
Samuel Johnson (1944)

DENIS DIDEROT

1 7 1 3 — 1 7 8 4

THE LIBERTIES OF THOUGHT

Qu'il fasse beau, qu'il fasse laid, c'est mon habitude d'aller sur les cinq heures du soir me promener au Palais-Royal. C'est moi qu'on voit toujours seul, rêvant sur le banc d'Argenson. Je m'entretiens avec moi-même de politique, d'amour, de goût ou de philosophie. J'abandonne mon esprit à tout son libertinage. Je le laisse maître de suivre la première idée sage ou folle qui se présente, comme on voit dans l'allée de Foy nos jeunes dissolus marcher sur les pas d'une courtisane à l'air éventé, au visage riant, à l'œil vif, au nez retroussé, quitter celle-ci pour une autre, les attaquant toutes et ne s'attachant à aucune. Mes pensées, ce sont mes catins.

Rain or shine, it is my custom towards five o'clock in the afternoon to walk in the Palais-Royal. There I may be observed, always alone, musing on the bench by the Hôtel d'Argenson. I am my own interlocutor, and discuss politics, love, taste, and philosophy. I give my mind full fling: I let it follow the first notion that presents itself, be it wise or foolish, even as our wild young rakes in Foy's Alley pursue some courtesan of unchastened mien and welcoming face, of answering eye and tilted nose, and then quit her for another, touching all and cleaving to none. My thoughts are my wantons.

Le Neveu de Rameau (1773)
Translated by Mrs. Wilfrid Jackson

There is no greater precision of expression.

RENÉ DOUMIC
Études sur la littérature française (1896)

LAURENCE STERNE

1 7 1 3 — 1 7 6 8

THE DEATH OF LE FEVER

Thou hast left this matter short, said my uncle Toby to the corporal, as he was putting him to bed,—and I will tell thee in what, Trim.—In the first place, when thou madest an offer of my services to Le Fever,—

as sickness and travelling are both expensive, and thou knowest he was but a poor lieutenant, with a son to subsist as well as himself out of his pay,—that thou didst not make an offer to him of my purse; because, had he stood in need, thou knowest, Trim, he had been as welcome to it as myself.—Your honour knows, said the corporal, I had no orders;—True, quoth my uncle Toby,—thou didst very right, Trim, as a soldier,—but certainly very wrong as a man.

In the second place, for which, indeed, thou hast the same excuse, continued my uncle Toby,—when thou offeredst him whatever was in my house,—thou shouldst have offered him my house too:—A sick brother officer should have the best quarters, Trim, and if we had him with us,—we could tend and look to him:—Thou art an excellent nurse thyself, Trim,—and what with thy care of him, and the old woman's, and his boy's, and mine together, we might recruit him again at once, and set him upon his legs.—

—In a fortnight or three weeks, added my uncle Toby, smiling,—he might march.—He will never march, an' please your honour, in this world, said the corporal:—He will march, said my uncle Toby, rising up from the side of the bed, with one shoe off:—An' please your honour, said the corporal, he will never march but to his grave:—He shall march, cried my uncle Toby, marching the foot which had a shoe on, though without advancing an inch,—he shall march to his regiment.—He cannot stand it, said the corporal;—He shall be supported, said my uncle Toby;—He'll drop at last, said the corporal, and what will become of his boy?—He shall not drop, said my uncle Toby, firmly.—A-well-o'-day,—do what we can for him, said Trim, maintaining his point,—the poor soul will die:—He shall not die, by G—, cried my uncle Toby.

—The Accusing Spirit, which flew up to heaven's chancery with the oath, blushed as he gave it in;—and the Recording Angel, as he wrote it down, dropped a tear upon the word, and blotted it out for ever.

—My uncle Toby went to his bureau,—put his purse into his breeches pocket, and having ordered the corporal to go early in the morning for a physician,—he went to bed, and fell asleep.

The sun looked bright the morning after, to every eye in the village but Le Fever's and his afflicted son's; the hand of death pressed heavy upon his eye-lids,—and hardly could the wheel at the cistern turn round its circle,—when my uncle Toby, who had rose up an hour before his wonted time, entered the lieutenant's room, and without preface or apology, sat himself down upon the chair by the bed-side, and, independently of all modes and customs, opened the curtain in the manner an old friend and brother officer would have done it, and asked him how he did,—how he had rested in the night,—what was his complaint,—where was his pain,—and what he could do to help him:—and without giving him time to answer any one of the enquiries, went on, and told him of the little plan which he had been concerting with the corporal the night before for him.—

—You shall go home directly, Le Fever, said my uncle **Toby,** to my house,—and we'll send for a doctor to see what's the matter,—and we'll have an apothecary,—and the corporal shall be your nurse;—and I'll be your servant, Le Fever.

There was a frankness in my uncle Toby,—not the effect of familiarity,—but the cause of it,—which let you at once into his soul, and shewed you the goodness of his nature; to this, there was something in his looks, and voice, and manner, superadded, which eternally beckoned to the unfortunate to come and take shelter under him; so that before my uncle Toby had half finished the kind offers he was making to the father, had the son insensibly pressed up close to his knees, and had taken hold of the breast of his coat, and was pulling it towards him.—The blood and spirits of Le Fever, which were waxing cold and slow within him, and were retreating to their last citadel, the heart—rallied back,—the film forsook his eyes for a moment,—he looked up wishfully in my uncle Toby's face,—then cast a look upon his boy,— and that ligament, fine as it was,—was never broken.————

Nature instantly ebbed again,—the film returned to its place,—the pulse fluttered—stopped—went on—throbbed—stopped again—moved— stopped—shall I go on?—No.

The Life and Opinions of Tristram Shandy (1760–67)

It is as pure a reflection of mere natural feeling as literature has ever given, or will ever give.

WALTER BAGEHOT
Literary Studies (1878)

WILLIAM SHENSTONE

1 7 1 4 — 1 7 6 3

BLOOM THE JASMINES

If through the garden's flowery tribes I stray,
    Where bloom the jasmines that could once allure,
'Hope not to find delight in us,' they say,
    'For we are spotless, Jessy; we are pure.'

Elegy xxvi

WILLIAM WORDSWORTH

1 7 7 0 — 1 8 5 0

SPRINGTIME WITH ONE LOVE

'Ah, why,' said Ellen, sighing to herself,
'Why do not words, and kiss, and solemn pledge;
And nature that is kind in woman's breast,
And reason that in man is wise and good,
And fear of him who is a righteous judge,—
Why do not these prevail for human life,
To keep two hearts together, that began
Their spring-time with one love, and that have need
Of mutual pity and forgiveness, sweet
To grant, or be received; while that poor bird—
O come and hear him! Thou who hast to me
Been faithless, hear him, though a lowly creature,
One of God's simple children that yet know not
The universal Parent, how he sings
As if he wished the firmament of heaven
Should listen, and give back to him the voice
Of his triumphant constancy and love;
The proclamation that he makes, how far
His darkness doth transcend our fickle light!'

The Excursion (1814), vi

The perfection of both these passages, as far as regards truth and tenderness of imagination in the two poets, is quite insuperable.

JOHN RUSKIN
Modern Painters (1856)

THOMAS GRAY

1 7 1 6 — 1 7 7 1

ELEGY WRITTEN IN A
COUNTRY CHURCHYARD

The Curfew tolls the knell of parting day,
  The lowing herd wind slowly o'er the lea,
The plowman homeward plods his weary way,
  And leaves the world to darkness and to me.

Now fades the glimmering landscape on the sight,
　　And all the air a solemn stillness holds,
Save where the beetle wheels his droning flight,
　　And drowsy tinklings lull the distant folds;

Save that from yonder ivy-mantled tow'r
　　The moping owl does to the moon complain
Of such as, wand'ring near her secret bow'r,
　　Molest her ancient solitary reign.

Beneath those rugged elms, that yew-tree's shade,
　　Where heaves the turf in many a mould'ring heap,
Each in his narrow cell for ever laid,
　　The rude Forefathers of the hamlet sleep.

The breezy call of incense-breathing Morn,
　　The swallow twitt'ring from the straw-built shed,
The cock's shrill clarion, or the echoing horn,
　　No more shall rouse them from their lowly bed.

For them no more the blazing hearth shall burn,
　　Or busy housewife ply her evening care:
No children run to lisp their sire's return,
　　Or climb his knees the envied kiss to share.

Oft did the harvest to their sickle yield,
　　Their furrow oft the stubborn glebe has broke;
How jocund did they drive their team afield!
　　How bow'd the woods beneath their sturdy stroke!

Let not Ambition mock their useful toil,
　　Their homely joys, and destiny obscure;
Nor Grandeur hear with a disdainful smile,
　　The short and simple annals of the poor.

The boast of heraldry, the pomp of pow'r,
　　And all that beauty, all that wealth e'er gave,
Awaits alike th' inevitable hour:
　　The paths of glory lead but to the grave.

Nor you, ye Proud, impute to These the fault,
　　If Memory o'er their Tomb no Trophies raise,
Where through the long-drawn aisle and fretted vault
　　The pealing anthem swells the note of praise.

Can storied urn or animated bust
    Back to its mansion call the fleeting breath?
Can Honour's voice provoke the silent dust,
    Or Flatt'ry soothe the dull cold ear of death?

Perhaps in this neglected spot is laid
    Some heart once pregnant with celestial fire;
Hands, that the rod of empire might have sway'd,
    Or waked to ecstasy the living lyre.

But Knowledge to their eyes her ample page
    Rich with the spoils of time did ne'er unroll;
Chill Penury repress'd their noble rage,
    And froze the genial current of the soul.

Full many a gem of purest ray serene
    The dark unfathom'd caves of ocean bear:
Full many a flower is born to blush unseen,
    And waste its sweetness on the desert air.

Some village Hampden that with dauntless breast
    The little tyrant of his fields withstood,
Some mute inglorious Milton, here may rest,
    Some Cromwell guiltless of his country's blood.

Th' applause of list'ning senates to command,
    The threats of pain and ruin to despise,
To scatter plenty o'er a smiling land,
    And read their history in a nation's eyes,

Their lot forbade: nor circumscribed alone
    Their growing virtues, but their crimes confined;
Forbade to wade through slaughter to a throne,
    And shut the gates of mercy on mankind,

The struggling pangs of conscious truth to hide,
    To quench the blushes of ingenuous shame,
Or heap the shrine of Luxury and Pride
    With incense kindled at the Muse's flame.

Far from the madding crowd's ignoble strife
    Their sober wishes never learn'd to stray;
Along the cool sequester'd vale of life
    They kept the noiseless tenor of their way.

Yet ev'n these bones from insult to protect
    Some frail memorial still erected nigh,
With uncouth rhymes and shapeless sculpture deck'd,
    Implores the passing tribute of a sigh.

Their name, their years, spelt by th' unletter'd muse,
    The place of fame and elegy supply:
And many a holy text around she strews,
    That teach the rustic moralist to die.

For who, to dumb Forgetfulness a prey,
    This pleasing anxious being e'er resign'd,
Left the warm precincts of the cheerful day,
    Nor cast one longing ling'ring look behind?

On some fond breast the parting soul relies,
    Some pious drops the closing eye requires;
E'en from the tomb the voice of Nature cries,
    E'en in our Ashes live their wonted Fires.

For thee, who, mindful of th' unhonour'd dead,
    Dost in these lines their artless tale relate;
If chance, by lonely contemplation led,
    Some kindred spirit shall inquire thy fate,

Haply some hoary-headed Swain may say,
    'Oft have we seen him at the peep of dawn
Brushing with hasty steps the dews away
    To meet the sun upon the upland lawn.

'There at the foot of yonder nodding beech
    That wreathes its old fantastic roots so high,
His listless length at noontide would he stretch,
    And pore upon the brook that babbles by.

'Hard by yon wood, now smiling as in scorn,
    Mutt'ring his wayward fancies he would rove,
Now drooping, woeful wan, like one forlorn,
    Or crazed with care, or cross'd in hopeless love.

'One morn I miss'd him on the custom'd hill,
    Along the heath and near his fav'rite tree;
Another came, nor yet beside the rill,
    Nor up the lawn, nor at the wood was he;

'The next with dirges due in sad array
    Slow through the church-way path we saw him borne.
Approach and read (for thou canst read) the lay
    Graved on the stone beneath yon aged thorn.'

THE EPITAPH

Here rests his head upon the lap of Earth
*   A Youth to Fortune and to Fame unknown.*
Fair Science frown'd not on his humble birth,
*   And Melancholy mark'd him for her own.*

Large was his bounty, and his soul sincere,
*   Heav'n did a recompense as largely send:*
He gave to Mis'ry all he had, a tear,
*   He gain'd from Heav'n ('twas all he wish'd) a friend.*

No farther seek his merits to disclose,
*   Or draw his frailties from their dread abode,*
(There they alike in trembling hope repose,)
*   The bosom of his Father and his God.*

(1750)

For wealth of condensed thought and imagery, fused into one equable stream of golden song by intense fire of genius, the Editor knows no poem superior to this ELEGY,—none quite equal.

FRANCIS TURNER PALGRAVE
The Children's Treasury of English Song (1875)

THOMAS GRAY

1716 — 1771

SUPREME DOMINION

Tho' he inherit
Nor the pride, nor ample pinion,
That the Theban Eagle bear
Sailing with supreme dominion
Thro' the azure deep of air.

The Progress of Poesy (1754)

Among the most liquid lines in any language.

ALFRED LORD TENNYSON
Alfred Lord Tennyson: A Memoir by Hallam Tennyson (1897)

929

THOMAS GRAY

1 7 1 6 — 1 7 7 1

THE LANGUAGE OF THE AGE

As to matter of stile, I have this to say: The language of the age is never the language of poetry; except among the French, whose verse, where the thought or image does not support it, differs in nothing from prose. Our poetry, on the contrary, has a language peculiar to itself; to which almost every one, that has written, has added something by enriching it with foreign idioms and derivatives: Nay sometimes words of their own composition or invention. Shakespear and Milton have been great creators this way; and no one more licentious than Pope or Dryden, who perpetually borrow expressions from the former. Let me give you some instances from Dryden, whom every body reckons a great master of our poetical tongue.——Full of *museful mopeings*—unlike the *trim* of love—a pleasant *beverage*—a *roundelay* of love—stood silent in his *mood*—with knots and *knares* deformed—his *ireful mood*—in proud *array*—his *boon* was granted—and *disarray* and shameful rout—*wayward* but wise—*furbished* for the field—the *foiled dodderd* oaks—*disherited*—*smouldring* flames—*retchless* of laws—*crones* old and ugly—the *beldam* at his side—the *grandam-hag*—*villanize* his Father's fame.
——But they are infinite: And our language not being a settled thing (like the French) has an undoubted right to words of an hundred years old, provided antiquity have not rendered them unintelligible. In truth, Shakespear's language is one of his principal beauties; and he has no less advantage over your Addisons and Rowes in this, than in those other great excellencies you mention. Every word in him is a picture. Pray put me the following lines into the tongue of our modern Dramatics:

> But I, that am not shaped for sportive tricks,
> Nor made to court an amorous looking-glass:
> I, that am rudely stampt, and want love's majesty
> To strut before a wanton ambling nymph:
> I, that am curtail'd of this fair proportion,
> Cheated of feature by dissembling nature,
> Deform'd, unfinish'd, sent before my time
> Into this breathing world, scarce half made up—

And what follows. To me they appear untranslatable; and if this be the case, our language is greatly degenerated.

Correspondence (1742)

It is impossible for a poet to lay down the rules of his own art with more insight, soundness, and certainty. Yet at that moment in England there was perhaps not one other man, besides Gray, capable of writing the passage just quoted.

MATTHEW ARNOLD
Essays in Criticism, Second Series (1888)

HORACE WALPOLE

1 7 1 7 — 1 7 9 7

TO THE REVEREND WILLIAM COLE

Arlington Street, April 27, 1773

I had not time this morning to answer your letter by Mr Essex, but I gave him the card you desired. You know, I hope, how happy I am to obey any orders of yours.

In the paper I showed you in answer to Masters, you saw I was apprised of Rastel's *Chronicle,* but pray do not mention my knowing of it, because I draw so much from it, that I lie in wait, hoping that Milles or Masters or some of their fools will produce it against me, and then I shall have another word to say to them which they do not expect, since they think Rastel makes for them.

Mr Gough wants to be introduced to me! Indeed! I would see him as he has been midwife to Masters, but he is so dull that he would only be troublesome—and besides you know I shun authors, and would never have been one myself, if it obliged me to keep such bad company. They are always in earnest, and think their profession serious, and dwell upon trifles, and reverence learning. I laugh at all those things, and write only to laugh at them and divert myself. None of us are authors of any consequence, and it is the most ridiculous of all vanities to be vain of being mediocre. A page in a great author humbles me to the dust, and the conversation of those that are not superior to myself reminds me of what will be thought of myself. I blush to flatter them or to be flattered by them, and should dread letters being published sometime or other, in which they should relate our interviews, and we should appear like those puny conceited witlings in Shenstone's and Hughes's Correspondence, who give themselves airs from being in possession of the soil of Parnassus for the time being, as peers are proud because they enjoy the estates of great men who went before them. Mr Gough is very welcome to see Strawberry Hill, or I would help him to any scraps in my possession that would assist his publications, though he is one of those industrious who are only reburying the dead—but I cannot be acquainted with him. It is contrary to my system and my humour; and besides I know nothing of barrows, and Danish entrenchments, and Saxon barbarisms, and Phoenician characters—in short I know nothing of those ages that knew nothing—then how should I be of use to modern *literati*? All the Scotch metaphysicians have sent me their works. I did not read one of them, because I do not understand what is not understood by those that write about it, and I did not get acquainted with one of the writers. I should like to be intimate with Mr Anstey, even though he wrote *Lord Buckhorse,* or with the author of the *Heroic Epistle*—I have no thirst to know the rest of my cotemporaries, from the absurd bombast of Dr Johnson down to the silly Dr Goldsmith, though the latter changeling has had bright gleams of parts, and the former had sense till he changed it for words and sold it for a pension. Don't think me scornful. Recollect that I have seen Pope, and lived with Gray. Adieu!

Yours ever,
H. WALPOLE

The best letter-writer in the English language.

SIR WALTER SCOTT
Horace Walpole (1821)

CHRISTOPHER SMART

1 7 2 2 — 1 7 7 1

A SONG TO DAVID

O thou, that sit'st upon a throne,
With harp of high majestic tone,
    To praise the King of kings:
And voice of heav'n-ascending swell,
Which, while its deeper notes excel,
    Clear, as a clarion, rings:

To bless each valley, grove and coast,
And charm the cherubs to the post
    Of gratitude in throngs;
To keep the days on Zion's mount,
And send the year to his account,
    With dances and with songs:

O Servant of God's holiest charge,
The minister of praise at large,
        Which thou may'st now receive;
From thy blest mansion hail and hear,
From topmost eminence appear
        To this the wreath I weave.

Great, valiant, pious, good, and clean,
Sublime, contemplative, serene,
        Strong, constant, pleasant, wise!
Bright effluence of exceeding grace;
Best man!—the swiftness and the race,
        The peril, and the prize!

Great—from the lustre of his crown,
From Samuel's horn, and God's renown,
        Which is the people's voice;
For all the host, from rear to van,
Applauded and embrac'd the man—
        The man of God's own choice.

Valiant—the word, and up he rose—
The fight—he triumph'd o'er the foes,
        Whom God's just laws abhor;
And arm'd in gallant faith he took
Against the boaster, from the brook,
        The weapons of the war.

Pious—magnificent and grand;
'Twas he the famous temple plann'd:
        (The seraph in his soul)
Foremost to give the Lord his dues,
Foremost to bless the welcome news,
        And foremost to condole.

Good—from Jehudah's genuine vein,
From God's best nature good in grain,
        His aspect and his heart;
To pity, to forgive, to save,
Witness En-gedi's conscious cave,
        And Shimei's blunted dart.

Clean—if perpetual prayer be pure,
And love, which could itself inure
        To fasting and to fear—
Clean in his gestures, hands, and feet,
To smite the lyre, the dance complete,
        To play the sword and spear.

Sublime—invention ever young,
Of vast conception, tow'ring tongue,
    To God th' eternal theme;
Notes from yon exaltations caught,
Unrivall'd royalty of thought,
    O'er meaner strains supreme.

Contemplative—On God to fix
His musings, and above the six
    The sabbath-day he blest;
'Twas then his thoughts self-conquest prun'd,
And heavenly melancholy tun'd,
    To bless and bear the rest.

Serene—to sow the seeds of peace,
Rememb'ring, when he watch'd the fleece,
    How sweetly Kidron purl'd—
To further knowledge, silence vice,
And plant perpetual paradise
    When God had calm'd the world.

Strong—in the Lord, who could defy
Satan, and all his powers that lie
    In sempiternal night;
And hell, and horror, and despair
Were as the lion and the bear
    To his undaunted might.

Constant—in love to God THE TRUTH,
Age, manhood, infancy, and youth—
    To Jonathan his friend
Constant, beyond the verge of death;
And Ziba, and Mephibosheth,
    His endless fame attend.

Pleasant—and various as the year;
Man, soul, and angel, without peer,
    Priest, champion, sage and boy;
In armour, or in ephod clad,
His pomp, his piety was glad;
    Majestic was his joy.

Wise—in recovery from his fall,
Whence rose his eminence o'er all,
    Of all the most revil'd;
The light of Israel in his ways,
Wise are his precepts, prayer and praise,
    And counsel to his child.

His muse, bright angel of his verse,
Gives balm for all the thorns that pierce,
     For all the pangs that rage;
Blest light, still gaining on the gloom,
The more than Michal of his bloom,
     Th' Abishag of his age.

He sung of God—the mighty source
Of all things—the stupendous force
     On which all strength depends;
From whose right arm, beneath whose eyes,
All period, pow'r, and enterprise
     Commences, reigns, and ends.

Angels—their ministry and meed,
Which to and fro with blessings speed,
     Or with their citterns wait;
Where Michael with his millions bows,
Where dwells the seraph and his spouse,
     The cherub and her mate.

Of man—the semblance and effect
Of God and Love—the Saint elect
     For infinite applause—
To rule the land, and briny broad,
To be laborious in his laud,
     And heroes in his cause.

The world—the clust'ring spheres he made,
The glorious light, the soothing shade,
     Dale, champaign, grove, and hill;
The multitudinous abyss,
Where secrecy remains in bliss,
     And wisdom hides her skill.

Trees, plants, and flow'rs—of virtuous root;
Gem yielding blossom, yielding fruit,
     Choice gums and precious balm;
Bless ye the nosegay in the vale,
And with the sweet'ners of the gale
     Enrich the thankful psalm.

Of fowl—e'en ev'ry beak and wing
Which cheer the winter, hail the spring,
     That live in peace or prey;
They that make music, or that mock,
The quail, the brave domestic cock,
     The raven, swan, and jay.

Of fishes—ev'ry size and shape,
Which nature frames of light escape,
    Devouring man to shun:
The shells are in the wealthy deep,
The shoals upon the surface leap,
    And love the glancing sun.

Of beasts—the beaver plods his task;
While the sleek tigers roll and bask,
    Nor yet the shades arouse:
Her cave the mining coney scoops;
Where o'er the mead the mountain stoops,
    The kids exult and brouse.

Of gems—their virtue and their price,
Which hid in earth from man's device,
    Their darts of lustre sheathe;
The jasper of the master's stamp,
The topaz blazing like a lamp
    Among the mines beneath.

Blest was the tenderness he felt
When to his graceful harp he knelt,
    And did for audience call;
When satan with his hand he quell'd,
And in serene suspense he held
    The frantic throes of Saul.

His furious foes no more malign'd
As he such melody divin'd,
    And sense and soul detain'd;
Now striking strong, now soothing soft,
He sent the godly sounds aloft,
    Or in delight refrain'd.

When up to heav'n his thoughts he pil'd,
From fervent lips fair Michal smil'd,
    As blush to blush she stood;
And chose herself the queen, and gave
Her utmost from her heart, "so brave,
    "And plays his hymns so good."

The pillars of the Lord are sev'n,
Which stand from earth to topmost heav'n;
    His wisdom drew the plan;
His WORD accomplish'd the design,
From brightest gem to deepest mine,
    From CHRIST enthron'd to man.

Alpha, the cause of causes, first
In station, fountain, whence the burst
	Of light, and blaze of day;
Whence bold attempt, and brave advance,
Have motion, life, and ordinance,
	And heav'n itself its stay.

Gamma supports the glorious arch
On which angelic legions march,
	And is with sapphires pav'd;
Thence the fleet clouds are sent adrift,
And thence the painted folds, that lift
	The crimson veil, are wav'd.

Eta with living sculpture breathes,
With verdant carvings, flow'ry wreathes
	Of never-wasting bloom;
In strong relief his goodly base
All instruments of labour grace,
	The trowel, spade, and loom.

Next Theta stands to the Supreme—
Who form'd, in number, sign, and scheme,
	Th' illustrious lights that are;
And one address'd his saffron robe,
And one clad in a silver globe,
	Held rule with ev'ry star.

Iota's tun'd to choral hymns
Of those that fly, while he that swims
	In thankful safety lurks;
And foot, and chapitre, and niche,
The various histories enrich
	Of God's recorded works.

Sigma presents the social droves,
With him that solitary roves,
	And man of all the chief;
Fair on whose face, and stately frame,
Did God impress His hallow'd name,
	For ocular belief.

OMEGA! GREATEST and the BEST,
Stands sacred to the day of rest,
	For gratitude and thought;
Which bless'd the world upon his pole,
And gave the universe his goal,
	And clos'd th' infernal draught.

O DAVID, scholar of the Lord!
Such is thy science, whence reward,
    And infinite degree;
O strength, O sweetness, lasting ripe!
God's harp thy symbol, and thy type
    The lion and the bee!

There is but One who ne'er rebell'd,
But One by passion unimpell'd,
    By pleasures unentic't;
He from himself his semblance sent,
Grand object of his own content,
    And saw the God in CHRIST.

Tell them, I am, JEHOVAH said
To MOSES; while earth heard in dread,
    And, smitten to the heart,
At once above, beneath, around,
All nature, without voice or sound,
    Replied, O Lord, THOU ART.

Thou art—to give and to confirm,
For each his talent and his term;
    All flesh thy bounties share:
Thou shalt not call thy brother fool;
The porches of the Christian school
    Are meekness, peace, and pray'r.

Open, and naked of offence,
Man's made of mercy, soul, and sense;
    God arm'd the snail and wilk;
Be good to him that pulls thy plough;
Due food and care, due rest, allow
    For her that yields thee milk.

Rise up before the hoary head,
And God's benign commandment dread,
    Which says thou shalt not die:
"Not as I will, but as thou wilt,"
Pray'd He whose conscience knew no guilt;
    With whose bless'd pattern vie.

Use all thy passions!—love is thine,
And joy, and jealousy divine;
    Thine hope's eternal fort,
And care thy leisure to disturb,
With fear concupiscence to curb,
    And rapture to transport.

Act simply, as occasion asks;
Put mellow wine in season'd casks;
 Till not with ass and bull:
Remember thy baptismal bond;
Keep from commixtures foul and fond,
 Nor work thy flax with wool.

Distribute: pay the Lord his tithe,
And make the widow's heart-strings blithe;
 Resort with those that weep:
As you from all and each expect,
For all and each thy love direct,
 And render as you reap.

The slander and its bearer spurn,
And propagating praise sojourn
 To make thy welcome last;
Turn from old Adam to the New;
By hope futurity pursue;
 Look upwards to the past.

Control thine eye, salute success,
Honour the wiser, happier bless,
 And for thy neighbour feel;
Grutch not of mammon and his leaven,
Work emulation up to heaven
 By knowledge and by zeal.

O DAVID, highest in the list
Of worthies, on God's ways insist,
 The genuine word repeat.
Vain are the documents of men,
And vain the flourish of the pen
 That keeps the fool's conceit.

PRAISE above all—for praise prevails;
Heap up the measure, load the scales,
 And good to goodness add:
The gen'rous soul her Saviour aids,
But peevish obloquy degrades;
 The Lord is great and glad.

For ADORATION all the ranks
Of angels yield eternal thanks,
 And DAVID in the midst;
With God's good poor, which, last and least
In man's esteem, thou to thy feast,
 O blessed bridegroom, bidst.

For ADORATION seasons change,
And order, truth, and beauty range,
    Adjust, attract, and fill:
The grass the polyanthus cheques;
And polish'd porphyry reflects,
    By the descending rill.

Rich almonds colour to the prime
For ADORATION; tendrils climb,
    And fruit-trees pledge their gems;
And Ivis with her gorgeous vest
Builds for her eggs her cunning nest,
    And bell-flowers bow their stems.

With vinous syrup cedars spout;
From rocks pure honey gushing out,
    For ADORATION springs:
All scenes of painting crowd the map
Of nature; to the mermaid's pap
    The scaléd infant clings.

The spotted ounce and playsome cubs
Run rustling 'mongst the flow'ring shrubs,
    And lizards feed the moss;
For ADORATION beasts embark,
While waves upholding halcyon's ark
    No longer roar and toss.

While Israel sits beneath his fig,
With coral root and amber sprig
    The wean'd advent'rer sports;
Where to the palm the jasmin cleaves,
For ADORATION 'mong the leaves
    The gale his peace reports.

Increasing days their reign exalt,
Nor in the pink and mottled vault
    Th' opposing spirits tilt;
And, by the coasting reader spy'd,
The silverlings and crusions glide
    For ADORATION gilt.

For ADORATION rip'ning canes
And cocoa's purest milk detains
    The western pilgrim's staff;
Where rain in clasping boughs inclos'd,
And vines with oranges dispos'd,
    Embower the social laugh.

Now labour his reward receives,
For ADORATION counts his sheaves
         To peace, her bounteous prince;
The nectarine his strong tint imbibes,
And apples of ten thousand tribes,
         And quick peculiar quince.

The wealthy crops of whit'ning rice
'Mongst thyine woods and groves of spice,
         For ADORATION grow;
And, marshall'd in the fencéd land,
The peaches and pomegranates stand,
         Where wild carnations blow.

The laurels with the winter strive;
The crocus burnishes alive
         Upon the snow-clad earth.
For ADORATION myrtles stay
To keep the garden from dismay,
         And bless the sight from dearth.

The pheasant shews his pompous neck;
And ermine, jealous of a speck,
         With fear eludes offence:
The sable, with his glossy pride,
For ADORATION is descried,
         Where frosts the wave condense.

The cheerful holly, pensive yew,
And holy thorn, their trim renew;
         The squirrel hoards his nuts:
All creatures batten o'er their stores,
And careful nature all her doors
         For ADORATION shuts.

For ADORATION, DAVID'S Psalms
Lift up the heart to deeds of alms;
         And he, who kneels and chants
Prevails his passions to control,
Finds meat and med'cine to the soul,
         Which for translation pants.

For ADORATION, beyond match,
The scholar bulfinch aims to catch
         The soft flute's iv'ry touch;
And, careless on the hazel spray,
The daring redbreast keeps at bay
         The damsel's greedy clutch.

For ADORATION, in the skies,
The Lord's philosopher espies
      The Dog, the Ram, and Rose;
The planet's ring, Orion's sword;
Nor is his greatness less ador'd
      In the vile worm that glows.

For ADORATION on the strings
The western breezes work their wings,
      The captive ear to soothe.—
Hark! 'tis a voice—how still, and small—
That makes the cataracts to fall,
      Or bids the sea be smooth.

For ADORATION, incense comes
From bezoar, and Arabian gums;
      And from the civet's furr:
But as for pray'r, or ere it faints,
Far better is the breath of saints
      Than galbanum and myrrh.

For ADORATION, from the down
Of dam'sins to th' anana's crown,
      God sends to tempt the taste;
And while the luscious zest invites,
The sense, that in the scene delights,
      Commands desire be chaste.

For ADORATION, all the paths
Of grace are open, all the baths
      Of purity refresh;
And all the rays of glory beam
To deck the man of God's esteem,
      Who triumphs o'er the flesh.

For ADORATION, in the dome
Of Christ the sparrows find an home;
      And on his olives perch:
The swallow also dwells with thee,
O man of God's humility,
      Within his Saviour's CHURCH.

Sweet is the dew that falls betimes,
And drops upon the leafy limes;
      Sweet Hermon's fragrant air:
Sweet is the lily's silver bell,
And sweet the wakeful tapers smell
      That watch for early pray'r.

Sweet the young nurse with love intense,
Which smiles o'er sleeping innocence;
    Sweet when the lost arrive:
Sweet the musician's ardour beats,
While his vague mind's in quest of sweets,
    The choicest flow'rs to hive.

Sweeter in all the strains of love,
The language of thy turtle dove,
    Pair'd to thy swelling chord;
Sweeter with ev'ry grace endu'd,
The glory of thy gratitude,
    Respir'd unto the Lord.

Strong is the horse upon his speed;
Strong in pursuit the rapid glede,
    Which makes at once his game;
Strong the tall ostrich on the ground;
Strong through the turbulent profound
    Shoots xiphias to his aim.

Strong is the lion—like a coal
His eyeball—like a bastion's mole
    His chest against the foes:
Strong the gier-eagle on his sail,
Strong against tide, th' enormous whale
    Emerges, as he goes.

But stronger still, in earth and air,
And in the sea, the man of pray'r;
    And far beneath the tide;
And in the seat to faith assign'd,
Where ask is have, where seek is find,
    Where knock is open wide.

Beauteous the fleet before the gale;
Beauteous the multitudes in mail,
    Rank'd arms and crested heads:
Beauteous the garden's umbrage mild,
Walk, water, meditated wild,
    And all the bloomy beds.

Beauteous the moon full on the lawn;
And beauteous, when the veil's withdrawn,
    The virgin to her spouse:
Beauteous the temple deck'd and fill'd,
When to the heav'n of heav'ns they build
    Their heart-directed vows.

Beauteous, yea beauteous more than these,
The shepherd king upon his knees,
    For his momentous trust;
With wish of infinite conceit,
For man, beast, mute, the small and great,
    And prostrate dust to dust.

Precious the bounteous widow's mite;
And precious, for extreme delight,
    The largess from the churl:
Precious the ruby's blushing blaze,
And alba's blest imperial rays,
    And pure cerulean pearl.

Precious the penitential tear;
And precious is the sigh sincere,
    Acceptable to God:
And precious are the winning flow'rs,
In gladsome Israel's feast of bow'rs,
    Bound on the hallow'd sod.

More precious that diviner part
Of David, ev'n the Lord's own heart,
    Great, beautiful, and new:
In all things where it was intent,
In all extremes, in each event,
    Proof—answ'ring true to true.

Glorious the sun in mid career;
Glorious th' assembled fires appear;
    Glorious the comet's train:
Glorious the trumpet and alarm;
Glorious th' almighty stretch'd-out arm:
    Glorious th' enraptur'd main:

Glorious the northern lights astream;
Glorious the song, when God's the theme;
    Glorious the thunder's roar:
Glorious hosanna from the den;
Glorious the catholic amen;
    Glorious the martyr's gore:

Glorious—more glorious is the crown
Of Him, that brought salvation down
    By meekness, call'd thy Son;

Thou at stupendous truth believ'd,
And now the matchless deed's achiev'd,
DETERMIN'D, DAR'D, and DONE.

(1763)

The top-most pinnacles of poetry.

WILLIAM CLYDE DE VANE
A Browning Handbook (1935)

MAURICE MORGANN

1 7 2 6 — 1 8 0 2

SHAKESPEARE

Shakespeare is a name so interesting, that it is excusable to stop a moment, nay it would be indecent to pass him without the tribute of some admiration. He differs essentially from all other writers: Him we may profess rather to feel than to understand; and it is safer to say, on many occasions, that we are possessed by him, than that we possess him. And no wonder;—He scatters the seeds of things, the principles of character and action, with so cunning a hand yet with so careless an air, and, master of our feelings, submits himself so little to our judgment, that every thing seems superior. We discern not his course, we see no connection of cause and effect, we are rapt in ignorant admiration, and claim no kindred with his abilities. All the incidents, all the parts, look like chance, whilst we feel and are sensible that the whole is design. His Characters not only act and speak in strict conformity to nature, but in strict relation to us; just so much is shewn as is requisite, just so much is impressed; he commands every passage to our heads and to our hearts, and moulds us as he pleases, and that with so much ease, that he never betrays his own exertions. We see these Characters act from the mingled motives of passion, reason, interest, habit and complection, in all their proportions, when they are supposed to know it not themselves; and we are made to acknowledge that their actions and sentiments are, from those motives, the necessary result. He at once blends and distinguishes every thing;—every thing is complicated, every thing is plain. I restrain the further expressions of my admiration lest they should not seem applicable to man; but it is really astonishing that a mere human being, a part of humanity only, should so perfectly comprehend the whole; and that he should possess such exquisite art, that

945

whilst every woman and every child shall feel the whole effect, his learned Editors and Commentators should yet so very frequently mistake or seem ignorant of the cause. A sceptre or a straw are in his hands of equal efficacy; he needs no selection; he converts every thing into excellence; nothing is too great, nothing is too base. Is a character efficient like *Richard,* it is every thing we can wish: Is it otherwise, like *Hamlet,* it is productive of equal admiration: Action produces one mode of excellence and inaction another: The Chronicle, the Novel, or the Ballad; the king, or the beggar, the hero, the madman, the sot or the fool; it is all one;—nothing is worse, nothing is better: The same genius pervades and is equally admirable in all. Or, is a character to be shewn in progressive change, and the events of years comprized within the hour;—with what a Magic hand does he prepare and scatter his spells! The Understanding must, in the first place, be subdued; and lo! how the rooted prejudices of the child spring up to confound the man! The Weird sisters rise, and order is extinguished. The laws of nature give way, and leave nothing in our minds but wildness and horror. No pause is allowed us for reflection: Horrid sentiment, furious guilt and compunction, air-drawn daggers, murders, ghosts, and inchantment, shake and *possess us wholly.* In the mean time the *process* is completed. *Macbeth* changes under our eye, *the milk of human kindness is converted to gall; he has supped full of horrors,* and his *May of life is fallen into the sear, the yellow leaf;* whilst we, the fools of amazement, are insensible to the shifting of place and the lapse of time, and till the curtain drops, never once wake to the truth of things, or recognize the laws of existence.—On such an occasion, a fellow, like *Rymer,* waking from his trance, shall lift up his Constable's staff, and charge this great Magician, this daring *practicer of arts inhibited,* in the name of *Aristotle,* to surrender; whilst *Aristotle* himself, disowning his wretched Officer, would fall prostrate at his feet and acknowledge his supremacy. —O supreme of Dramatic excellence! (*might he say,*) not to me be imputed the insolence of fools. The bards of *Greece* were confined within the narrow circle of the Chorus, and hence they found themselves constrained to practice, for the most part, the precision, and copy the details of nature. I followed them, and knew not that a larger circle might be drawn, and the Drama extended to the whole reach of human genius. Convinced, I see that a more compendious *nature* may be obtained; a nature of *effects* only, to which neither the relations of place, or continuity of time, are always essential. Nature, condescending to the faculties and apprehensions of man, has drawn through human life a regular chain of visible causes and effects: But Poetry delights in surprize, conceals her steps, seizes at once upon the heart, and obtains the Sublime of things without betraying the rounds of her ascent: True Poesy is *magic,* not *nature;* an effect from causes hidden or unknown. To the Magician I prescribed no laws; his law and his power are one; his power

946

is his law. Him, who neither imitates, nor is within the reach of imitation, no precedent can or ought to bind, no limits to contain. If his end is obtained, who shall question his course? Means, whether apparent or hidden, are justified in poesy by success; but then most perfect and most admirable when most concealed.

An Essay on the Dramatic Character of Sir John Falstaff (1777)

The passage where he breaks away exultantly from his main subject to write in sheer delight of Shakespeare's essential difference from all other writers and his imperishable gifts, is one of the great things in the whole range of English criticism. There is nothing greater—perhaps nothing so great—in Coleridge or Hazlitt.

D. NICHOL SMITH
Shakespeare Criticism (1916)

EDMUND BURKE

1 7 2 9 — 1 7 9 7

THE PROPOSITION IS PEACE

For that service, for all service, whether of revenue, trade, or empire, my trust is in her interest in the British constitution. My hold of the colonies is in the close affection which grows from common names, from kindred blood, from similar privileges, and equal protection. These are ties, which, though light as air, are strong as links of iron. Let the colonies always keep the idea of their civil rights associated with your government;—they will cling and grapple to you; and no force under heaven will be of power to tear them from their allegiance. But let it be once understood, that your government may be one thing, and their privileges another; that these two things may exist without any mutual relation; the cement is gone; the cohesion is loosened; and every thing hastens to decay and dissolution. As long as you have the wisdom to keep the sovereign authority of this country as the sanctuary of liberty, the sacred temple consecrated to our common faith, wherever the chosen race and sons of England worship freedom, they will turn their faces towards you. The more they multiply, the more friends you will have; the more ardently they love liberty, the more perfect will be their obedience. Slavery they can have any where. It is a weed that grows in every soil. They may have it from Spain, they may have it from Prussia. But until you become lost to all feeling of your true interest and your natural dignity, freedom they can have from none but you. This is the com-

947

modity of price, of which you have the monopoly. This is the true act of navigation, which binds to you the commerce of the colonies, and through them secures to you the wealth of the world. Deny them this participation of freedom, and you break that sole bond, which originally made, and must still preserve, the unity of the empire. Do not entertain so weak an imagination, as that your registers and your bonds, your affidavits and your sufferances, your cockets and your clearances, are what form the great securities of your commerce. Do not dream that your letters of office, and your instructions, and your suspending clauses, are the things that hold together the great contexture of this mysterious whole. These things do not make your government. Dead instruments, passive tools as they are, it is the spirit of the English communion, that gives all their life and efficacy to them. It is the spirit of the English constitution, which, infused through the mighty mass, pervades, feeds, unites, invigorates, vivifies, every part of the empire, even down to the minutest member.

Is it not the same virtue which does every thing for us here in England? Do you imagine then, that it is the land tax act which raises your revenue? that it is the annual vote in the committee of supply, which gives you your army? or that it is the mutiny bill which inspires it with bravery and discipline? No! Surely no! It is the love of the people; it is their attachment to their government from the sense of the deep stake they have in such a glorious institution, which gives you your army and your navy, and infuses into both that liberal obedience, without which your army would be a base rabble, and your navy nothing but rotten timber.

All this, I know well enough, will sound wild and chimerical to the profane herd of those vulgar and mechanical politicians, who have no place among us; a sort of people who think that nothing exists but what is gross and material; and who therefore, far from being qualified to be directors of the great movement of empire, are not fit to turn a wheel in the machine. But to men truly initiated and rightly taught, these ruling and master principles, which, in the opinion of such men as I have mentioned, have no substantial existence, are in truth every thing, and all in all. Magnanimity in politics is not seldom the truest wisdom; and a great empire and little minds go ill together. If we are conscious of our situation, and glow with zeal to fill our places as becomes our station and ourselves, we ought to auspicate all our public proceedings on America, with the old warning of the church, *Sursum corda!* We ought to elevate our minds to the greatness of that trust to which the order of Providence has called us. By adverting to the dignity of this high calling, our ancestors have turned a savage wilderness into a glorious empire; and have made the most extensive, and the only honorable conquests; not by destroying, but by promoting the wealth, the number, the happiness, of the human race. Let us get an American revenue as we have got an American empire. English privileges have made it all that it is; English privileges alone will make it all it can be.

In full confidence of this unalterable truth, I now (*quod felix faustum-que sit*)—lay the first stone of the temple of peace.

Speech on Moving Resolutions for Conciliation with the Colonies
(March 22, 1775)

If delivered under the conditions of a later period, when it would have been read in every household on the day following, [it] could not but have reacted with power on both House and government. As it is, it remains some compensation to English literature for the dismemberment of the British empire. Whether we reflect on the art with which it is constructed, the skill with which the speaker winds into the heart of his subject and draws from it the material of his splendid peroration on 'the spirit of the English constitution' and its power to unite, invigorate and vivify the British empire in all its diverse members; or reflect on the temper, passionate and moving yet restrained and conciliatory, in which the argument is conducted; or recall simply the greater flights of picturesqu eloquence, the description of American industry and enterprise, the imagery in which the speaker clothes his conception of the spirit of the English constitution and the sovereign authority of parliament—the speech takes its own place beside the greatest masterpieces of our literature, the plays of Shakespeare and the poems of Milton.

HERBERT J. C. GRIERSON
Edmund Burke, in The Cambridge History of
English Literature (1914)

WILLIAM COWPER

1 7 3 1 — 1 8 0 0

TO THE REV. JOHN NEWTON

March 29, 1784.

My dear Friend,——

It being his Majesty's pleasure that I should yet have another opportunity to write before he dissolves the parliament, I avail myself of it with all possible alacrity. I thank you for your last, which was not the less welcome for coming, like an extraordinary gazette, at a time when it was not expected.

As when the sea is uncommonly agitated, the water finds its way into creeks and holes of rocks, which in its calmer state it never reaches, in like manner the effect of these turbulent times is felt even at Orchard side, where in general we live as undisturbed by the political element, as shrimps or cockles that have been accidentally deposited in some hollow beyond the water mark, by the usual dashing of the waves. We were sitting yesterday after dinner, the two ladies and myself, very composedly, and without the least apprehension of any such intrusion in our snug parlour, one lady knitting, the other netting, and the gentleman winding worsted, when to our unspeakable surprise a mob appeared before the window; a smart rap was heard at the door, the boys haloo'd, and the maid announced Mr. Grenville. Puss * was unfortunately let out of her box, so that the candidate, with all his good friends at his heels, was refused admittance at the grand entry, and referred to the back door, as the only possible way of approach.

Candidates are creatures not very susceptible of affronts, and would rather, I suppose, climb in at a window than be absolutely excluded. In a minute the yard, the kitchen, and the parlour were filled. Mr. Grenville advancing toward me shook me by the hand with a degree of cordiality that was extremely seducing. As soon as he and as many more as could find chairs were seated, he began to open the intent of his visit. I told him I had no vote, for which he readily gave me credit. I assured him I had no influence, which he was not equally inclined to believe, and the less, no doubt, because Mr. Ashburner, the drapier, addressing himself to me at this moment, informed me that I had a great deal. Supposing that I could not be possessed of such a treasure without knowing it, I ventured to confirm my first assertion by saying, that if I had any I was utterly at a loss to imagine where it could be, or wherein it consisted. Thus ended the conference. Mr. Grenville squeezed me by the hand again, kissed the ladies, and withdrew. He kissed likewise the maid in the kitchen, and seemed upon the whole a most loving, kissing, kind-hearted gentleman. He is very young, genteel, and handsome. He has a pair of very good eyes in his head, which not being sufficient as it should seem for the many nice and difficult purposes of a senator, he has a third also, which he wore suspended by a ribband from his button-hole. The boys haloo'd, the dogs barked, Puss scampered, the hero, with his long train of obsequious followers, withdrew. We made ourselves very merry with the adventure, and in a short time settled into our former tranquillity, never probably to be thus interrupted more. I thought myself, however, happy in being able to affirm truly that I had not that influence for which he sued; and which, had I been possessed of it, with my present views of the dispute between the Crown and the Commons, I must have refused him, for he is on the side of the former. It is comfortable to be of no consequence in a world where one cannot exercise any without disobliging somebody. The town, however, seems

---

* His tame hare.

to be much at his service, and if he be equally successful throughout the county, he will undoubtedly gain his election. Mr. Ashburner, perhaps, was a little mortified, because it was evident that I owed the honour of this visit to his misrepresentation of my importance. But had he thought proper to assure Mr. Grenville that I had three heads, I should not, I suppose, have been bound to produce them.

Mr. Scott, who you say was so much admired in your pulpit, would be equally admired in his own, at least by all capable judges, were he not so apt to be angry with his congregation. This hurts him, and had he the understanding and eloquence of Paul himself, would still hurt him. He seldom, hardly ever indeed, preaches a gentle, well-tempered sermon, but I hear it highly commended: but warmth of temper, indulged to a degree that may be called scolding, defeats the end of preaching. It is a misapplication of his powers, which it also cripples, and teases away his hearers. But he is a good man, and may perhaps outgrow it.

Many thanks for the worsted, which is excellent. We are as well as a spring hardly less severe than the severest winter will give us leave to be. With our united love, we conclude ourselves yours and Mrs. Newton's affectionate and faithful

W. C.
M. U.

The best of English letter-writers.

ROBERT SOUTHEY
The Life of William Cowper, Esq. (1839)

JOHN LANGHORNE

1 7 3 5 — 1 7 7 9

POETIC MOMENT

Where longs to fall that rifted spire,
As weary of th' insulting air.

Fable vii, The Wall-Flower

He has in the italicised line a "poetic moment" which is, for its poetic quality, as free of the poetic Jerusalem as "We are such stuff," or the dying words of Cleopatra. He has hit "what it was so easy to miss," the passionate expression, in articulate music, unhit before, never to be poetically hit again save by accident, yet never to perish from the world of poetry. It is only a grain of gold ("fish-scale" gold, even, as the mining

951

EDWARD GIBBON

1 7 3 7 — 1 7 9 4

GRAVE AND TEMPERATE IRONY

Within these limits the almost invisible and tremulous ball of orthodoxy
was allowed securely to vibrate.

When the Arian pestilence approached their frontiers, they were
supplied with the seasonable preservative of the Homoousion, by the
paternal care of the Roman pontiff.

The prerogatives of the King of Heaven were settled, or changed,
or modified, in the cabinet of an earthly monarch.

The *circumincessio* is perhaps the deepest and darkest corner of
the whole theological abyss.

Future tyrants were encouraged to believe that the blood which they
might shed in a long reign would instantly be washed away in the
waters of regeneration.

The Decline and Fall of the Roman Empire (1776–88)

Flaubert could not hunt more nicely for the right word.

OLIVER ELTON
A Survey of English Literature 1730–1780 (1928)

GLOSSARY

abrayde, started up
achaat, buying
achátours, buyers
after oon, of uniform quality
alderbest, best of all
alenge, miserable
Algezir, Algeciras
Alisaundre, Alexandria
aller cok, rooster's crow for all
anlaas, dagger
apikèd, trimmed
appele, accuse
arewe, in a row
asterte, escape
astronomye, astrology
áventure, chance

bachelor, young knight
baite, resting-place
baundoun, power
bawdryk, belt
Belmarye, Benmarin
bemès, trumpets
bismótered, stained
bitore, bittern
biwreyè, betray
boote, remedy
bord bigonne, seat of honor
bote, unless
bourde, jest
bracér, arm-guard
briddès, birds
broukè, have the use of
buen, be
bulte it to the bren, sift it to the bran
burdoun, base accompaniment

carl, man
catel, property
ceint, girdle
chapèd, mounted

chaunterie, a job singing daily masses
ches, chose
chevyssaunce, dishonest deals
chyvachie, cavalry raid
cleped, called
clerk, student
coillons, testicles
colpons, bunches
complecciouns, temperaments
conscïence, feelings
contekes, fights
cope, top
coráges, hearts
cote, cottage
coude, knew
countour, auditor
covyne, tricks
coy, modest
croys of latoun, cross of copper and zinc
    alloy
crulle, curled

daunger, control
daungerous, arrogant
dawngerouse, haughty
dees, dice
delyvere, agile
depeint, soiled
despitous, scornful
deye, dairy woman
dissaite, deceit
drecchèd, troubled
drede, doubt
dreynt, drowned

eek, also
embrouded, embroidered
engyned, racked
envynèd, stocked with wine
estatlich, dignified
evene, average
ey, egg

faldyng, coarse wool
faren in londe, gone to the country
farsed, stuffed
fee symple, absolute possession
fen, chapter
fernè, distant
ferrer twynne, go farther
ferthyng, speck
fetisly, precisely
fetys, handsome
feye, stricken
floytynge, fluting
flytt, fled
foo, foe
foond, provided for
for-dronke, very drunk
forneys of a leed, furnace under
  a caldron
forpynèd, wasted by suffering
fors, attention
forslewthen, waste
forthi, for this
forwake, tired out
forward, agreement
fother, load
fredom, generosity
fynch eek koude he pulle, have his own
  concubine
fyne, cease

galle, sore spot
galyngale, a spice
gamed, prospered
gargat, throat
gat-tothèd, teeth widely spaced
gauded, gauds or large beads
Gernade, Grenada
geynest, fairest
gipser, purse
girlès, both sexes
gise, manner
goliardeys, teller of dirty stories
gore, garment
Gretè See, Mediterranean
grope, test
ground, texture
grys, costly gray fur
gypon, tunic

habergeon, coat of mail
halwès, shrines
hap, lot
harre, hinges
haunt, skill
he, she; the knight
hele, conceal
hendy, happy
hente, obtain; took
herberwe, inn
here, their
hett, promised
heu, color
hierde, herdsman
hightè, named
holt, farm
hyre, her

iantilnesse, waywardness
ichabbe, I have
icham, I am
ichot, I wot
in feere, together

janglere, noisy talker
jet, fashion

knarre, stout fellow
kowthe, known

lele, loyal
lemes, flames
lent, turned away
lesynges, lies
lette, prevented
Lettow, Lithuania
letuaries, medicines
levedi, lady
libbe, live
licóur, sap
lith, limb
lode-menage, piloting
loh, laughed
Looth, Lot
losengeour, flatterer
lossom, lovable
love-dayes, arbitration days
lud, voice

Lyeys, Ayas
lyht, has lighted
lymytour, licensed to beg in a limited area
lyven, live

make, mate
makeles, matchless
male, bag
mareys, marsh
mede, reward
mekyl, much
mene, pity
mette, dreamed
meynee, followers
middel, waist
moot I thee, may I thrive
moote sterven wood, may die mad
mort, dead
mortreux, stew
morwenynges, mornings
Myda, Midas
myster, craft

narette, blame
narre, nearer
ne, not
nis, is not
nones, occasion
normal, a sore
not-heed, closely cut hair
nyghtertale, nighttime

on, in
ounces, strands
overeste courtepy, upper short coat

paas, walking pace
pace, go; surpass
Palatye, Balat
Parvys, lawyers' meeting place
pers, blue-gray
philosophre, alchemist
pilèd, scanty
pilwè-beer, pillowcase
pistel, word
pocok, peacock

poraille, poor people
poudrè-marchant, a sour seasoning
preevè, experience
prikasour, hunter on horseback
proprè, own
prow, profit
Pruce, Prussia
purchas, money from begging
purtreye, draw
pyned, tortured

rage, play around
rakè-stele, rake handle
raughte, reached
recche, interpret
reed, advice; adviser
remes, realms
rethor, author
reve me, rob me of
reysèd, raided
roun, song
rouncy, a nag
rownèd, whispered
Ruce, Russia

Satalye, Attalia
sautrie, psaltery
sawcèfleem, pimply
scathe, a pity
scoleye, attend school
see, protect
seeke, sick
semlokest, loveliest
senténce, meaning
sette hir aller cappe, fooled them all
sewed, pursued
seynd, broiled
sheeldès, French coins
shentè, harmed
shoope, planned
Significavit, writ of arrest for excommunication
siker, certain
sikerly, certainly
sithes, times
so, as
soond, sand
soote, refreshing

sownynge, emphasizing
spicèd, overscrupulous
stape, advanced
stent, stopped
stepe, protruding
sterve, die
stevene, voice
stoor, stock
strondes, shores
stuwe, fishpond
swelte, swooned
swevene, dream
swithe, quickly
swych, such
swynk, work
swynkere, worker
swyre, neck

taille, credit
talen, tell tales
tappestere, barmaid
Tapycer, tapestry weaver
targe, shield
temple, law school
theech, may I thrive
tho, those
tholien whyle sore, to endure for a time
tollen, take toll for grinding
tombesteres, dancing girls
toon, toes
toune, season
toverbyde, outlive
Tramyssene, Tremessen
tretys, neat

undermelès, afternoons
undren, forenoon
unkyndèly, unnaturally

vavasour, squire
vernycle, copy of St. Veronica's hand-
    kerchief bearing the face of Christ
verray, true
vertú, power
vigiliès, religious services

warice, cure
wastel, fine white
Webbe, weaver
wende, turn
wight, person
wlatsom, loathsome
wonges, cheeks
wonyng, dwelling
wonynge, living
wood, crazy
wore, weir
wowyng, wooing
wyter, wise

yeddynges, singing contests
yede, went
yën, eyes
yerne, eagerly
yhent, won
y-lad, drawn
y-lymèd, caught
yore, long
y-purfiled, trimmed
y-yerned, yearned

INDEXES

INDEX OF AUTHORS AND CRITICS

The names of critics are printed in italics

INDEX OF TITLES

INDEX OF FIRST LINES
OF POEMS AND PLAYS

lxi